INTERNATIONAL BUSINESS NEGOTIATIONS

THEORY AND PRACTICE

PERVEZ N. GHAURI

Professor of International Business, University of Birmingham, UK

URSULA F. OTT

Professor of International Business, Nottingham Trent University, UK

HUSSAIN G. RAMMAL

Associate Professor of International Business and Strategy, University of Technology Sydney, Australia

Cheltenham, UK • Northampton, MA, USA

Published by
Edward Elgar Publishing Limited
The Lypiatts
15 Lansdown Road
Cheltenham
Glos GL50 2JA
UK

Edward Elgar Publishing, Inc.
William Pratt House
9 Dewey Court
Northampton
Massachusetts 01060
USA

A catalogue record for this book
is available from the British Library

Library of Congress Control Number: 2020944284

ISBN 978 1 78897 837 8 (cased)
ISBN 978 1 78897 839 2 (paperback)
ISBN 978 1 78897 838 5 (eBook)

Typeset by Servis Filmsetting Ltd, Stockport, Cheshire
Printed and bound in Great Britain by TJ Books Limited, Padstow, Cornwall

CONTENTS IN BRIEF

FULL CONTENTS

FIGURES

TABLES

ABOUT THE AUTHORS

Pervez N. Ghauri is Professor of International Business at the University of Birmingham, UK. He is the founding Editor-in-Chief of *International Business Review*. He has published 30 books on marketing and international business topics. He has published in journals such as *Journal of International Business Studies, Journal of World Business, Journal of Organizational Behaviour, International Marketing Review, Journal of Business Research* and *Industrial Marketing Management*. He also provides consultancy services to several multinational firms on international business negotiations and entry strategies.

Ursula F. Ott is Professor of International Business at Nottingham Trent University, UK. She is the Head of the Research Group in International Business, Strategy and Decision Making (IBSD). She has won awards for her work in international negotiations and bargaining. She has published research monographs and articles in leading journals. Her publications appear in journals such as *Journal of Management Studies, Journal of International Business Studies, Journal of Business Research, Organization Studies, Sociology* and *International Business Review*.

Hussain G. Rammal is Associate Professor of International Business and Strategy at the University of Technology Sydney, Australia. He is the Co-Editor-in-Chief of *Review of International Business and Strategy* and founding editor of the *Emerging Issues in International Business and Global Strategy* book series. He has published research books and articles on international business topics including business negotiations, talent management and internationalisation of service firms. His research has been published in journals such as *Journal of World Business, Journal of Business Ethics, International Business Review, International Marketing Review, Journal of Knowledge Management, Management Decision* and *European Journal of Finance*.

PREFACE

Negotiations are an essential part of the managerial process and are highly relevant to the implementation of business strategies. International marketers are thus increasingly business negotiators who regularly discuss and make deals across national borders with a variety of actors: business partners, buyers, suppliers, government institutions and even competitors. The explosion of international trade, outsourcing and foreign direct investment has increased the importance of negotiation skills that managers need to possess, as without negotiations none of the above can be achieved. These deals are not just arrived at in formal or informal discussions but need to be drafted through extensive give-and-take between traders and businesspeople from around the world with different backgrounds and cultural and psychological characteristics.

Managers across cultures and borders need to overcome verbal and non-verbal issues as well as challenges in terms of different norms of interaction and behaviour to do business in the international marketplace. Establishing, maintaining and fostering relationships are therefore of prime importance for the market transactions to take place. Business negotiations thus occupy a prominent place in international deals because any transaction is in some way negotiated even though on a limited range of issues. Complex international deals are very challenging; this does not only include sales agreements, but also the discussion of agency and distribution contracts in foreign markets, joint ventures and licensing agreements, as well as selling huge projects and package deals.

In addition, the emergence of information technology (IT) provides exceptional opportunities and challenges for negotiators, generating a culture of continuous readiness. However, in spite of technological developments, complexity could potentially appear when partners come from different national and cultural backgrounds and do not share the same native language, yet still have a major interest in dealing with each other.

Our aim in writing this textbook is to give our students and readers tools for dealing with international business negotiations. The book will help students and readers to:

1. identify and understand the factors influencing international business negotiations;
2. understand the process of international business negotiations;

3. develop an understanding of the issues at stake and the importance of proper preparations;
4. develop skills for being a successful international negotiator.

This book is thus divided into four parts: (I) the importance of international business negotiations; (II) factors influencing international negotiations; (III) negotiation process; (IV) negotiating effectively.

The first part is designed to cover the basics of international business negotiations. Chapter 1 gives an overview of the fundamentals of negotiations and proposes some warm-up questions used further in the text. Emergence of conflict is explained in Chapter 2, where conflict resolution is presented as an illustration of resolving mismatches that arise in the interaction between the negotiators who come from different countries and belong to different cultures. The cultural and strategic misalignments between intercultural negotiators may be due to social distance and lack of social awareness. Chapter 3 deals with different theoretical underpinnings, particularly game theory and how it can help resolve conflict.

Part II deals with the factors that influence business negotiations. Chapter 4 discusses the crucial role of culture in a variety of strategies employed by negotiators in the international business arena. This is followed by an explanation of cultural differences and how national culture and organisational culture impact buyer–seller interactions. It sets in perspective the respective roles of country, corporate and individual variables in shaping negotiation behaviour at the international level. Culture is a major determinant of strategies and tactics in international business negotiation. Chapter 5 explains the importance of communication, both verbal and non-verbal, and discusses how the patterns of communication differ across cultures. Chapter 6 looks at the effects of social interaction on negotiation outcomes and how people, their background and different personalities influence business negotiations. This chapter also discusses the role of individuals in the selection of negotiation styles and how personality could impact the outcome for negotiation teams.

The third part begins with the negotiation process and how it should be handled. The first two chapters (Chapters 7 and 8) present the theoretical bases to provide a framework for the negotiation process and the stages it goes through and discuss the pre-negotiation stage, the face-to-face negotiation and the post-negotiation stage and the activities that are undertaken in each stage.

Since there are several types of strategies and tactics in business negotiations, the most important strategies, including tough, soft, reciprocity and good cop/bad cop, are delivered in Chapter 9. Chapter 10 reviews the ethical challenges and the tactics that can be used to protect the code of conduct and handle ethical dilemmas faced by international business negotiators. Different types of contracts and negotiations for these contracts are discussed in the next chapter. International sales, export transactions, licensing agreements and the role of agents are articulated in Chapter 11. The chapter shows how cooperative negotiation works as an asset for the future ventures.

The fourth and final part of the book provides some practical guidelines for international business negotiations. Chapter 12 has a more regional focus, looking at how negotiations should be managed with people from various geographical areas, though it also builds on cultural factors as well as content-oriented aspects of international business negotiations. We could not be exhaustive here and decided to concentrate on major countries and areas that make up a quite significant part of world trade. Some general guidelines are provided in Chapter 13. This last chapter synthesises the lessons from previous chapters and provides some general rules that can be followed while negotiating across cultures.

Pervez N. Ghauri London	Ursula F. Ott Nottingham	Hussain G. Rammal Sydney

PART I

THE IMPORTANCE OF BUSINESS NEGOTIATIONS

1 The nature of negotiations

Negotiating is a process whereby two or more parties, who have their own objectives and demands, discuss these in order to achieve as many of these objectives as possible. Negotiation is an activity people participate in on a daily basis in order to manage their relationships. Negotiations take place between a husband and wife, over who will do the school run, between a child and parent, over whether the child will get to have the latest video-game console, between employers and employees, about the nature of a task, between a buyer and seller, over the price of a commodity, and between business associates, over the strategic direction of their company.

Some of these negotiations are simple day-to-day arrangements and neither negotiator feels the need to pre-plan the process or the outcome, but in some cases, as is the case in business relationships, the stakes can be high and it is essential that negotiators prepare, plan and pursue their objectives and preferred outcomes more carefully. In all business relationships, including international business relationships, parties negotiate in the belief they are able to influence the process in such a way that they can get a better deal than simply accepting or rejecting what the other party is offering. Negotiation is thus a voluntary process of reciprocity where both parties modify their own offers and expectations to reach an outcome that satisfies everyone involved.

Self-reference criteria: the unconscious belief that one's own culture, values and norms are the most appropriate ones.

Negotiations between two parties coming from two different cultures/countries are different from negotiations between parties coming from the same culture/country. The uniqueness of international business negotiations stems from the fact that these negotiations are influenced by a diversity of environments, business norms and perspectives of different people about what is reasonable, appropriate or even right or wrong. This is due to the fact that each party's behaviour is determined by his/her own *self-reference criteria* – an unconscious belief that one's own culture, values and norms are the most appropriate.[1]

Negotiation skills are not genetic characteristics. Negotiation is an art/skill that can be learnt and developed through study and practice.[2] International negotiations demand an understanding of social, cultural, political and economic systems, as well as knowledge of individual characteristics of the opposite party. Negotiations are thus a process of reaching agreement between two or more parties, where each party tries to achieve its objectives. However, both parties quite often know it is not possible to achieve all their objectives. Moreover, each party is aware that to achieve its objectives it must accept some of the

EXAMPLE 1.1
BREXIT NEGOTIATIONS

Britain has had a love-hate relationship with Europe for more than fifty years. Back in the early 1960s Britain's entry to Europe's common market was denied twice. Britain was allowed to enter in 1973. However, the idea was put to a referendum in 1975 that was convincingly won by the "Join EU" side.

During the election campaign for a second term, UK Prime Minister David Cameron announced that, if he won the election, he would hold a referendum to remain in or leave the EU. Cameron thus had to hold a referendum in 2016, which was won by the leave side by a margin of 3.8 per cent, thus initiating Brexit. After the referendum, it took almost three years and two elections to get Parliament's approval to exit from the European Union. Britain had a transition period of one year to negotiate the details of the exit deal.

Ideally, the UK wants single market access and special agreements to be negotiated for financial services, security issues and the Northern Ireland border, and no free movement of people. The EU wants to prevent the UK from undercutting it with trade agreements with its partners, agreement on state aid to companies, labour standards and environmental rules. It also wants some governance system for future conflict through the European Court of Justice. The UK demands that it must take control of its fishing waters that the EU wants to have access to with some quotas. Considering the opposing positions on these concerns, and issues such as services, public procurement, data rules, transport and aviation, it seems that the parties are heading towards a no-deal Brexit.

It seems that if the UK can be flexible on issues such as fisheries and EU rules, the EU might also be flexible on issues such as subsidies to companies, workplace rules and financial services. Negotiations, after all, mean "give" and "take" and compromise. However, both parties seem to have different priorities and preferences: while the EU is more concerned about economics and trade implications, the UK seems mainly to be concerned about sovereignty and independence. In other words, while the EU wants to take a rational approach, the UK's negotiation strategy is based on an emotional approach.

Discussion Point: Discuss the negotiating strategies of the UK and EU and suggest the best possible approach that the parties could take.

demands of the other party. In other words, negotiations are a process of give and take to achieve as many of one's objectives as possible. This process is illustrated in Example 1.1.

Due to an increased interdependence of world economies, the nature of international production systems, with their expanded value chains and focus on outsourcing, has changed.[3] This has increased the need for international business negotiations between buyers and suppliers and between buyers and distributors/sellers. In these negotiations, parties need to not only think about their own benefits but also about those of the other parties. This is often described through a dual concern model as shown in Figure 1.1.

As we can see, in a buyer and seller negotiation the seller cannot only aim to achieve a sale but also has to ensure that the buyer gets a beneficial outcome too. S/he has to convince the buyer that the deal s/he is getting is the best possible for him/her. In other words, s/he needs to behave as a joint problem solver. The more that buyer believes that s/he is getting a

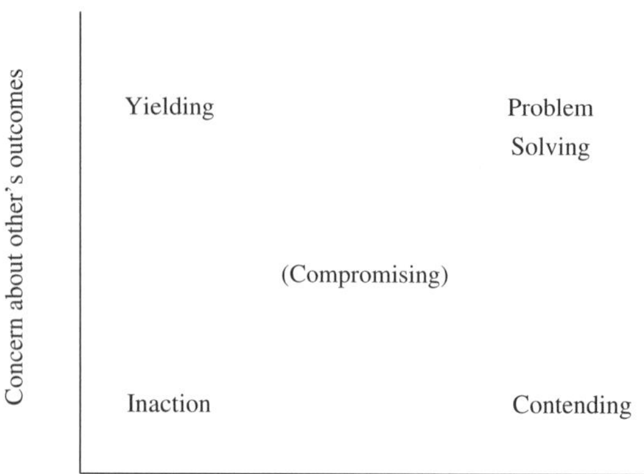

Source: Adapted from Rubin et al. (1994).[4]

Figure 1.1 The dual concern model

beneficial deal the greater the chances that s/he will continue doing business with the same seller. This means that to achieve a long-term, sustainable business, the parties need to work with a dual concern model and not only for their own benefit. As shown in Figure 1.1, the more the parties are concerned with their own benefit, the more they want to stay towards the right of the horizontal axis. While the more they think about a joint benefit (their own as well as of the other party), the more they will be towards the left of the horizontal axis. However, depending upon their interaction, most probably the parties will end up somewhere in the middle. We can see that there are five different behaviours/strategies parties can adopt.[5]

1. Contending/Competing: Here a party pursues its own benefits and is not concerned with the other party's benefits.
2. Yielding/Accommodating: Here a party is less concerned about his/her own benefits and is more concerned that how the other party can achieve its objectives.
3. Inaction/Avoiding: Here both parties show indifference, as if they are not concerned whether they or the other party can achieve their own goals or not.
4. Problem Solving/Collaborative: Here both parties are concerned with making a deal and that both should achieve their goals. In this case both parties aim to achieve the maximum joint benefit.
5. Compromising: Here both parties are moderately interested in achieving their objectives and are willing to give and take so that both can achieve some of their objectives.

As we can see, there are several negotiation strategies and behaviours available to parties in business negotiations. It is often suggested that in business negotiations, parties should adopt a problem-solving negotiation behaviour.[6]

We can now define a negotiation as a process through which parties make joint decisions about their future behaviour towards each other. Two elements are almost universal in any negotiation: the first that parties share a common interest; the second that parties have some conflicting interests that need to be resolved.[7] In international business negotiations the stakes are sometimes not that high and the parties do not have to go through lengthy negotiations. Sometimes, however, the stakes are extraordinarily high, and parties need to discuss at length all the details and foreseeable conflicts that may arise, including delayed payments, delayed deliveries and the terms of payment. International business negotiations thus have some characteristics that are different from other types of negotiation. These include:

1. The negotiation process has inherent conflict as agreeing a higher price leads to a higher profit for one negotiating party but a lower profit for the others as the higher price means an increase in expenses.
2. There are always two or more parties. In high-stakes business negotiations there can often be more than two parties involved in the deal; this could either be direct or indirect involvement.
3. The exchange of information between parties is relatively open compared to other types of negotiation. Both parties inform one another about what they want to achieve and what their present situation is. Furthermore, both parties explain what their ideal position on a number of issues, such as product or service characteristics, delivery time, price and means of payment (cash up front, credit, payments in instalments, etc.), would be.
4. Both parties understand that they cannot get entirely what they demand, and they will have to make some concessions in order to arrive at the best possible outcome. Both sides are thus willing to adjust their demands over the course of the negotiation.[8]
5. Parties believe that they can achieve better results through negotiating rather than not negotiating or by adopting a take it or leave it approach. Businesses always want to have long relationships with their clients where possible, whether these be suppliers or customers.
6. Parties understand that the negotiation taking place at any one time is taking place not only to resolve the conflict that exists in the here and now, or even the specific, identifiable conflict, but also to prepare the ground for any future deals with the other party.
7. Business negotiations are *always* voluntary processes. This means that if one party does not see any benefit in negotiating, it can simply withdraw without any serious difficulty, so-called "walk away". This explains why international business negotiations are *always* win-win: both parties benefit and if one party does not perceive there to be any benefit it can simply choose to withdraw from the negotiations.

In the literature, bargaining and negotiation are sometimes used interchangeably. To us, however, they mean different things. Bargaining refers to haggling and bartering more suited to the "bazaar" than the international marketplace. Bargaining is akin to competitive, auction-like bidding; it is a *distributive* approach that divides a fixed resource. The objective of distributive bargaining is to maximise one's own benefit and acquire as much as possible, frequently at the expense of the other party. This is a win-lose situation. In these cases, parties are reluctant to share information with each other; in fact there are incentives to try to conceal important details from the other side. This is contradictory to the nature of an international business negotiation.

Negotiations on the other hand refer to joint problem solving, in which both parties look for a win-win outcome that is beneficial to everyone involved. This calls for an *integrative* approach. An integrative approach creates a situation in which both parties can achieve their objectives. When negotiations are not handled efficiently, both sides can end up with a mutually inferior outcome. The international business negotiations that receive attention in this book are integrative negotiations.[9]

Negotiations that follow a distributive or competitive approach do not achieve optimal results for any party. In these cases, parties believe that their objectives are opposed and cannot be achieved simultaneously. In reality, however, each party's goals may not be in opposition with, or contradictory to, one another. It is easier to see communality of objectives if parties adopt an integrative approach. In international business negotiations parties are interdependent; one party cannot do business on its own and has to involve the other. A distributive approach can only be used when business is being negotiated for just a single transaction and there is no intention or desire to do long-term business. In most business situations both buyers and sellers have other options, and if the deal is not completed with one party it will likely go through with another.

It is only through an integrative approach that parties can convince one another that this is the best deal possible and each party can influence the other to readjust its limits and demands. In the integrative approach parties can present and look at different offer packages and try different combinations. In this case parties can look together at different options and even discuss the give and take of each offer. Using the integrative approach, parties are more inclined to discuss commonalities than differences and show that they are committed to satisfying each other's needs. In this case parties are also more willing to exchange information than in the distributive approach.[10] Using the integrative approach, parties are also more willing to think about the underlying interests and intangible content of a particular deal that will help the discovery of innovative solutions to the satisfaction of each party, thus paving the way for a win-win outcome. There are several ways of creating a win-win solution to negotiations, some of which are summarised in Table 1.1. All these demand working together with the other party, which will by itself improve the possibility of achieving an integrative and problem-solving solution.

1.1 BEST ALTERNATIVE TO A NEGOTIATED AGREEMENT (BATNA)

The possibility of deadlocks and agreements during the negotiation process need to be anticipated. If the current negotiation reaches an impasse, what are the best outside options? Most seasoned negotiators understand the value of evaluating their BATNA, or their "best alternative to a negotiated agreement".[11] The awareness of BATNA can give a negotiator the confidence to walk away from a subpar agreement.[12] Negotiation experts have always considered bargaining power and BATNA as relevant factors in the negotiation outcome.

Table 1.1 Creating win-win solutions in international business negotiations

Approach	Description
Expand the pie	A shortage of resources is often a major concern in a negotiation that hinders both parties in their attempts to achieve their goals. One way to get around this problem is to suggest a different division of resources among the parties.
Unbundle the issue	Partition an issue that is causing major conflict into several smaller issues and then arrange these according to each party's priorities. Such action will disclose several new solutions.
Non-specific compensation	Let one party achieve its goal on one issue and "pay off" the other party in another way that is related to an unconnected issue. For example, if a party is asking for a 7 per cent discount on the price of machinery, offer a 15 per cent reduction in price on future purchases of replacement or spare parts if they accept the price you want; or offer free maintenance for the next five years.
Bridge the gap	Establish what the underlying issues for each party are. For each party, list their priorities from high to low. Understanding the relative priorities of both sides will produce a solution that is acceptable to both sides.
Think outside the box	At times negotiators persist in trying to convince one another that their proposal is the one that should be accepted and ratified when actually the ideal solution is to be found outside of the proposal they are making. Consider the story of two people quarrelling in a library. One wants the window open, the other wants to keep it shut. The two individuals argue about how much the window should be open: all the way, half open, or slightly open. After listening to their squabbling, the librarian asks one individual why they want to have the window open – the reply is to get some fresh air. When the other individual is asked why they want the window closed, the reply is to avoid sitting in a draft. The librarian then walks to the next room and opens a window in there, allowing fresh air to circulate without producing a draft.[13]

Source: Adapted from Lewicki (1994).[14]

BATNA can be assessed in a four-step process: considering alternatives, evaluating alternatives, establishing BATNA and choosing a course of action that would have the highest expected value in case the current deal fails.[15] Moreover, it is imperative to calculate the reservation value, which is the lowest-valued deal the negotiator is willing to accept. An evaluation of the best alternative to a deal is critical, if the negotiator is to establish the threshold at which they will reject an offer. Effective negotiators determine their BATNAs before talks begin, as costly mistakes can occur, such as rejecting a deal that should have been accepted or accepting one which it would have been wise to reject. In negotiation, it is important to have high aspirations and to fight hard for a good outcome. However, it is just as critical to establish a walk-away point that is firmly grounded. If the value of the deal proposed is lower than the reservation value, it is better to reject the offer and pursue the BATNA. These dispute resolution mechanisms are a valuable way of highlighting the importance of atmosphere and background factors before, during and after negotiations. Furthermore, the core of a negotiation process is not only information sharing, preparation and cooperative constructs, but also deadlocks and conflict resolution to have an efficient negotiation process and a satisfying outcome.[16]

1.2 DEAL MAKING

Deal making considers cooperative behaviour[17] between the parties and brings a positive aspect to negotiations. International negotiations will move across stages and are followed by trade deals and bilateral investment treaties. For this reason, conflict resolution and negotiation techniques will be important to this process. Here it is important to consider the mirror-image rule, negotiator authority and intention, as well as to ensure that deals do not later collapse on technical grounds. This means that every deal must have an offer, a counteroffer (give and take) and an acceptance. The parties add some value for each other to make a deal enforceable through contract law.

Combining psychological and political science perspectives of conflict resolution provided us with a basis for the frameworks in international business negotiations discussed in the following chapters.

1.3 SUMMARY

This chapter provides an overview of the nature of negotiations. Negotiating effectively is a highly valued skill that is learnt and improved by practice over time. In international settings, negotiators have to consider the influence of the cultural, political and institutional differences on the negotiation process. Negotiations are a complex process that involve two or more parties getting together to create a new relationship or discussing issues relating to their existing relationship. The elements of both cooperation and conflict are inherently present in all negotiations as parties attempt to maximise the benefits and outcomes for their organisation. A win-win approach to negotiation involves parties working towards a positive outcome for all those involved. However, if parties take a win-lose approach to negotiations, they risk a lose-lose outcome for all sides involved in the process.

QUESTIONS

1. What are the limitations of negotiators using self-reference criteria?
2. Explain the dual concern model as it applies to business negotiations.

3. What are some of the differences between an integrative and distributive bargaining approach?
4. What are some of the ways that win-win outcomes can be achieved in negotiations?

NOTES

1. Ghauri, P. and Cateora, P. (2014) *International Marketing*. 4th ed. London, McGraw-Hill.
2. Kapoor, A. (1975) *Planning for International Business Negotiations*. Cambridge MA, Ballingers Publishing Co.
3. Buckley, P. and Ghauri, P. (2004) Globalization, economic geography and the strategy of multinational enterprises. *Journal of International Business Studies*. **35**(2), 81–98.
4. Rubin, J., Pruitt, D. and Kim, S.H. (1994) *Social Conflict Escalation, Stalemate and Settlement*. 2nd ed. Boston MA, McGraw-Hill.
5. Lewicki, R., Barry, B. and Saunders, D. (2007) *Essentials of Negotiations*. 4th ed. New York, McGraw-Hill.
6. Lewicki, R. (1992) Negotiating strategically. In: Cohen, A. (ed.) *The Portable MBA in Management*. New York, John Wiley & Sons, pp. 147–89.
7. Ilke, F.C. (1964) *How Nations Negotiate*. New York, Praeger.
8. Lewicki et al. (2007) op. cit.
9. Ghauri, P.N. and Usunier, J.-C. (eds) (2003) *International Business Negotiations*. 2nd ed. Oxford, Pergamon/Elsevier.
10. Kelly, H.H. (1966) A classroom study of the dilemma in inter-personal negotiations. In: Archibald, K. (ed.) *Strategic Interaction and Conflict, Original Papers and Discussion*. Berkley, Institute of International Studies, pp. 49–73.
11. Fisher et al. (1991) op. cit.
12. Fisher et al. (1991) op. cit.; Subramanian, G. (2007) Bargaining in the shadow of PeopleSoft's (defective) poison pill. *Harvard Negotiation Law Review*, Winter.
13. Fisher, R., Ury, W. and Patton, B. (1991) *Getting to Yes: Negotiating Agreement without Giving In*. London, Penguin.
14. Lewicki, R.J., Litterer, J.A., Minton, J.W. and Saunders, D.M. (1994) *Negotiation*. 2nd ed. Burr Ridge, Irwin.
15. Fisher et al. (1991) op. cit.; Malhotra, D. (2004) Risky business: trust in negotiation. *Negotiation*. **7**(2).
16. Ghauri, P.N. (2003) A framework for international business negotiations. In: Ghauri, P.N. and Usunier, J.-C. (eds) *International Business Negotiations*. 2nd ed. Oxford, Pergamon/Elsevier, pp. 3–22; Ott, U.F., Prowse, P., Fells, R. and Rogers, H. (2016) The DNA of negotiations as a set theoretic concept: a theoretical and empirical analysis. *Journal of Business Research*. **69**(9), 3561–71.
17. Raiffa, H., Richardson, J. and Metcalfe, D. (2002) Negotiation Analysis: The Science and Art of Collaborative Decision Making. Cambridge MA, The Belknap Press of Harvard University Press; Subramanian, G. (2006) Contracts 101: what every negotiator should know about contract and agency law. *Harvard Business Review*. Available from: https://store.hbr.org/product/contracts-101-what-every-negotiator-should-know-about-contract-and-agency-law/N0602D.

FURTHER READING

Agndal, H., Åge, L. and Eklinder-Frick, J. (2017) Two decades of business negotiation research: an overview and suggestions for future studies. *Journal of Business and Industrial Marketing*. **32**(4), 487–504.

Fells, R., Rogers, H., Prowse, P. and Ott, U.F. (2015) Unraveling business negotiations using practitioner data. *Negotiation and Conflict Management Research*. **8**(2), 119–36.

Luomala, H.T., Kumar, R., Singh, J.D. and Jaakkola, M. (2015) When an intercultural business negotiation fails: comparing the emotions and behavioural tendencies of individualistic and collectivistic negotiators. *Group Decision and Negotiation*. **24**(3), 537–61.

Wang, Y., Wang, K.Y. and Ma, X. (2016) Understanding international business negotiation behavior: credible commitments, dispute resolution, and the role of institutions. *International Negotiation: A Journal of Theory and Practice*. **21**(1), 165–98.

2
Conflict resolution

This chapter highlights the differences between cooperation and conflict. Conflict resolution models exist for international negotiations between countries, but also between companies and individuals. There are clear strategic possibilities related to the conflict mechanisms, and the early conflict resolution models are still relevant for international business negotiations, since they have been adapted by many international business negotiation scholars.

Cooperation and conflict are two essential parts of every negotiation. This chapter defines conflict and reviews the theoretical frameworks to categorise conflict resolution strategies. The conflict resolution mechanisms used in international negotiations are highlighted at the end of the chapter to give the reader a tool for understanding, analysing and solving conflicts in a real-life business context.[1]

2.1 WHAT IS CONFLICT?

The definition of *conflict* reflects numerous attempts from scholars across the fields (psychology, sociology, political science). The similarities of these definitions are based around:[2]

> Conflict is a state in which people differ in their preferences on how to reach objectives and the differences impede each party's ability to get what they want.

1. People differ in their preferences regarding how to accomplish an objective.
2. These differing preferences impede each side's ability to get what they want.

At the core of the definition of conflict is that the *disputing parties* are trying to seek an outcome which satisfies their preferences. Conflict is a social force that has shaped, and continues to shape, the world we live in. The outcome of prior conflict, whether that conflict has been economic, ideological, ethnic or even international (the most extreme example of which is war), has profoundly affected us all: our ideas, our welfare and even the languages that we use to communicate with one another. The effect that conflict has had on the world and the complexity of the concept is to some extent belied by the simplicity of the word's basic definition, which the Merriam-Webster dictionary gives as "a struggle for power". Even the fuller definition of conflict provided by the Merriam-Webster dictionary, namely a "fight, battle, war", is very simple and straightforward. The difficulty with simplicity is that it can often be misleading and omit important information. For instance, neither the basic nor the fuller definition of conflict provide information about what the sources or the reasons for conflict are. Nor do they provide any information about the scale or scope that conflict may assume, nor even at what level or unit of society conflict may occur. Conflicts, however, vary in their bases, their duration, their mode of settlement, their outcomes and their consequences.[3] In order to properly comprehend these issues, and understand why conflict is an important element of international business negotiations, a more sophisticated definition of conflict is required.

Defining conflict in the first instance as either a struggle or a fight does have one significant advantage – it focuses attention on the fact that conflict is essentially about disagreement, the opposition of two entities. The entities in opposition to each other can take various forms: they can be an opposition of ideas, interests or values. The important point is, however, that conflict is an interactive process; it is the engagement of two interests or concerns that are incompatible with one another and as such are unable to mutually co-exist.[4] The psychologists Karen Jehn and Corinne Bendersky have provided a broad definition of conflict, namely "perceived incompatibilities or discrepant views among the parties involved", that relates well to this first definition of conflict.[5] A further important element when defining conflict is provided by the Nobel Laureate Thomas Schelling, who in his book *The Strategy of Conflict*[6] argues that conflict situations are bargaining situations, emphasising that in addition to conflict being the divergence of interests over certain variables in dispute,[7] there is a powerful common interest inherent in conflict to reach an outcome that is not enormously destructive to both sides. Schelling supports this by arguing that a successful employees' strike is not one that financially destroys the employer. Rather, it could in fact be one that never even takes place. The definition of conflict as a process in which there has been a divergence of interests so that one "party perceives that its interests are being opposed or negatively affected by another party" has been reiterated subsequently.[8]

Reviewing and summarising these various definitions it is possible to state five key criteria that for the purposes of international business negotiations define conflict. These are:

1. Conflict is a struggle.
2. Conflict is a perceived disagreement between two opposing entities.
3. Conflict is interactive; it is the engagement of two interests that are unable to mutually co-exist and are thus incompatible.
4. Conflict situations are bargaining situations where interests have diverged.
5. Ultimately, both parties will benefit from finding a constructive outcome.

Negotiation is a means of managing conflict as defined by these criteria. Negotiation seeks to resolve the struggle, end disagreement, synchronise interests that previously were unable to mutually co-exist, and, through bargaining, enable the interests of the conflicting parties to converge, allowing a constructive outcome to be reached.

Now a definition of conflict has been established based on these five key criteria, the next step required to establish a complete understanding of conflict, and its function in international business negotiations, is to determine the levels at which conflict may develop. In this respect, Rahim[9] has differentiated between conflict that develops at the intra-organisational level, and that which develops at the inter-organisational level. Refining and developing a taxonomy first presented in a co-authored article published in 1979, Rahim classifies four different sub-levels at which intra-organisational conflict may originate:[10]

1. Intrapersonal (conflict occurs within an individual)
2. Interpersonal (conflict occurs between two or more individuals)
3. Intragroup (conflict occurs within a group)
4. Intergroup (conflict occurs between two or more groups).

The first of the four sub-levels, intrapersonal conflict, is a psychological form of conflict that occurs within, and is confined to, an individual. For example, one can be conflicted about whether one believes in God or not, or about whether one should revise for a test or party with my friends.[11] While there is no denying that intrapersonal conflict is an important level of conflict, socially, conflict is more clearly and accurately described as involving at least two parties.[12] Conflict that arises between two parties aligns more closely with the five key criteria that have been used to define conflict above. Moreover, within the context of international business negotiations, defining conflict as occurring between two or more parties allows for far greater scope, and generalisability. Interpersonal, intragroup and intergroup conflict are, therefore, all levels at which intra-organisational conflict between two or more parties may occur.

Interpersonal conflict is the conflict that exists, or is perceived to exist, between two individuals, such as a husband and wife, a buyer and a seller in a transaction, or the president and vice-president of a company.

The next level at which conflict between two or more parties can be manifest is at the intragroup level. Intragroup conflict is a type of conflict that can occur among a company's top management team, within a premier league football team or between members of a university's research ethics committee. Guetzkow and Gyr[13] were the first to make a conceptual difference between two types of conflict that could arise within groups: one rooted in the substance of the task a group is undertaking, and one deriving from the emotional, affective aspects of the group's interpersonal relations. More recently, Karen Jehn has reformulated and elaborated on this distinction, differentiating between two different types of intragroup conflict: relationship conflict and task conflict.[14] Relationship conflict exists when there are interpersonal incompatibilities among group members – which typically include tension, animosity and annoyance among members within a group. Task conflict exists when there are disagreements among group members about the content of the tasks being performed, including differences in viewpoint, ideas and opinion. Amongst certain groups, such as top management teams, task conflict is unavoidable.[15] Successfully resolving intragroup conflict, however, is of great importance, as it affects the ability of the group to resolve its internal disputes and achieve its goals effectively.[16]

The fourth level at which intra-organisational conflict between two or more parties can arise is at the intergroup level. Intergroup conflict may arise between labour and management, between retail stores and the head office, or between the marketing and finance departments.

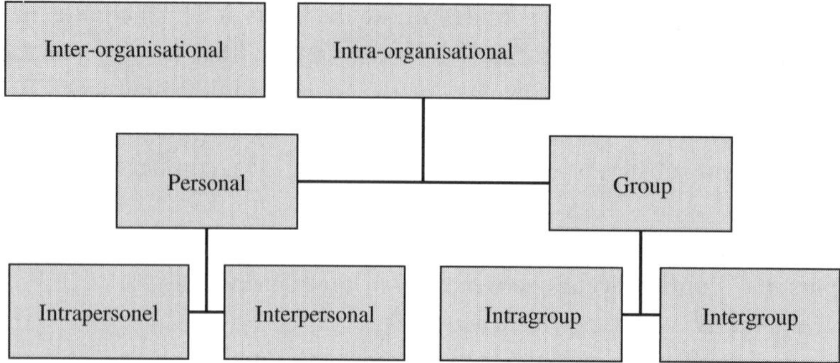

Figure 2.1 Classification of the levels at which conflict can appear

Like interpersonal conflict, intergroup conflict can be understood using the techniques of game theory. This is because a group is simply an aggregate set of individuals who identify with each other rather than through negotiations conducted by the groups as a whole.[17]

Finally, conflict that arises at the inter-organisational level, in Figure 2.1, should not be neglected. Indeed, conflict is not only a key characteristic of inter-organisational relationships,[18] but in international business theory, inter-organisational conflict between organisations such as multinational enterprises (MNEs) and a home- or host-country government regarding distributional issues and the power of the MNE versus the home state, or at a more general level between markets (driven by the actions of MNEs) and governments, is of great importance.[19] To be even more specific, the type of conflict that arises between partners in an international strategic alliance is a significant type of inter-organisational conflict that belongs uniquely to the subject of international business negotiations.

2.2 WHAT ARE THE SOURCES OF CONFLICT?

So far five key criteria that define conflict, and the five levels at which conflict may arise, have been established. Yet, up to this point, the sources of conflict have not been discussed. This section focuses on this topic. Identifying what the sources of conflict are is vitally important for a successful resolution; if the reasons for disagreement and the divergence of interests are not known, it is not possible to seek a solution to the conflict, or to conduct a successful negotiation that produces a constructive outcome for both parties. There are three potential triggers of conflict: opportunity, preference and perception.[20]

2.2.1 Opportunity

Opportunity may be the cause of conflict because one party believes a scenario has presented itself in which there are prospects for gain, or for it to improve upon its current situation. This gain or improvement might, however, only be attained at the expense of, or with negative effects for, another, second, party. To illustrate how opportunity may trigger conflict, suppose

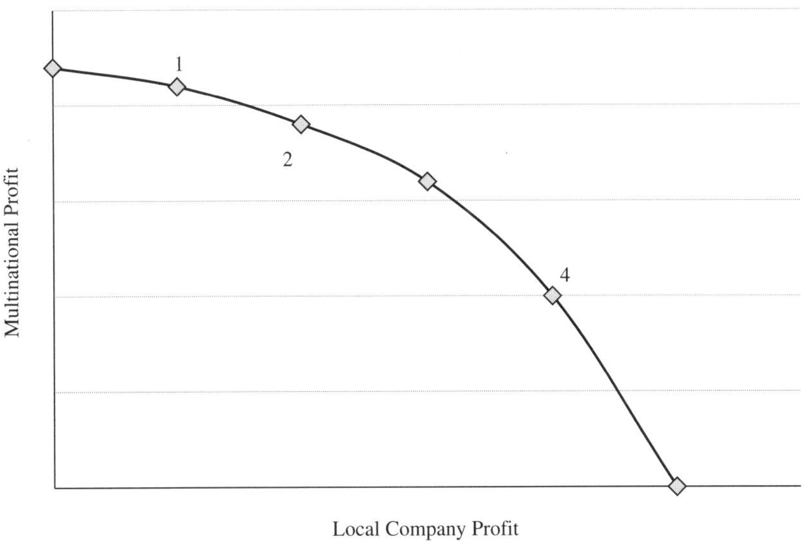

Figure 2.2 Profit allocation of partnership between an MNE and a local company

a large, mature multinational decided to expand into a foreign country's market for the first time. While this multinational has experience of operating in foreign markets generally, it does not in this instance possess the infrastructure necessary to sell its product in the particular country in which it is about to launch operations.[21] A local company does, however, possess suitable infrastructure that the multinational can use in order to sell its product in the foreign market. In return for giving the multinational access to this infrastructure, the local firm is allocated a proportion of the profits, illustrated by point 4 in Figure 2.2. Initially, the terms on which profits are allocated are favourable to the local company, reflecting the fact that at this stage the multinational has no other viable option but to partner with the local company.

Subsequently, an opportunity presents itself for the multinational to establish and develop its own infrastructure in the host country. Now an alliance with the local company is no longer the multinational's only viable option: it has the opportunity to operate by itself and have full control over the profits generated by the venture. The multinational has however received praise from the host country's government and received positive media coverage in its home country for the relationship it has forged with the local company. Moreover, establishing the necessary infrastructure would involve considerable capital investment, and several board members and key shareholders are uneasy at the large cost of such an uncertain project; they would much prefer a larger dividend or a share buyback.

As a result, the multinational's senior managers propose to the local company that rather than terminate the alliance altogether in light of the opportunity that has presented itself, the local company accept instead a smaller share of the alliance's profits, indicated at point 1 on Figure 2.2. The local company is, however, disappointed that it is going to receive a smaller portion of the profits than it had been receiving up to this point. Changing the terms of the profit allocation might even disrupt future investment plans that the local company had made. Instead, the local company proposes to the multinational that rather than profits being allocated at point 1 on Figure 2.2, they be allocated at point 2.

Whether the multinational and the local company reach an agreement isn't important at this stage. What is important is that the conflict between the two parties has arisen from a set of circumstances that presented itself to one of the parties that would have allowed it to improve its own circumstances but with a cost for, and to the detriment of, the second party. It is also useful to note that both the multinational and the local company have a mutual interest in reaching an outcome that is satisfactory for them both. There are potential benefits to both through the continuation of joint production, and potential disadvantages to both for not reaching a mutually satisfactory outcome.

2.2.2 Preferences

A second potential source of conflict is the preferences of a particular party. These preferences are the principles, assumptions and values that an individual, a group or an organisation is committed to above all others. Such preferences can incorporate anything from universal ideals such as truth, liberty and justice to subjective, context-specific ideas about maximising shareholder value, or operating in a sustainable and environmentally concerned way. Corporate preferences are frequently expressed in a company's mission statement. Twitter for example states that its mission is "to give everyone the power to create and share ideas and information instantly without barriers", but since the company's inception it has incurred significant operating losses, and as of 31 December 2014 the accumulated deficit of Twitter was $1.57 billion. Twitter's preference, for the time being at least, is not necessarily generating profit, but rather to "democratise content creation and distribution, enabling any voice to echo around the world instantly and unfiltered".[22]

The basis for an individual's, group's or organisation's preferences can seemingly be irrational, but every culture, or subculture, is defined by its own set of common values, its own set of agreed upon preferences. Without a nucleus of common values, a culture cannot exist, and society is classified into cultures and subcultures precisely because it is possible to identify groups and individuals who share common values.[23] By their very nature, however, such preferences can create instances where one party's interests are opposed to another. Twitter, for instance, is officially blocked in China; the preferences of the company and the country are opposed. This may have less to do with Twitter's commitment to barrier-free information and idea sharing, however, and more to do with the Chinese government's economic preference for the growth of the Chinese-based Sina Weibo.

During a conflict or a bargaining situation, a set of ingrained beliefs or preferences can lead to different values being placed on different aspects of the conflict situation and its outcome: what one party needs (A_1) or wishes does not necessarily align with what the other party needs or wishes (A_2); what may be the highest priority for one of the parties (B_3), may be a fairly low priority for the other party whose highest priority (B_4) is on an entirely different issue. While one party may value and want to see truth and humility from its negotiating partner, that partner might act deceptively or brashly in order to achieve the outcome it desires most, and believes (mistakenly) that the way to achieve this outcome is to act in such a manner.

2.2.3 Perception

The third potential source of conflict is perception. Perception is about information, and how individuals, groups or organisations "tune in" to their environment and ascribe meaning to messages.[24] The actions of individuals or groups are frequently based on their perceptions of the environment they are in and the context in which events occur. Commercially, this might lead a business to mistakenly overestimate the relative strength of one of its products, and simultaneously underestimate the strength of a competitor's product. Alternatively, a consumer may perceive that a company is an ethical, trustworthy and socially responsible organisation, when in reality it is no such thing! Flawed or inaccurate perceptions can lead to suboptimal outcomes, for industries, consumers and society.

Perception can be a source of conflict because one party mistakenly believes that it can secure a better outcome than the existing one through initiating a conflict (bargaining) situation. An extreme example of this is provided by the case of the Vietnam War, where the United States engaged in an enormously destructive conflict based on the perception that "victory might come easily and with little pain".[25] On a different level, two managers may be conflicted over their perceptions of uncertainty in a foreign market, and the extent to which their product would be viable and profitable.

Returning to the previous example of the multinational and the local company, the opportunity may never have arisen for the multinational to develop and build its own infrastructure (such is the nature of an opportunity). Nonetheless, the multinational's senior management may feel it can secure a higher share of the profits (point 1) if it threatens to withdraw from the alliance, leaving its local partner high and dry. The multinational behaves in such a way because it perceives that without the alliance the fortunes and profit of the local company would be irrevocably damaged. This perception may be correct, and the local company may agree to allocate the multinational a higher share of the profit, but by the same token such a perception may be false. The local company's profit and fortunes may be perfectly satisfactory *without* the alliance, and the local company may therefore refuse to be dictated to by the multinational, refuse to allocate the multinational a higher proportion of the profits, and terminate the alliance. The multinational is left with no profits and no means of operating in that market, while the local company can continue as before.

In a conflict situation, accurate perception is liable to be distorted by preconceived opinions about an individual or a group. These preconceived ideas form the basis for stereotypes and prejudice. A stereotype is the collected beliefs about the characteristics of a group of people:[26] Germans are efficient and always win penalty shoot-outs, the Swiss are punctual, Japanese people are very polite. Prejudice, meanwhile, is a stored-up attitude towards another person, group or organisation. Here, attitude implies an evaluation of a stimulus object (the colour of skin, an accent, the way a person is dressed) on a positive–negative scale; thus, while traditionally prejudice has mostly been a negative attitude and associated with a disposition to act negatively towards another group, more recently it has been treated as a dimension that refers to both positive and negative evaluation.[27] In conflict situations, stereotypes and prejudice are simultaneously outcomes of previously acquired hostility between the groups or people involved and nourished by the maintenance of conflict.

2.2.4 Stimulants of conflict: the influence of emotion and the importance of communication

Conflict can thus be triggered by opportunity, preference or perception, but it is sustained, advanced and intensified by an emotional reaction to, or emotional involvement with, an issue or dispute. Emotions such as ambition, pride, vanity and anger can all influence a conflict situation. The members of an environmental campaign group, for example, who care deeply about the environment, may allow the depth of their feeling for the issue to dominate their interaction and entrench a conflict they have with a resource extraction company. Emotion begets emotion, and as feelings begin to dominate, the actual substance of the conflict begins to diminish and no resolution may be found; the negotiation ends in a stand-off with neither side willing to seek a constructive outcome.[28]

Most research on emotional involvement in conflict and bargaining (negotiating) situations has focused on the intrapersonal effects of a negotiator's emotional state.[29] A negotiator may be happy, angry or emotionally neutral. A seminal study by Carnevale and Isen[30] demonstrated that negotiators with positive feelings engaged in more productive negotiations and produced more optimal solutions than emotionally neutral negotiators. Inversely, a high degree of anger (a negative emotion) and a low degree of compassion (a positive emotion) has been shown to pose serious disadvantages to a negotiation: it reduces the gains for both of the negotiating parties.[31]

2.2.5 Emotion adversely effects communication

The most serious threat emotion poses to the successful resolution of conflict situations is that it adversely affects the ability of each party to communicate with the other. As communication between the conflicting parties is impaired, little confidence is placed in the information one party receives from the other; instead, suspicion and thoughts of misinformation begin to grow. As a result, instead of communication producing a satisfactory outcome for both parties, the differences and points of divergence between the two conflicting parties are reinforced and amplified as communication becomes increasingly to be seen as futile. As the conflict becomes ever more intractable, communication only serves to magnify the differences between the parties.

2.2.6 As communication decreases conflict escalates

The conflict is escalated as communication becomes merely a repeated experience of further disagreement and rejection of solutions that erodes belief that the two parties can ever be reconciled and a unifying outcome reached. Instead, each party seeks to enhance their own position and power, while seeking to reduce the power and position of the other. This negative, self-perpetuating destructive cycle is displayed in Figure 2.3 and originates from the work of the social psychologist Morton Deutsch.[32]

In order to avoid this destructive cycle in a conflict situation, it is necessary to recognise the importance of emotion and begin to attempt to control it through an awareness of one's

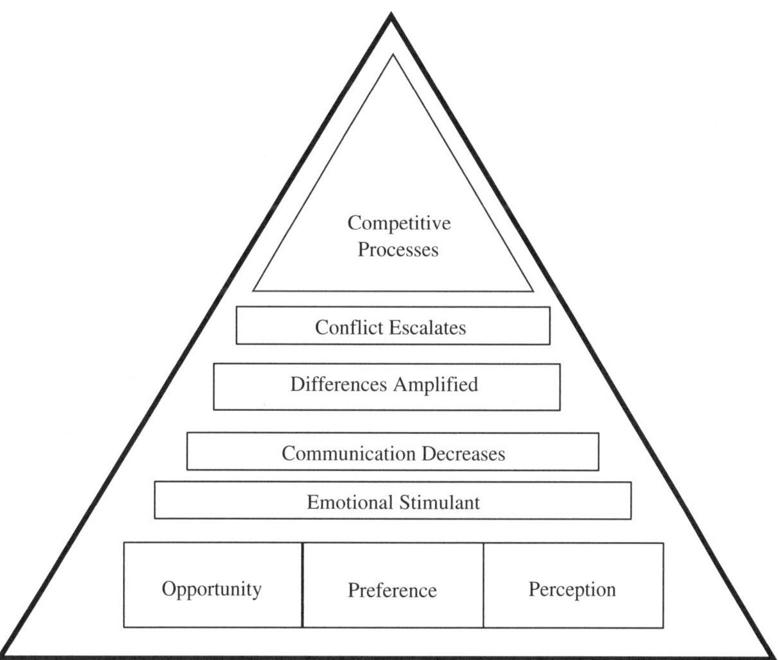

Figure 2.3 The negative conflict escalation pyramid

own emotional state, and the emotional state of the other party. Research has recently shown that emotion is actually expressing information on how to respond. What is imperative is choosing an appropriate response. Communication skills are necessary to express one's own state of mind, and to listen to the other party's emotional expressions, both verbal and non-verbal. If communication between the two parties is poor, or one party elects not to engage, then the differences between the two are magnified, conflict escalates and the two parties compete in open hostility. The failure to communicate or correctly interpret the message of the other party is therefore critical to ensuring an outcome to the conflict is reached that is not enormously destructive to both sides.

2.3 CAN CONFLICT BE POSITIVE?

In the Orson Welles movie, *The Third Man*, Welles's character, the villain Harry Lime, trades in the black market for medicinal drugs. When he tells the man, Holly Martins, who has previously been his friend and idolised him, the truth of his illicit activities, Martins is understandably upset. Lime, though, instructs Martins not to be so gloomy about the truth, because after all, "in Italy, for thirty years under the Borgias, they had warfare, terror, murder and bloodshed, but they produced Michelangelo, Leonardo da Vinci and the Renaissance. In Switzerland, they had brotherly love, they had five hundred years of democracy and peace – and what did that produce? The cuckoo clock."

This chapter has so far proceeded on the assumption that conflict is a negative, disruptive force that is detrimental to any social unit in which it arises. A body of research, however, suggests that in reality this is far from the case; that conflict when managed well may have positive outcomes, breathing life and energy into relationships, strengthening parties' interdependence and bolstering productivity, creativity and innovation.[33] Theoretically, the positive value of conflict has a long history.[34] Of particular importance to those who study and participate in international business negotiations is the idea that conflict can have a positive influence by creating unity between isolated individuals,[35] or by bringing together previously isolated groups to form a coalition.[36] Such coalitions can be formed into more permanent institutions through common values, norms and the shared experience of a struggle endured together. Such progress, however, requires compromise and the willingness of all parties to cooperate with one another. Fostering cooperation and creating cooperative goals are fundamental to positive conflict.[37]

2.3.1 Cooperation

In international business it is imperative that cooperation is analysed as simultaneously both an input and an output of a conflict or bargaining situation, and it is very important to differentiate between cooperation as an input and cooperation as an output. The input aspect of cooperation is the awareness by both sides that a problem exists and a *willingness* on the part of the parties involved in the conflict process to address the issues that need addressing. Cooperation can be regarded as an output, as the commitment and initial willingness demonstrated by one party creates increased trust and belief in the commitment of all parties to the venture that they are involved in together.[38] In order to produce cooperation, though, parties first need to communicate their willingness and their intent to cooperate to their partners. All cooperating partners need to be fully cognisant of the issues and matters that require settlement in order to produce a satisfactory outcome. Such communication is an integral part of the negotiation process.

2.3.2 Willingness to cooperate

That an initial indication of willingness to cooperate is the essential first step in establishing and sustaining cooperation, and through cooperation producing positive conflict, is shown through consideration of the tit-for-tat strategy. Using the example of the prisoner's dilemma game, the tit-for-tat strategy relies on the game being played not just once, but an indefinite number of times. This is a more realistic setting for the game as in both free market and hierarchical economic exchanges, actors can never be sure how long any relationship will last. The tit-for-tat strategy begins with player 1 making a move that cooperates with the other player, that is, player 1 does not confess to the police. In subsequent games, however, player 1 mimics player 2's previous move. So if player 1's opening move is cooperative but it is met with a non-cooperative move by player 2, that is, if player 2 defects and confesses to the police that she and player 1 are guilty, then the next time player 1 plays, they will not cooperate with the other player, and will confess to the police. Player 1 will only become cooperative again with player 2 when their previous move has been cooperative.[39]

2.3.3 Demonstrate willingness

The key point of the tit-for-tat strategy is that the initial willingness to cooperate, and communication of that willingness to another player in an iterated environment, should encourage the other player to adapt and change their behaviour from non-cooperation to cooperation. The initial willingness to cooperate has to be properly understood, though, and this can be difficult in the "noisy" environment of the real world. Misunderstanding the initial gesture of cooperation, or erroneous implementation of cooperative behaviour, can lead to the failure of a party to change or adapt their behaviour.[40] How then to manage such noise so that the initial cooperative move is not lost and a cooperative result can be achieved?

While such noise can never be entirely eradicated, it can be reduced by correctly attributing the thoughts, intentions and motivations to the words or actions that are being communicated. Correct attribution of meaning relies on interpersonal intelligence, which is "the ability to notice and make distinctions among other individuals and, in particular, among their moods, temperaments, motivations, and intentions".[41]

Positive conflict leads to increases in interpersonal intelligence, and in so doing it strengthens and develops individuals, groups and organisations. Accordingly, positive conflict is a part of testing and assessing the strength of an individual, group or organisation,[42] and enables conflicting parties to accomplish things together that they never thought were possible. Furthermore, positive conflict may itself initiate the positive conflict process, through increasing awareness of a problem that requires change.[43]

How positive conflict develops, and the actions necessary to exploit its potential, are summarised in Figure 2.4. The weight or power cooperative processes have is distributed throughout the structure that supports it: the structure is built in the first instance on both parties' awareness that a problem exists. Both parties then need to communicate their willingness to cooperate and adapt their behaviour accordingly. The adaption of behaviour creates empathy and the ability to see the problem through the eyes of the other party. This broadening of horizons leads to the growth of individuals separately and collectively as they work together towards conflict resolution. The whole cooperative process leads to far more positive outcomes than would be the case if conflict was allowed to grow and no joint actions were taken.

2.4 CONFLICT RESOLUTION FRAMEWORKS: PSYCHOLOGY PERSPECTIVE

International business negotiations draw from the psychological, economics and political science conceptual and theoretical approaches and benefit from these different perspectives. This section deals with the psychological frameworks for conflict resolution. The psychological literature distinguishes two frameworks – the dual concern model and the interest–rights–power (IRP) theory.

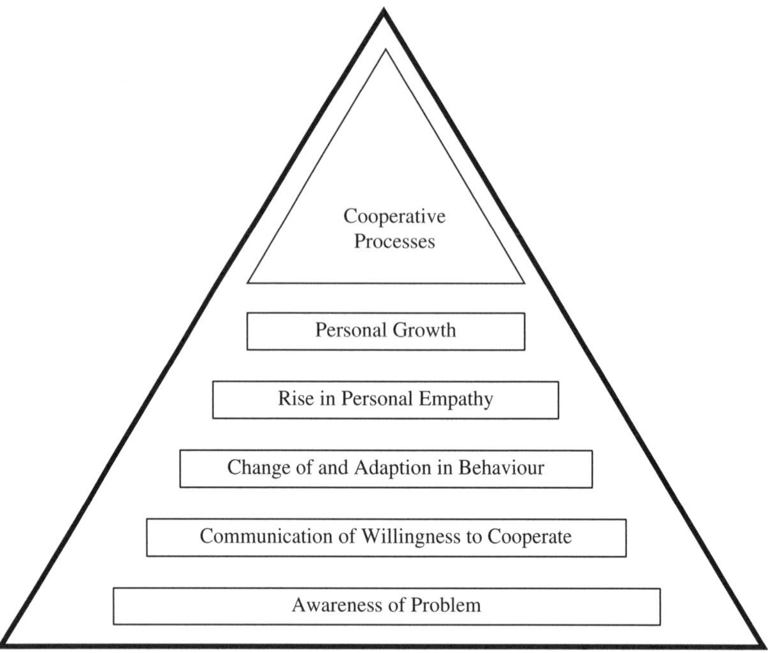

Figure 2.4 The positive conflict pyramid

2.4.1 The dual concern model

The dual concern model was briefly introduced in Chapter 1; here we explain it further. The concern and welfare of the "self" and the "other" reflects the strategic choices of the disputants. Combining these concerns with a classification of strategies on how to handle conflict, the parties can choose:[44]

1. Domination
2. Integration
3. Compromise
4. Suppression
5. Avoidance.

Domination strategy: The concern is more about the self of the focal party than the other party. The contrary is happening in the suppression or subordinance of one's needs.
Integration strategy: The disputant is highly interested in meeting both parties' welfare.
Compromise strategy: The disputant is moderately interested in meeting both parties' welfare.
Suppression strategy: For the benefit of the counterparty, the disputant suppresses their own needs.
Avoidance strategy: The disputant is unconcerned about the well-being of the other party. The disputant does not talk to other the party about their differences.

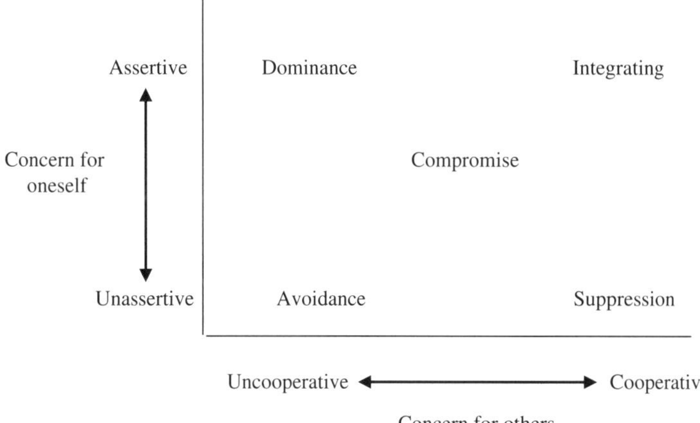

Sources: Adapted from De Dreu (2004);[45] Shapiro and Kulik (2004);[46] Saner (2003);[47] and Elgoibar et al. (2017).[48]

Figure 2.5 The basic dual concern model

Apart from avoidance strategy, all other strategy choices involve concession making. Long-lasting agreements are often based on strategies involving mutual concessions as they lead to more satisfying outcomes. De Dreu[49] combined the dual concern model into a diagram of self-concern and concern for others with the respective strategies (Figure 2.5).

In Example 2.1 we apply this framework to Apple's apology in China to show the working.

EXAMPLE 2.1
APPLE APOLOGY IN CHINA

On 15 March 2013, a Chinese television network highlighted that Apple was giving iPhone customers in China a short warranty and charging consumers to replace faulty back covers on iPhones. Other media outlets joined in, and the public outcry grew. Some speculated that the complaints were a calculated campaign by the local competitors to weaken Apple's market position. Apple initially failed to respond to the accusations against its warranty policies.

In April 2013, the *New York Times* reported that Apple CEO Timothy D. Cook made the unusual move of apologising to Chinese customers for his company's warranty policy and promised to make amends. An open letter was released in Chinese in which Cook admitted that his company's lack of communication had led to a perception that "Apple is arrogant and doesn't care or value consumers' feedback." The letter continued, "We sincerely apologize for any concern or misunderstanding this has brought to the customers."

The application of the dual concern model to the Apple China apology is shown in Figure 2.6.

Discussion Point: The strategies used were integrating and compromising. Are there any other possible scenarios? Try to give some other views and find similar cases.

Dominance
(Apple does not care/arrogant)
Integrating (Apology)
Concern for Apple
Compromise (Apology)
Avoidance
(Apple does not respond)
Suppression
(adjusts to Chinese)
Concern for Chinese

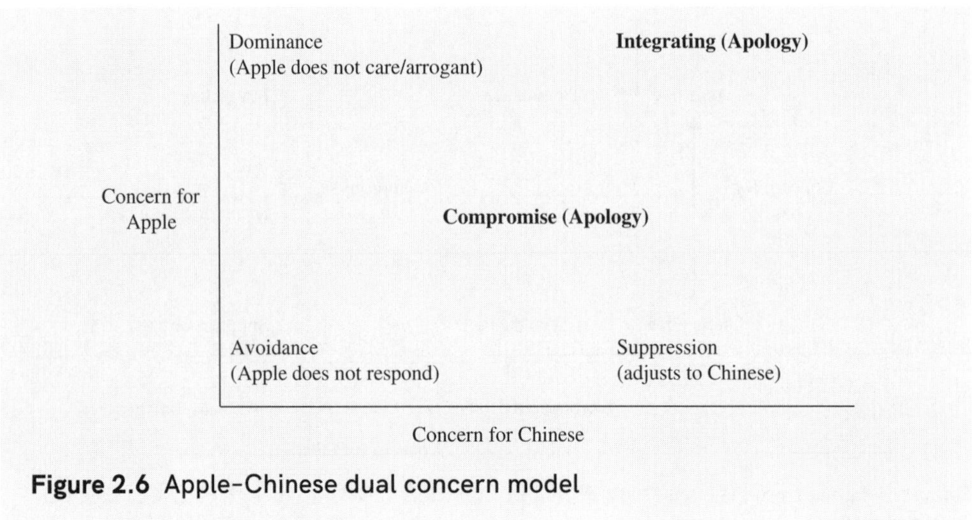

Figure 2.6 Apple-Chinese dual concern model

The dual concern model for conflict resolution can align the various approaches and provides a good basis for analysis.

International negotiations have concern for self and others integrated in their approach to bridge cultural differences. The cultural differences in international business negotiations often comprise different conflict and cooperation strategies depending on whether they have an individualistic or collectivistic cultural background. The concern for self and others is part of the tragedy of the commons which is inherently a conflict scenario of individualistic and collectivistic approaches. Figure 2.7 can be seen as an underlying possibility to position the different approaches in international business negotiations.

Dominance
Tough Demands, Low Concessions
Persuasion, Threats
Focus on Positions not Interests
Integrating
Package Negotiations
Information Exchange, Expanding the Pie
Focus on Interests not Position
Self-concern
Compromise
Avoidance
No Demands or Concessions
Downplaying Issue Importance
Ignoring Requests and Deadlines
Suppression
Low Demands and Concessions
Downplaying Self-interest
Ingratiation and Subordinance
Concern for others

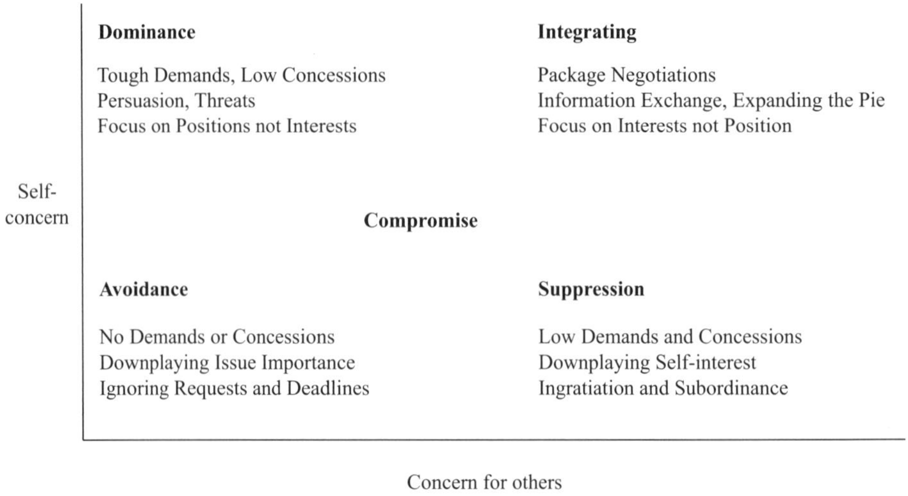

Figure 2.7 Dual concern model for negotiations

2.4.2 The interest-rights-power (IRP) theory

Another conflict resolution framework is based on communication between the parties and how to resolve the conflict in different ways through their messages. Originally, Ury, Brett and Goldberg suggested that when disputants communicate three types of messages tend to be conferred:[50]

1. **I**nterest-oriented messages – when the conflict resolution message is sent or given it integrates the preferences of the parties.
2. **R**ights-oriented messages – the substance of the conflict resolution message refers to rules, laws, norms and standards which guide the conflict resolution process.
3. **P**ower-oriented messages – the substance of the conflict resolution message is threatening in nature.

These messages in the conflict resolution situation can occur in parallel and in combination. Rights- and power-oriented messages can be used at the same time and lead to an escalation of conflict. Conflict resolution experts advise to refrain from using rights and power expressions early in the conflict resolution process. The most effective way to stop conflict is to combine a power-oriented with an interest-oriented message. In cross-cultural contexts, the communication patterns matter, as cultural differences add to the complexities of conflict resolution. When using new technologies (internet, chat rooms) in which the disputes are not resolved face to face, the nature of conflict and dispute resolution moves to another level. In this case the parties need to move from a dual concern model to a multiple concern model in which collective interests and well-being are considered. Indirect strategies are much more relevant than those found in conventional models.

In Example 2.2 we use the same conflict situation of Apple in China and solve it with the IRP framework.

EXAMPLE 2.2
APPLE APOLOGY IN CHINA

On 15 March 2013, Apple was criticised for giving iPhone customers in China a short warranty and for charging consumers to replace faulty back covers on iPhones. Other media outlets joined in, and the public outcry grew. Some speculated that the complaints were a calculated campaign by Chinese competitors.

Apple initially failed to respond to the accusations against its warranty policies. In April 2013, the *New York Times* reported that Apple CEO Timothy D. Cook made the unusual move of apologising to Chinese customers for his company's warranty policy and promised to make amends. An open letter was released in Chinese in which Cook admitted that his company's lack of communication had led to a perception that "Apple is arrogant and doesn't care or value consumers' feedback." The letter continued, "We sincerely apologize for any concern or misunderstanding this has brought to the customers."

Interest-oriented messages: With the letter the conflict was moved to resolution by using an approach which is particularly important in collectivist cultures – the apology.

Rights-oriented messages: Warranty policy and legal rules based messages between Apple and the Chinese government are leading to a conflict situation.

Power-oriented messages: The Chinese government displays its power over Apple, which originally seemed more powerful than the Chinese customers.

A rights-oriented and power-oriented message would have failed in the cross-cultural conflict resolution.

Conflict can be positive in many ways. It reveals the different preferences of the parties and demonstrates the ability and willingness to find a solution to an underlying problem. Conflict will lead to creative solution strategies, an awareness of careful planning, information exchange and the use of deadlock situations to find alternative paths to a negotiation outcome.

Discussion Point: Find some positive examples of conflict from your own experience.

2.5 THE CONFLICT RESOLUTION MODEL FOR INTERNATIONAL NEGOTIATIONS: POLITICAL ANGLE

To use a more abstract approach to start with, the international relations literature deals with conflict between states. This shows the highest level of interaction in international negotiations. The outcome of an international crisis can lead to war and therefore mediation is an essential part of the negotiation between governments. *International crisis* is defined as:[51]

1. A change that occurs in the type and/or intensity of disruptive (hostile verbal or physical) interaction between two or more states, with a heightened probability of military hostilities;
2. These changes in turn destabilise the states' relationship and challenge the structure of the international system.

Mediation shortens the crisis and leads to better outcomes and a peaceful setting. Cultural differences in this stream are associated with unsuccessful outcomes.

The definitions of conflict, conflict management and conflict resolution highlight the differences in their agenda. *Conflict management* deals with conflict and escalation, whereas *conflict resolution* means reduction, elimination or solving of a conflict. For conflict resolution to take place, the parties need to communicate and exchange their views, transform the situation, change the rules, actors or the structure or even bring in a third party as mediator. Conflict resolution processes occur in negotiations and mediation.[52]

Conflict management deals with conflict and escalation.

Conflict resolution reduces, eliminates or solves conflict. Communication and exchange of views is essential.

Conflict resolution in international negotiations goes back a long time, and many scholars have come up with similar structures of international negotiations when it comes to highlighting the dispute resolution process. The *Journal of Conflict Resolution* published a very early comprehensive model of international negotiations which highlights the stages of the negotiation. It focuses on the actors, the activities, the strategies and the outcome, but also the implementation. In 1966, Randolph conceptualised international negotiations in a conflict resolution setting. Randolph's conceptualisation can be recognised in many international negotiation frameworks, as shown in Table 2.1.[53]

This conceptualisation of the conflict situation inherent in international negotiations shows the relevance of understanding the phases of international negotiations. The pre-negotiation phase influences the rest of the negotiation in terms of conflict and cooperation over the duration of a negotiation. The conflict resolution literature refers to international political conflicts and crisis. For this chapter, the conflict resolution relates to both the political dimension between countries and the conflict between individuals in international groups and corporations. In any case, the degree of conflict arises because of the influence of different cultures in social interactions. For conflict resolution and culture, we dedicate

Table 2.1 A conflict resolution model for international business negotiations

A suggested model of international negotiations			
Pre-negotiation phase	**Negotiation phase**	**Agreement phase**	**Implementation phase**
Ability to negotiate Number of actors; Goals achievable; Negotiation issues; Resources possessed and desired; Capability to trade; Values and communication; Mutual trust; Others: Time, non-interference, non-preoccupation, agents present	**The parties** Individual parties; Symmetrical negotiations; Friendly parties; Bilateral or polarised multilateral negotiations	**The settlement** Compromise; Parties got acceptable satisfaction at tolerable risk; Absence of ambiguity and escape clauses; Settlement on the merits	**Voluntarism by use of:** Symmetrical negotiations; Casuistry; Expanding the benefits
Willingness to negotiate Parties with direct interest; A priori pledge to negotiate; Certainty to obtain goals or Capability to enhance the certainty	**Proposals** Goals desired over the long term; General proposals; Moderate changes in the status quo	**After-effects** Moderate changes in the status quo; Terms made legitimate to the constituencies; Terms allowing task and issue expansion, definite obligations and indefinite benefits	**The agreement** As one of a series or one arising by spillover; Conferral of positive benefits (high satisfaction for participants)

Table 2.1 (continued)

Pre-negotiation phase	Negotiation phase	Agreement phase	Implementation phase
	Compromise A trade of similar goods; Future focus; Upgrading the common interest		**Post-agreement phase** Maintenance of optimal pressure on participants; Absence of reprisals to prevent enforcement; Non-occurrence of outside event to prevent enforcement
	After-effects Capability for legitimisation of constituency; Non-crisis negotiations		

Source: Adapted from Randolph (1966).[54]

a section later to this important topic. Pragmatically, conflict resolution deals with conflict situations to solve the dilemma that has arisen and/or the crisis that has occurred.

What needs to be done to solve a conflict, or better still, to avoid even getting into one? Using Randolph's international conflict resolution concept, the pre-negotiation phase asks for careful planning, the negotiation stage should look into the conflict resolution strategies with their conflict handling approaches discussed earlier, the agreement phase will consider deal making as a conflict resolution mechanism, and finally the implementation stage will need to consider best alternatives to a negotiated agreement (BATNA). This framework could be applied to the crisis in Cyprus outlined in Example 2.3.

The Cyprus conflict can be analysed with the Randolph conflict resolution model, and each part of the conflict in the negotiation process can be assigned to its elements in the international negotiations. Fill in the blank spaces in Table 2.2 and discuss in class.

Another application could be the EU multiparty dispute set out in Example 2.4.

EXAMPLE 2.3
CYPRUS CRISIS

On 19 March 2013, the economy of Cyprus was on the verge of collapse; its lawmakers rejected a €10 billion international bailout package, leaving the nation's president, Nicos Anastasiades, to come up with a Plan B. Cypriot banks had amassed huge losses over the past few years in its dealings with Greece. The Cypriot government closed the banks to prevent a run on the nation's financial institutions. The International Monetary Fund (IMF), the European Central Bank (ECB) and the European Commission offered a bailout package that required Cyprus to come up with a substantial portion of the funds via a one-time tax on ordinary Cypriot bank depositors. Citizens took to the streets in protest, and the parliament rejected the plan. Cyprus was left with three options: "sell its soul to Russia, default and possibly quit the euro, or patch together a new deal with the euro zone".

Option 1, a bailout from Russia in exchange for energy industry rights to Cyprus's potentially rich offshore natural gas reserves would amount to Cyprus "turning its back on modernity".

Option 2, to leave its banks hanging - the banks could have collapsed, yet another unappealing alternative.

Option 3, was to renegotiate its deal with Europe.

Ultimately, Cyprus agreed to a modified European bailout, and the government began confiscating 9.9 per cent of the assets of anyone holding more than $136,000 in a Cyprus bank.

Exploring possible agreements on multiple fronts is, in international negotiation, the only avenue available to accepting that the best deal one can get may be better than no deal at all.

Table 2.2 An application of the conflict resolution model to the Cyprus conflict

A suggested model of international negotiations			
Pre-negotiation phase	**Negotiation phase**	**Agreement phase**	**Implementation phase**
Ability to negotiate	**The parties**	**The settlement**	**Voluntarism by use of:**
Actors:	Polarised multilateral negotiations in this case:	Compromise:	Symmetrical negotiations:
Goals achievable:		All parties got acceptable satisfaction at tolerable risk:	
Negotiation issues:	Cyprus		Resolving of moral problems:
Resources:			
Capability to trade:		Absence of ambiguity and escape clauses:	Expanding the benefits
Compatible values:			
Communication:		Settlement on the merits:	

Table 2.2 (continued)

Pre-negotiation phase	Negotiation phase	Agreement phase	Implementation phase
Mutual trust:			
Time: non-interference, non-preoccupation, agents present			
Willingness to negotiate	**The proposals**	**After-effects**	**The agreement**
Parties with direct interest:	Goals desired over the long term:	Moderate changes in the status quo:	As one of a series or one arising by spillover:
A prior pledge to negotiate:	General proposals: Moderate changes in the status quo	Terms made legitimate to the constituencies:	Conferral of positive benefits (high satisfaction for participants):
Certainty to obtain goals:		Terms allowing task and issue expansion, definite obligations and indefinite benefits:	
Capability to enhance the certainty:			
	The compromise		**Post-agreement phase**
	Future focus:		Maintenance of optimal pressure on participants:
	Upgrading the common interest		Absence of reprisals to prevent enforcement:
			Non-occurrence of outside event to prevent enforcement
	After-effects		
	Capability for legitimisation of constituency:		
	Non-crisis negotiations		

EXAMPLE 2.4
EU MULTIPARTY DISPUTES

Multiparty negotiations are complicated, challenging and often require a very good BATNA (best alternative to a negotiated agreement). A European Union summit held in late October 2013 failed to make headway towards more coordination of economic policies. Facing resistance from Germany in particular, European officials grew pessimistic regarding their odds of negotiating a deal over the next year to lay the foundation for a banking union for the 17 nations that use the euro. The proposed banking union would pool assets to allow the nations to engage in shared spending and borrowing, among other activities. The plan for greater financial coordination was conceived at the height of the European financial crisis in 2012. As consensus grew that a shared currency with 17 different economic policies was unsustainable, the European Union began looking for ways to prevent future disasters. Those who support greater integration sought a model similar to the American system of federalism. A working group negotiated plans to set up a central budget that would cushion countries hit by crisis - as Spain and Ireland had been - through measures such as funding the costs of unemployment benefits. Yet as the financial crisis subsided, Germany, Belgium and France began to push back against proposals for greater financial unity.

Multiparty agreements are difficult to negotiate. It is important to find out how the decisions will be made and agreed upon. The negotiation process and voting procedures need to be clarified at the beginning. In this respect the coalition possibilities need to be planned carefully. In business settings, joint ventures and alliances are examples for multiparty negotiations and the respective outcome.

Three issues make multiparty negotiations more complex than two-party talks: (1) coalition formation, (2) process-management issues, and (3) each party's best alternative to a negotiated agreement (BATNA).

Source: Adapted from Program on Negotiation.[55]

Discussion Point: What kinds of approaches can be chosen for this scenario in terms of dual concern theory and IRP theory? How can this conflict be shown in the international negotiation model according to Randolph? Provide insights into deal making, dispute resolution and BATNA for the case.

2.6 CONFLICT RESOLUTION IN INTERNATIONAL BUSINESS NEGOTIATIONS

2.6.1 Modes of conflict management

In an earlier section it was established that well-managed conflict may have positive outcomes, which satisfy all parties, and lead to all sides emerging from the process feeling as though they have obtained something worthwhile. In order to achieve these positive outcomes, it is imperative to manage conflict appropriately. A number of analytical frameworks are now introduced to help achieve an appropriate conflict resolution in international business negotiations.

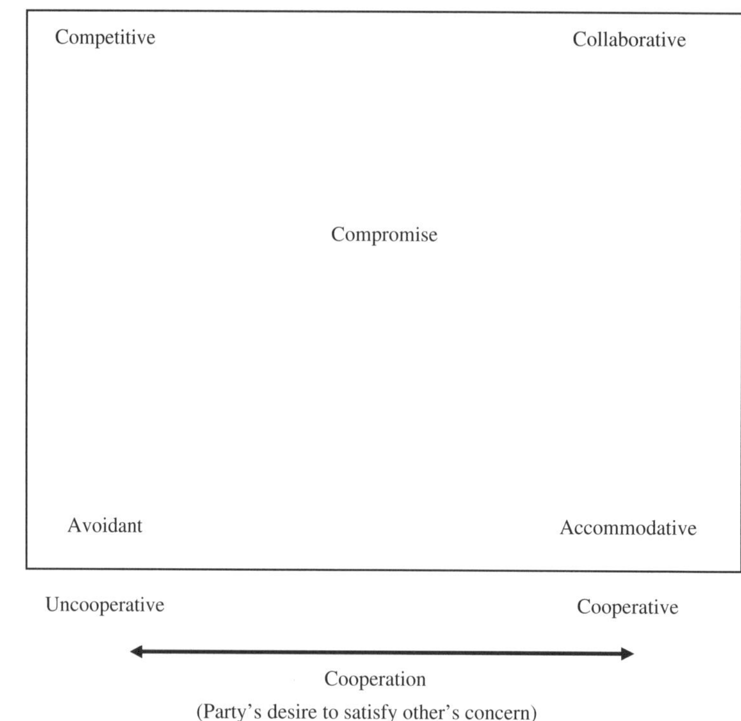

Figure 2.8 Modes of conflict management

One of the most frequently used frameworks is the managerial grid, derived from the psychological conflict resolution perspective. Initially developed as a framework for analysing managerial conduct,[56] among other aspects of managerial style assessed, the grid classifies five different approaches to conflict management.[57] These are based on two key variables: concern for production, which is plotted on the horizontal axis, and concern for people, plotted on the vertical axis.[58] The managerial grid has subsequently been reinterpreted, and five conflict-handling orientations were proposed based on two underlying dimensions: assertiveness and cooperation. This basic framework for managing conflict is presented in Figure 2.8.[59] The vertical axis charts assertiveness, which captures the attempts a party makes to satisfy its own concern, while cooperation, plotted on the horizontal axis, captures a party's desire to satisfy the other's concern.

The first of the five orientations for handling conflict in this schema in the lower-left corner is the avoidant category. Being avoidant is both unassertive (a party has a low desire to satisfy their own concerns) and uncooperative (a party has a low desire to satisfy the concerns of the other party). Directly above in the upper-left corner is competitive, which is extremely assertive (a party has a high desire to satisfy their own concerns) but also uncooperative (a party has a low desire to satisfy the concerns of the other party). In the lower-right corner is the accommodative orientation, which is unassertive (a party has a low desire to satisfy their own concerns) but very cooperative (a party has a high desire to satisfy the other party's concerns). Above, in the top-right hand corner, is the collaborative orientation. Being collaborative is both extremely assertive (a party has a high desire to satisfy their own concerns) and highly cooperative (a party has a high desire to satisfy the concerns of the other party). Finally, in the middle there is compromise, which balances assertiveness and cooperation. In order to appreciate these five orientations further, each is now explored in greater detail.

Competitive

The competitive orientation exemplifies an adversarial approach where a party is highly concerned with achieving its own purposes and reaching its individual targets, but has little or no regard for the purposes or targets of another party. Typically, such an orientation is defined by absolutism; there is minimal scope for nuance or manoeuvre: it is a case of my way or the highway. Such an orientation should be understood in terms of a party's willingness to stake out a tough, extreme position and wait for the other party to yield in the expectation that they will.[60] As such there is no flexibility in this orientation and it is not receptive to indications of cooperation.[61] The competitive orientation is associated with forceful behaviour and pressure tactics in order to achieve success.[62] Competitive behaviour is displayed by parties who believe that they are in a strong position; as such they behave with the expectation that the other party will make concessions. The competitive orientation comes close to a zero-sum game where the gains of one party represent direct losses to the other.

Avoidant

The avoidant orientation is characterised by withdrawal and acceptance of defeat. Avoidance is expressed through disinterest and, eventually, the conscious departure of the avoiding party from the conflict situation.[63] Avoidance signifies low levels of concern both for the conflict situation itself (the avoiding party is apathetic towards the problem) and for securing an outcome to the conflict that will satisfy both parties.[64] The avoidant orientation implies that even if a party had a solution to the problem they would suppress it rather than offer it. The outcome of avoidance for both parties is roughly comparable; it has low utility and neither side are happy. Avoidance tactics involve minimising discussion about the conflict, evading critical concerns and delaying. Avoidance is an orientation that avoids both cooperation and antagonism in an attempt to maintain the status quo. Avoidance attempts to maintain maximum flexibility in the future by circumventing tough choices, in the expectation that at a later stage the choice the parties have to make may not be so stark or difficult.

Accommodative

The accommodative orientation is defined by a party's willingness to sacrifice their own interests and objectives in favour of helping the other party achieve their objectives. It is thus the antithesis of the competitive orientation, being highly responsive to the wishes of the others. This is an orientation which may be associated with culpability or the fact that when all other considerations are taken into account, it is much more important that the other party achieve what they need to achieve.[65] The focus is on appeasement and obedience, accepting and incorporating the needs of others.[66] As such the orientation could be misunderstood as a sign of a party's weakness or softness. Accommodating parties are both highly flexible and highly receptive to indications of cooperation. Kenneth Boulding has described a party who adopted this orientation as a "conflict absorber", who reacted to high hostility with low hostility and even friendliness.[67] Tactics that the accommodating party might employ are subservient in nature: unreserved agreement and making extra efforts above and beyond what is required.

Collaborative

The collaborative orientation illustrates the efforts of both the conflicting parties to show familiarity with the root cause of the problem and work jointly to reach a solution that has high utility for all.[68] The focus of the orientation is on commonality of purpose and shared goals rather than on individual motivation and self-serving interests. Collaboration involves working through the conflict situations together as one, with both sides demonstrating a degree of flexibility and openness to indications of cooperation.[69] The collaborative orientation signifies high levels of concern both for the conflict situation itself (the collaborative parties are eager to solve the problem) and for securing an outcome of the conflict that will be satisfactory for both parties; it is thus the antithesis of the avoidant orientation. Collaborative tactics include learning from each other, offering well-thought-through, constructive propositions and proposing and participating in activities designed to relieve tension.

Compromise

The compromise orientation is an intermediate position which produces an outcome that is somewhat but not totally satisfactory for the parties involved: it is a halfway house, a middle-of-the-road solution. The emphasis in compromise is on fairness and equity, where both sides give a little. Parties compromise when they view the conflict issue in fixed-sum terms; it is a satisfactory rather than an optimal solution that has average utility.[70] A party may feel it necessary to adopt a compromise orientation if the problem that has caused conflict is not a particularly high priority for them and they do not want the disruption of competition or to commit the resources necessary to collaborate. Alternatively, compromise may be a good solution when the conflict situation is a highly pressurised one, where any outcome is better than no outcome. Compromise tactics involve offers of give and take, emphasis that the compromise is only a short-term solution from which further agreement may be reached, and prominence being given to the maximisation of wins and the minimisation of losses.[71] Compromise is an outcome that can be achieved when both parties feel as though they are equally powerful and the goals of each are mutually exclusive.[72] Finally, compromise can be a useful fallback orientation when attempts at either collaboration or competition have been tried without any success.

Deciding on an orientation

Different scenarios and different contexts mean that at different times parties must assume different orientations and adapt their behaviour accordingly. For instance, in order to preserve a relationship with a key supplier, an accommodating orientation may be the best choice. Alternatively, if a company requires that cost savings be made in an overseas subsidiary, the management team may decide a competitive orientation is the most appropriate. A framework that can be used to systematically assess each conflict situation on its merits

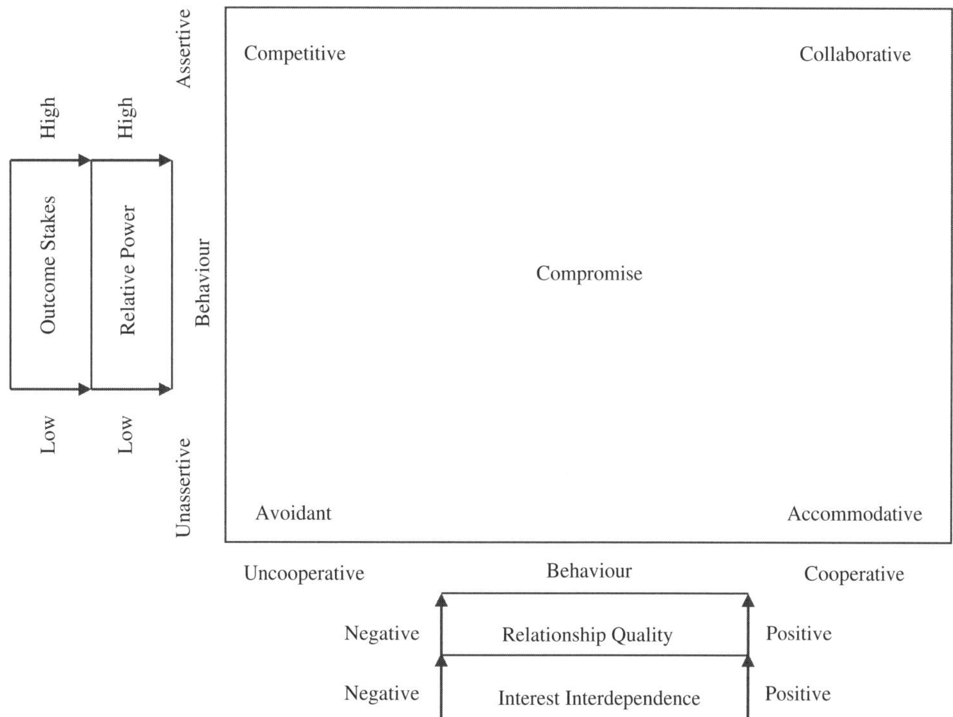

Figure 2.9 Determinants of conflict behaviour

and the factors influencing the potential resolution of the conflict, and thus allows the most suitable orientation to be adopted, is presented in Figure 2.9.

Outcome and interest interdependence

In the first instance the determinants of conflict behaviour framework advances the simple modes of conflict management framework presented in Figure 2.8 by differentiating between the degree of party *interest interdependence* plotted on the horizontal axis in Figure 2.9 and *outcome stakes* plotted on the vertical axis. *Interest interdependence* relates to the extent to which the two conflicting parties rely, or are dependent, on each other to attain their goals. A positive interdependence indicates that the realisation of each party's objectives is highly interrelated. If the two parties have positive interdependency, they are more likely to be accommodating or collaborative, depending upon what the outcome stakes are. If the two conflicting parties have negative interdependency, however, then the orientation of each party is likely to be avoidant or competitive, again depending on what the outcome stakes are.

Outcome stakes essentially relates to how much each party has invested in, or is concerned about, the way in which the conflict transpires and what the implications of the conflict settlement are. Outcome stakes range from low to high. When the outcome stakes for a party are high, they are more likely to adopt a competitive or collaborative orientation. When the outcome stakes are low, an avoidant or accommodative orientation is more probable.

Table 2.3 Conflict orientation as a product of interest interdependence and outcome stakes

Interest interdependence	Outcome stakes	Conflict orientation
Positive	High	Collaborative
Positive	Low	Accommodative
Negative	Low	Avoidant
Negative	High	Competitive
Zero	Moderate	Compromise

The appropriate orientation for conflict resolution as indicated by the interaction between interest interdependence and outcome stakes is shown in Table 2.3.

When interest interdependence is positive and outcome stakes are high, the collaborative orientation is most probable. If the outcome stakes are low, but interest interdependence is still positive, then the most appropriate orientation is accommodation. Negative interest interdependence and low outcome stakes generate an avoidant orientation, while negative interest interdependence combined with high outcome stakes mean that a competitive orientation is most probable. When interest interdependence is neither positive nor negative, and the outcome stakes are only moderately important, then a compromise orientation is most fitting.

This analysis necessarily raises the question, what determines the extent of party interest interdependence, and outcome stakes? As the framework indicates, there are two variables that are associated with whether interest interdependence is positive or negative, and whether outcome stakes are high are low. Interest interdependence is linked to the characteristics of the relationship (shown as relationship quality in Figure 2.9), while outcome stakes are associated with the degree of relative power each party has.

Relationship quality and behaviour

The extent to which two parties are dependent upon each other to achieve their goals is related to the features of the relationship that the two parties have with one other. Relationship characteristics are affected by a number of factors including:

- The length of time that the two parties have been associated with one another.
- The success or failure of previous ventures that the parties have had together.
- The reputation of the two parties.
- Whether there is ownership of a common resource or not.
- The extent of the investment each party has in the venture.

If the relationship has many positive characteristics, then the interests of the two parties are more likely to be positively aligned than if there are negative facets to the relationship. Positive interest interdependence built upon a relationship defined by positive characteristics leads to cooperative behaviour, while negative interest interdependence built upon a relationship defined by negative characteristics leads to uncooperative behaviour, as shown in Table 2.4.

Table 2.4 Conflict orientation and behaviour as a product of interest interdependence based on relationship quality and outcome stakes based on relative power

Interest interdependence	Relationship quality	Behaviour	Outcome stakes	Relative power	Behaviour	Conflict orientation
Positive	Positive	Cooperative	High	High	Assertive	Collaborative
Positive	Positive	Cooperative	Low	Low	Unassertive	Accommodative
Negative	Negative	Uncooperative	Low	Low	Unassertive	Avoidant
Negative	Negative	Uncooperative	High	High	Assertive	Competitive
Zero	Zero	Mediated	Moderate	Moderate	Moderate	Compromise

Relative power and behaviour

The degree to which each party ascribes value to the outcome of the conflict is associated with the relative power of each party. Factors affecting the power of one party relative to the other include:

- The financial strength of the respective parties.
- The knowledge each party possesses.
- Whether the power of each party is recognised as legitimate or not.
- The capacity of one party to exercise coercion or incentivisation over the other.
- The viability and availability of alternative options.

EXAMPLE 2.5
INTERCULTURAL CONFLICT

(Soon-to-be) New Owner: You guys never make decisions in time.

(Soon-to-be) Former Partner: Speedy decisions are not everything. Consensus is more important.

N.O.: Well, just tell the dealers that our products are the best in the world. Tell them that they sell everywhere except here.

F.P.: But the dealers complain that your products are just okay, not great. Even worse, they are not really tailored to the needs or aesthetic preferences of local customers.

N.O.: Nonsense. What customers buy, everywhere in the world, is the physical performance of the product. No one matches us in performance.

F.P.: Perhaps. Still, the dealers report that your products are not neatly packaged and often have scratches on the surface.

N.O.: But that has no effect on performance.

F.P.: Tell that to the dealers. They say they cannot readily see - or sell - the performance difference you're talking about, so they have to fall back on aesthetics, where your products are weak. We will have to reduce the price.

N.O.: Don't you dare. We succeeded in the United States and in Europe by keeping our prices at 5 per cent above those of our competitors. If we're having trouble in Japan it's because of you. Your obvious lack of effort, knowledge, even confidence in our products - that's what keeps them from selling. Besides, your parent keeps on sending our joint venture group a bunch of bumbling old incompetents for managers. We rarely get the good people. Maybe the idea is to kill off our relationship entirely so they can start up a unit of their own making imitation products.

F.P.: Well, if you feel that way, there is not much point in our continuing on together.

N.O.: Glad you said that. We'll buy up the other 50 per cent of the equity and go it on our own.

F.P.: Good luck. By the way, how many Japanese-speaking managers do you have in your company - that is, after we pull out all the "bumbling old incompetents" from our joint venture?

N.O.: None. But don't worry. We'll just hire a bunch of headhunters and get started up in record time.

Source: Adapted from Ohmae (1989, p. 148).[73]

Discussion Point: Discuss this exercise with the above conflict resolution grid for international business negotiations in mind.

If one party has greater power relative to the other party, and both sides recognise this to be genuine, then the party with high relative power will behave in a more assertive manner than the party whose relative power is quite low.

2.6.2 Conflict resolution in international business negotiations

The conflict resolution literature combines different streams of research, such as that on international relations and cross-cultural psychology. Conflict in international business negotiations derives from the differences between the actors regarding their cultural backgrounds, attitudes, behaviour and norms. The clash of cultures often leads to an awareness of dealing with the culturally determined conflicts in international negotiations. To mediate conflicts, the sections above highlight different strategies and concepts.

The definition of mediation goes back to Bercovitch, Anagnoson and Wille:[74] *Mediation* is "a process of conflict management where disputants seek assistance of, or accept an offer of help from, an individual, group, state or organization to settle their conflict or resolve their differences without resorting to physical force or invoking the authority of law". Mediation is a distinct form of negotiation, in which a third party is involved to help find a solution or contribute to an agreement. International negotiations need mediation in the form of third parties when culturally different understandings are having an impact on the outcome of a negotiation. You will find more details and examples on mediation in a negotiation context in Chapter 7.

The cross-cultural psychology literature explores the impact of culture on mediation and negotiation. Many researchers[75] have evaluated and classified characteristics of different cultures from religious to organisational and leadership behaviour. These will be dealt with later. This chapter deals with culture and mediation and therefore sets the parameters for the later treatment of culture. The definitions of culture deal with the complexity of the whole of culture, the layers of culture, mental schemes and what is acceptable behaviour in groups. Inman et al.[76] observe and analyse the impact of culture on mediation. They highlight two approaches: (1) to quantify cultural distance and differences between the conflicting parties in mediation and (2) to test the impact of specific cultural values on the outcome. The study concludes that cultural differences have a considerable impact on the ability of third parties to get the disputants to accept mediation. Yet, once at the negotiation table these differences only affect the mediated negotiations in a negligible way. The awareness of the cultural differences has a greater effect on the mediation strategies and process. Cultural differences in terms of language, race, religion and values surface in mediation between countries. Interestingly, democracies will more often use mediation to solve conflicts and are less likely to have a bias towards religious differences. Religious differences have little impact on whether mediation occurs. Weaker states might be expected to use mediation as a method of conflict resolution, whereas stronger states would not opt for the interference of third parties. Moving away from a country perspective, business conflicts are often dealt with in stages, with a strategic approach taken towards conflict resolution. The same rules which apply to constructive debate are necessary for mediation in conflict resolution situations:[77]

1. Provide psychological safety.
2. Avoid moral outrage.
3. Avoid being provoked into an emotional response.
4. Don't abandon cooperative strategies.
5. Use time to your advantage.

Example 2.6 shows conflict between cultures by way of a dialogue.

Two polar yet interdependent strategies[78] are known as distributive and integrative negotiation. *Distributive negotiation* means that activities are instrumental to the attainment of one party's goals when they are in basic conflict with those of the other party. *Integrative negotiation* means that parties' activities are oriented to finding common or complementary interests and to solving problems confronting both parties. Integrative and distributive negotiations describe the conflict resolution processes in negotiations best, and especially in international negotia-

EXAMPLE 2.6

DIALOGUE: CONFLICT BETWEEN CULTURES - YAMADA DISTRIBUTORS

Mr Smith: Since we have a few minutes left in our meeting, I would like to bring up the subject of Yamada distributors.

Mr Masami: Yamada? What about them?

Mr Smith: Well, I don't think any of us are that pleased with their services. I think we should find a new distributor. I've heard that Inoue Corporation is quite good.

Mr Masami: I wonder what others think. Have you discussed this with anyone else?

Mr Smith: Not really. That's why I'm bringing it up now, to get your opinions.

Mr Masami: Yes, we should get people's opinions before we make a decision.

Mr Smith: Good. So what do you think, Masami-san?

Mr Masami: I couldn't really say.

Source: Adapted from Sorti (1994).[79]

To help solve this conflict, the following cultural differences and conflict resolution are added:

1. The Japanese do not like to be surprised at meetings, especially to be asked to make a public statement of one's views.
2. Decisions are made by consensus in Japan; it is not appropriate to voice strong opinions for risk of losing face.
3. For the American, Mr Smith, it is simply an issue of comparing the merits between two distributors and finding the best one.
4. There are sensitive issues in this situation, including who recommended the company, whether this person will be shamed, who is pushing the other company, and whether the choice against the distributing company will have an impact on that person. Seniority matters in Japanese companies.
5. Finally, keiretsu - an interconnected network of relationships between manufacturers, suppliers and distributors - is carefully constructed and nurtured to benefit all participants. This means if one player is changed the structure of the network is affected. This is often an issue when negotiation teams are concerned that in the Western world it does not matter to change someone.

Discussion Point: Try to find a solution for this situation using the dual concern and IRP models and then continue the dialogue.

Table 2.5 A conflict resolution model for international business negotiations aligned to the psychological and political frameworks

International business negotiations			
Pre-negotiation phase	**Negotiation phase**	**Agreement phase**	**Implementation phase**
Ability and willingness to negotiate	The parties The proposals The compromise The after-effects	The settlement The after-effects	The agreement Post-agreement phase
CAREFUL PLANNING	CONFLICT RESOLUTION (managerial, psychological models)	BATNA (Best Alternative to a Negotiated Agreement)	DEAL MAKING

tions these strategies are relevant for the tone of the negotiation and the outcomes. Overall then, all international business negotiations need some basic rules and aspects, including careful planning, dispute resolution, deal making and best alternative to a negotiated agreement (BATNA). International business negotiations follow the path shown in Table 2.5.

Careful planning

To start with, careful planning by negotiators means they must consider three relevant approaches:

1. weighing up the long-term results of various options,
2. evaluating structures promoting short-term thinking at the expense of future implications,
3. negotiating in stages.

It is therefore important to consider incremental progress, beginning with the exit negotiations and then following that with the deals. Although it could lead to some deadlocks, this is in line with good negotiation practices and would be the best way to negotiate.[80] Careful planning is part of the conditions leading to a successful outcome, and anticipating difficulties is part of a conflict resolution mechanism. Especially in international business negotiations, understanding the other party and their cultural values, norms, attitudes and behaviour is part of a successful negotiation process.

Conflict resolution

Following careful planning, the procedures, techniques and dispute resolution mechanisms must be considered. The best way to do this is to stick to dispute resolution approaches and apply power-based and interest-based ways of handling conflict (see IRP theory as well).

Strategies of dispute resolution are competitive strategies and have an impact on the atmosphere between the negotiators.[81] Resolving disputes can be achieved by improving communication between the parties, by introducing a third party as a mediator and by shifting the perception from a zero-sum game to one of win-win.[82]

It is still possible, however, that during the process negotiators will have to deal with difficulties arising from the characteristics of the negotiators, from differences in the objectives, strategies and expected outcomes. Important suggestions for dealing with such difficulties are to build a golden bridge to save the face of the counterpart, to reframe the problem,[83] to involve the counterpart in finding a solution, to offer choices and to emphasise joint interests. Many authors suggest presenting ways of finding value in a seemingly intractable dispute,[84] exploring differences in preferences, priorities and resources, and providing each side with appropriate incentives throughout the life of the deal.

2.7 SUMMARY

This chapter lays the groundwork for international business negotiations. It outlines the conflict aspect between parties and then provides conflict resolution mechanisms. Conflict between individuals, groups, organisations and nations is at the centre of the discussions. It starts with inter- and intrapersonal conflicts, then it deals with inter- and intragroup conflicts. The conflict resolution models from a psychological and political perspective provide mechanisms to overcome conflict and lead to cooperation. Early work has already integrated conflict resolution in political science with international negotiation, although on a country level. It still can be seen in international business negotiation frameworks. Similarly, the psychological grounding of the conflict management grid is very prominent and supports the systematic analysis of the conflict resolution strategies. This chapter provides a good basis for moving on to the rational theoretical aspects of international business negotiations.

QUESTIONS

1. Where does conflict come from?
2. What kind of conflict resolution mechanisms can be used in international business negotiations?
3. How can social dilemmas be solved?
4. How can you enlarge dispute resolution when culture and conflict occur?
5. What communication processes are found in negotiations?

NOTES

1. Shapiro, D.L. and Kulik, C.T. (2004) Resolving disputes between faceless disputants: new challenges for conflict management theory. In: Gelfand, M.J. and Brett, J.M. (eds) *The Handbook of Negotiation and Culture*. Stanford, Stanford Business Books, pp. 177–92.
2. Shapiro and Kulik (2004) ibid.
3. Kriesberg, L. (1973) *The Sociology of Social Conflicts*. Englewood Cliffs, Prentice Hall.

4. Rahim, M.A. (2002) Toward a theory of managing organizational conflict. *International Journal of Conflict Management.* **13**(3), 206–35.
5. Jehn, K. and Bendersky, C. (2003) Intragroup conflict in organizations: a contingency perspective on the conflict–outcome relationship. *Research in Organizational Behavior.* **24**, 187–242.
6. Schelling, T. (1960) *The Strategy of Conflict.* Cambridge MA, Harvard University Press.
7. Inherent in Schelling's conceptualisation of conflict is that there is an element of contention or quarrel and that one party is seeking to settle this decisively through contention.
8. Wall, J.A. and Callister, R.R. (1995) Conflict and its management. *Journal of Management.* **25**(3), 515–58.
9. Rahim, M.A. (2001) *Managing Conflict in Organizations.* London, Quorum.
10. Rahim, M.A. and Bonoma, T.V. (1979) Managing organizational conflict: a model for diagnosis and intervention. *Psychological Reports.* (44), 1323–44.
11. Deutsch, M. (1969) Conflicts: productive and destructive. *Journal of Social Issues.* **25**(1), 7–42.
12. Boulding, K. (1957) Organisation and conflict. *Conflict Resolution.* **1**(2), 122–34.
13. Guetzkow, H. and Gyr, J. (1954) An analysis of conflict in decision-making groups. *Human Relations.* **7**(3), 367–82.
14. Adapted from: Jehn, K.A. (1994) Enhancing effectiveness: an investigation of advantages and disadvantages of value based intragroup conflict. *International Journal of Conflict Management.* **5**(3), 223–38; and Jehn, K.A. (1995) A multimethod examination of the benefits and detriments of intragroup conflict. *Administrative Science Quarterly.* **40**(2), 256–82.
15. Amason, A.C. (1996) Distinguishing the effects of functional and dysfunctional conflict on strategic decision making: resolving a paradox for top management teams. *Academy of Management Journal.* **39**(1), 123–48.
16. Lewicki, R.J., Saunders, D.M., Minton, J.W. and Barry, B. (2003) *Negotiation: Readings, Exercises and Cases.* 4th ed. Boston MA, McGraw-Hill.
17. Blake, R.R. and Mouton, J.S. (1961) Reactions to intergroup competition under win-lose conditions. *Management Science.* **7**(4), 420–35.
18. Lumineau, F., Eckerd, S. and Handley, S. (2015) Inter-organizational conflicts: research overview, challenges, and opportunities. *Journal of Strategic Contracting and Negotiation.* **1**(1), 42–64.
19. See especially Hymer, S.H. (1976) *The International Operations of National Firms: A Study of Direct Foreign Investment.* Cambridge MA, MIT Press; Dunning, J.H. and Rugman, A.M. (1985) The influence of Hymer's dissertation on the theory of foreign direct investment. *American Economic Review.* **75**(2), 228–32; Buckley, P.J. and Ghauri, P.N. (2004) Globalisation, economic geography and the strategy of multinational enterprises. *Journal of International Business Studies.* **35**(2), 81–98.
20. Hirshleifer, J. (2001) *The Dark Side of the Force.* Cambridge, Cambridge University Press.
21. Hennart, J.F. (1991) The transaction cost theory of joint ventures: an empirical study of Japanese subsidiaries in the United States. *Management Science.* **37**(4), 483–97.
22. Twitter Inc. (2014) *Annual Report.*
23. Boulding, K. (1962) *Conflict and Defense: A General Theory.* New York, Harper.
24. Lewicki, R.J. and Litterer, J.A. (1985) *Negotiation.* Homewood, Irwin.
25. Deutsch (1969) op. cit.
26. Hamilton, D.L. and Sherman, J.W. (1994) Stereotypes. In: Wyer, R.S. and Srull, T.K. (eds) *Handbook of Social Cognition*, Vol. 2, *Applications.* Hillsdale, Erlbaum, pp. 1–68.
27. Adapted from: Mackie, D.M. and Smith, E.R. (1998) Intergroup relations: insights from a theoretically integrative approach. *Psychological Review.* **105**(3), 499–529; Zanna, M.P. and Rempel, J.K. (1988) Attitudes: a new

look at an old concept. In: Bar-tal, D. and Kruglanski, A. (eds) *The Social Psychology of Knowledge*. Cambridge, Cambridge University Press, pp. 315–44; Bar-tal, D. and Teichman, Y. (2005) *Stereotypes and Prejudice in Conflict: Representations of Arabs in Israeli Jewish Society*. Cambridge, Cambridge University Press.

28. Fisher, R., Ury, W. and Patton, B. (1981) *Getting to Yes. Negotiating Agreement without Giving In*. New York, Penguin.
29. Van Kleef, G.A., De Dreu, C.K.W. and Manstead, A.S.R. (2004) The interpersonal effects of emotions in negotiations. *Journal of Personality and Social Psychology*. **87**(4), 510–28.
30. Carnevale, P.J.D. and Isen, A.M. (1986) The influence of positive affect and visual access on the discovery of integrative solutions in bilateral negotiation. *Organizational Behavior and Human Decision Processes*. **37**(1), 1–13.
31. Allred, K.G., Mallozzi, J.S., Matsui, F. and Raia, C.P. (1997) The influence of anger and compassion on negotiation performance. *Organizational Behavior and Human Decision Processes*. **70**(3), 175–87.
32. Deutsch, M. (1973) *The Resolution of Conflict: Constructive and Destructive Processes*. New Haven, Yale University Press.
33. Tjosvold, D. (1997) Conflict within interdependence: its value for productivity and individuality. In: De Dreu, C.K.W. and Van de Vliert, E. (eds) *Using Conflict in Organizations*. London, SAGE, pp. 23–7.
34. Cf. Hirschman, A.O. (1994) Social conflicts as pillars of democratic market society. *Political Theory*. **22**(2), 203–18.
35. Simmel, G. (1968) *The Conflict in Modern Culture, and Other Essays. Translated, with an Introduction by K. Peter Etzkorn*. New York, Teachers College Press.
36. Coser, L. (1956) *The Functions of Social Conflict*. London, Routledge & Kegan Paul.
37. Tjosvold, D. (1998) Cooperative and competitive goal approach to conflict: accomplishments and challenges. *Applied Psychology*. **47**(3), 285–313.
38. Buckley, P.J. and Casson, M. (1988) A theory of cooperation in international business. In: Contractor, F.J. and Lorange, P. (eds) *Cooperative Strategies in International Business: Joint Ventures and Technology Partnerships between Firms*. Lexington, Lexington Books, pp. 31–54.
39. Axelrod, R. (1985) *Evolution of Cooperation*. New York, Basic Books.
40. Adapted from: Tazelaar, M.J.A., Van Lange, P.A.M. and Ouwerkerk, J.W. (2004) How to cope with "noise" in social dilemmas: the benefits of communication. *Journal of Personality and Social Psychology*. **87**(6), 845–59; Van Lange, P.A.M., Ouwerkerk, J.W. and Tazelaar, M.J.A. (2002) How to overcome the detrimental effects of noise in social interaction: the benefits of generosity. *Journal of Personality and Social Psychology*. **82**(5), 768–80.
41. Gardner, H. (2011) *Frames of Mind: The Theory of Multiple Intelligences*. New York, Basic Books.
42. Deutsch, M. (1971) Toward an understanding of conflict. *International Journal of Group Tensions*. **1**, 42–54.
43. Litterer, J.A. (1966) Conflict in organizations: a re-examination. *Academy of Management Journal*. **9**(3), 178–86.
44. See De Dreu, C. (2004) Motivation in negotiation: a social psychological analysis. In: Gelfand, M.J. and Brett, J.M. (eds) *The Handbook of Negotiation and Culture*. Stanford, Stanford Business Books, pp. 114–35; Pruitt, D.G. and Carnevale, P.J. (1993) *Negotiation in Social Conflict*. Mapping Social Psychology. Pacific Grove CA, Thomson Brooks/Cole Publishing, pp. 104–106; Rahim (2001) op. cit., pp. 27–30.
45. See De Dreu (2004) op. cit.
46. Shapiro and Kulik (2004) op. cit.
47. Saner, R. (2003) Strategies and tactics in international business negotiations. In: Ghauri, P.N. and Usunier, J.-C. (eds) *International Business Negotiations*. 2nd ed. Oxford, Pergamon/Elsevier, pp. 51–74.
48. Elgoibar, P., Euwema, M. and Munduate, L. (2017) Conflict management. *Oxford Research Encyclopedia of Psychology*. Oxford, Oxford University Press.

49. De Dreu (2004) op. cit.
50. Ury, W.L., Brett, J.M. and Goldberg, S.B. (1988) *Getting Disputes Resolved.* San Francisco, Jossey-Bass; Ury, W. (1991) *Getting Past No: Negotiating with Difficult People.* New York, Bantam Books.
51. Wilkenfeld, J., Young, K., Asal, V. and Quinn, D. (2003) Mediating international crisis: cross-national and experimental perspectives. *Journal of Conflict Resolution.* **47**, 279–301.
52. Elgoibar et al. (2017) op cit.
53. Adapted from: Ghauri, P.N. (2003a) A framework for international business negotiations. In: Ghauri, P.N. and Usunier, J.-C. (eds) *International Business Negotiations.* 2nd ed. Oxford, Pergamon/Elsevier, pp. 3–22; Ghauri, P.N. (2003b) The role of atmosphere in negotiations. In: Ghauri, P.N. and Usunier, J.-C. (eds) *International Business Negotiations.* 2nd ed. Oxford, Pergamon/Elsevier, pp. 205–19; Manrai, L.A. and Manrai, A.K. (2010) The influence of culture in international business: a new conceptual framework and managerial implications. *Journal of Transnational Management.* **15**(1): 69–100.
54. Randolph, L. (1966) A suggested model of international negotiation. *Journal of Conflict Resolution.* **10**, 344–53.
55. PON staff (2017) Top international multiparty negotiations: dissent in the European Union, *Program on Negotiation*, 21 February.
56. Blake, R.R. and Mouton, J.S. (1964) *The Managerial Grid.* Houston, Gulf.
57. Thomas, K.W. (1992) Conflict and conflict management: reflections and updates. *Journal of Organisational Behaviour.* **13**(3), 265–74.
58. Blake and Mouton (1964) op. cit.
59. Thomas, K.W. (1983) Conflict and conflict management. In: Dunnette, M.D. (ed.) *Handbook of Industrial and Organisational Psychology.* New York, Wiley, pp. 889–935.
60. Rubin, J.Z. (1994) Models of conflict management. *Journal of Social Issues.* **50**(1), 33–45.
61. Saner (2003) op. cit.
62. Rahim, M.A. and Magner, N.R. (1995) Confirmatory factor analysis of the styles of handling interpersonal conflict: first-order factor model and its invariance across groups. *Journal of Applied Psychology.* **80**(1), 122–32.
63. Blake and Mouton (1964) op. cit.
64. Tjosvold, D. and Sun, H.F. (2002) Understanding conflict avoidance: relationship, motivations, actions and consequences. *International Journal of Conflict Management.* **13**(2), 142–64.
65. Rahim, M.A. (1985) A strategy for managing conflict in complex organizations. *Human Relations.* **38**(1), 81–9.
66. De Dreu, C.K.W., Evers, A., Beersma, B., Kluwer, E.S. and Nauta, A. (2001) A theory-based measure of conflict management strategies in the work place. *Journal of Organizational Behavior.* **22**(6), 645–68.
67. Boulding (1962) op. cit.; Rahim (2001) op. cit.
68. Saner (2003) op. cit.
69. Montes, C., Rodríguez, D. and Serrano, G. (2012) Affective choice of conflict management styles. *International Journal of Conflict Management.* **23**(1), 6–18.
70. Lewicki and Litterer (1985) op. cit.
71. Montes et al. (2012) op. cit.
72. Rahim and Bonoma (1979) op. cit.
73. Ohmae, K. (1989) The global logic of strategic alliances. *Harvard Business Review*, March–April, 143–55.
74. Bercovitch, J., Anagnoson, J. and Wille, D. (1991) Some conceptual issues and empirical trends in the study of successful mediation in international relations. *Journal of Peace Research.* **28**(1), 7–17.

75. Hofstede, G. (1980) *Culture's Consequences: International Differences in Work-Related Values*. Newbury Park CA, Sage Publications; House, Robert J., Hanges, Paul J., Javidan, Mansour, Dorfman, Peter W. and Gupta, Vipin (2004) *Culture, Leadership, and Organizations: The GLOBE Study of 62 Societies*. Thousand Oaks CA, Sage Publications, Inc.; Inglehart, R. and Baker, W. (2000) Modernization, cultural change, and the persistence of traditional values. *American Sociological Review*. **65**, 19–51; Schwartz, S.H. (1994) Beyond individualism/ collectivism: new cultural dimensions of values. In: Kim, U., Triandis, H.C., Kâğitçibaşi, Ç., Choi, S.-C. and Yoon, G. (eds) *Individualism and Collectivism: Theory, Method, and Applications*. Cross-Cultural Research and Methodology series, Vol. 18. Thousand Oaks CA, Sage Publications, Inc., pp. 85–119.
76. Inman, M., Roudabeh, K., Wilkenfeld, J., Gelfand, M. and Salmon, E. (2014) Cultural influences on mediation in international crises. *Journal of Conflict Resolution*. **58**(4), 685–712.
77. Peterson, R. (2019) Three rules for constructive debate, *Financial Times*, 15 May; Shonk, K. (2019) 3 negotiation strategies for conflict resolution. *Program on Negotiation*, 21 January. Available from: https://www.pon.harvard.edu/daily/dispute-resolution/3-negotiation-strategies-for-conflictresolution/?utm_source=WhatCountsE-mail&utm_medium=jsweekly&utm_date=2019-02-02-14-30-00&mqsc=W4028742.
78. Walton, R.E. and McKersie, R.B. (1965) *A Behavioral Theory of Labor Negotiations: An Analysis of a Social Interaction System*. New York, McGraw-Hill.
79. Sorti, C. (1994) *Cross Cultural Dialogues: 74 Brief Encounters of Cultural Differences*. Boston MA, Intercultural Press.
80. Subramanian, G. (2006) A contingent contract? Weigh the costs and benefits of making a "bet". *Negotiation Briefings*, 24–26 August; Subramanian, G. (2007a) Contracts 101: what every negotiator should know about contract and agency law. *Negotiation Briefings*, 2–7 November; Subramanian, G. (2007b) Taking BATNA to the next level. *Negotiation Briefings*, 17–20 November; Ott, U.F., Prowse, P., Fells, R. and Rogers, H. (2016) The DNA of negotiations: a configurational approach. *Journal of Business Research*. **69**(9), 3561–71.
81. Malhotra, D. (2004) Accept or reject? Sometimes the hardest part of negotiation is knowing when to walk away. *Negotiation* newsletter, August 2004.
82. Ghauri (2003b) op. cit.; Manrai and Manrai (2010) op. cit.
83. Hackley, S. (2004) When life gives you lemons: how to deal with difficult people. *Negotiation*, 3–5 November; Ury (1991) op. cit.
84. Bordone, R.C. and Moffitt, M.L. (2006) Create value out of conflict. *Negotiation*, 5–7 June.

FURTHER READING

Fisher, R., Ury, W. and Patton, B. (1991) *Getting to Yes: Negotiating Agreement without Giving In*. London, Penguin.

Randolph, L. (1966) A suggested model of international negotiation. *Journal of Conflict Resolution*. **10**, 344–53.

Shapiro, D.L. and Kulik, C.T. (2004) Resolving disputes between faceless disputants: new challenges for conflict management theory. In: Gelfand, M.J. and Brett, J.M. (eds) *The Handbook of Negotiation and Culture*. Stanford, Stanford Business Books, pp. 177–92.

Wilkenfeld, J., Young, K., Asal, V. and Quinn, D. (2003) Mediating international crisis: cross-national and experimental perspectives. *Journal of Conflict Resolution*. **47**, 279–301.

3
Theoretical bases for international business negotiations

The theoretical underpinning for international negotiations is not only disciplinary, but also interdisciplinary. To identify the many directions influencing decision making, and interactive decision making specifically, this chapter provides an overview, as well as a basic understanding, of the psychological, economic and decision-science streams of literature which influence international negotiation research. The psychological and anthropological perspective in international business negotiations considers the rules of exchange and the social and economic relationships developed in a negotiation setting. Social exchanges are understood and made during most business negotiations. At the same time, economics and cost–benefit analysis are an integral part of business negotiations. Decision science, as an individual process of deriving a decision, provides another important theoretical lens for international business negotiation. Whether market entry decisions via export and import or foreign direct investment, the decisions are made from an individual, strategic, organisational or interactive perspective. Social exchange theory, transaction cost economics, decision analysis, game theory and negotiation analysis are all dealt with in this chapter.

3.1 SOCIAL EXCHANGE THEORY

The social exchange paradigm is one of the most influential theoretical underpinnings from an organisational behaviour perspective. The idea of social exchange goes back to the work of the famous anthropologist Malinowski in the 1920s, and then to Homans's work within social psychology from the late 1950s. They agree that *social exchange* is defined as a series of social interactions that generate obligations. These interactions are interdependent and contingent on the actions of another person. Negotiations are therefore very clearly part of this social exchange paradigm. The explanatory power of social exchange is that it has rules and norms of exchange, that resources are exchanged and that relationships emerge. All of this forms part of negotiations and the basis of any negotiation between people, companies and countries. Further complexities arise when these exchanges are made between

> Social exchange is a series of social interactions that generate obligations.

people/organisations from different cultures in international negotiations. In social exchange theory, the purpose of these exchanges is to maximise the benefit and minimise the costs, and this applies to international exchanges as well. Homans highlights that people weigh up the potential rewards as well as the risks of social exchange. This also happens in international negotiations, in which the complexities of dealing with other companies and cultures are multiplied due to differences in understanding the norms, behaviour and attitudes of the counterparts.

The best-known exchange rule is reciprocity, or repayment in kind. The nature of reciprocity regarding exchange takes three forms:[1]

1. Reciprocity as a transactional pattern of interdependent exchange;
2. Reciprocity as a folk belief;
3. Reciprocity as a moral norm.

> Reciprocity is an interdependent exchange that is connected to the human interaction with another person.

Reciprocity as interdependent exchange is connected to the human interaction with another person, which can be either independent, dependent or interdependent. The first two do not relate to social exchange, since social exchange needs to go in both directions. This interdependency in social exchange highlights cooperation and reduces risk. This also lies at the heart of business negotiations as both buyer and seller want an exchange to take place.

Reciprocity as a folk belief involves the cultural expectation that in the long run relationships reach an equilibrium and that everyone gets what they deserve, punishment for bad behaviour and reward for good behaviour. This promotes long-term business relationships beyond transactional exchange.

Reciprocity as a moral norm has as its centre of interest the quality of how people should behave. There is strong evidence of cultural and individual differences when norms are followed, and people are supposed to behave accordingly. For example, in some cultures gift giving is a norm while in others it is not. Negotiated agreements are more detailed than reciprocated exchanges. The obligations are more precise and clearly understood in negotiated outcomes compared to reciprocated exchanges. Economic transactions are often negotiated exchanges. Economic outcomes are financial and tangible. Socioemotional outcomes are often connected to social and esteem needs.

Resources are exchanged in economic transactions and relationships are exchanged in social transactions. In international business negotiations both types of transactions are necessary and need to be considered. Table 3.1 shows a model of social and economic exchange.

Social exchange examples touch many areas, from human relationships to work employment situations, business relationships and international conflicts. The main focus is on the differences between the benefits and costs to the parties. Distinguishing between relations and transactions, as shown in Table 3.1, has shown that conflicts can be approached from a social–social, social–economic, economic–social and economic–economic perspective. Negotiation scenarios can therefore be broken down into these elements and solved with this perspective in mind.

Table 3.1 Social and economic exchange: type of relationship and transaction

		Type of transaction	
		Social exchange	**Economic exchange**
Type of relationship	**Social exchange**	Social Transaction in a Social Relationship *Negotiation outcome is a relationship*	Economic Transaction in a Social Relationship *Negotiation outcome is a future trading relationship*
	Economic exchange	Social Transaction in an Economic Relationship *Reputational effect of good trading*	Economic Transaction in an Economic Relationship *Trading contract*

Source: Adapted from Cropanzano and Mitchell (2005).[2]

Social Transaction in a Social Relationship: At the heart of the exchange is the social relationship, such as between friends, partners and colleagues. The rational weighing of costs and benefits also has a place in this setting. Humans put effort into these relationships and expect a benefit in return.

Social Transaction in an Economic Relationship: An employee who thinks his hard work is not being acknowledged in the office may switch jobs to one that is more rewarding, or where he gets the same benefits for less effort.

Economic Transaction in a Social Relationship: A vegetable farmer and a dairy farmer can benefit if they enter into a relationship to exchange their goods.

Economic Transaction in an Economic Relationship: When a buyer needs a product which is sold by two suppliers, then one supplier often benefits at the expense of the other. The second supplier may offer more concessions, putting up with more costs to attract the customer, when he realises that the other one will end up with all the profit.

Example 3.1 shows a practical example of social exchange.

EXAMPLE 3.1
COUNTRY-COUNTRY NEGOTIATIONS: THE US AND CHINA TRADE DISPUTE

The world's two largest economies have imposed tariffs on billions of dollars' worth of one another's goods. The United States has long accused China of unfair trading practices and intellectual property theft. Whereas in China, there is a perception that the United States is trying to curb its rise.

Negotiations are ongoing but have proven difficult. The two sides remain far apart on issues including how to roll back tariffs and enforce a deal. The uncertainty is hurting businesses and weighing on the global economy.

What tariffs have been imposed? The United States' tariffs policy aims to encourage consumers to buy American by making imported goods more expensive. The United States has imposed tariffs on more than $360 billion (£296 billion) of Chinese goods, and China has retaliated with tariffs on more than $110 billion of US products.

The United States delivered three rounds of tariffs in 2018, and a fourth one in September 2019. This latest round targeted Chinese imports from meat to musical instruments with a 15 per cent duty.

China has hit back with tariffs ranging from 5 to 25 per cent on US goods, such as a 5 per cent levy on US crude oil, the first time fuel has been hit in the trade battle.

Source: Adapted from BBC (2019).[3]

Discussion Point: Find a solution path which fits this type of conflict. How can this negotiation be classified in terms of social exchange? Would it help to position this negotiation in this way?

Conflict over scarce resources is particularly tricky to resolve. Business negotiators facing this type of resource division may be able to avoid conflict by spending time thinking about each party's contributions and claims. Putting oneself into the shoes of another party can be a good starting point for conflict resolution, as can considering how to split the pie. The situation can be solved in terms of social exchange theory or using the transaction cost approach, but also in a rational game theoretical or negotiation analytical manner.

3.2 TRANSACTION COST ECONOMICS

Transaction costs bring order in terms of governance to mitigate conflict and create joint gains in transactions regarding economic exchange.

Transaction cost economics goes back to Oliver E. Williamson, who received a Nobel Prize for his seminal work. *Transaction cost economics* can be anchored in economics as a discipline, but is interdisciplinary as it connects economics, law and organisation theory. It deals with bringing order in terms of governance (the governance perspective) to mitigate conflict and create mutual gains in transactions (business deals) regarding economic exchange. Private ordering plays a prominent role in transaction cost economics in that the parties to an exchange have an incentive to design contract-specific safeguards to avoid contractual hazards and create mutual gains.

International negotiations are touched by transaction cost economics in that they aim to come to an agreement which is implemented as a contract. Thus, views relating to transaction cost economics are relevant and focus not only on the transaction, but also on the human actors behind the process. The view that transaction cost economics is a useful tool has endured from the 1970s to the present day.[4]

Hennart emphasises the strength of transaction cost theory in international business topics such as multinational enterprises (MNEs) and their international, organisational interdependencies, asset specificity and information asymmetries.[5]

In terms of negotiations or bargaining, it is useful to understand *transaction costs.*[6] The application of transaction costs to negotiations can be useful due to the fact that:

STRENGTH OF TRANSACTION COST ECONOMICS

Williamson highlighted the following strengths of transaction cost economics:

1. Transaction cost economics focuses on vertical integration: the make-or-buy decision has been a fundamental problem for business firms. This has two advantages: first, it addresses the theory of the firm problem to which Coase (1937) referred,[7] and without transaction costs the market is always best to solve the coordination problem; and second, the transactions in intermediate product markets are less identified by contractual complications (such as asymmetries of information, resources, expertise and risk aversion) than are other transactions such as day-to-day buying and selling.
2. The transaction is the basic unit of analysis, with an emphasis on asset specificity, contractual disturbances (uncertainty) and frequency.
3. In terms of autonomous and coordinated adaptation, alternative modes of governance are described as internally consistent attributes to which distinctive strengths and weaknesses accrue.
4. Transactions, which differ in their attributes, are aligned with governance structures, differing in their cost and competence to the effect that a transaction cost economises the outcome.
5. Any issue that arises, or can arise, as a contracting problem can be interpreted in transaction cost economising terms.
6. Transaction cost economics invites, and has benefited from, empirical testing. Indeed, "transaction cost economics stands on a remarkably broad empirical foundation" (Geyskens, Steenkamp and Kumar, 2006, p. 531).[8] Transaction cost economics has been influential because of the empirical work that it has produced.
7. Transaction cost economics has also transformed public policy by working up the efficiency/inefficiency consequences of transaction cost economics for complex economic organisation.

1. Agreements may occur rapidly compared to the outcome in the pure discounting model. The rapid settlement rates may simply be due to positive transaction costs.
2. When transaction costs increase, the duration of negotiations decreases, but also the frequency of termination increases. It would be less costly to opt out when we would have higher costs to consider in the next negotiation stage. Thus, to opt out would be the solution to this dilemma. However, if sunk costs exist for the parties, then it is better to continue to negotiate.
3. As transaction costs increase, the seller's *ex ante* payoff declines slowly, and the buyer's payoff increases slowly. The bargaining efficiency declines as transaction costs increase, yet the decline is small.
4. Termination of negotiations may occur because of positive transaction costs. Termination, however, always occurs at the outset of negotiations. This is because the buyer has full information about the size of the gains from trade. Uncertainty, however, complicates the situation.
5. Patience is usually a virtue: as the buyer's cost advantage increases, the seller's payoff declines, and the buyer's payoff increases. Eventually, the seller will however benefit

from higher transaction costs, in which case the seller can terminate negotiations. Higher transaction costs makes it easier for the seller to commit to walking away following a rejection by the buyer.

6. Transaction costs may be used to make threats credible. If a seller prefers to employ a costly agent to conduct the negotiation, then that makes terminating negotiations credible if the initial offer is rejected. This point has empirical relevance. Threats to terminate negotiations if demands are not met are commonly observed in negotiations. Termination arises naturally once transaction costs are introduced.

Example 3.2 provides a practical example for transaction costs.

EXAMPLE 3.2
AXIATA AND TELENOR ABANDON MOVE TO MERGE ASIAN OPERATIONS

Axiata, Malaysia's telecommunications conglomerate, and Telenor, the Norwegian telecoms operator, have abandoned plans to merge their Asian operations in a deal that would have created a group with 300 million customers from Thailand to Indonesia.

In separate statements on Friday, the companies blamed the ending of the talks, which started four months ago, on "complexities". The merged group would have generated $13 billion in annual revenues and would have been the biggest telecoms operator in South East Asia. Under the plan, Telenor would have owned 56.5 per cent of the combined entity while Axiata would have held the rest. The collapse of the talks comes after Malaysia's prime minister voiced concerns about potential job losses to the country's sovereign wealth fund of which he is chairman and which is Axiata's main shareholder. Axiata's chief executive had said that the company would offer voluntary separation schemes to its staff in Malaysia if the deal had gone through; there would have been no forced job cuts. The companies expected cost savings of $5 billion from the proposed merger. The companies were looking to finalise the transaction this quarter. Telenor shares slid more than 6 per cent in Oslo, while trading in Axiata's stock was halted before the ending of talks was disclosed. Both companies said that "a future transaction could be possible". Axiata would "continue to actively explore possible consolidation and portfolio optimisation opportunities". The deal would have given the combined group operations across nine countries and 14 key entities. Both groups have operations in Malaysia, Thailand, Bangladesh, Pakistan and Myanmar. Axiata is also present in India, Indonesia, Sri Lanka, Cambodia and Nepal. The Bangladesh operations of Axiata would have been excluded from the deal. Earlier this year, Bloomberg reported a third party had expressed interest in taking over Edotco, Axiata's wireless tower business, at a $3 billion valuation while the Malaysian conglomerate was working on the merger with Telenor. Telenor said it would not comment on another party's interest. Telenor, majority-owned by the Norwegian government, has sold off a number of stakes in Central and Eastern Europe as it seeks to concentrate on the Nordic and Asian regions after being embroiled in a damaging bribery scandal in Russia.

Source: Adapted from Palma (2019).[9]

Discussion Point: What transaction costs might have occurred? Does transaction cost economics explain the merger talks situation?

3.3 DECISION ANALYSIS

In 1968, Howard Raiffa published his book *Decision Analysis*, which launched this field. Decision analysis offers a robust, accessible way of making decisions under uncertainty.[10] It is based on individual decision making. The *decision analytical* problem is disaggregated into a sequence of uncertain events and choices together with a clear description of the possible consequences of each choice and each uncertain event in combination with the decision maker's attitude towards time and risk. Decision analysis uses many influential concepts from game theory and economics and is based on how people behave, which was originally classified as descriptive. Decision analysis deals with descriptive, prescriptive and normative decision making. This means that the behaviour of individuals is analysed, whether it is based on how people behave (*descriptive*), or how they should wish to behave once they have thought hard about the solution (*prescriptive*), in comparison to the rationally logically disciplined manner (*normative*) of game theoretical reasoning.

In negotiations, the descriptive angle comes across when the negotiators' behaviour is linked to characteristics in terms of personality or culture. The prescriptive behaviour highlights how they should choose their strategies to come to a conclusion, whether a deal or a break-up. Finally, the normative angle of negotiations focuses on the rational behaviour of super-humans who are able to anticipate and follow a clearly designated path to an outcome (see Figure 3.1).

Decision analysis tends to prescribe a systematic decomposition of the problem of decision making under uncertainty. It structures and sequences the party's chance events and choices, then it separates and assesses the probabilities, risks, values and time preferences subjectively.

The *expected utility* criterion created by von Neumann and Morgenstern[11] proves a simple method to aggregate the elements into a measure that explicitly ranks possible actions to determine the optimal choice. The uncertainties are not interactive, meaning that they are not influenced by other parties.

For international negotiations, decision analysis can be used for individual choices under uncertainty. This will affect the negotiation party and the individual choices for the negotiation process as well as the anticipation of the negotiation outcome.

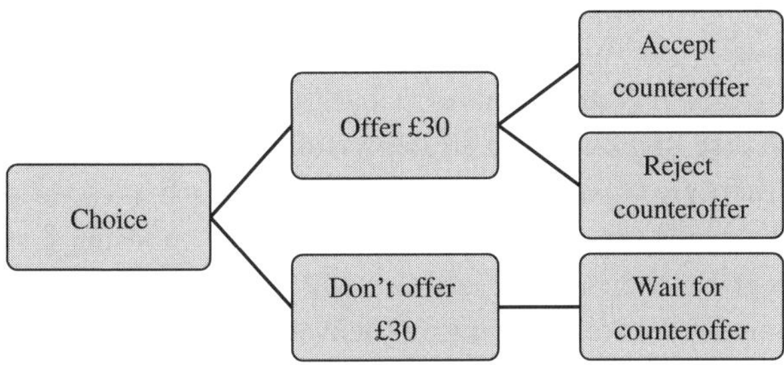

Figure 3.1 Decision analysis of the choice to offer

3.4 GAME THEORY

In previous sections, game theoretical reasoning has already been touched upon. In the case of transaction cost economics, bounded rationality was introduced to give the rationality assumption a more realistic lens. The rationality assumption in game theory is one of its criticisms, since the individual decision maker will make the decision in line with a logical system in a disciplined way. For international business negotiations, *game theoretical reasoning* is relevant, because it highlights interactive decision making. Each party anticipates choices which affect themselves as well as the other party. Howard Raiffa's initial focus was on game theory.[12] *Game theory* offers a rational and logically consistent analysis of interdependent decision making among actors.[13]

Here the description of the course of actions for each player is called "*strategy*". An analysis of these strategies leads to an outcome or an "*equilibrium*". This is especially useful for repeated interactions in negotiations. The importance is that the interactions are well structured. Likewise, game theory is important for understanding the design of auctions, bidding mechanisms, voting behaviour and other economic and social contexts. Game theory goes back to the seminal work of John von Neumann and Oskar Morgenstern (1944), who wrote the book the *Theory of Games and Economic Behavior* in which they offered a simple method of aggregating game theoretical elements to rank the possible actions in order to determine the optimal choice. This is especially useful when it comes to decisions under uncertainty. Systematically, the problem is structured and sequenced with the players' choices and chance events. Probabilities, risk, values and time preferences are then separated and individually assessed. Many have criticised the rationality assumption and the difficulty for real people to behave like super-rational players. Besides the seminal work of von Neumann and Morgenstern, game theory has produced many Nobel Prize winners (John Nash, Reinhard Selten, John Harsanyi, Robert Aumann, Thomas Schelling, Roger Myerson), as they have applied game theoretical analysis to real-life situations. Their contribution to game theory ranges from subgame perfect to cooperative and incomplete information games, using the various angles of analysis and contributing to the knowledge of rational players. Table 3.2 illustrates different approaches with equilibria concepts for negotiations.

3.4.1 Games with perfect information

A small example can show how a game theoretical approach can identify the problems and provide the payoffs to a strategy set of negotiators I and II. The negotiators know their own strategies (soft or tough). They need to assign to their counterpart the probability of choosing either the soft or the tough strategy. This goes back to a discussion about optimal strategies and payoffs. In our case, the choice of strategy is directly related to the way game theory develops the rules: there are two or more players (N), they each have a strategy profile (S_1, S_2) and they each have payoffs (π_1, π_2). The probability, p, of choosing a strategy is included. In a rational assumption, the expected utilities will be calculated. Apart from the rational assumption, the game theoretical solution can deliver a solution which is *Pareto-optimal* for the players, which means no player is made better off than the other one.

Table 3.2 Classification of game theoretical solution concepts

Games	Complete information	Incomplete information
Static games	Nash Equilibrium *Prisoner's dilemma,* Nash (1950, 1952) Perfect information between the players: "I know that you know that I know" Example: Competitive advantage between a duopoly	Bayesian Nash Equilibrium Harsanyi (1967–8) Nature is introduced as a dummy player to show uncertainty around the players' preferences Example: Auctions
Dynamic games include time as a factor	Subgame Perfect Equilibrium Selten (1975) The subgames can be played by themselves and over time in which strategies can be adapted and changed Example: Market entry game	Perfect Bayesian Equilibrium Harsanyi (1967–8) Uncertainty about a player's type or preferences is played over time and beliefs can be updated (signalling games) Example: Bargaining mechanisms under uncertainty

Source: Adapted from Ott (2013).[14]

The prisoner's dilemma game was first developed by A. Tucker in 1955,[15] then in 1957 R. Duncan Luce and Howard Raiffa picked it up in their book *Games and Decisions.*[16] Below is a good example of a rational approach towards solving a two-player non-cooperative situation in which the payoffs need to be maximised considering the other player's choices. It is a perfect information game, since both players know their own and their counterpart's strategy and payoff. The prisoners sit in different cells and have to consider their punishment. If neither player chooses to cooperate, then in the case where player II also does not cooperate both players get one year in jail. If both players cooperate, they both get three years in jail. If player I does not cooperate and player II cooperates, then player I gets two years in jail and player II gets five years, and vice versa. The Nash equilibrium is therefore to not confess (1, 1).

In the "classic" version of this game the police have arrested two suspects A and B, or in our case the famous criminal couple Bonnie and Clyde, for a serious crime (with them ending up in a cell rather than being shot). Both are guilty, but the police do not have enough evidence to prove the guilt of either Bonnie (A) or Clyde (B). Instead, the police interrogate each suspect in a separate room. Bonnie and Clyde are not, nor have they been, allowed to communicate. The concern of each individual is to maximise his or her own payoff. No matter what the other does, both Bonnie and Clyde can improve their own position by confessing. If both confess (A2, B2) they will both get jail sentences, but reduced ones, for helping the authorities. If either Bonnie or Clyde confesses, the other should confess also, because if he or

Table 3.3 The Nash equilibrium

		Clyde	
		Not confess	**Confess**
Bonnie	**Not confess**	(2, 2)	(10, 1/2)
	Confess	(1/2, 10)	(5, 5)

she does not (A1, B2; A2, B1), the player who does not confess will be punished by receiving the longest jail sentence possible. If neither Bonnie nor Clyde confess (A1, B1), the police cannot fully prove the guilt of either party and each prisoner will only receive a short jail sentence. The payoff matrix of this game is shown in Table 3.3.

The prisoner's dilemma in this form is a non-zero-sum or mixed-motive game (it is possible for both players to win, neither player to win, or for one player to win and the other player to not win) in which the gains or losses incurred by each player are a function of the choices of the other party as well as the choices made by the individual.[17] The outcomes of the prisoner's dilemma for each player are, therefore, both conflicting and compatible.[18] In contrast, the outcome of a zero-sum game means that the victory of one player by necessity entails the loss of the other player.

In this form the prisoner's dilemma is also a non-cooperative game, as A and B are unable to communicate with each other; if they were allowed to communicate the game would be cooperative and the players, it is assumed, would attempt to settle on either both confessing or both not confessing.

Now, removing the condition that both A and B are not allowed to communicate, it might be supposed that prior to interrogation both players will agree not to confess and thus cooperate with each other. After reaching this agreement, A and B are separated and interrogated in separate rooms. In spite of the agreement the two players had made with each other to not confess, the dominant strategy for both players, paradoxically, remains to confess to the police and defect on their agreement with each other. Thus, renaming the "confess" choice as "defect" and the "not confess" choice as "cooperate", the dominant strategy even if communication is allowed would be to defect – even though the welfare of both individuals is improved if they chose to cooperate. This is the paradox of the prisoner's dilemma.

Example 3.3 highlights an international business negotiation dilemma.

A negotiation situation which looks like the above prisoner's dilemma but considers the probability of strategies used by the players will be shown in Table 3.5.[19]

It is different in that the criteria of rationality are not sufficient to define the optimal strategy. The game can be played in many ways. This representation shows why optimal strategies are definable only if the opponent's behaviour is predictable. If one of the players knows that the probability of the opponent playing soft is p, then the expected payoff could be maximised, which is sufficient to define the optimal strategy. Bartos[20] introduced soft and tough strategies and we can use this to align Bartos's classification with strategies (see later chapters) often used in international business negotiations to show cultural differences.[21]

EXAMPLE 3.3
NEGOTIATIONS BETWEEN AMERICAN BUSINESSWOMAN AND JAPANESE BUSINESSMAN

(The American woman Ms Field is discussing with her colleague Ms Jones the negotiations with the Japanese businessman Mr Teryaki)

Ms Jones: How did the negotiation go?

Ms Field: Not so well. We were taken.

Ms Jones: What happened?

Ms Field: Well, I proposed our starting price, and Teryaki did not say anything.

Ms Jones: Nothing?

Ms Field: He just sat there, looking very serious. So I brought the price down.

Ms Jones: And?

Ms Field: Still nothing. But he looked a little surprised. So I brought it down to our last offer... and just waited. I could not go any lower.

Ms Jones: What did he say?

Ms Field: Well, he was quiet for about a minute, and then agreed.

Ms Jones: Well, at least we got a deal. You should be pleased.

Ms Field: I guess so. But later I learnt that he thought our first price was very generous.

We transfer the negotiation discussed between Ms Field and Ms Jones into a dilemma, solved in a rational manner in Table 3.4.

Discussion Point: The difference between no communication and communication in negotiations needs to be shown in the game theoretical approach. What are strategies and payoffs? (d, d) is the disagreement point. Assume that the numbers are monetary values for price offers.

Table 3.4 A decision problem: international negotiations between an American businesswoman and a Japanese businessman

		Mr Teryaki	
		No communication	**Communication**
Ms Field	**No communication**	(1, 1) - (d, d)	(2, 5)
	Communication	(5, 2)	(3, 3)

To show this: the row player assumes her opponent plays soft with probability p. If the row player plays soft, then the expected payoff is $3p+2$; if she plays tough, it is $8p$. The maximisation of the expected payoff means that he should be soft $3p+2>8p$, which is $p>2/5$. If $p<2/5$, then she should be tough, and if $p=2/5$ then the players could toss a coin. The payoff matrix shows in general that if a player is soft, then the opponent is likely to be tough and vice versa. This strategy profile matrix shows that it is only possible to define negotiation strategies when the counterpart's behaviour is predictable. In a symmetrical situation, the rational approach is easier to use, whereas when we deal with asymmetric preferences and strategies, then other ways need to be considered. International negotiations with their asymmetries regarding cultural backgrounds make it much more difficult to predict and prescribe behaviour (see Table 3.5).

Table 3.5 A decision problem: soft or tough strategy

		Negotiator II		
		Soft strategy **p**	**probabilities**	**Tough strategy** **(1 – p)**
Negotiator I	**Soft strategy**	(5, 5)		(2, 8)
	Tough strategy	(8, 2)		(0, 0)

Source: Adapted from Bartos (1967).[22]

Nevertheless, for international business negotiations, the interactive side of the negotiations has relevance when it is used as an analytical tool for strategic interactions between one or many players.

Even though game theory assumes rational behaviour, game theoretical solution concepts also use an approach to deal with real-life problems and how to solve them. Market behaviour and bargaining relies on solutions from game theory. Incomplete information and the use of time give the problems a more relevant direction. The section below deals with solution concepts which are useful for international business negotiations, such as bargaining, signalling and market entry.

3.4.2 Games with imperfect information

International business negotiations have characteristics of uncertainty and dynamics. We therefore introduce the game theoretical approaches for these applications. Bargaining games can be shown in normal form (see the matrix of the prisoner's dilemma) or in extensive form as a game tree. The latter is a sequence of offers and counteroffers: sequential bargaining. In bargaining there needs to be consistency, such that one should never ask for something later that has been rejected before and one should never reject something now that is planned to be asked for later.

In Figure 3.2 a practical case can be shown as an alternating offer game. There is a specific sum of money M on the table and there are two periods of negotiations. We use Richard Branson's attempt to get $1 billion from an investor for his endeavours to get to space as a bargaining scenario (see Figure 3.2).

This alternating offer game was developed by Rubinstein[23] and reflects a business situation. In Figure 3.2, to the box in which Branson rejects can now be added further boxes with every offer and counteroffer. The costs of time and reduction of offers as concessions are made lead to a smaller pie.

Every time an offer is rejected a counteroffer will be made until they either complete the deal or end their negotiations. This is a sequential bargaining game over several periods. Haggling in a bazaar would look like the game tree in Figure 3.3.[24]

Consider a seller facing a buyer in a two-period game. In the first period, the seller makes an offer to sell at price p_1 and the buyer accepts or rejects. If the buyer accepts the offer, the

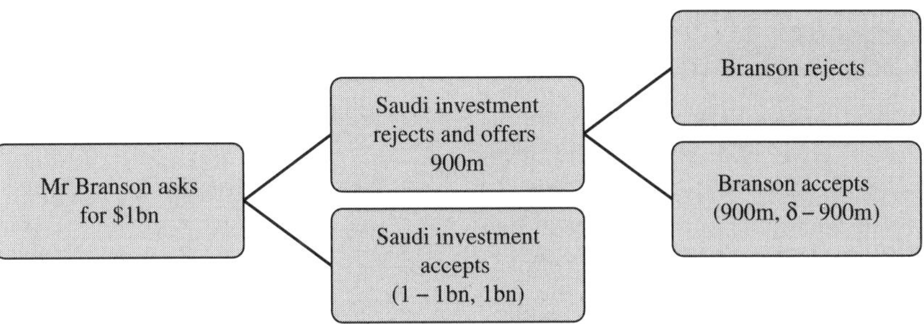

Figure 3.2 Alternating offer game for the case of Richard Branson requesting funding for space travel

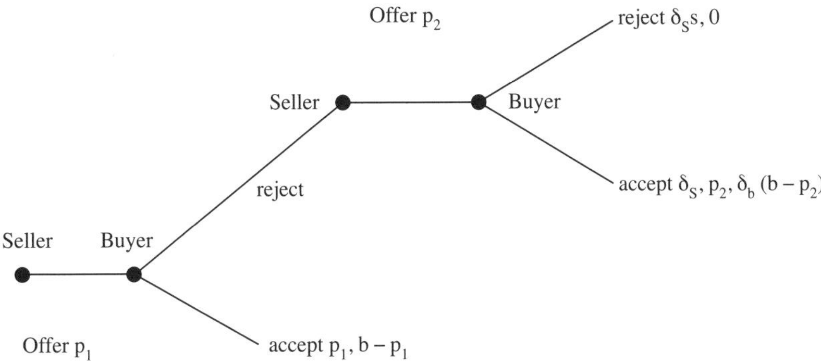

Figure 3.3 Haggling in a bazaar situation

exchange is made and the game is over. The deal is done. If, however, the buyer rejects the offer, then the seller makes another offer p_2 and the buyer accepts or rejects. In a bazaar, the interactions are quick and involve many rounds of offer and counteroffer before an agreement is made or the haggling process breaks up. The goods are known to both the buyer and the seller and are often displayed in front of them.

Adding uncertainty to the situation, there will be a signalling game in which the parties need to find out the preferences and values which are not disclosed among them. In international business negotiations, uncertainty about the players and the environment is a major factor. The game in Example 3.4 is called the caveat emptor game, in which the buyer does not know the quality of the goods and it is his responsibility to check this before the purchase.

3.5 NEGOTIATION ANALYSIS

The next step in the theoretical underpinning section focuses on negotiation analysis, which was introduced by Howard Raiffa in his book *The Art and Science of Negotiations*.[25] He is one of the most acclaimed negotiation scholars, since his background is in decision science

EXAMPLE 3.4
CAVEAT EMPTOR GAME[26]

The uncertainty of the quality is in this case indicated by the player called Nature, who throws the die on whether the quality is good or bad with probability p(good) and p(bad). The notation is p for price, v for value for the good item for which the buyer pays price p: v - p. The bad item has worth w for the buyer from which the price is deducted: w - p. Costs (c) is for the bad-type seller. There are four possible equilibria in this game:

1. Complete market failure: All sellers are concerned about rejection of the buyer.
2. Complete market success: Only sellers with good items offer them for sale. Separating equilibrium in which the type is revealed.
3. Partial market success: All sellers offer their items for sale, and all buyers buy whatever is offered.
4. Near market failure: Some but not all bad-type sellers offer their items for sale. Buyers buy what is offered for sale.

Figure 3.4 shows this graphically.

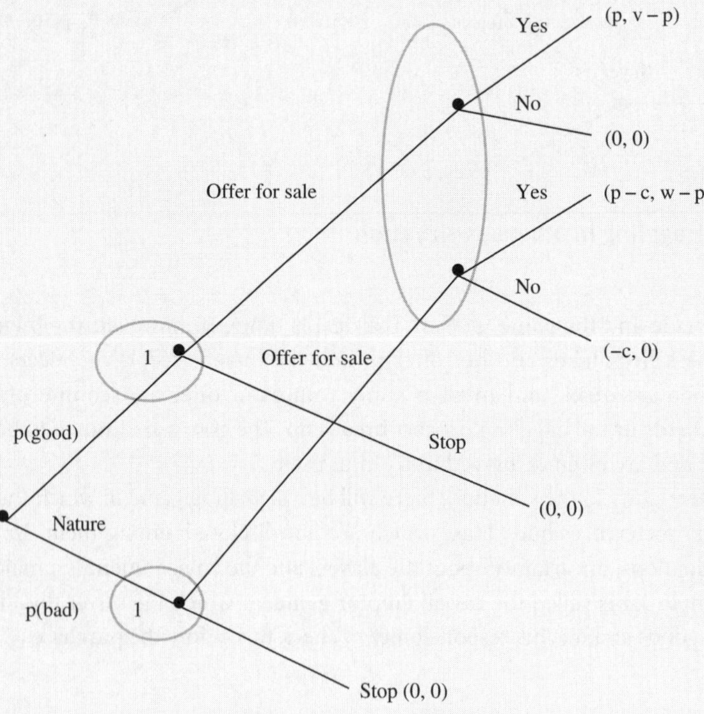

Figure 3.4 A simple signalling game in business

and game theory. He could see the advantages and disadvantages of both and therefore positioned negotiation analysis between decision science, game theory and psychology.

Negotiators show purposeful behaviour towards understanding each other's position; they move significantly from the "idealized, super-rational" behaviour of game theoretical making to the joint decision making of negotiators. Raiffa found it more important to consider the interactive problems in which joint decisions of the negotiators influence the outcomes.[27] This led to "*negotiation analysis*", which combines the divided fields of descriptive and prescriptive work. The negotiation analytical direction provides an integrative approach which is asymmetrically descriptive/prescriptive. This means that one side knows what to do under the conditions and how the counterpart is going to behave. Negotiation analysis decomposes the problem into characteristic elements. It assesses:

1. The involved parties.
2. Their potential coalitional alignments.
3. Their underlying interests.
4. Their alternatives to a negotiated agreement.

The tensions between competitive actions to claim value individually and/or cooperative actions to create value jointly are productively dealt with. The negotiation analysis perspective has carefully worked out the precise analytical relationships between these factors and a range of technical tools to evaluate and move them into prescriptions. The full (game theoretical) rationality is complemented by the findings of behavioural science and experimental economics. This approach expects intelligent goal-seeking action by the parties, but not full rationality. The possible strategies and tactics are evaluated by focusing on the changes in perception of the "zone of possible agreement" and the distribution of negotiated outcomes conditional on the various actions. Negotiation analysis considers "parties" instead of "players" in a joint decision-making situation. Different to game theory, negotiation analysis views that:[28]

1. *Joint decisions* are not binding or enforceable – a verbal agreement, a handshake, an exchange of assets and even a contract may not be enough to make the parties stick to the agreement. It is important to develop mechanisms for enforcement.
2. *Joint payoffs* are determined by the joint decisions of the parties that are also relevant/acceptable for each party.
3. *Reciprocal communication* of interests, aspirations, expectations, beliefs and visions of the future are relevant rather than simultaneous choices. Even though full, open and truthful exchange is dealt with towards maximising joint gains, communication is not always seen as good. Bluffing, threat, trickery, exaggeration, concealment, half-truths and lies are part of negotiations. Negotiations are determined by the truthful exchange of information and interests, while the parties proceed in separate and interacting moves in an extensive game.
4. *Creativity* allows a less tightly defined perspective on the existence of predetermined strategies and payoffs. Assumptions about common knowledge are relaxed.

5. *Decision* perspectives of negotiations are composed of individual, interactive and joint decision-making approaches. These three perspectives cannot lead to an integrated analysis since negotiations are far too complex. The best solutions can be achieved by finding a balance between analytical endeavours and cognitive capabilities. Bargaining skills, the power of persuasion, knowledge and communication skills, willingness to use creativity, inventiveness, and skills in drafting agreements are crucial elements of business negotiations.
6. *Negotiator's dilemma* is derived from the situation where a large slice of the pie needs to be created jointly with the counterpart. The complexity in business negotiations is that this created value is linked to value claiming.

Negotiation analysis is a collaborative approach which adopts FOTE (Full, Open, Truthful Exchange) to reach the goals between the parties. In cooperative situations, there can be differences in value, perceptions, bargaining power and time preferences. If all parties agree to negotiate with common knowledge and in a FOTE manner, there can be still cases in which the parties do not tell the full truth and might withhold information. At this point, the negotiation analysis can be conducted in a POTE (Partly, Open, Truthful Exchange) manner. Therefore, there are cases when the parties cannot be trusted. All these manners and elements of negotiation are possible in international business negotiations, in which the complexities of cultural background, negotiation styles, preferences, communication patterns and time preferences are even more exposed than in domestic negotiations.

3.6 A THEORETICAL APPLICATION TO INTERNATIONAL BUSINESS NEGOTIATIONS – FOR THE MATHEMATICALLY INCLINED

International business negotiations are characterised by having parties from different cultural backgrounds, which has an impact on the strategies and negotiation styles used in the negotiation process. The expectation of the outcome is different as well: some might want a long-term relationship and others a short-term contract. From an interactive decision-making perspective, game theoretical reasoning would help in considering the different paths for the players.

A game theoretical framework for different activity types[29] maps the cultural diversity and considers three categories of culture:[30]

1. Linear-active cultures (L): task-oriented planners who prefer data and information. They use logic to argue their case, interrupt rarely and take one action at a time. They set the initial offer they want to receive and have a short-term perspective.
2. Multi-active cultures (M): people-oriented interlocuters who prefer human action and emotions in their interactions. They use emotional argumentation, interrupt often and combine tasks. They tend to offer a high price, considering a longer bargaining time horizon.

3. Reactive cultures (R): respect-oriented listeners who prefer both human interaction and data in order to get the bigger picture. They rarely interrupt, don't want to lose face and react to the counterpart's actions. They are inclined to respond to the counterpart's behaviour and have a long bargaining horizon to develop relationships.

The payoffs are dependent on the price, the costs and the discount factor involved in the bargaining process. The initial offer for each culture type p_0 is basically the proposal including the margin the players anticipate being put on top dependent on their type $p_0 = \{p_{L,} p_{M,} p_R\}$. The costs of bargaining are a product of the length of bargaining shown as discount factor δ, which is different for the three types such that $0 \le \delta_L < \delta_M < \delta_R \le 1$. We have δ_L for the impatient linear-active type, δ_M for the multi-active type and δ_R for the patient reactive type.

The initial price offer is dependent on the types (linear-active, multi-active or reactive) $p_0 = \{p_{L,} p_{M,} p_R\}$ as can be explained in the following:

1. The linear-active seller wants $p_{L,}$ his initial price, which includes a small margin *L* to cover a short period of bargaining.
2. The multi-active seller offers p_M, in which M is a fixed margin considered to be on top of the price, anticipating bargaining costs over the period of time.
3. The reactive seller makes his initial offer p_R, considering R as a margin on top of the seller's price to cover the costs of delay.

The payoffs amount to the price minus the costs involved. Since we expect the price to be the result of a bargaining procedure, the final price may be either the precise expected final price or, in case of difficulties during the procedure, the price p* with a margin based on the time horizon. The latter occurs because of asymmetries in the bargaining behaviour. With respect to the disagreement point after several periods of bargaining, this outcome includes negative payoffs due to the high bargaining costs. The interval between the offers Δ plays another important role in distinguishing between the three types. Thus, we have $\Delta_L \to 0$ for a short bargaining linear-active type, $\Delta_R \to 1$ for a patient reactive type and $\Delta_M \in \{0,1\}$ for a multi-active type. Since the empirical findings show that the time interval between offers is dependent on the type of player, we can add to the price function the time interval Δ dependent on the type of player.

Finally, the *payoff functions* are therefore different for the sellers and buyers with different cultural activity types. The payoffs for the sellers are $p - c$ and for the buyers $v - p$. This shows that the sellers have to deduct the costs from the price negotiated and the buyers will need to get a lower price than the value placed on the good in order to deal with each other. The negotiated price covers costs and value of the products.

The specific properties of the linear-active, multi-active and reactive sellers and buyers are used for the contingencies of bargaining scenarios. Table 3.6 provides the overall framework for sellers and buyers with either different cultural bargaining strategies (complete information) or different cultural activity types (incomplete information).

Using a multi-active seller who negotiates with linear-active, multi-active or reactive buyers, Figure 3.5 shows the acceptance points and where trade can occur. From a

Table 3.6 A framework for activity-based negotiations

	Buyer/seller cultures	Buyer (player II)		
		Linear-active American/ German	**Multi-active Brazilian/ Italian**	**Reactive Japanese/ Finnish**
Seller (player I)	Linear-active American/ German	Similar cultural background with refinements *"Time is money" approach* $(p_L - c_L; v_L - p_L)$	Seller linear-active and buyer multi-active $(p_L - c_L; v_M - p_M)$	Seller linear-active and buyer reactive $(p_L - c_L; v_R - p_R)$
	Multi-active Brazilian/ Italian	Seller multi-active and buyer linear-active $(p_M - c_M; v_L - p_L)$	Similar cultural background with refinements *"Haggling" approach* $(p_M - c_M; v_M - p_M)$	Seller multi-active and buyer reactive $(p_M - c_M; v_R - p_R)$
	Reactive Japanese/ Finnish	Seller reactive and buyer linear-active $(p_R - c_R; v_L - p_L)$	Seller reactive and buyer multi-active *Scenario 9* $(p_R - c_R; v_M - p_M)$	Similar cultural background with refinements *"Building trust" approach* $(p_R - c_R; v_R - p_R)$

Source: Adapted from Ott (2011).[31]

negotiation analytical perspective, the seller uses a strategy which gets an early acceptance by the linear-active buyer, a holding-out and relationship-building approach by the reactive buyer, and a haggling approach by the similar type – the multi-active buyer.

Connected to the strategies discussed earlier, the strategies used by linear-active, multi-active and reactive sellers and buyers fall into the tough and soft strategy category. Later chapters will add the intermediate strategy, which is already present in the three-activity typology.

This typology can be applied to business cases. The Microsoft–Nokia Deal demonstrates the activity-based typology ideally. The information in Example 3.5 can be used to identify the scenario in the framework (Table 3.6) with the respective diagram (Figure 3.5).

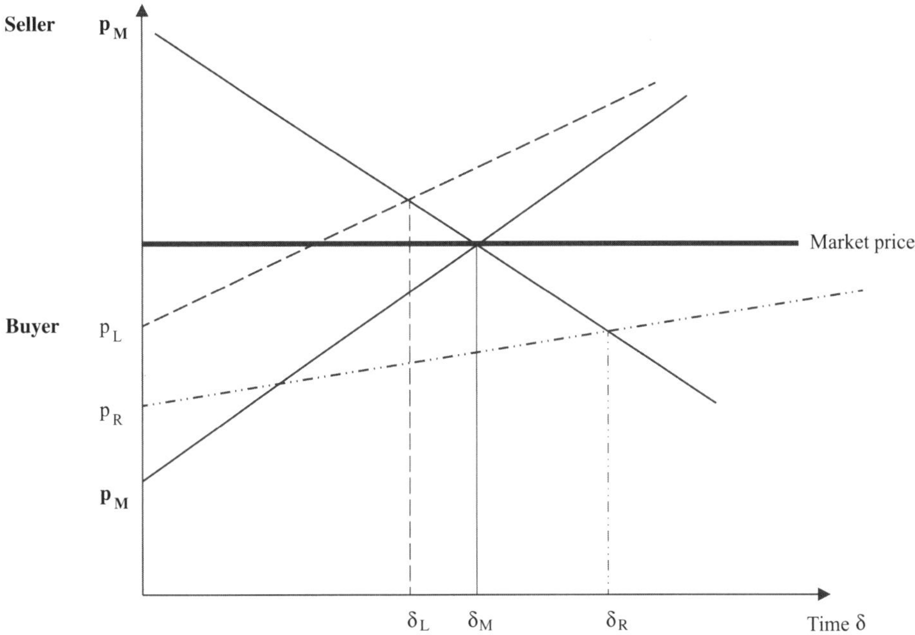

Source: Adapted from Ott (2016).[32]

Figure 3.5 Multi-active seller negotiates with LMR buyer

EXAMPLE 3.5
THE MICROSOFT-NOKIA DEAL

Microsoft announced a deal to acquire the handset and services business of Finnish mobile phone company Nokia for $7.2 billion. This agreement marked a bold move by Microsoft to upgrade its presence in handheld devices and signals. It should mark an end to Nokia's long struggle to enter the hyper-competitive (and extremely lucrative) smartphone market. The dynamics behind the negotiations reveal Nokia's and Microsoft's negotiation styles, since both sides had strong incentives to get together. Nokia had lost significant ground in recent years to smartphone manufacturers such as Samsung and Apple, and had failed to keep up with innovations, for instance touch screens. Nokia planned to focus on telecommunications equipment, its mapping business and its patent portfolio, after getting rid of the underperforming handset business. During the Mobile World Congress industry conference in Barcelona, Steve Ballmer, CEO of Microsoft, approached Nokia CEO Stephen Elop about a possible acquisition. Then, in 2013, Ballmer and Nokia chairman Riisto Siilasmaa conducted negotiations across the globe in a methodological and discreet manner. The complexity of international business negotiations involving different cultures (US American versus Finnish) was particularly relevant in this case. Not only do these two companies belong in the ranks of the world's largest firms, but the complexity of merging the cultures of the two distinct home countries also added to the difficulties. The challenges of integrating employees from different cultures needed to be tackled after signing the contract.

From a negotiation analytical perspective, it pays to view negotiators as individuals and not as cultural ambassadors. It often makes sense to maintain each organisation's unique identity and borrow from the best of both. Based on expected cultural norms, the bargaining process is a holistic procedure aimed at creating value and agreements.

In the end, Microsoft acquired Nokia, but it turned out to be "monumental mistake" and Microsoft ended up writing off billions of dollars as an "impairment charge". The write-off, which amounted to $7.6 billion, was almost the amount Microsoft paid for Nokia and its patents.

Sources: Adapted from *New York Times*, Program on Negotiation, Microsoft and Nokia webpages.

Discussion Point: Can this deal be categorised as social exchange, transaction cost economics, game theory and negotiation analysis? What kind of scenario would fit this deal in the activity-based negotiation framework?

3.7 SUMMARY

This chapter deals with rational behaviour and joint decision making in international business negotiations. Social exchange theory and transaction cost theory position the negotiation problem in terms of social and economic interactions and cost–benefit analysis of the motives to trade. The game theoretical perspective suggests that people make their decisions in a rational manner with the prisoner's dilemma, bargaining and signalling games as interesting applications to international business settings. Negotiation analysis positions the problem as joint decision making between individuals and highlights that real-life applications are possible with full and partial disclosure of information. At the end of the chapter, an application to activity-based negotiations in international business consolidates the theoretical underpinnings of this chapter.

QUESTIONS

1. What paradigms have influenced international business negotiations?
2. How are psychological and economic perspectives in international business negotiations connected?
3. Why is it important to approach international business negotiations from a game theoretical perspective?
4. What are the differences between decision analytical, negotiation analytical and bargaining theoretical approaches in international negotiations? Highlight the benefits of each of them and the different outcomes, respectively.

NOTES

1. Homans, G.C. (1958) Social behaviour as exchange. *American Journal of Sociology*. **63**(6), Emile Durkheim-Georg Simmel, 1858–1958 (May, 1958), pp. 597–606.
2. Cropanzano, R. and Mitchell, M.S. (2005) Social exchange theory: an interdisciplinary review. *Journal of Management*. **31**, 874–900.
3. BBC (2019) A quick guide to the US–China trade war. *BBC News*, 2 September.
4. See here Williamson, O.E. (1971) The vertical integration of production: market failure considerations. *American Economic Review*. **61**(May), 112–23; Williamson, O.E. (1975) *Markets and Hierarchies: Analysis and Antitrust Implications*. New York, Free Press; Williamson, O.E. (2002a) The lens of contract: private ordering. *American Economic Review*. **92**(May), 438–43; Williamson, O.E. (2002b) The theory of the firm as governance structure: from choice to contract. *Journal of Economic Perspectives*. **16**(Summer), 171–95; Williamson, O.E. (2005a) The economics of governance. *American Economic Review*. **95**(2), 1–18; Williamson, O.E. (2005b) Transaction cost economics and business administration. *Scandinavian Journal of Management*. **21**, 19–40.
5. Hennart, J.-F. (2010) Transaction cost theory and international business. *Journal of Retailing*. **86**(3), 257–69.
6. Crampton, P. (1991) Dynamic bargaining and transaction costs. *Management Science*. **37**, 1221–33.
7. Coase, R.H. (1937) The nature of the firm. *Economica*. **4**(16), 386–405.
8. Geyskens, I., Steenkamp, J.E.M. and Kumar, N. (2006) Make, buy, or ally: a meta-analysis of transaction cost theory. *Academy of Management Journal*. **49**(3), 519–43.
9. Palma, S. (2019) Axiata and Telenor abandon move to merge Asian operations. *Financial Times*, 6 September.
10. Sebenius, J.K. (2009) Negotiation analysis: from games to inferences to decisions to deal. *Negotiation Journal*. **25**, 449–65.
11. Von Neumann, J. and Morgenstern, O. (1944) *The Theory of Games and Economic Behavior*. Princeton, Princeton University Press.
12. Luce, R.D. and Raiffa, H. (1957) *Games and Decisions*. New York, John Wiley & Sons.
13. Von Neumann and Morgenstern (1944) op. cit.; Nash, J. (1950) The bargaining problem. *Econometrica*. **18**(1), 155–62; Nash, J. (1951) Noncooperative games. *Annals of Mathematics*. **54**, 289–95; Nash, J. (1953) Co-operative games. *Econometrica*. **21**, 128–40; Selten, R. (1960) Spieltheoretische Behandlung eines Oligopolmodells mit Nachfragetragheit. *Zeitschrift fur die gesamte Staatswissenschaft*. **121**, 301–24 and 667–89; Harsanyi, J. (1967–8) Games with incomplete information played by Bayesian players. *Management Science*. **14**, 159–82, 320–34 and 486–502; Myerson, R.B. (1991) *Game Theory: Analysis of Conflict*. Cambridge MA, Harvard University Press; Ott, U.F. (2013) International business research and game theory: looking beyond the prisoner's dilemma. *International Business Review*. **22**(2), 480–91; Ott, U.F. (2011) The influence of cultural activity types on buyer–seller negotiations – a game theoretic framework for international negotiations [Special Issue on Culture and Negotiations]. *International Negotiation Journal*. **16**(3), 427–50.
14. Ott (2013) op. cit.
15. Tucker, A.W. (1955) *Game Theory and Programming*. Stillwater, Department of Mathematics, Oklahoma Agricultural and Mechanical College.
16. Luce and Raiffa (1957) op. cit.
17. Deutsch, M. (1973) *The Resolution of Conflict: Constructive and Destructive Processes*. New Haven, Yale University Press.
18. Lewicki, R.J. and Litterer, J.A. (1985) *Negotiation*. Homewood, Irwin.
19. Bartos, O. (1967) How predictable are negotiations? *Journal of Conflict Resolution*. **4**, 481–96.
20. Bartos (1967) ibid.

21. Ghauri, P.N. (2000) Negotiating international industrial projects: MNCs vs emerging markets. In: Woodside, A. (ed.) *Advances in Business Marketing and Purchasing*, Vol. 9. Stanford CA, JAI Press, pp. 187–201; Ott (2011) op. cit.
22. Bartos (1967) op. cit.
23. Rubinstein, A. (1982) Perfect equilibrium in a bargaining game. *Econometrica*. **50**, 97–109.
24. Gintis, H. (2009) *Game Theory Evolving*. Princeton, Princeton University Press.
25. Raiffa, H. (1983) *The Art and Science of Negotiation*. Cambridge MA, The Belknap Press of Harvard University Press.
26. Gardner, R. (2003) *Games for Business and Economics*. Hoboken, John Wiley & Sons.
27. Raiffa (1983) op. cit.; Raiffa, H., Richardson, J. and Metcalfe, D. (2002) *Negotiation Analysis: The Science and Art of Collaborative Decision Making*. Cambridge MA, The Belknap Press of Harvard University Press.
28. Raiffa (1983) op. cit.; Raiffa et al. (2002) ibid.; Sebenius (2009) op. cit.
29. Ott (2011) op. cit.; Ott, U.F. (2016) The art and economics of international negotiations: haggling meets hurrying and hanging on in buyer–seller negotiations. *Journal of Innovation and Knowledge*. **1**(1), 51–61.
30. Lewis, R.D. (2006, 2018) *When Cultures Collide: Leading across Cultures*. London, Nicholas Brealey Publishing; Ott (2011) op. cit.
31. Ott (2011) op. cit.
32. Ott (2016) op. cit.

FURTHER READING

Cropanzano, R. and Mitchell, M.S. (2005) Social exchange theory: an interdisciplinary review. *Journal of Management*. **31**, 874–900.

Ott, U.F. (2011) The influence of cultural activity types on buyer–seller negotiations: a game theoretic framework for international negotiations [Special Issue on Culture and Negotiations]. *International Negotiation Journal*. **16**(3), 427–50.

Raiffa, H. (1983) *The Art and Science of Negotiation*. Cambridge MA, The Belknap Press of Harvard University Press.

Williamson, O.E. (2005) The economics of governance. *American Economic Review*. **95**(2), 1–18.

4
Culture in international business negotiations

Culture is considered to be one of the most influential factors in international business negotiations. The business practices, the patterns of communication and the negotiation process followed by people in a country are influenced by the cultural norms and behaviours prevalent in society. In Chapters 4 and 5 we will explore how culture influences the international business negotiation activities and the communication process.

We begin this chapter by defining culture and explaining the various forms of cultures that are observed in business activities, including negotiations. We then provide an overview of the various studies on culture undertaken in international business and discuss how the dimensions of culture influence negotiator behaviour, the negotiating environment and the negotiation process across national boundaries.

4.1 WHAT IS CULTURE?

Culture is seen to be complex and therefore there is no one agreed upon definition. There is much debate about an individual's culture and cultural identity, especially in today's society where migration is increasing, and terms like biculturalism (seeing oneself as part of two cultures) and multiculturalism (the view that various cultures in a society merit equal respect) are used to explain the population in many countries. In this book, we follow the definition used commonly in international business that states that culture is a system of values, norms and beliefs that a group of people share and identify with and provides guidance on how society would work and expectations about individuals' behaviours.

Culture: a system of values, norms and beliefs that a group of people share and identify with.

There are many levels of culture that run deep, and when looking at another culture, one may only observe the visible aspects. Anthropologists give the analogy of the iceberg,[1] where only the tip of the iceberg is visible but the underlying aspects of culture that influence behaviour and norms in a society lie below the surface. As depicted in Figure 4.1, culture can be divided into three levels:

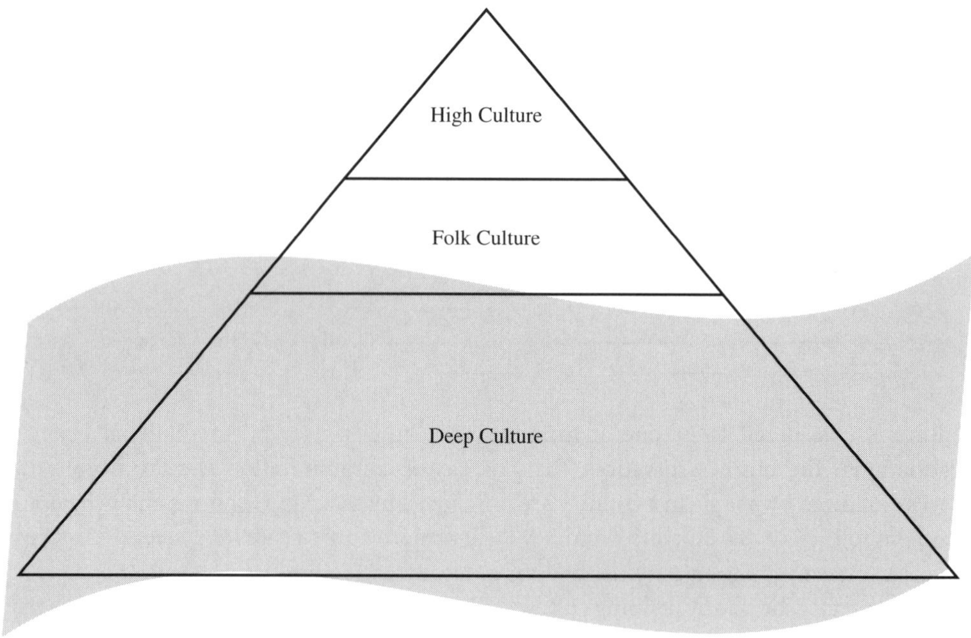

Source: Adapted from Cavusgil et al. (2014).[2]

Figure 4.1 The iceberg levels of culture

- High culture: the visible cultural aspects that includes arts, music and literature.
- Folk culture: cultural aspects that one is aware of, such as religion, humour and etiquettes.
- Deep culture: the cultural aspects that one is unaware of, such as family relationships, gender roles and non-verbal communication.

Culture is therefore learnt and dictates what people see as right or wrong. Therefore, the tacit behaviour and knowledge of an individual can be seen as directly influenced by the culture they most commonly associate with. However, culture is slow to change and changes to the norms and behaviours observed in the society can be seen as a gradual process. Therefore, cultural norms and values that are foreign to a society cannot be forced upon its members. Many successful organisations understand the importance of adapting to local cultural norms and follow the idea of "thinking global and acting local", or *Glocal*. One such example is that of KFC in China, which successfully adapted its menu to cater to the needs of the local population (see Example 4.1).

4.2 FORMS OF CULTURES

When culture is discussed in international business, the emphasis tends to be on the national culture level. Classifying cultures along national differences has been a significant stream

EXAMPLE 4.1
KFC IN CHINA: FROM STANDARDISATION TO ADAPTATION

Opening its first restaurant in 1987 in Beijing, KFC became the first American fast food chain to launch in China. It now operates 5,000 restaurants in over 1,000 cities in China. At a time when street vendor options in China were the norm, KFC restaurants introduced Chinese consumers to a comfortable dine-in experience. The consumers also appreciated the cleanliness of the restaurants and the freshness of the food.

The key to KFC's success in China, however, has been its ability to combine standard menu offerings with meal options that appealed to the tastes of the local population. So, a family visiting KFC in China could order the company's trademark fried chicken option or opt for congee. While the entry of other fast food chains has reduced KFC's overall market share, the company continues to introduce new localised menu options and holds a dominant position in China.

Sources: Adapted from Jacobs (2018);[3] and Pillai (2019).[4]

Discussion Point: How would you describe KFC's understanding of the Chinese culture and consumer market? Can you think of examples of other Western companies that have been successful in the Chinese market?

of research in international business and the influence of these differences on international business negotiations has been highlighted in many studies. In particular, research on negotiations in China, Japan and many developing countries has used differences in national culture as the central issue in explaining the negotiating behaviour.

National cultures influence the way business is done in a society and how individuals are expected to behave. By studying the cultural differences across countries, we can increase cultural empathy and understand why individuals behave the way they do. However, there are other forms of culture that need to be understood in the context of international business negotiations. In this chapter, we highlight and discuss some of the forms of cultures: national culture, business culture, organisational/corporate culture and professional/occupational culture.

4.2.1 National culture

In many countries, there is diversity in the population along the lines of geography, language, religious beliefs and ancestry and these differences lead to the existence of subcultures. These subcultures can be a result of historical diversity, as seen in countries like China, India and Indonesia, or a result of migration over time, such as in countries like Australia, Canada, the United Kingdom and the United States. Therefore, when the term *national culture* is used, it refers to the dominant culture practised in the country.

For example, the Malaysian population consists of three ethnic groups: the Malays, the Chinese and the Indians. In some cities of Malaysia, like George Town in the state of Penang, the Chinese ethnic population is in the majority. However, the *bumiputera* (a

National culture: the dominant culture practised in a country.

term used to describe the local Malay population, literal meaning "son of the land") population represents the largest ethnic group and its customs, behaviours and religious beliefs are what we associate as being the national culture of Malaysia.

4.2.2 Business culture

Business culture: the norms of how business activities are undertaken in a country.

The way business is conducted in a culture is referred to as the *business culture* of the country. The business practices followed in a country tend to reflect the widely held norms and beliefs found in a country's national culture. For example, if a country's national culture tends to emphasise respect for an individual's experience and age, then this is likely to be reflected in the business culture of the country, where senior managerial positions and key negotiations would be led by people of a certain age and experience.

Japan provides us with an example of a country where the emphasis on seniority and long-term planning meant that some large Japanese firms until the 1990s offered lifetime employment opportunities to their employees and implemented seniority-based promotion programmes. This was also reflected in international business negotiations involving Japanese managers, where the lead negotiator from Japan tends to be someone who has been with the organisation for a long period of time.

4.2.3 Corporate/organisational culture

Corporate/organisational culture: culture applied by a company throughout their network.

Companies that have a presence in more than one country face the challenge of managing operations across national cultures. These challenges can include differences in work expectation, decision-making process, and expected outcomes and rewards for individuals and groups. To ensure a consistent approach to work, and to align expectations, companies can create their own distinctive set of norms, values, beliefs and modes of behaviour known as *corporate or organisational culture.*

Companies attempt to foster a strong organisational culture to ensure that there is consistency in the way things are done within the organisation regardless of where the individual or team is based. Hence, organisations attempt to maximise efficiency by creating an identity for their employees at work that can limit the influence of other cultures. In some instances, companies may send managers from head office as expatriate country managers to ensure that the corporate/organisational culture is applied in the new overseas subsidiary. Toyota is one such organisation that places a strong emphasis on its corporate culture, and this is reflected in their consistent management and production programme called "The Toyota Way", which emphasises continuous improvement and respect for people as the key areas of focus of the organisation (see Example 4.2). IKEA is another such company that emphasises IKEA culture in all of its markets and follows a certain code of doing business called I-WAY or IKEA-Way.[5]

EXAMPLE 4.2
TOYOTA'S GLOBAL CULTURE

Toyota is one of the world's leading automotive firms. Its name is synonymous with Japanese quality and efficiency. Toyota's organisational values reflect the national culture values of Japan and are reflected in Toyota's framework called the *Toyota Way*. The framework defines the fundamental values and business methods that are applied in Toyota's operations and these form the foundations of the company's culture. The framework is built on two pillars: continuous improvement that emphasises high quality, and respect for people. The focus on people specifically highlights respect and teamwork, which reflects Japan's cultural emphasis on collectivism. Toyota applies these values worldwide and expects contributions to be made by individuals in a team environment regardless of whether the operations are in a collectivist or individualistic society.

Source: Adapted from Toyota (2019).[6]

Discussion Point: How can organisations like Toyota create a culture that can bring consistency to their international operations? What are some of the challenges that organisations can face in attempting to create a global culture?

4.2.4 Professional/occupational culture

The final form of culture that we cover in this book relates to the shared knowledge, norms and behaviour that people from the same profession or occupation share. For many professions, the training that is imparted is standardised around the world, and therefore people sharing the same code of ethics and values are said to have the same *professional or occupational culture*. Such professional groups include accountants, lawyers, doctors and engineers, whose values and beliefs transcend national boundaries.

This means that individuals sharing the same professional background and culture across nations would have more common beliefs about work than people from different professional backgrounds living in the same country. Professional culture can, therefore, be a useful way to achieve effective intra-organisational communication and knowledge flow in the company, and the use of shared knowledge and technical language can limit the problems associated with the interpretation of words and their meaning in cross-cultural communication.

4.3 OVERVIEW OF CULTURAL DIMENSIONS

As we discussed earlier, there have been many studies that attempt to classify cultures into dimensions to help explain national and sub-national differences. In this section, we provide an overview of the key dimensions identified across a number of studies and using these dimensions we discuss how culture affects negotiations and negotiating behaviours in the next section.

The studies by Geert Hofstede,[7] Trompenaars and Hampden-Turner,[8] and the Global Leadership and Organizational Behavior Effectiveness (known more popularly as GLOBE)[9] study are considered to be some of the most influential in international business. Many of the cultural dimensions identified by these researchers have been found to share similarities across the studies. In this chapter, we focus on the cultural dimensions identified in the seminal study by Geert Hofstede as these dimensions have been widely studied and tested.

Geert Hofstede, a Dutch social psychologist, published the findings from his analysis of the worldwide survey of IBM's employees' values. Despite the organisational and occupational cultures being the same, Hofstede found differences in the responses to the survey questions across countries, which he explained as a reflection of the national culture influence. The findings were published by Hofstede in his book *Culture's Consequences*, which introduced four cultural dimensions: Power Distance; Individualism versus Collectivism; Uncertainty Avoidance; and Masculinity versus Femininity.[10] A fifth dimension was added later and is known as Long-term versus Short-term Orientation. Although a sixth dimension (Indulgence versus Restraint) was added more recently in 2010, there has not been sufficient research yet to make inferences about how this dimension affects negotiations. We briefly discuss each of these five dimensions here.

Power Distance: The power distance dimension describes the acceptance of a power differential in society between leaders and followers. In cultures that have a high power distance, the decisions made by leaders tend not to be questioned, and titles and positions are acknowledged and respected. In contrast, in countries with low power distance, titles do not matter, decisions by managers can be questioned and there is less acceptance of power inequality.

Individualism versus Collectivism: Cultures that emphasise self-interest and independence of the individual are categorised as being individualistic. In such societies, work-related tasks and rewards are focused on the individual's capabilities and performance. In collectivist societies, the emphasis is on strong links and relations with other members of the in-group, such as work colleagues and broader social networks. Tasks and rewards in collectivist societies are set for groups or teams rather than individuals.

Uncertainty Avoidance: The level of comfort a society has with ambiguous and uncertain situations is captured in the dimension of uncertainty avoidance. Cultures that are categorised as low uncertainty avoidance tend to demonstrate a higher level of comfort when faced with ambiguity, whereas cultures with high uncertainty avoidance tend to rely on experts and have a dislike for change.

Masculinity versus Femininity: This dimension measures whether a society tends to accept values that are regarded as predominantly masculine or feminine. Cultures that place emphasis on task, acquisition of wealth and material possessions, and are accepting of assertive behaviour to achieve these goals, are classified as demonstrating masculinity. However, if a culture encourages nurturing behaviour, values intrinsic rewards and discourages conflict at work then such a society is classified as having a higher level of femininity.

Long-term versus Short-term Orientation: The initial survey was undertaken in the 1960s when IBM did not have a subsidiary in China. Therefore, the original study did not include China. Michael Bond, a researcher at the Chinese University of Hong Kong, attempted to replicate the Hofstede study using Chinese executives as the sample population. While the four dimensions identified by Hofstede were validated in China, the study also identified a new dimension that explored whether a culture placed emphasis on short-term tasks and rewards or long-term tasks and rewards. Bond's Chinese Values Survey (CVS) was then undertaken across 23 countries and linked to the notion of Confucianism in the society. The dimension was initially labelled as Confucian Dynamism. However, Hofstede used the label of long-term versus short-term orientation and studies.

4.4 HOW DOES CULTURE INFLUENCE NEGOTIATIONS?

Having highlighted and explained the cultural dimensions, we now turn our attention to how they influence international business negotiations. As mentioned in earlier chapters, international business negotiations involve two or more parties, at least one of them from a different country, who come together to negotiate or renegotiate a deal. The influence of culture can be observed in the negotiation process, especially due to the beliefs and values of the negotiators. Therefore, knowing who the negotiators are, and their cultural background, is critical for the success of international business negotiations. In particular, we need to understand the dynamics of decision making that negotiators from certain cultures would as individuals or as part of a team of negotiators follow. We highlight these issues by presenting them under the headings of relationship-building; treatment of time and culture; how to handle time effectively; negotiators' cultural background; and approach to negotiations.

4.4.1 Relationship-building

In many cultures, building relationships between the negotiating parties is an important element of the negotiation process and considered to be a prerequisite of the formal commencement of business discussions. The expectations for relationship-building reflect the way societies conduct their day-to-day and business activities. In particular, in societies that display collectivist cultural values and where the formal institution environment is underdeveloped or in infancy, business networks are highly valued and the relations between individuals act as a way of developing trust between the negotiating parties. This exercise is also relevant when the parties are attempting to negotiate a long-term deal and are willing to invest time for this activity.

The relationship-building aspect of negotiations in highly collectivist societies allows organisations to not only develop a working relationship with the other party or parties but to also have access to their social capital and networks, including relationships that the company would like to use to strengthen and expand its business activities. Business and social networks can provide a way for negotiators to find things that they share in common and can help the parties discuss business activities despite the cultural differences. At a very broad level, these can include shared interests, mutual contacts, or institutional affiliation such as alma mater of the negotiators. However, these networks can also be formed at a much deeper and historical level, including beliefs, such as religious background, or the negotiators' family background or membership of a clan or tribe. For example, in China, *guanxi* (loosely translated as business networks) has been acknowledged as a critical aspect of doing business in the country. The roots of *guanxi* can be traced back to Confucian texts such as the *Lunyu* (Confucian Analects), which refers to *lun* (relations). Historically, China has been an agrarian society, and people tend to see their position in society on the basis of blood, kinship and geography.[11] Family or group obligations are therefore emphasised in all activities including business, with people being members of either an in-group or an out-group. To be successful in markets like China requires developing relations with in-group members in order to gain access to their networks.

China is not unique in the use of business networks, with similar networks found in Russia (known as *blat*), Japan (*wa*), Korea (*inhwa*) and the Arab world (*wasta*). Negotiators who share faith-based values and religion may also find it easier to build trust and be more flexible in their negotiated outcomes. For example, Muslim negotiators from Malaysia demonstrate flexibility when dealing with other Muslim negotiators.[12] The common belief they share is that the completion of a task or reaching an agreement depends on whether it is the will of Allah (the word *Inshallah*, or God willing, is commonly used across the Muslim world). Therefore, the parties tend not to engage in aggressive bargaining tactics when negotiating with each other.

These networks can raise concerns about nepotism and cronyism as they seem to encourage supporting members of the in-group and excluding others. Negotiators should also be cautious about possible claims made by the other party about their networks to try to influence negotiation outcomes.[13] This is particularly true in the case of agents, who may attempt to oversell their networks when offering their services to organisations with limited local cultural knowledge. Regardless of whether the relationships are built by individuals from the organisation or through agents, the process requires a substantial investment of time.

4.4.2 Treatment of time and culture

Historically, time has been treated differently in different cultures and mostly been influenced by commercial observations. In ancient societies a week had a different number of days depending upon when the farmers and artisans brought their products to the marketplace. For example, a Roman week consisted of eight days as the farmers brought their products to the city every eighth day, while in Central America and East India a week consisted of five days.

Different cultures also have different temporal orientations towards time. Some cultures are past oriented, meaning that people value and emphasise their past and their decisions are made based on past experiences. Europeans are typically past oriented and value their museums, old buildings and history. Many Asians such as Chinese and Japanese are more future oriented than past oriented, while many religious societies, such as those of the Middle East and India, are present oriented as they are rather fatalistic in their behaviour and decision making. It is, therefore, important to understand the time orientations and culture of the

Table 4.1 Practical tips for handling past-, present- or future-oriented cultures

Recognising the differences		
Past	**Present**	**Future**
Talk about history, origin of family, business and nation historically	Activities and enjoyments of the moment are most important	Talk of prospects, potentials, aspirations, future achievements
Motivated to recreate a golden age	Plans not objected to, but rarely execute	Planning and strategising done enthusiastically
Show respect for ancestors, predecessors and older people	Show intense interest in present relationships "here and now"	Show great interest in the youthful and in future potentials
Everything viewed in the context of tradition or history	Everything viewed in terms of its contemporary impact and style	Present and past used, but for future advantages

people with whom one is going to negotiate. A number of scholars have provided guidelines for handling negotiators from different time orientations; this is illustrated in Table 4.1.

Monochronic time system: followed by societies where task completion is prioritised over relationships, people tend to do one thing at a time, and deadlines are strictly adhered to.

Polychronic time system: followed by societies where relationships are valued more than task completion, people tend to do many things simultaneously, and deadlines are seen to be flexible.

To demonstrate the link between time and relationship-building in a culture, we need to understand what time system is followed by that society. Based on their understanding and use of time, Edward T. Hall classified national cultures as followers of monochronic or polychronic time systems.[14] Cultures that follow the *monochronic time system (M-time)* tend to prioritise the completion of tasks over relationships, with deadlines being firmly set, and people tend to undertake and complete a task before commencing another one. Countries such as Germany, Switzerland and the United States are examples of societies that follow a monochronic time system. The *polychronic time system (P-time)* classification suggests that people tend to value relationships as being more important than the completion of tasks. In such cultures, deadlines are seen as being flexible as the support for the relationship takes precedence over the completion of a task. Countries in the Middle East, South Asia and South America tend to follow the polychronic time system (see Example 4.3). Differences in the time systems are observable when M- and P-time cultures negotiate with each other. This often leads to frustration between the parties as the M-time negotiators expect meetings to commence and finish on time, with discussions surrounding the task and firm deadlines, such as delivery dates in the buyer–seller relationship, whereas P-time system cultures would interpret strict deadlines to be rigid and inflexible, and negotiators would have apprehensions about the fast pace of the negotiations due to the lack of effort to build trust between the parties.

4.4.3 How to handle time efficiently

In cross-cultural negotiations, it is important to understand how negotiators from the other side treat time. Some scholars believe that Germans and Japanese are relatively more *monochronic*.[15] While other scholars believe that cultures that use a low-context communication pattern use monochronic time while cultures that use a high-context communication pattern use *polychronic* time,[16] and also that in polychronic cultures people give more importance to people than to the task at hand. Considering all these intricacies about how different cultures treat time, negotiators may be puzzled. However, for the sake of simplicity, we believe that while negotiating business internationally, the following guidelines may help negotiators to use their time more efficiently.[17]

Tolerance about time: As different cultures treat time differently, making and keeping appointments can be somewhat flexible in some cultures. This means that negotiators should be prepared for the possibility that the other party might be late for the meeting by 30 minutes and might not even apologise for that. This should not create a negative atmosphere or intolerant behaviour from one side. In the same vein, in some cultures there is often no end time to a meeting. This regularly happens in Spain and France, where there is a start time for a meeting but no end time. On the other hand, in Germany and Nordic countries there is always a start time and an end time for the meeting (for example, 10:00–12:00) and if the meeting is not finished by that time some people might start leaving as they are booked for another meeting from 12:00 onwards.

Time for small talk: Negotiators should be aware that in some cultures meetings do not immediately start with the task or the agenda at hand. Instead, the parties first spend several minutes on small talk such as asking about each other's well-being. In some cultures, people talk about the weather or sports (e.g. the previous evening's football match) before they start the meeting.[18] Several authors advocate for such preliminaries to allow the parties to get acquainted with each other, while others suggest that personal relations should be developed, or informalities completed, outside the meeting room and not during meetings.[19]

Creating a positive atmosphere: Time can be efficiently used as a tactical move in the process by every now and then introducing some small talk or making small concessions to lighten up the mood, alleviate tension and create a positive atmosphere. It is thus important for the negotiators to keep aside a few small concessions (agreement points) or "goodies" to use in the process if needed. Although some cultures, for example Americans, might consider it as time wasting, negotiators often use this as a tactical move or to delay things, as they know that Westerners/Americans are in a hurry and will make more concessions closer to the end of the meeting or the deadline.[20]

Patience is a virtue: As we have discussed, many negotiators use delaying tactics. However, some cultures do take a longer time as they want to digest things properly before making a decision. Also, they do not have the same urgency as seemingly displayed by many Western negotiators. It is therefore important not to rush the other party and allow them, and yourself, plenty of time. Negotiations is a process and it has to take

EXAMPLE 4.3
TIME AND BUSINESS IN THE ARAB WORLD

Experienced international negotiators report that negotiating a business deal in the Arab world requires patience and time. The Arab world is collectivist in nature and places emphasis on relationship-building. The countries also tend to follow the polychronic time system and to undertake many tasks simultaneously.

It is also important to understand how time is used for observance of religious obligations and business. Many international managers get caught out when in the middle of a meeting the Arab manager may excuse themselves to observe one of the five obligatory daily prayers. Managers should also be aware that business activities are limited during the month of Ramadan, when Muslims observe fasting from sunrise to sunset. Being informed about the use of time for religious obligations would allow international managers to be flexible in their planning of meetings and any deadlines they may set for business activities.

Sources: Adapted from Abbasi and Hollman (1993);[21] and Zoubir (2000).[22]

Discussion Point: How can negotiators plan for cultural differences and the use of time when negotiating across different cultures? Should Western negotiators avoid business activities with Arab negotiators during Ramadan? Why or why not?

its course. If things are agreed quickly, often negotiators do not feel comfortable as they feel they have not properly discussed the issues at hand. The negotiation process always takes longer than expected and the points/issues that you might have considered settled/agreed might come back on the table.

Don't disclose your time limit: It is important that negotiators do not disclose that they are in a hurry or have a deadline to meet. If this is done, then the other party will definitely use it tactically to their advantage. While travelling abroad, it is wiser not to disclose your timetable or when you are going back. If asked, perhaps the best answer is to say "we are here as long as it takes", or to travel with an open return ticket. In cases where you have to set deadlines for yourself or for the process as a whole, these should be realistic and not based on wishful thinking.

Cultural empathy: the capacity to identify with the feelings, thoughts and behaviour of individuals from other cultures.

For negotiators, there are a few guidelines for approaching international business negotiations in ways that are inclusive of the focus on relationships and the use of time. Exhibit 4.1 provides a summary of these guidelines. First, take time to get to know the other party. Cross-cultural differences are often neither predicted nor understood until the negotiators meet in person. To be able to understand the perspectives of the other parties, negotiators need to develop and demonstrate *cultural empathy*, which is the capacity to identify with the feelings, thoughts and behaviour of individuals from other cultures.[23] The time it takes to build relations in cultures where it is highly valued should be seen as a long-term investment. Even though it may seem as if more time is spent on developing relationships than conducting business

EXHIBIT 4.1
GUIDELINES FOR BUILDING AND MAINTAINING RELATIONSHIPS IN INTERNATIONAL BUSINESS NEGOTIATIONS

1. Invest time to build relationships.
2. Ensure meeting times and deadlines accommodate and meet the expectations of all negotiating parties.
3. Find effective ways of transferring the relationships and networks developed by individual negotiators or agents to the organisations.
4. Continue to nurture and grow the relationship with the other parties after the conclusion of formal negotiations.

discussions, in the long run these relationships can help reduce the time required for business transactions and future negotiations.

Second, one should not assume that the other parties follow the same time systems. Therefore, any deadlines agreed to need to be realistic, achievable and accommodating of the time expectations of all parties involved. Negotiators should also plan carefully regarding the time required for negotiations and should be flexible when it comes to organising their travel plans and accommodation as the process can be time-consuming.

Third, ensure that the relations being built are not limited to just the individuals but are also transferred at the organisational level. Since negotiations are conducted by individuals, there is a risk that the relations built between the parties are in fact between the individuals, and any change in personnel may require the relations to be rebuilt. However, the parties can address this issue by transferring this relation to the organisational level through visits, increased collaboration between teams and so on. The issue of relationship-building is another limitation associated with the use of agents to conduct negotiations on behalf of a company. The limited interaction with the company means that the trust is built between the other party and the agent.

Finally, negotiations should not be seen as having reached their conclusion even when an agreement seems to be forthcoming. As highlighted earlier, the need for relationship-building is higher in societies where the formal institutional environment is not very stable or institutional regulations are not fully implemented. Therefore, the relations between the parties need to be nurtured and enriched beyond the formal negotiation stage to ensure a long-term working relationship. Example 4.4 highlights how the Renault–Nissan alliance was built despite the cultural differences between the two sides.

4.4.4 Negotiators' cultural background

Knowing who will be negotiating on behalf of the other parties can help organisations prepare for the expected dynamics of the negotiations and the behaviour that the individuals may display. The cultural background of the individual negotiators can influence the negotiation process, and as we discussed earlier, the pace at which the discussions are held. Earlier, we discussed how professional or occupational culture transcends national boundaries and individuals from different countries who share the same profession would find it easier to communicate and negotiate. While these individuals would generally be part of the

EXAMPLE 4.4
RENAULT-NISSAN ALLIANCE NEGOTIATIONS

The Renault-Nissan alliance began on 27 March 1999. At the time of the alliance the car industry was transitioning through a consolidation phase with car manufacturers acquiring smaller brands or forming alliances. The Daimler-Chrysler merger a year earlier in 1998 was undertaken with the explicit goal of becoming the world's largest car manufacturer.

In the case of the Renault-Nissan alliance, the two sides collaborated to improve their financial viability and to find synergies to enhance innovation. The large cultural distance between these two firms - one French, the other Japanese - meant that many in the industry believed that the negotiations for the alliance would fail.

Despite some initial reservations about the deal, the parties were able to successfully reach an agreement. So how did the parties manage to bridge the cultural differences? The Renault executives claimed that the credit for the success goes to the efforts that were made to build trust between the parties. It began with representatives from the two companies meeting to explore avenues where they could collaborate with each other. Once the details were agreed upon, the senior executives from the companies met to finalise the agreement. They took the opportunity to meet in person and to build a rapport that would serve them well in the future.

Since the cultural differences between France and Japan is high, Carlos Ghosn and other executives from Renault spent time learning about the Japanese culture and took daily language classes. This approach to developing cultural empathy helped the executives understand the perspective of the Nissan executives. Both Renault and Nissan shared a common vision that the alliance was to be one that would last for the long term. Therefore, instead of rushing into an agreement, the parties spent six months working together before the agreement was signed. This allowed the two sides to experience first-hand what the alliance's operations would be like in the future.

The companies were rewarded for their investment of time and resources in the alliance, with the alliance (which subsequently included Mitsubishi) becoming one of the largest manufacturers in the world in 2018. The success of the alliance demonstrates that with appropriate preparation and the willingness to collaborate, firms can address the challenges of cultural differences. These relationships, though, are not without their challenges and require constant communication. In 2019, Renault proposed a merger with Fiat Chrysler (FCA). However, the discussions were stalled as the French government, which holds a 15 per cent share in Renault, raised objections about the impact on the Nissan alliance. To address these concerns, Renault's chairman Jean-Dominique Senard arrived in Tokyo in May 2019 to discuss and sell the proposed merger to Nissan. These discussions are progressing slowly as all parties involved attempt to achieve a positive outcome without hurting their current relationship.

Sources: Adapted from Donnelly et al. (2005);[24] Jie and Takahashi (2019);[25] Weiss (2011);[26] and Winton (2019).[27]

Discussion Point: What are the challenges in negotiating and managing international alliances? What are some of the key cultural differences between France and Japan?

negotiating team to provide views on the technical aspects of the projects, the other team members, including senior executives, may not necessarily share a common professional culture with members of the other negotiating parties. In such instances, the influence of the negotiators' national culture becomes even more prominent during meetings.

The society's emphasis on collectivism determines the individual's role within the negotiating team. In cultures that tend to have lower levels of collectivism, individual negotiators would have a preference for a negotiated outcome that they believe would be beneficial not only for the organisation but also for themselves. Negotiators from such societies tend to be vocal and express their individual opinions during negotiations. In contrast, negotiators from collectivist cultures see themselves as part of the in-group and the outcomes they seek are those that benefit the entire group. The loyalty to the team members means that even if there were an opportunity to gain individual benefit during negotiations, the individual would forgo that opportunity if the overall outcome was more beneficial for the group. The pace of the negotiations with teams from collectivist societies tend to be slower as team members seek to confer with their colleagues before making any commitments.

Negotiations are not limited to discussions in the board room, and in many collectivist societies business negotiations can continue in an informal setting after hours, such as in a restaurant over dinner. Being aware of these differences can help negotiators avail themselves of opportunities to further discuss business.

Identifying how the decision is made and by whom is another issue that is influenced by the national culture. Does the negotiating team make concessions during negotiations as a team decision with each member participating in the discussion or are these decisions made by one individual in the group? Does the negotiating team even have the authority to make any changes to the proposed offer or do they need to seek permission from the head office? These are some of the questions to consider when attempting to understand the decision-making process followed by the other parties. The level of power distance accepted in a society can help explain who makes the decision. In high power distance societies, the decisions would be made by the individual in the team with the highest position of power. The collectivist nature of some societies would mean that the decision by the leader is taken in consultation with other team members. However, such consultations with team members are more often than not mere formalities as subordinates in high power distance societies do not question the decisions of the leaders. Knowing who in the other negotiating team makes the decision helps negotiators to make their offer targeted to the individual with the power, or in the case of teams from low power distance countries, to address the relevant concerns of the individuals in the team.

So far, we have discussed international business negotiations involving individuals from monoculture backgrounds and highlighted cultural differences as a challenge for negotiators to address. However, we are witnessing an increasing number of *biculturals* negotiating on behalf of their organisations. Biculturals are individuals who have been exposed to, and have successfully internalised, two or more cultures.[28] These individuals have the ability to use the norms and attitudes that are common across the two cultures. Global migration has been a strong driver for the rise in multiculturalism

Biculturals: individuals who have successfully internalised two or more cultures.

in societies, and this in turn has led to an increase in the number of bicultural managers working in international organisations. Countries like Australia, Canada, the United States and the United Kingdom are some of the countries that have a sizeable migrant population.

Biculturals can help the negotiating parties bridge the cultural gap, and their ability to relate to both cultures can be an asset for organisations in developing the required business relations. This ability to shift from one cultural mindset to another, known as cultural frame switching (CFS), can be a key resource during international business negotiations. CFS helps bicultural individuals to be more flexible with other negotiators coming from different cultures and can help break down the cultural barriers that exist between the parties.

4.4.5 Approach to negotiations

The bargaining approach followed by negotiators determines the level of cooperation or conflict between the parties during negotiations. For example, negotiators from masculine societies focus on maximising the benefit for them and their organisation. They display aggression during negotiations to achieve their goal, even though it may risk the other party giving up more of their benefits. This win-lose approach to negotiations has a limited appeal in international business negotiations, especially when multiple parties take the same distributive bargaining strategy, resulting in a lose-lose negotiation tactic. Instead, a win-win approach to negotiations is preferred if the negotiating parties can realise mutual benefits and work towards them.

How do negotiators react to the threat of the potential deal failing? Are they willing to make concessions in order to keep the deal alive? The cultural dimension of uncertainty avoidance is what helps answer these questions. If one party believes that the other side has a high level of discomfort with uncertainty and ambiguity, then tactics such as delays and threats to end the deal could be used to gain an advantage during negotiations.

The approach to negotiations is also influenced by the occupational and organisational cultures of the negotiators. In some developing countries, like Myanmar, senior government positions (including those related to trade and foreign investment) are held by current and former military officials. These individuals bring elements of the occupation culture to the negotiating table, which can influence the approach to bargaining that the teams take. Similarly, the organisational culture can influence the process and negotiated outcomes between the parties. For example, if an organisation tends to take a long-term view towards business and prefers to work with buyers and suppliers over an extended period of time, then the approach during negotiations would be more integrative. However, if the parties display short-term orientation behaviour, then the approach to negotiations will be distributive, with each side attempting to maximise their return.

4.5 GUIDELINES FOR MANAGING CULTURAL DIFFERENCES

This chapter has highlighted how culture influences the way individuals behave and how business is conducted in a society. The globalised nature of contemporary business activities means that individuals are expected to manage employees and negotiate business deals in cultures that are distinct from their own. We suggest some steps that can be taken to manage cross-cultural differences.

4.5.1 Ethnocentrism versus cultural relativism

International managers face the challenge of balancing their responses to cultural differences by choosing between ethnocentrism and cultural relativism. Ethnocentrism is the belief that one's own culture is superior to that of others and therefore the home country context should be applied to the way work and personal activities are undertaken.[29] This approach is unsuitable in cross-cultural management as it ignores local norms and customs and discounts the cultural differences without understanding why certain activities are undertaken.

The opposite of ethnocentrism is cultural relativism,[30] which proposes that each culture is unique and a universal approach to understanding culture is flawed. This approach helps managers adapt better to the local culture and demonstrate cultural empathy. The limitation of this approach is that certain cultural norms and practices followed in a host country may be appropriate and acceptable in that society, but it may be in direct conflict with the beliefs and practices of the home country.

Managers can balance these differences by highlighting the best practices and make their decisions based on the maximisation of the benefits for the majority of the population. For certain activities, such as those concerning the equality and safety of employees, the best standards should be applied universally, and where host-country norms have to be taken into consideration, such as when meetings should be scheduled, or the way messages are communicated, adapting the behaviour to suit the local culture would be appropriate.

4.5.2 Managing motivations

Another challenge faced in cross-cultural situations is ascertaining the motivations of employees and negotiators from the other party. Maslow's hierarchy of needs model highlights the various factors that motivate individuals and influence their behaviour. However, recent studies have demonstrated that the influence of these motivational factors varies across cultures, and managers need to understand that the factors that are effective in their own culture may not work in others.[31] Perhaps one of the most common motivation/reward programmes used in Western cultures relates to material rewards such as increased income, promotions and so on. In international business negotiations this may translate into negotiators seeking a short-term deal with the outcome focused on maximising the benefits for their party. In contrast, in many collectivist cultures, negotiators may seek a longer-term relationship between the parties and are more inclined to offer concessions to develop trust.

4.5.3 Flexibility

Finally, while cultural studies and culture scores provide a guide for how the majority of the population in a country may behave, individual behaviour can vary, and it would be a folly for negotiators and managers to stereotype every negotiator in society by assuming they would all follow the same cultural norms.

The key to success in cross-cultural situations is to demonstrate flexibility.[32] Managers may find themselves in situations where they are either negotiating with individuals who do not necessarily follow the cultural norms or demonstrate behaviours that one would associate with the particular culture, or the negotiating side is represented by individuals from a third culture. Being flexible and able to adapt to the behaviour of the members of the other party is another critical skill that managers can develop to minimise the influence of cross-cultural differences in business activities.

4.6 SUMMARY

A deep understanding of the forms and dimensions of culture that influence negotiations is a prerequisite to successful international business negotiations. Organisations can prepare for the technical aspects and requirements of the products, but they cannot control the cultural factors that are in play during the negotiations between the parties. Negotiators can prepare for the potential differences by attempting to understand the cultural perspectives of the other parties by developing cultural empathy. Identifying the influence of culture on the negotiator's behaviour, the importance of relations and business networks, and the approach to negotiations can help reduce impediments to negotiations.

QUESTIONS

1. What is the popular definition of culture?
2. What are the various forms of culture?
3. How does the time system followed in a country influence the negotiation process?
4. "Business networks are forms of nepotism and cronyism." Discuss this statement.
5. What role can biculturals play in the negotiation process?

NOTES

1. Hall, E.T. (1976) *Beyond Culture*. New York, Doubleday.
2. Cavusgil, S.T., Knight, G., Riesenberger, J.R., Rammal, H.G. and Rose, E.L. (2014) *International Business*. London, Pearson.
3. Jacobs, H. (2018) KFC is by far the most popular fast food chain in China and it's nothing like the US brand – here's what it's like. *Business Insider Australia*, 16 April.
4. Pillai, M. (2019) China's KFC gives up and starts selling Chinese street food. *RADII*, 19 July.
5. Hofstede, G. and Hofstede, G.J. (2005) *Cultures and Organizations: Software of the Mind, Intercultural Cooperation and Its Importance for Survival*. New York, McGraw-Hill.
6. Trompenaars, F. and Hampden-Turner, C. (1998) *Riding the Waves of Culture: Understanding Diversity in Global Business*. 2nd ed. New York, McGraw-Hill.

7. IKEA (2019) *Our Way of Conduct*. Available from: https://www.ikea.com/ms/en_AU/about_ikea/our_responsibility/iway/.
8. Toyota (2019) *The Toyota Way*. Available from: https://www.toyota-europe.com/world-of-toyota/this-is-toyota/the-toyota-way.
9. House, R.J., Hanges, P.J., Javidan, M., Dorfman, P. and Gupta, V. (eds) (2004) *Culture, Leadership and Organisations: The GLOBE Study of 62 Societies*. London, SAGE.
10. Hofstede, G. (1980) *Culture's Consequences: International Differences in Work-Related Values*. Beverly Hills, SAGE.
11. Guo, Y., Rammal, H.G., Benson, J., Zhu, Y. and Dowling, P.J. (2018) Interpersonal relations in China: Expatriates' perspective on the development and use of *guanxi*. *International Business Review*. **27**(2), 455–64.
12. Richardson, C. and Rammal, H.G. (2018) Religious belief and international business negotiations: does faith influence negotiator behaviour? *International Business Review*. **27**(2), 401–9.
13. Khakhar, P. and Rammal, H.G. (2013) Culture and business networks: international business negotiations with Arab managers. *International Business Review*. **22**(3), 578–90.
14. Hall, E.T. (1981) *Beyond Culture*. New York, Doubleday.
15. Potter, R.E. and Balthazard, P.A. (2000) Supporting integrative negotiation via computer mediated communication technologies: an empirical example with geographically dispersed Chinese and American negotiators. *Journal of International Consumer Marketing*. **12**(4), 7–32.
16. Hall, E.T. (1983) *The Dance of Life*. New York, Doubleday.
17. Usunier, J.-C. (2003) The role of time in international business negotiations. In: Ghauri, P.N. and Usunier, J.-C. (eds) *International Business Negotiations*. 2nd ed. Oxford, Pergamon/Elsevier, pp. 171–204.
18. Hall (1981) op. cit.
19. Burt, D.N. (1984) The nuances of negotiating overseas. *Journal of Purchasing and Material Management*. **20**(4), 2–8.
20. Usunier, J.-C. and Lee, J.L. (2005) *Marketing across Cultures*. 4th ed. Essex, Pearson Education; Adler, N. (2002) *International Dimension of Organizational Behaviour*. 4th ed. Cincinnati, Thomson Learning.
21. Abbasi, S. and Hollman, K. (1993) Business success in the Middle East. *Management Decision*. **31**(1), 55–9.
22. Zoubir, Y.H. (2000) Doing business in Egypt. *Thunderbird International Business Review*. **42**(3), 329–47.
23. Alon, I., Boulanger, M., Meyers, J. and Taras, V. (2016) The development and validation of the Business Cultural Intelligence Quotient. *Cross Cultural and Strategic Management*. **23**(1), 78–100.
24. Donnelly, T., Morris, D. and Donnelly, T. (2005) Renault-Nissan: a marriage of necessity? *European Business Review*. **17**(5), 428–40.
25. Weiss, S. (2011) Negotiating the Renault–Nissan alliance: insights from Renault's experience. In: Benoliel, M. (ed.) *Negotiation Excellence: Successful Deal Making*. Singapore, World Scientific Publishing Company, pp. 315–40.
26. Jie, M. and Takahashi, M. (2019) Renault and Nissan enter talks over proposed Fiat Chrysler merger. *Los Angeles Times*, 29 May.
27. Winton, N. (2019) Renault, FCA may revive merger but PSA could score a late winner. *Forbes*, 12 August.
28. Mahadevan, J. (2015) Understanding the process of intercultural negotiations through liminality: insights on biculturality, marginality and cultural expertise from a Sino-German business context. *International Journal of Cross-Cultural Management*. **15**(3), 239–58.
29. Ferraro, G. and Briody, E. (2017) *The Cultural Dimension of Global Business*. London, Routledge.
30. Demuijnck, G. (2015) Universal values and virtues in management versus cross-cultural moral relativism: an education strategy to clear the ground for business ethics. *Journal of Business Ethics*. **128**(4), 817–35.

31. Zhao, B. and Pan, Y. (2017) Cross-cultural employee motivation in international companies. *Journal of Human Resource and Sustainable Studies*. **5**, 215–22.
32. Bartel-Radic, A. and Giannelloni, J.-L. (2017) A renewed perspective on the measurement of cross-cultural competence: an approach through personality traits and cross-cultural knowledge. *European Management Journal*. **35**(3), 632–44.

FURTHER READING

Ghauri, P.N. and Fang, T. (2001) Negotiating with the Chinese: a socio-cultural analysis. *Journal of World Business*. **36**(3), 303–25.

Graham, J.L. (1985) The influence of culture on the process of business negotiations: an exploratory study. *Journal of International Business Studies*. **16**(1), 81–96.

Hofstede, G., Hofstede, G.J. and Minkov, M. (2010) *Cultures and Organizations: Software of the Mind*. 3rd ed. New York, McGraw-Hill.

Kong, D.T. and Yao, J. (2019) Advancing the scientific understanding of trust and culture in negotiations. *Negotiation and Conflict Management Research*. **12**(2), 117–30.

End of Part I cases

CASE 1
SOFTBANK VISION FUND (SAUDI ARABIA AND ABU DHABI) AND GUAZI (CHINA)

A deal between the SoftBank Vision Fund and Guazi may be announced within the next few weeks. The SoftBank Vision Fund is in late-stage negotiations to invest up to $1.5 billion in Guazi, one of China's largest used-car trading sites, which would value the five-year-old start-up at $8.5 billion. The deal would be the second time that Softbank's Vision Fund has backed a used-car platform, having invested €460 million into Germany's Auto1 last year at a valuation of €2.9 billion, though the business models between the two companies are different.

Guazi operates a peer-to-peer platform that matches car buyers with car sellers in China's automobile market. Guazi is run as a subsidiary of 58.com, the Chinese holding company that operates a variety of online classifieds and listings platforms. The deal would be the latest investment in China by the near $100 billion Vision Fund, which is primarily backed by the governments of Saudi Arabia and Abu Dhabi. The fund hired Eric Chen, formerly of private equity firm Silver Lake, to run its China-based investment team.

China's new-car market is languishing, following the removal of government subsidies, weaker consumer sentiment and the impact of US–China trade tensions. Car sales in China recorded their first annual decline in almost three decades last year. China's second-hand platforms, like other Chinese tech companies, have heavy cash burn as they spend money trying to bring on new customers.

Source: Adapted from Massoudi and Lucas (2019).[1]

DISCUSSION QUESTIONS

1. Are the conflicts between the parties personal, group or organisation specific?
2. What kinds of conflict resolution mechanisms can be used (dual concern model, conflict management grid, and so on)? Show the strategies which are followed.
3. Are there any other strategies on offer?

CASE 2
HOSTILE TAKE-OVER NEGOTIATIONS: VERSUM (USA) AND MERCK (GERMANY)

In a negotiation between two chemicals companies, Entegris offering to buy US-based Versum Materials for a $4.5 billion deal, German company Merck offered $5.9 billion in a move that could deliver a blow to its rival. This unexpected counter bid for Versum, which makes critical components used in semiconductors, would bolster Merck's performance materials unit as chipmakers.

Merck offered to pay $48 a share in cash for Versum, roughly 52 per cent above Versum's share price before its all-stock deal with Entegris was announced and 16 per cent higher than its closing level on Tuesday.

The $5.9 billion deal value includes the assumption of Versum's outstanding debt. Versum was part of industrial-gas company Air Products & Chemicals before 2016. It generated $1.4 billion in sales in its last fiscal year and counts Samsung and Intel among its largest customers. The group supplies high-tech chemicals used in the production of circuit boards and wafers. The combination of Merck and Versum would strengthen both companies, as artificial intelligence and the rise of the internet drives demand for semiconductors. Merck's board unanimously backed the bid and was ready to proceed to due diligence and negotiations. Versum was not aware of the bid and said it continued to believe in the rationale of its merger with Entegris, but that it would "thoroughly review" the proposal.

Versum shares climbed 17 per cent to $48.56 in early trading in New York, whereas Entegris stock slid 3 per cent to $36.54, while Merck shares fell 4 per cent to €91.46.

Family-backed Merck has sought to strengthen its performance materials business in recent years, buying London-listed speciality chemicals group AZ Electronics for £1.6 billion, including debt. The group, which also makes materials for liquid crystal displays, has faced intensifying competition from Chinese manufacturers in that business. A successful offer to Versum would create a more balanced split between the company's three core divisions of healthcare, life sciences and performance materials. Merck estimates its net leverage could increase to 2.9 times its earnings before interest, taxes, depreciation and amortisation. The bid from Merck is the latest in a rapidly rising number of hostile takeover bids since the start of the year. Companies across the world have become bolder in their pursuit of assets that are perceived as game-changing in their sectors.

Source: Adapted from Platt et al. (2019).[2]

DISCUSSION QUESTIONS

1. In which scenario of the activity-type framework would this problem fit? Explain your decision and note as many solutions are possible.
2. What theoretical and conflict resolution possibilities are offered in this situation?

NOTES

1. Massoudi, A. and Lucas, L. (2019) SoftBank fund in talks to invest up to $1.5bn in Chinese used car site. *Financial Times*, 1 February.
2. Platt, E., Fontanella-Khan, J. and Neville, S. (2019) Merck gatecrashes Versum-Entegris deal with $5.9bn offer. *Financial Times*, 27 February.

PART II

FACTORS INFLUENCING INTERNATIONAL NEGOTIATIONS

5 The importance of communication in negotiations

Negotiations involve the exchange of information between the negotiating parties that is communicated through messages. Therefore, communication is an integral part of the negotiation process, and the success or failure of the negotiations can be linked to it. However, communication is a complex activity that requires much thought and planning about what message needs to be delivered, the best channel to facilitate it, and the ability of the individuals involved to communicate effectively. The complexity and challenges of communicating increases when the negotiation activity is undertaken with another culture. The differences in the spoken language and the use of non-verbal cues can cause problems when attempting to interpret the true meaning of the messages being communicated. In this chapter, we identify these issues and suggest strategies for firms to address these concerns.

In the following section we discuss the communication process and detail the model of communication. The chapter then discusses how differences in context can lead to communication failure. Non-verbal communication is then discussed, and the chapter concludes by highlighting key communication issues found in contemporary international business negotiation practices.

5.1 THE COMMUNICATION MODEL

Communication process: the encoding, transfer and decoding of information delivered through various channels.

Communication can be best described as the process by which information, ideas, opinions and thoughts are exchanged between the sender and the receiver of messages. Everyone engages in some form of communication on a daily basis, whether it involves sending and receiving emails, ordering a cup of coffee, discussing work-related issues with colleagues, or interacting with family or friends over a meal. However, this process is complex, and there are many factors that can influence the effective communication of a message. Although the transmission of messages can be challenging even in a domestic setting, the complexity can be exaggerated when undertaking such a process in the international context. Not only does the intended meaning of the messages being communicated need to be interpreted by the receiver, but the dynamic nature of the negotiation process means that multiple messages are being relayed by various parties simultaneously, adding to the complexity of the process.

There are various factors that can influence the *communication process*, including culture. We explain the communication process by dividing it into four steps (see Figure 5.1):

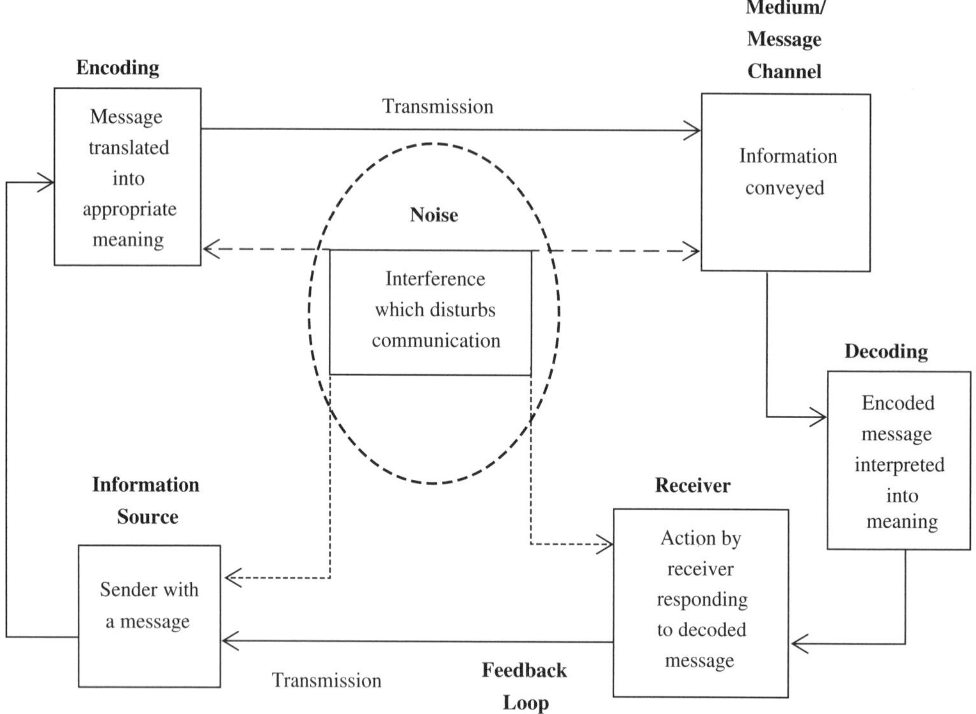

Figure 5.1 The communication process

1. The way messages are encoded.
2. Selecting the appropriate medium.
3. The decoding of the message.
4. The use of the feedback loop.

The process commences when the sender attempts to convey information through a message. The sender determines the nature of the message and encodes it into words that they believe would be understood by the receiver. The *encoding* step involves choosing the words and expressing them in a way that the sender believes will convey the true meaning of the message when interpreted by the receiver. For example, in response to an initial enquiry by a buyer, the seller may respond by sending a message that expresses their interest in pursuing further discussions about the quantity of the goods required, the terms and other details of the agreement.

The next step in the communication process involves selecting the appropriate *medium* to deliver the message. The medium refers to the channel that is used to deliver the message. The sender has to decide whether the message would be understood if it was delivered in the written form or whether a combination of spoken and written words helps deliver the message more effectively. The choice of the medium is influenced by the nature of the communication being

Encoding: converting a message into words.

Medium: the channel used to deliver a message.

undertaken. If the negotiating parties are exchanging their initial offers through a formal proposal, then the written form of communication would be expected. However, during face-to-face negotiations, where the parties discuss the details of the offers and terms, a combination of spoken and written forms of communication may be more appropriate.

The third step in the process involves the *decoding* of the message by the receiver. The message is deemed to be successfully communicated if the receiver is able to decode or break down the message and interpret the meaning as was intended by the sender. But how can the sender and receiver check that the communication process was completed successfully when the message is unidirectional from the sender to the receiver? The possibility of communication failure increases if the process is limited to the transfer of a message without providing for the opportunity to verify whether the message decoded by the receiver is, in fact, understood in the way it was meant to be at the time of the encoding.

> Decoding: interpreting the words to find the meaning of the message.
>
> Noise: anything that distorts the transmission of the message.

The meaning of a message can be distorted in international communication due to *noise.* The sources of "noise" include multiple messages being simultaneously received that have similar words but may have distinct meanings. The interpretation of these messages can be influenced by the different cultural background of the sender and the receiver. Even if the sender and receiver use the same language to communicate, such as English, the use of the words and their meaning in the way they are expressed can vary from one culture to another, and this can be a source of confusion when the receiver attempts to decode the message (see Example 5.1). We discuss this issue further in section 5.2.

EXAMPLE 5.1
"PREPONING" MEETINGS IN INDIA

A legacy of the British rule in India was the introduction of the English language and its use as an official language for business. India boasts one of the largest numbers of English-language speakers in a country. With English the preferred mode of communication in higher education, language proficiency is considered to be high, and this has been one of the advantages for Indian firms and professionals involved in international business activities.

However, the use of certain words and expressions are unique to communication in India and other neighbouring countries in South Asia. For example, the word "postpone" is commonly used to describe the delay of some event or activity to another time in the future. However, in some parts of India, the word "prepone" is also used in business communication. The word "prepone" refers to a situation where a meeting or event is brought forward to occur earlier than the initially scheduled time. So, a meeting scheduled for 10 am on Tuesday morning may be "preponed" to the day earlier, on Monday afternoon at 4:30 pm.

The use of such terms, while understood by managers in India, may prove to be a source of confusion for individuals from other countries.

Source: Adapted from Yano (2006).[1]

Discussion Point: Is there a universal language that can be used for negotiations? What steps can negotiators take to minimise "noise" in communication?

Using a rigid, one-way communication process can limit the ability of the participants in the communication process to verify whether the interpretation of the message is correct. For example, an instruction from a manager to an employee asking for a report to be submitted by *the end of the week* could be interpreted in different ways. Does the end of the week refer to the start of the last working day on Friday? Or by the end of Friday? Or does it mean that it should be completed before the beginning of the workday on Monday? Therefore, having a feedback loop that allows the receiver to verify with the sender that they have successfully decoded the meaning can be useful in ensuring the successful transfer of the message.

5.2 CONTEXT IN COMMUNICATION

A common source of "noise" is the contextual differences in cross-cultural communication. Context refers to the way words are used by individuals to express their feelings and meanings through communication. Do individuals in society express themselves in an explicit fashion, or do they communicate in an implicit manner? Recall from Chapter 4 that we looked at the classification of culture by Edward T. Hall based on how society uses time. Hall also classified countries according to the way they communicate. According to Hall, cultures can be low-context or high-context communication societies.

Low-context cultures: societies where communication is direct/explicit.

In *low-context cultures*, communication is direct, and the meaning of the message is made explicit to avoid any ambiguity. This form of communication is found in countries that are found to be task focused and where there is a separation between work and personal relationships. Due to the nature of the message, the communication process is shorter as there is a chance of confusion when interpreting messages. Such a form of communication can be found in cultures that tend to score high on masculinity (emphasis on completion of the task and the competitive nature of work) but low on power distance (appropriate to question decisions made and flat structures). The use of this form of communication in high power distance countries that typically have a hierarchical structure tends to be unidirectional and top-down in nature. Countries such as Switzerland and Germany are classified as users of the low-context form of communication.

High-context cultures: societies where communication is indirect/implicit.

In contrast, communication in *high-context cultures* takes into consideration both personal and work relations, and therefore messages are communicated in a more implicit and indirect manner. There is also elaborate use of words to ensure that the message does not come across as being too abrupt or direct. Therefore, reading and understanding the message requires digging through the deep layers of words used to find the real meaning of the message. The use of non-verbal cues is also of significance in the communication (we discuss these further in section 5.3), and silences and pauses in the communication process may also have meanings that the receiver of the messages needs to attempt to understand. High-context communication societies tend to be found in cultures that are collectivist in nature and value interpersonal relations. Japan, China and the Arabic-speaking countries are some of the countries that use the high-context form

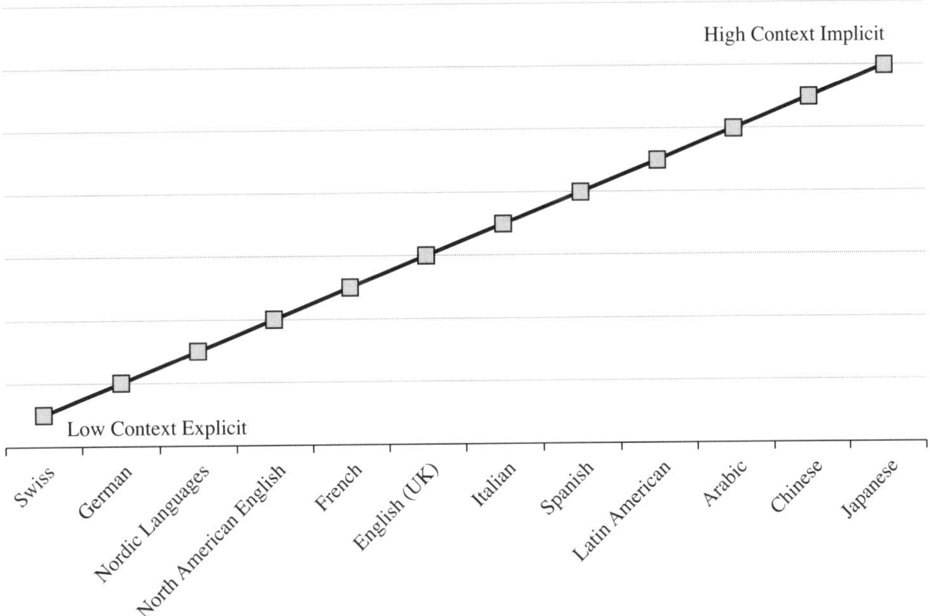

Source: Adapted from Hall (1976).[2]

Figure 5.2 High-/low-context cultures

of communication. These characteristics manifest themselves in the national and regional languages used to communicate in the country. Figure 5.2 shows the findings from Hall's study.

The contextual differences can be a source of confusion and frustration during cross-cultural communication. These issues are not limited to interpersonal communication but are often observed in marketing communication failure by well-known global multinational enterprises (MNEs). Some of these failed communication messages are highlighted in Example 5.2.

Negotiators from a low-context culture may find conversations and discussions with negotiators from a high-context culture to be slow, formal, and the meaning of the message difficult

EXAMPLE 5.2
FAILED MESSAGES

Apple, Samsung, McDonalds, Mercedes, Gucci and other brands have built up a strong brand name and image and they are instantly recognised by consumers worldwide. But this global recognition also means that any communication mistakes made by such firms are highlighted, and in this age of social media communication, instantly shared globally.

A few recent examples of such communication errors in specific markets that became worldwide news include the "chopsticks" ads by Dolce & Gabbana and Burger King. In 2018, Italian luxury brand Dolce & Gabbana was accused of being culturally insensitive in their video ad campaign that showed a Chinese model struggling to eat spaghetti and pizza with chopsticks. The ad was seen as playing with cultural stereotypes and Chinese e-commerce websites stopped selling the company's products.

In 2019, Burger King reignited the controversy when its New Zealand franchisee uploaded a video ad on its Instagram account that showed diners attempting to eat its new "Vietnamese Sweet Chilli Tendercrisp Burger" with large chopsticks with the caption: "take your taste buds all the way to Ho Chi Minh City". Like the Dolce & Gabbana ad, Burger King was accused of stereotyping that consumers in East and South East Asia only consumed food with chopsticks. The ad was subsequently removed by the company but not before it was shared widely on social media platforms and made news headlines around the world.

Sources: Adapted from Patton and Green (2019);[3] and Pfeiffer and Mayes (2018).[4]

Discussion Point: How can global organisations avoid such communication blunders when messages meant for one market may be accessed and interpreted differently by people in another country?

to interpret. On the other hand, negotiators from high-context cultures may find negotiators from low-context cultures to be too direct, with a lower emphasis on interpersonal relations. However, it is not only differences in the use of language and the context that can add to the noise in the transmission of the message, with non-verbal differences also adding to the complexity of the cross-cultural communication. We discuss these differences next.

5.3 NON-VERBAL COMMUNICATION

Non-verbal communication is usually associated with the part of the message that is not encoded in words and is conveyed through gestures, vocal tone and other forms. Although non-verbal messages are usually accompanied by a verbal message, some studies suggest that 65 per cent of the communication consists of the non-verbal part.[5] Therefore, we tend to communicate more non-verbally than we do with words. However, as we do with words, the way we interpret non-verbal cues and messages is influenced by our cultural context. As we discussed earlier, "noise" can distort the communication of a message. When negotiators who speak a different native language attempt to communicate using a *lingua franca*, they attempt to look for non-verbal cues that may be familiar to them. This is due to the fact that if the verbal part of a message does not match the non-verbal part, then there is a tendency to believe the non-verbal part. Non-verbal messages are communicated through a number of different means. Some of these include kinesics, paralanguage, space and proximity, and artefacts.

Kinesics: the transfer of non-verbal messages through body movements.

Kinesics refers to non-verbal messages communicated through body movements such as those of the hand, head and face (that is, facial expressions). Kinesics can help reinforce the message being sent. For example, a nodding of the head can be a sign of approval in some cultures and can complement a verbal agreement during negotiations. However, if one presumes that non-verbal cues are universal and can be interpreted accordingly, then the chances of failure in communication increases. Example 5.3 highlights some of these differences in relation to negotiations between American and Japanese negotiators.

EXAMPLE 5.3
GIVING THE "NOD" TO A DEAL

There are many non-verbal cues that can be thought of as being universal. Facial expressions that highlight pain or tears to express sorrow can perhaps be easier to understand across different cultures. However, many other non-verbal cues are not that easy to translate across cultures and may be confusing for the receiver of a message. For example, the nod of the head in parts of India that actually takes the form of a side-to-side motion (also known as the head bobble) can indicate an agreement or a disagreement to a statement. The context of communication is important in deciphering the meaning of the non-verbal cue.

In low-context cultures, where messages are communicated explicitly, understanding non-verbal cues and periods of silence may be difficult and can be uncomfortable. In such situations, negotiators may revert to using ethnocentrism to seek meaning in the other party's behaviour based on what they expect in their own culture. One such example is that of American negotiators communicating with Japanese negotiators in the 1970s and 1980s. The Japanese culture emphasises respect for authority and is a high-context culture. As such, Japanese negotiators tend not to be explicit in showing their feelings and emotions and tend to choose their words carefully to ensure that the parties do not lose face. For American negotiators, communicating in such a context was a challenge, and they sought to find meanings in the non-verbal actions of the Japanese negotiators. One of the observations they made was that when they presented their proposal, they noticed the Japanese team member nodding in the affirmative. This was the signal they needed to confirm that the Japanese side agreed with the details of the proposals. However, it was later when the negotiations continued on and further discussions were taking place that they realised that the nodding was a sign from the Japanese side that they understood what the American negotiators were saying but unlike the way the nod is used in America, it did not signal an agreement to the proposal.

Sources: Adapted from Graham (1999);[6] and Graham and Sano (1999).[7]

Discussion Point: Do you believe kinesics still hold the same importance in today's increasingly electronic-communication-based business environment? Can individuals learn to observe and interpret non-verbal cues used in other cultures?

Paralanguage: the use of vocal qualities to affect the way something is said.

The use of vocal qualities to affect the way something is being said rather than what is being said is known as paralanguage. *Paralanguage* can help emphasise the key points and feelings of the speaker in a verbal message. For example, a person speaking excitedly about their holiday would be confirming their verbal message and its meaning, whereas people may view with suspicion a salesperson's verbal message when spoken too quickly.[8]

Proximity: the use of space to transmit a message.

A culture's use of space and the message it communicates refers to *proximity*. Cultures differ in their expectation of, and the way they interpret, personal space. Some cultures are comfortable with close physical contact between individuals, which sends a message of closeness and an intimate relation between the parties. In contrast, other cultures are more comfortable with maintaining a larger personal space and people tend to limit physical contact. Based on their preference for physical contact, Hall classified countries as being either high-contact or low-contact cultures.[9] High-contact cultures are those that are comfortable with close contact between individuals. The Arab countries, Latin American countries, Greece and Italy are considered to be high-contact cultures. Low-contact cultures tend to maintain a wider individual space, and thus physical contact is kept to a minimum.[10] The United Kingdom and Japan are examples of countries that have a low-contact culture. The distance and level of contact between individuals can be viewed at various levels: intimate, personal, social and public. The more intimate the interpersonal relations between the individuals, the less the space between them, extending to a large distance and less physical contact between individuals when the interaction is at the public level.

Artefacts: use of objects to convey non-verbal messages about image and style.

And finally, *artefacts* are objects that are used to convey non-verbal messages of image, style and self-concept. Such messages are conveyed through the way people dress, company logos and symbols found on business cards and documents. The ritualistic nature of undertaking certain activities is also part of the artefacts. For example, the way business cards are exchanged is also unique to cultures, and the ritual of the exchange can signal to the other party the level of formality that would be expected in the negotiations.

An individual's body can convey messages in different situations. Particularly expressive in this respect is the interaction between a person's hands and their face. Figure 5.3 depicts three common gestures that involve the interaction between the hand and the face. Certain gestures can be revealing about negotiators when they are communicating something that is either not entirely correct or they are uncomfortable with, as well as about their reaction to a

Source: Adapted from Pease and Pease (2004).[11]

Figure 5.3 Hand and face interaction

piece of information that does not sit well with them. One such gesture is the covering of the mouth with one's hand depicted in Figure 5.3. It suggests that the person is not comfortable with the words they are saying so they want to disguise them. If a certain point is being discussed in the negotiation that one of the parties is not comfortable hearing, they may start rubbing their ear as depicted in the figure.

Finally, the rubbing of the eye communicates the fact that a person does not want to see what is staring them in face. While hand–face interaction reveals a lot about a person's thought process in response to various stimuli, the movement of the hands alone can be extremely revealing. There are two basic palm positions: upward facing palms displaying openness and downward facing palms exhibiting power, control and authority.

The use a negotiator makes of their hands relates to how they speak to and behave in the space they occupy. But humans also have a natural tendency to mark and protect their territory and the physical setting of a room can reflect this instinct. In a negotiation room, sitting on opposite sides of a table automatically creates a competitive atmosphere, which is reinforced by the verbal and non-verbal cues that are communicated by the individuals. In a negotiation, sitting on opposite sides of the table is therefore not a good idea, as it increases the level of competition and emphasises the impression that the parties are not on the same side but on opposite sides.[12] Where it is not possible to prevent the parties from sitting across the table from each other, it is important to try to diffuse the situation by ensuring that there are refreshments, a sculpture or plants on the table, as long as they do not obstruct visibility. Alternatively, one could try to break the barriers between the parties by demonstrating more cooperative behaviour, such as standing up and walking to a more neutral position when making a pitch, or by using artefacts such as a whiteboard, a computer presentation or printed documents.

From the preceding discussion, it is useful to be mindful of the following five non-verbal strategies when preparing and conducting negotiations in international business. While observing these five strategies, keep an eye on the body language of the other party, and be mindful of communication – both verbal and non-verbal. This will aid accurate judgement of the message and offers the other side present so that any response will be appropriate.

1. Be aware of the cultural meaning of different signs and gestures. A thumbs up and/or ok hand signal are not positive in all cultures. In Greece, for example, a thumbs up gesture is considered as a vulgar gesture and in Brazil making an ok sign is thought of as obscene.
2. If you are expecting a tense negotiation, try to sit so that you and your party do not have your back towards the door. Research has shown that not facing the door when seated increases stress, feelings of stress and raises blood pressure. It has been known for some negotiators to deliberately place the other party with their backs to the door.
3. Resist crossed arms, which is thought to expose a closed "defensive" mindset. Furthermore, do not place your elbows on the table – this is a matter of etiquette but may also be interpreted as an indication that the person with their elbows on the table is trying to unbalance the discussion. Instead, have open palms facing upwards as this shows openness and honesty; palms down is a projection of authority.
4. Raising one's hands above one's shoulders should be avoided – it may be seen as a signal of defeat, surrender or exasperation.

5. If wearing a suit jacket during the negotiations, do not sit or stand with the jacket buttoned up. Opening the jacket button signals openness, a willingness to cooperate and that the person does not intend to leave quickly.

5.4 COMMUNICATION ISSUES IN INTERNATIONAL BUSINESS NEGOTIATIONS

As we discussed at the beginning of this chapter, communication is an integral part of the negotiation process. We have also discussed how contextual factors can influence the communication process. In this section, we highlight some of the issues related to cross-cultural communication in contemporary international business negotiations.

One of the issues affecting international business negotiations relates to the use of technology as a medium of transfer of information between parties during the communication process. Historically, the negotiating parties have used phone conversations, written letters or, more recently, emails to make initial contact to express interest in pursuing a business opportunity. However, once the parties decide to pursue further discussions, negotiators have tended to meet in person to discuss the proposals. For firms, the cost of international travel to undertake face-to-face meetings has reduced in the last few decades. But despite the lowering of cost, the use of video conferencing and other forms of communication is on the rise, and virtual meetings are increasingly preferred by many firms as an alternative to physical meetings. This trend can add to the "noise" in communication, as the opportunity to build interpersonal relations and to read and decipher non-verbal cues to interpret the message can be limited in virtual meetings.

Another issue related to communication is the influence of the negotiators. The ability to communicate successfully depends on a number of factors, including the personality of the negotiator, and their previous experience. In international business negotiations, the role of the negotiators is critical as not only do they need to able to present their arguments in a professional and effective way, but they should also demonstrate active listening to help negotiators from the other party feel comfortable during the negotiation process (see Example 5.4). But how can negotiators demonstrate active learning and successfully interpret the message when they are not communicating in their native language?

In such circumstances, firms that use bilingual negotiators may benefit. As we discussed in Chapter 4, bicultural negotiators can act as a bridge between the negotiating parties. Similarly, bilingual negotiators are able to understand their counterparts better and can help express terms in the other party's native language. Language is key to understanding a culture and having bilingual negotiators in the negotiating team can reduce the influence of "noise" in the communication process.

There are, however, further issues that need to be considered. What if a firm does not have bilingual/multilingual negotiators in their organisation and the use of *lingua franca* during negotiations is limited due to the challenges of language proficiency of the negotiators? In such instances, a firm may feel that the use of an interpreter or a local agent to conduct business on their behalf either individually or as part of the firm's team is appropriate. The

EXAMPLE 5.4
ACTIVE LISTENING

Active Listening (AL) can be used in negotiations to cultivate a collaborative relationship with the other party. AL is based on empathetic, genuine and non-judgemental attitudes. Open-mindedness is a key asset for AL, the final aim being to enable the other side to freely, openly and completely express its needs, preferences and priorities. AL requires the individual to be free of any prejudice, and they should demonstrate attentiveness and refrain from interrupting. Asking clarifying and open questions and rephrasing the negotiating partner's statements without distorting the meaning can help make AL a collaborative conversational tool rather than a passive approach to negotiation.

As Saner emphasises: "Active Listening and requests for clarification strengthen the conviction that the agreement sought is in fact attainable. While the less experienced negotiator will skirt around tricky or unclear points, for fear of jeopardizing the agreement, the professional [negotiator] is thinking about the possible problems of practical application while the negotiation is still going on."

Sources: Adapted from Worthington (2016);[13] and Saner (2000).[14]

arguments for the use of interpreters and agents need to be balanced against the criticism that the external actors would not be as invested in achieving the best outcome for the firm as the employees would.

5.5 SUMMARY

In this chapter we have highlighted how the communication process works and the challenges associated with transmitting messages successfully across national boundaries. Skilled and experienced negotiators realise that communication involves both the spoken word and non-verbal cues. Many of the factors that can become a source of noise and distort the meaning of a message can be linked to the contextual differences between cultures. Negotiators can attempt to address these issues by developing active listening skills and avoiding ethnocentrism in an attempt to make sense of the differences in communication. Organisations also have to pay attention to the individual profiles of the negotiators and decide whether it might be better to involve an interpreter or agent in the process or even to use them to conduct negotiations on behalf of the firm.

QUESTIONS

1. Using the communication model, explain how information can be transmitted from the sender to the receiver.
2. How do contextual differences between cultures influence the negotiation process?
3. How does "noise" distort the message being communicated? What are some of the sources of this "noise"?

4. "Non-verbal communication holds less value today due to the increase in the virtual nature of communication." Discuss this statement.
5. How can active listening improve the effectiveness of cross-cultural communication?

NOTES

1. Yano, Y. (2006) Cross-cultural communication and English as an international language. *Intercultural Communication Studies*. **15**(3), 172–9.
2. Hall, E.T. (1976) *Beyond Culture*. New York, Doubleday.
3. Patton, L. and Green, J. (2019) Burger King drops chopsticks ad after accusations of cultural insensitivity. *Time*, 9 April.
4. Pfeiffer, T. and Mayes, J. (2018) Marketing fail: a history of costly blunders by big names. *The Sydney Morning Herald*, 23 November.
5. Birdwhistell, R.L. (1970) *Kinesics and Context: Essays on Body Motion Communication*. Philadelphia, University of Pennsylvania Press.
6. Graham, J. (1999) Vis-a-vis: international business negotiations. In: Ghauri, P.N. and Usunier, J.-C. (eds) *International Business Negotiations*. Oxford, Pergamon/Elsevier, pp. 69–90.
7. Graham, J. and Sano, Y. (1999) Business negotiations between Japanese and Americans. In: Ghauri, P.N. and Usunier, J.-C. (eds) *International Business Negotiations*. Oxford, Pergamon/Elsevier, pp. 353–68.
8. Dwyer, J. (2005) *Communication in Business: Strategies and Skills*. 3rd ed. Frenchs Forest, Pearson Education Australia.
9. Hall, E.T. (1959) *The Silent Language*. New York, Doubleday.
10. Gudykunst, W. (1998) *Bridging Differences: Effective Intergroup Communication*. 3rd ed. Thousand Oaks, SAGE.
11. Pease, A. and Pease, B. (2004) *The Definitive Book of Body Language*. Buderim, Pease International.
12. Pease, A. (2003) *Body Language: How to Read Others' Thoughts by Their Gestures*. Bodmin, Sheldon.
13. Worthington, D. (2016) *Listening: Processes, Functions and Competency*. New York, Routledge.
14. Saner, R. (2000) *The Expert Negotiator*. The Hague, Kluwer.

FURTHER READING

Brannen, M.Y., Piekkari, R. and Tietze, S. (2014) The multifaceted role of language in international business: unpacking the forms, functions and features of a critical challenge to MNC theory and performance. *Journal of International Business Studies*. **45**(5), 495–507.

Hall, E.T. and Hall, M.R. (1990) *Understanding Cultural Differences*. Yarmouth, Intercultural Press.

Jolly, S. (2000) Understanding body language: Birdwhistell's theory of kinesics. *Corporate Communications: An International Journal*. **5**(3), 133–9.

Kendon, A. (2004) *Gesture: Visible Action as Utterance*. Cambridge, Cambridge University Press.

Sundaram, D.S. and Webster, C. (2000) The role of nonverbal communication in service encounters. *Journal of Services Marketing*. **14**(5), 378–91.

6
Individuals and personalities

This chapter focuses on the role of personalities in negotiations and why these are important. For that reason, the seminal work of Jung (1921) and the data base of Myers–Briggs (1975) are considered. The knowledge of one's own type and that of the counterpart is relevant and influences the strategies and styles of the negotiation process. The focus is then on differences in negotiation styles, professional differences in negotiation behaviour and negotiations in teams.

6.1 INDIVIDUALS AND PERSONALITIES: THEORETICAL UNDERPINNING

The desire to find typologies of individuals and personalities goes back to Carl Jung's early work, *Psychological Types*, published in 1921.[1] Jung suggested that "The further we go back in history the more we see personality disappearing behind the wrappings of collectivity." Collectivism is part of an indigenous setting, and a high level of community has also been necessary for survival in subsistence societies. The individual and individualism is only a phenomenon of recent times in human mind and humankind. From ancient times, four temperaments were used to classify people: the choleric, the sanguine, the melancholic and the phlegmatic. Then gnostic philosophy identified three types of basic psychological functions: thinking, feeling and sensation. Jung then developed his "extraverted" and "introverted" types and added thinking, feeling and sensation, as well as intuition, to each of these. He provided the following classifications (see also Figure 6.1):

- Extraverted Types:
  - Extraverted Rational Types (Extraverted Thinking Type and Extraverted Feeling Type)
  - Extraverted Irrational Types (Extraverted Sensation Type and Extraverted Intuition Type)
- Introverted Types:
  - Introverted Rational Types (Introverted Thinking Type and Introverted Feeling Type)
  - Introverted Irrational Types (Introverted Sensation Type and Introverted Intuition Type)

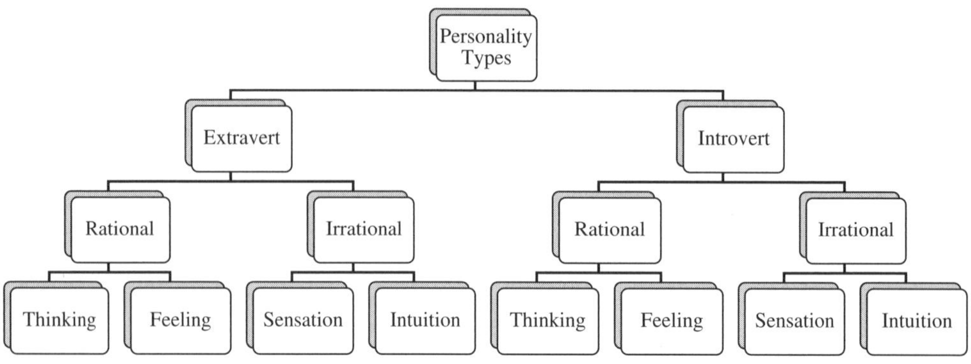

Figure 6.1 Jung's personality types

This was the basis for the development of the Myers–Briggs personality types that are now used in modern management consulting, job assessment and various managerial classifications. A more in-depth description and analysis of these personality types follows in the next section.

6.2 MYERS-BRIGGS PERSONALITY TYPES (MBTI)

Katharine Cook Briggs (1875–1968) found out about Jung's personality types and was intrigued to see her family as a reflection of these types. Her daughter, Isabel Myers (1897–1980), shared her enthusiasm and together they developed the Myers-Briggs Type Indicator® instrument. They intended to provide an understanding and appreciation of the differences between individuals, which should then improve harmony and productivity among individuals and in groups. The mother–daughter team started to observe different types over a period of two decades. Isabel Myers, a graduate of Swarthmore College, created a questionnaire to evaluate the types. The MBTI® instrument was the result of three decades of research into the behaviour of thousands of people. This research continues to the present day, in combination with studies published in articles and books each year. In 1975, Consulting Psychologists Press, Inc. (now called The Myers-Briggs Company) moved towards publishing the MBTI instrument for practical applications. The applications of the personality types have expanded nationally and internationally. The MBTI instrument has been officially translated into 30 languages and is used all over the world. The personality types describe the different ways in which people relate to situations, approach the world, make decisions, deal with information and tackle everyday tasks. Understanding their own type should help people to appreciate their strengths and weaknesses, but also to deal with differences with other people.[2] The essence of the theory is that much seemingly random variation in behaviour is actually quite orderly and consistent, being due to basic differences in the way individuals prefer to use their perception and judgement.

The identification and description of 16 distinctive Myers–Briggs personality types is a result from the way people see their outer world, called Extraversion (E) or Introversion (I).

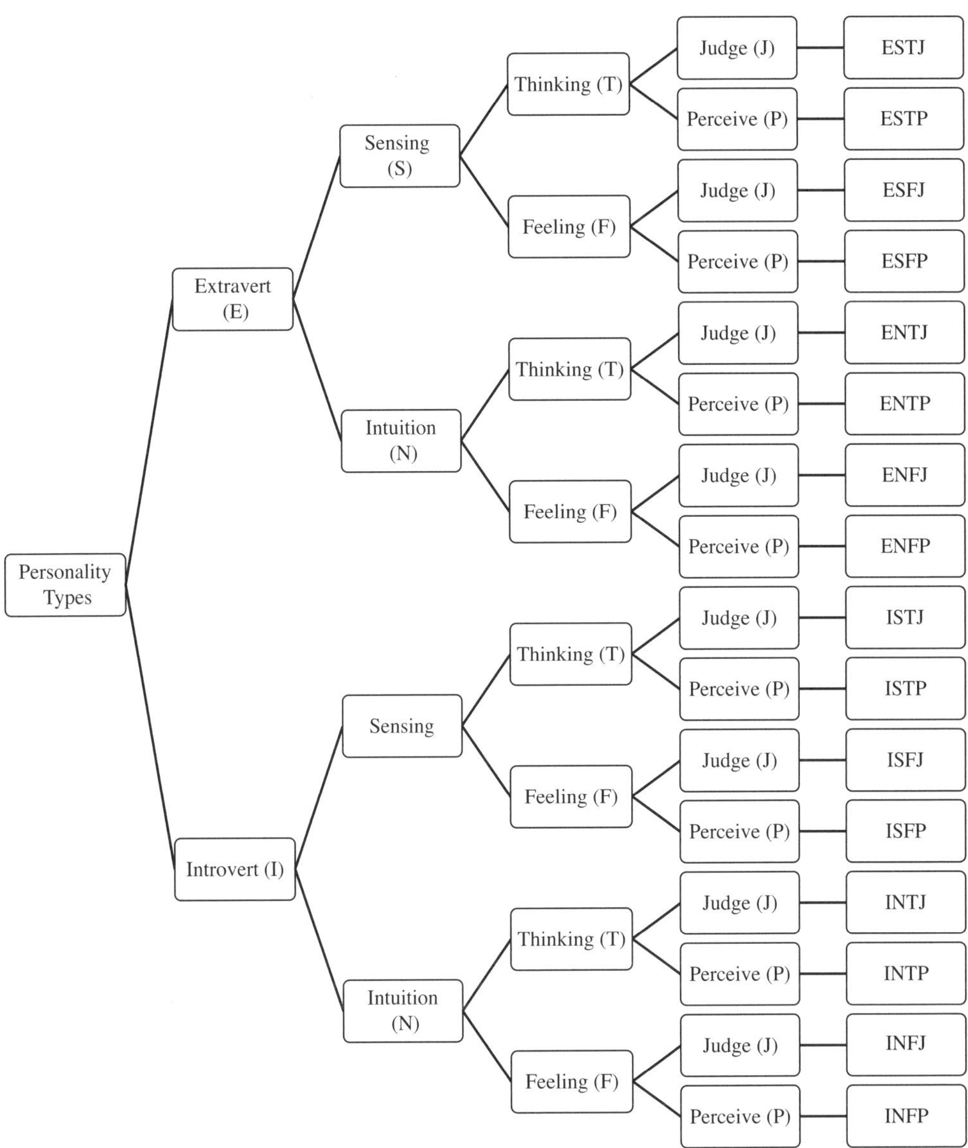

Source: Adapted from Myers–Briggs (1975).

Figure 6.2 Myers–Briggs personality types

The next level is then how information is taken in either through Sensing (S) or Intuition (N). Decision making is considered as well with Thinking (T) or Feeling (F), and finally the structure of the outer world in the way new options are processed is considered either by Judging (J) or Perceiving (P). By answering the questionnaire, the specific personality type is identified out of the 16 distinctive types denoted by a four-letter code as shown in Figure 6.2.

After 40 years of research into the types and classification of people, it is very important to highlight that all types are equal and refer to preferences and not character or ability. The goal of knowing about personality type is to understand and appreciate differences between people when making decisions and sharing information. The instrument has been proven as valid and reliable. This means it measures what it says it does (validity) and produces the same results when given more than once (reliability).

6.2.1 The Extravert types (E)

The Extravert type – Sensing (ES)

Extravert, Sensing, Thinking types with deviations in Judging and Perceiving
ESTJ: This personality type is decisive and quickly moves to implement decisions. They organise projects and people to get things done and focus on getting results in the most efficient way possible. This type takes care of routine details, has a clear set of logical standards, systematically follows them and likewise wants others to do so. They are practical, realistic and matter-of-fact.

ESTP: This personality type wants to act energetically to solve the problem and focuses on the here and now. They are spontaneous, enjoy each moment they can be active with others and learn best through doing. This type is flexible and tolerant, and takes a pragmatic approach focused on immediate results.

Extravert, Sensing, Feeling types with deviations in Judging and Perceiving
ESFJ: This personality type wants harmony in their environment and work to establish it. They like to work with others to complete tasks accurately and on time. This type notices what others need in their day-to-day lives and tries to provide it. They want to be appreciated for who they are and for what they contribute. This personality is warm-hearted, conscientious and cooperative.

ESFP: This personality type enjoys working with others to make things happen. They bring common sense and a realistic approach to their work and make work fun. They are flexible and spontaneous, and they adapt readily to new people and environments. This type learns best by trying a new skill with other people. This personality is outgoing, friendly, and accepting.

The Extravert type – Intuition (EN)

Extravert, Intuition, Thinking type with deviations in Judging and Perceiving
ENTJ: This personality type quickly recognises illogical and inefficient procedures and policies, and they develop and implement comprehensive systems to solve organisational problems. This type enjoys long-term planning and goal setting. They are usually well informed, well read and enjoy expanding their knowledge and passing it on to others. This personality is frank, decisive and assumes leadership readily.

ENTP: This personality type is resourceful in solving new and challenging problems, and is adept at generating conceptual possibilities and analysing them strategically. They are good at reading other people. This type is easily bored by routine, will seldom do the same thing the same way, apt to turn to one new interest after another. They are quick, ingenious, stimulating, alert and outspoken.

Extravert, Intuition, Feeling type with deviations in Judging and Perceiving
ENFJ: This personality type is highly attuned to the emotions, needs and motivations of others. They find potential in everyone and want to help others to fulfil their potential. This type may act as catalysts for individual and group growth. They are sociable, facilitate others in a group and provide inspiring leadership.

ENFP: This personality type makes connections between events and information very quickly, and confidently proceeds based on the patterns they see. They want a lot of affirmation from others, and readily give appreciation and support. They are spontaneous and flexible and often rely on their ability to improvise and their verbal fluency.

6.2.2 The Introvert types (I)

The Introvert type - Sensing (IS)

Introvert, Sensing, Thinking types with deviations in Judging and Perceiving
ISTJ: This personality type decides logically what should be done and works toward it steadily, regardless of distractions. They take pleasure in making everything orderly and organised – their work, their home, their life. They are quiet, serious and earn success by thoroughness and dependability. This type behaves in a matter-of-fact, realistic and responsible manner.

ISTP: This personality type quietly observes until a problem appears, then acts quickly to find workable solutions. They analyse what makes things work and readily get through large amounts of data to isolate the core of practical problems. They are interested in cause and effect, organise facts using logical principles and value efficiency.

Introvert, Sensing, Feeling types with deviations in Judging and Perceiving
ISFJ: This personality type is committed and steady in meeting their obligations. They are thorough and painstaking. They remember specifics about people who are important to them, and are concerned with how others feel. This type strives to create an orderly and harmonious environment at work and at home. They are quiet, friendly, responsible and conscientious.

ISFP: This personality type enjoys the present moment and what is going on around them. They like to have their own space and to work within their own time frame. This type is committed to their values and to people who are important to them. They dislike disagreements and conflicts, and do not force their opinions or values on others.

The Introvert type – Intuition (IN)

Introvert, Intuition, Thinking types with deviations in Judging and Perceiving

INTJ: This personality type has a great drive for implementing their ideas and achieving their goals. They quickly see patterns in external events and develop long-range explanatory perspectives. When committed, they organise a job and carry it through. They have high standards of competence and performance – for themselves and others.

INTP: This personality type seeks to develop logical explanations for everything that interests them. They are interested more in ideas than in social interaction. They have the unusual ability to focus in depth to solve problems in their area of interest. This type is sometimes critical, and always analytical.

Introvert, Intuition, Feeling types with deviations in Judging and Perceiving

INFJ: This personality type wants to understand what motivates people and develops a clear vision about how best to serve the common good. They are organised and decisive in implementing their vision. They seek meaning and connection in ideas, relationships and material possessions. This type is conscientious and committed to their firm values.

INFP: This personality type seeks to understand people and to help them fulfil their potential. They want an external life that is congruent with their values. They are quick to see possibilities and can be catalysts for implementing ideas. This type is adaptable, flexible and accepting unless a value is threatened.

We suggest you take a free test. Then you can understand the negotiation styles from that perspective.

6.2.3 What typology would be good for negotiations?

The typology of personalities can be useful for identifying the ideal types of actors for negotiations:

- *Extraversion* and *introversion* in international business negotiations are related to culture and are embedded in one's personality, but also in the personality of a cultural group as a result of their upbringing. Belonging to a group and having individualistic and collectivistic features is a distinct characteristic of cultural differences.
- *Sensing* and *intuition* are important cultural intelligence features and both are considered as emotions in negotiation.
- More importantly, *thinking* and *feeling* are often seen as antipodes in international negotiations as they lead to different paths in the negotiation process. Likewise, *judging* and *perceiving* are important elements in the background and atmosphere of negotiations. The judgement of a negotiation and the way the expectation of the outcome is perceived have a strong impact on the negotiation procedures. It would be therefore more appropriate to change the coding for negotiations to T and F, then to J and P.

EXAMPLE 6.1
MYERS AND BRIGGS, MASTERS OF TYPOLOGY AND ITS SCEPTICISM

The Myers-Briggs Type Indicator (MBTI) was the work of a singular mother-and-daughter pair of amateur psychologists. In 1943 Myers created her own paper-and-pencil test to assign people to one of 16 personality types. Early customers were companies like Lockheed Aircraft who were keen to introduce efficiencies. The questionnaire interested practitioners of a nascent branch of academic psychology concerned with personality. In 1959, the MBTI came under the purview of the Educational Testing Service (ETS), publishers of the SAT. Myers was employed by ETS as an adviser, but she set little store by "empirical validation"; Jung was drawing his theories from religion, philosophy and literature, but without empirical validation. Henry Chauncey, ETS's boss, made a prescient observation about its appeal, saying that without wishing to "dignify the hypotheses by speaking of them as a theory, it can be described in words that have meaning to the layman", and "isn't so complex or unusual that he throws his hands up". In 1975 the MBTI was ditched by ETS have been derided by a number of its own psychologists, but Myers found a publisher with no qualms about selling it to all-comers.

Today, the MBTI is variously criticised for spreading a kind of sense of selfhood and its susceptibility to gaming. Its popularity, though, still endures. Part of the appeal of MBTI-type was imagining that there were others out there like you.

Sources: Adapted from The Economist (2018);[3] and Ahmed (2016).[4]

Discussion Point: The sceptics and the fans of MBTI both have strong, but opposing, views about the typology and classification into 16 types. Would it be different if the thinking and feeling categories were the baseline rather than the extraverts and introverts categories? Try to develop the categories in line with sensing and intuition or thinking and feeling as the baseline. Would there be the same outcome?

EXAMPLE 6.2
MYERS-BRIGGS IN THE WORKPLACE

Myers-Briggs makes human resources into an algorithm: give your employee an online quiz, and within minutes you'll know whether they're social (E) or quiet (I), interested in details (S) or the big picture (N). Forget all the messy, expensive team off-sites and one-on-ones – how much easier is it to compress assessments into four little letters, puzzle pieces on the page? It's HR tailor-made for the Buzzfeed quiz generation.

Katherine Wang, 26, a consultant at one of the largest global management consulting firms (which asks its employees not to disclose their work affiliation to the press), said she found out her Myers-Briggs profile at her first company training. Immediately, she was seated with others who shared her type for a conversation on how their personality traits might affect their working styles. She quickly memorised her profile and others. Each time she began a new case, she'd study her teammates' Myers-Briggs before even considering the client's needs.

Ms Wang was sceptical of all the talk of INTJs and ENFPs when she first arrived on the job, but within a few months she came to appreciate the test's value. It provided a shorthand to talk about a whole range of personal needs: how much you like to fill your calendar, how you want your manager to give feedback, how personal you want to get with colleagues at the water cooler.

For Nerissa Clarke, 33, a researcher at a public policy group, her company's all-day training on the Insights Discovery test served as a much-needed reprieve from a routine of spreadsheet analysis. "We sit there crunching numbers in Excel so it's good for us to do team-building," Ms Clarke said, though perhaps efficiency comes at the expense of naturalness. "At my old job we had much more of a culture of people getting to know each other in an organic way."

At Harley-Davidson, the motorcycle company, Kelly Arnold, a 40-year-old project manager, said employees are required to learn their top five strengths through CliftonStrengths. These are then included on email signatures and hung on cubicles beneath nameplates.

Ms Arnold noted that Harley-Davidson's adoption of personality tests might come as a surprise to outsiders. Aren't its workers supposed to be gruff, leather-wearing biker dudes with no time for conversation on personality? But it showed, she said, that "we're in tune with our inner selves, just like any other company."

Source: Adapted from Goldberg (2019).[5]

Try to identify the clash between Extravert and Introvert Sensing types. Then find the negotiation style for them. What outcome do you anticipate?

Negotiation behaviour, negotiation styles and negotiation strategies are often interchangeably used and in order to see how personality influences these, we can now show that the negotiation styles are a function of one's personality and cultural background.

6.3 NEGOTIATION STYLES

Negotiation styles vary across cultures and personality types. Understanding differences in style is essential to improve negotiation outcomes.[6] People bring different negotiation strategies and styles to the table, which are mostly based on different personalities, beliefs, attitudes and experiences. A clash of cultures and styles happens when it is difficult to anticipate differences. Different social motives, cultural upbringing and preferences have an impact on the negotiation outcome.[7] Weingart[8] highlights four basic types of social motives which drive human behaviour in negotiation and other competitive situations and lead to four basic negotiation styles:

- *Individualistic negotiators* are seeking to maximise their own benefits with little regard for their counterpart's outcomes. Especially visible in the United States, and consistent with individualism and collectivist measures according to the psychologists De Dreu, Seoung Kwon and Weingart, about half of negotiators have an individualistic negotiating style.
- *Cooperative negotiators* are negotiators who strive to maximise their own and their counterpart's outcomes. About 25 to 35 per cent of negotiators belong to this type and want to see that resources are divided fairly.

- *Competitive negotiators* behave in a self-serving manner and often do not trust their counterparts to solve problems cooperatively. About 5 to 10 per cent of negotiators seek to get a better deal than their "opponent".
- *Altruistic negotiators* are very rare, since they put their counterpart's needs above their own.

Of those negotiation styles above, individualistic and cooperative styles are the most common. Negotiators with an individualistic style are more likely to make threats, argue their positions and make single-issue offers than negotiators with a cooperative style. Negotiators who are cooperative are more likely to engage in value-creating strategies such as offering information, asking questions and making multi-issue offers. In multi-issue negotiations, cooperators are likely to expand the pie of value for both sides.[9] When people with different negotiation styles meet at the negotiation table their approaches converge.[10] The mirror effect comes across in the way the negotiators tend to subconsciously mimic each other.[11]

At this point, we can go back to the personality types which have an impact on the characteristics of negotiation styles: extroversion versus introversion. The assumption is that extraverts – those who are outgoing and draw their energy from others – tend to be better negotiators than introverts, who generally are reserved and prefer to think things through on their own. Extraverts, like cooperators, have an ability to bring people together and respond skilfully to others' emotions. Many of the introverts' strengths[12] can be useful in negotiation, since they tend to listen closely without interruption and prepare thoroughly for negotiations. The insights into personality types and negotiation styles from a decision-making perspective have an impact on the solutions in negotiation processes. Negotiation styles are a consequence of personality, but also cultural adaptation. Individualism and collectivism influence negotiations styles (individualistic and competitive negotiation styles are more aligned to individualism, whereas cooperative and altruistic negotiation styles are rooted in collectivist behaviour). The consequences of different negotiation styles can be overcome by understanding the counterpart's style and adapting to the unfolding negotiation process. Combined with conflict resolution strategies, negotiation styles offer a wider opportunity to analyse negotiation processes and their outcomes. Deadlock situations are particularly useful for finding out whether individualist, cooperator, competitor or altruist styles are the underlying problem of the lack of progress. A mixture of styles and personality types will more likely lead to satisfying outcomes. For instance, if an individualist and competitor work on adding traditional distributive strategies to the value-creating strategies on which cooperatives rely, then a conflict resolution mechanism can lead to a better outcome. In Example 6.3 an application to the situation of Nissan can be analysed.

6.4 PROFESSIONAL BACKGROUND OF INDIVIDUALS AND THEIR NEGOTIATION BEHAVIOUR

Besides personality and national culture, negotiators have also developed a professional negotiation culture, which considerably facilitates the negotiation process.[13] Their professional

EXAMPLE 6.3

WHO CAN FIX NISSAN? THE CARMAKER WANTS A LEADER WHO CAN RESTORE A JAPANESE ICON AND BREAK FROM CARLOS GHOSN

The departure of Nissan's chief executive, Mr Saikawa, leaves the company looking for a leader who can resuscitate a Japanese icon, navigate a global merger and make a clear break with the Ghosn era. Mr Ghosn rescued the group from near bankruptcy in 1999. Back then, Nissan's financial troubles were even deeper, requiring a capital injection from Renault. But Mr Ghosn's solution, namely deep cuts in the workforce, car plants and suppliers, was straightforward at a time when the automotive industry was focusing on combustion engine vehicles.

With the shift towards electric and self-driving vehicles, two decades on Nissan's nomination committee is trying to find a new saviour from at least six candidates. Whoever gets the job will inherit a daunting task.

Background: The Japanese carmaker is struggling in almost all its key markets, and plans to cut 12,500 jobs globally in a broad overhaul. The management has been preoccupied with a ten-month internal investigation into Mr Ghosn and with a breakdown in ties with Renault. The Japanese group needs to find a permanent fix to its relationship with Renault, which was held together by Mr Ghosn's diplomatic skills. Mr Saikawa's exit could also revive negotiations over the future of an alliance that has the potential to evolve into the world's largest car group. While Nissan has been distracted with legal trials regarding falsifying Mr Ghosn's rewards, many deals between carmakers have taken place as the automotive industry shifts towards electric vehicles. Toyota invested in Uber's self-driving unit and smaller rival Suzuki, while Ford and Volkswagen have strengthened their ties to collaborate on electric vehicles and self-driving technology. Nissan's alliance with Renault was badly fractured by Mr Ghosn's abrupt arrest and subsequent abortive merger talks between its French partner and Italy's Fiat Chrysler Automobiles (FCA). With the FCA keen to revive talks with Renault, people close to Nissan say the new chief must possess an international background and tough negotiation skills to demand a fix to its capital structure with Renault before any such talks resume.

Renault owns a 43 per cent stake in Nissan, contrasting with the Japanese group's 15 per cent non-voting stake in the French carmaker. A change at the top at Nissan could provide a breath of fresh air for the strained alliance, according to people close to Renault. While Nissan searches for Mr Saikawa's successor, chief operating officer Yasuhiro Yamauchi will serve as caretaker CEO.

The Nissan CEO shortlist also includes:

PSA chief executive Carlos Tavares – the 61 year old successfully saved the French carmaker from collapse, thanks to a ferocious attitude to cost-cutting adopted during his time working under Mr Ghosn at Renault. His presence, however, would not be welcomed by Fiat Chrysler, which hopes to eventually restart merger talks with Renault.

Toyota executive Didier Leroy – he knows both Japan and his native France well, giving him the diplomatic skills to navigate the vagaries of the alliance. But Toyota is a fierce rival to Nissan, and with the potential for retirement looming, Mr Leroy, 61, may not want to switch jobs.

Former Nissan sales and marketing boss Daniele Schillaci – he left this year to run Italian supplier Brembo, but Mr Schillaci has extensive experience at both the Japanese group and Renault. He is said to be Mr Saikawa's preferred candidate, though that may no longer be an advantage.

Chief operating officer Yasuhiro Yamauchi - he has a purchasing career at Nissan spanning nearly 40 years, and is considered a solid caretaker CEO. Mr Yamauchi is considered more open to restoring Nissan's ties with the French carmaker and holding talks with FCA than Mr Saikawa was. He has experience as an alliance executive and member of Renault's board.

Former head of Nissan's China business Jun Seki - he was assigned the pivotal role of overseeing the company's recovery plan in May, prompting speculation that the 58-year-old executive was being groomed to replace Mr Saikawa.

Makoto Uchida - Mr Seki's successor as China boss, he spent more than ten years at a Japanese trading house before joining Nissan in 2003. Internally, he has been considered a candidate for the top job, with his role as China boss helping, since it is a critical market for the carmaker as it struggles in the United States.

Source: Adapted from Inagaki et al. (2019).[14]

Discussion Point: What kinds of personality types can you identify in this case? What type of CEO and negotiator for the Renault-Nissan alliance is it important to find?

What is your negotiation style? What characteristics of other negotiation styles might you adapt to reach better outcomes?

Which of the MBTI personality types would fit the four types of negotiation styles? Discuss and show why it makes sense to consider individualist and cooperative styles in negotiations as a basic negotiator characteristic?

culture is seen as more superficial than their national culture: it consists much more of commonly learnt behaviours and symbols than of shared values. Differences in negotiation style are found in the following professions: sales representatives, engineers, lawyers, diplomats, bureaucrats, politicians. Often it is easier to negotiate with colleagues from different countries than negotiators from different professions. Like professions, corporate identity influences the negotiation behaviour and style. International bodies, such as United Nations agencies, can play an important role because their internal culture facilitates communication. Organisational and professional cultures are not always an asset, and they can turn into a liability when blocking communication instead of facilitating it.

The next sections deal with sales negotiations, as the most direct form of negotiations; legal background in negotiation behaviour; technical background in negotiation behaviour; and the entrepreneur's negotiation behaviour, which is not often investigated.

6.4.1 Sales negotiations

Sales negotiations[15] are a good starting point to analyse the offer and counteroffer patterns leading to a deal. Being the one who makes the first offer is often a smart move. The first offer can be anchored and then have a powerful effect on the outcome. What if the other party starts first? Then the counteroffer needs to be framed carefully. Framing in negotiation is the crafting of an offer to improve its appeal. Framing a counteroffer with a strong rationale may increase the odds of re-anchoring the discussion. Sales negotiations are a good

EXAMPLE 6.4
EXPORT SALES NEGOTIATIONS

An exporter offers a unit price for a specific good (clothes) to an importer. Both negotiators know the market price. They have different preferences (high price for the exporter and low price for the importer). The exporter does not value the product as much as the importer does, whereas the exporter wants the costs covered by the price. Let's assume that the market price of a shirt is £20 (the production costs are £10). The exporter would have a margin of £10. Dependent on the value for the importer and the quantity, terms of delivery and payment, the two negotiate over a period of time to get the price which will bring both a good result.

way of relating export–import negotiations to the basic concept of negotiating a price (see Example 6.4).

Effective sales negotiation techniques include:

- *Frame counteroffers* for maximum advantage.
- *Choose the best rationale:* Two common types of rationales are (1) constraint rationales and (2) disparagement rationales. A constraint rationale focuses on what's holding one side back from accepting the other side's offer, such as not being able to afford what they're asking. By contrast, a disparagement rationale critiques what the other party is offering – for example, by suggesting the quality is low. In a recent study,[16] Alice J. Lee and Daniel R. Ames compared the effectiveness of these two types of rationales. Buyers' constraint rationales sway sellers more than their disparagement rationales. This is because sellers may view the criticism in a disparagement rationale as inaccurate or rude and react by sticking to the price. When buyers, however, describe their financial constraints, then sellers take it seriously when they say they can't afford the deal on the table. A buyer is therefore more likely to get a better deal if he accompanies his counteroffer with information about his financial constraints rather than diminishes the value of what's being sold. The seller might be similarly better off to highlight the financial constraints than being dismissive about the buyer's BATNA (best alternative to a negotiated agreement).
- *Highlight losses rather than gains:* Tversky and Kahneman[17] show that people are more motivated to avoid losses rather than they are to achieve gains. For instance, investigations[18] into homeowners who participated in a free energy audit and then listened to a sales pitch for insulation products and services that would lower their energy costs, showed that homeowners were significantly more likely to purchase insulation when it was pitched as avoiding losing money rather than when it was pitched as a way to save money. This is because loss aversion is more prominent in a human's mind than framing something as a gain.
- *Split up losses; combine gains:* Tversky and Kahneman also discovered in their research that people prefer to gain money in instalments, whereas they prefer to lose money in one lump sum. Thus, when making a concession it is a good idea to divide it into two

or more smaller concessions, whereas when asking for a concession on the price, then it makes more sense to demand one rather than two partial ones.

- *Justify:* In a study,[19] experimenters suggested that even a lame justification for a first offer can be more effective than none at all. For instance, to use a copier to make five copies, using the rather weak justification "May I use the Xerox machine, because I have to make some copies?" was far more successful than giving no justification at all for cutting in ("May I use the Xerox machine?"). People tend to rebel against more significant requests with weak justifications.[20] When a justification for an offer is easy to counter, it inspires a backlash. If a salesperson has already shown off the many attractive features of the product, the first price offer is justified.

6.4.2 Legal background in negotiations: legal experts in negotiations

International business negotiations deal with legal environments which are different to those in a domestic setting. Legal frameworks belong to the background of the international business negotiations and understanding Incoterms[21] is a tool for reducing complexities in export–import negotiations. It is useful to understand differences in legal terms, and it also helps to understand that in many negotiations the advice of legal experts is taken on board. In a lawyer's career,[22] no negotiation is the same – all negotiations are different in some ways and alike in others. Four "golden rules" can be identified for tackling legal issues with the aim of achieving productive negotiation outcomes. Each rule needs to be applied at different stages of the negotiation process, the different stages and the relevant rule being listed below:

- *The background homework:* Understand the interests and positions of the other side and relate them to one's own interests and positions. Preparation for these items and spending time to analyse them beforehand are important.
- *During the process:* If the negotiator is not fully knowledgeable about the counterpart's position, then it is important to stand firm on the initial position and give an explanation of the rationale. However, it is important not to give in too early on these points. In the negotiation process, both sides will start to reveal which issues are more important.
- *The stalemate:* Often in negotiations, there will come a point where it feels that there is no room for either side to move. This is a stalemate or deadlock situation. Both sides are stuck on their position and may lose sight of the overall objective of the negotiation. The logical paths have given way to an emotional approach. At this point there is also the possibility of overcoming the problems by offering new solutions.[23] When reaching this point, it might be a good idea to concede on this issue which is important to the other side in exchange for a concession on an unrelated point that is relatively more important to you. There is sometimes a bottom line which is usually negotiation currency outside of the last area one is focused on negotiating.
- *To close or not to close:* It is important to always let someone else walk away. In cases where one cannot be reconciled on key issues or one feels that the deal is too intense or that the other party is driving too hard a bargain, it is useful to make an offer and let the other side walk if they don't want it. This does not mean that one is being offensive;

rather, it gives an impression of being honest and straightforward on what one can do and what cannot be done.

6.4.3 Technical background in negotiations: engineers and inventors in negotiations

Sales representatives, marketeers, lawyers and engineers are some of the professionals that are often included in international business negotiations due to their expertise and daily exposure to negotiating deals, contracts and agreements. However, not all these professionals are skilled negotiators. The importance of negotiating skills is often neglected in engineering training.[24] For engineers it is important not only to come up with innovative ideas, but also to bring them to the market and implement them with business partners.

Having developed inventions and made a business plan, finding investors becomes important. This is where negotiations come in. With research and development (R&D) and innovation being used by the headquarters of multinational enterprises (MNEs), engineers are often included in the network of MNE ventures. Difficulties arise when engineers have to negotiate on their own. Negotiation skills are needed to bring an idea to market or to further innovative practices within an existing company. Many inventors or innovators repeat the same mistakes when they negotiate with investors or potential partners:[25]

- there is an assumption that inventors need to convince investors with the right evidence;
- there is not really an understanding that the other side has real constraints that limit the "zone of possible agreement";
- emotions get the better of inventors, who try to reduce uncertainty by generating "better" forecasts;
- finally, inventors concentrate exclusively on the terms of the deal and ignore the need to build trust and pay attention to relationships.

It is essential to build up trust and relationships in inventor–investor negotiations. Especially in international business negotiations when MNEs and technology experts work together, but also for small and medium-sized enterprise (SME) negotiations, the below are important aspects which lead to a better outcome in the long run.

- *Emotion:* It is important to avoid conducting negotiations with an emotional approach. This might be easier to understand for engineers, who often have a logical approach towards problem solving. Moreover, inventors often have spent countless hours on a project and are likely to take any criticism as a personal attack.
- *Dealing with uncertainty:* Investors, on the other hand, want to minimise risk and increase their rewards. Risk is different for inventors and investors, and key for inventors and innovators is to be ready with contingent proposals that will minimise the risk for their investors.
- *Handling technical complexity:* Investors do not understand the complexities of a prototype as well as the inventor does. For both sides it might be a good idea to engage

EXAMPLE 6.5
NEGOTIATING WITH THE RIGHT PEOPLE[26]

A technology owner decided to license technology to a foreign company through its own wholly owned subsidiary in the same country as the licensee. Agreements were drawn up and signed, which then had to be submitted to the Authorities for approval. The local subsidiary was essentially a promotional and sales-brokering company; its people knew nothing of technology licensing. The Authorities gave their approval subject to a reduction in the specified daily rates for technical/engineering services. The managing director of the local subsidiary company agreed without consulting his principals and the licence agreement took effect. As a result, services performed in support of the licence were rewarded at less than actual cost, seriously eroding the profit on the licence.

The lesson is of course to put proper controls in place if the technology owner who will perform the licence services is not the licensor.

in joint fact-finding. This could ensure that they have a shared understanding which is grounded in mutually acceptable data.

- *Building trust and working relationships:* Cooperation and trust are the main components of successful negotiations. During the negotiation process, inventors might over promise. To avoid distrust, claims need to be trustworthy. To achieve good working relationships, a successful negotiator knows that they need to say what they mean and mean what they say.

Problem solving for an engineer is breaking a problem into smaller parts and putting smaller solutions together. Negotiators, on the other hand, need to know how to keep multiple agenda items open as long as possible. This is a way of creating value, by incorporating different trades across multiple issues and developing packages. Experienced negotiators try to find low-cost ways of addressing their counterpart's most important interests and making the pie larger before attempting to divide it up.

6.4.4 Entrepreneurs' negotiation behaviour

Entrepreneurs and small businesses negotiate differently to managers in MNEs. Not much has been done on entrepreneurship negotiations, but in a recent study the authors Artinger et al.[27] highlight uncertainty as a strong issue in entrepreneurs' negotiation behaviour. Furthermore, argument, emotions, uncertainty, information and profit sharing influence the negotiation style of entrepreneurs. Not much has been done in finding out the differences between entrepreneurs and non-entrepreneurs. The experimental study, however, highlighted the importance of understanding the differences, which are discussed here:

- *Initial asking – anchors:* In the experiment, entrepreneurs did not choose to set the "anchor" for their negotiations more frequently than non-entrepreneurs. Their initial proposals were higher than those of non-entrepreneurs. They did not differ regarding their concession rates. Interestingly, entrepreneurs made significantly fewer offers than non-entrepreneurs and also rejected offers more often.

- *Arguments and persuasion:* Entrepreneurs use argument as a technique of persuasion more frequently than non-entrepreneurs; for instance, in the study for every 10 arguments that were made by non-entrepreneurs, on average 17 arguments were made by entrepreneurs. Most of the sellers' arguments dealt with covering costs of production, whereas buyers argued about the value the product would have for them. The participants' BATNAs (best alternative to negotiated agreement) were a special focus among the participants.
- *Information:* When complete information was available, arguments dealt primarily with fairness considerations; these were less often used by entrepreneurs.
- *Uncertainty and asymmetric information:* Among other elements of negotiations, it was tested whether entrepreneurs are better than non-entrepreneurs in using information asymmetries to their advantage. Private information was supplied about reservation prices in one scenario, and in another scenario private information was supplied about outside options. In the first scenario, entrepreneurs' profits were slightly lower than those of non-entrepreneurs, but slightly higher in the second scenario.
- *Emotions:* Entrepreneurs use more frequent and variable emotional expressions than non-entrepreneurs, changing from positive to negative more regularly throughout a negotiation process.
- *Profits and deals:* Entrepreneurs claim a higher variance in profit shares claimed, which is reflected in the fact that entrepreneurs close a lower number of deals. However, they have higher profits in their closed deals. Consequently, they more often receive zero profits than is the case for non-entrepreneurs. If a participant is particularly good at adjusting to different scenarios, then this will show in accumulated profits. The higher the adaptability of a participant, the higher is the accumulated profits. Logically, entrepreneurs' average accumulated profits were higher than those of non-entrepreneurs.

The following discussion point looks at the backgrounds of negotiators regarding personality types and negotiation styles in line with their professional identities. The examples included in this chapter provide a good basis for setting up different negotiation scenarios, and the business pages of the *Financial Times* and *The Economist* give good examples of business leaders and their negotiation behaviour in real-life cases. Many insights are possible.

Discussion Point: Use the explanations of the personality types above and discuss the following: A British innovator with an MBTI profile of ISTJ wants to negotiate a deal with an investor from the Far East with an MBTI profile of ENFP. Their negotiation styles are different, having an individualistic and cooperative style respectively, and there are cultural differences. Develop a description of the basic characteristics of the negotiators and highlight the potential pitfalls and difficulties that may arise in the negotiations. Are there any possible outcomes which can be anticipated at this stage?

Example 6.6 combines different negotiator types from a real-life scenario.

EXAMPLE 6.6

JACK MA RETIRES FROM ALIBABA: MOVE MARKS FIRST SUCCESSION AT ONE OF CHINA'S TECH GIANTS. JACK MA IS TO HAND THE REINS TO CHIEF EXECUTIVE DANIEL ZHANG

Alibaba, China's well-known public tech company, will mark its 20th birthday with a transition from its founder Jack Ma to chief executive Daniel Zhang, whereas other Chinese tech companies such as Tencent and Baidu are still run by their founders Pony Ma and Robin Li.

Mr Ma is a charismatic leader who built Alibaba from a shared apartment into a company worth $462 billion. On the other hand, his successor is a low-key former accountant. This has not affected Alibaba's investors, since the company's share price has risen 9.4 per cent in the year since the announcement of the retirement. Alibaba is woven into the fabric of daily life for hundreds of millions of Chinese. The company runs like a machine, combining the idealism and blue-sky thinking of Mr Ma with his successor's pragmatic, bottom-line approach. The succession has been carefully planned. It is part of Alibaba's deep talent pool. Mr Zhang has some targets to achieve, set by his predecessor: by 2036 the Alibaba "economy" will create 100 million jobs, support 10 million profitable businesses and serve 2 billion customers around the world, up from around 654 million currently. This year it is targeting $1 trillion in gross merchandise value, the value of the goods sold on its platforms, up from $853 billion last year.

The US-China trade war is souring globalisation - and has already claimed another Alibaba pledge - to create 1 million jobs in America by giving small businesses there a route to sell their goods in China. Alibaba's own globalisation efforts closer to home, in South East Asia and India, have yet to bear much fruit; e-commerce platform Lazada has been through various iterations since Alibaba acquired it. Overseas markets are key if Alibaba is to meet its target of 2 billion customers. Mr Ma did it with e-commerce, now a $2 trillion market in China, and in mobile payments, in a country where even beggars accept alms via Alipay. Mr Ma, in a debate with Tesla founder Elon Musk, pointed out that "We need heroes like you (who want to go to Mars), but we need heroes like us (who will fix Earth)", but then changed his tone more recently by making the statement "A lot of companies, I learnt why they fail. Because they want the next quarter. They want revenues, they want profit. They forget about dreams. It's important that Alibaba dreams."

Source: Adapted from Lucas (2019).[28]

Discussion Point: What are the personality types and negotiation styles of Mr Ma, Mr Zhang and Mr Musk? Are there professional differences? Analyse their behaviour.

Discussion Points:

1. Negotiations between strategic alliance partners, such as Renault–Nissan, Airbus and the NUMMI joint venture of GM and Toyota, need to be set up. The negotiation partners are chosen according to their MBTI scores. Find the combination of personalities which might work well together in an international joint venture (IJV) negotiation.
2. Add to the personality types from above the negotiation styles of the partners that fit with the MBTI scores.

3. Draw a decision tree for the negotiators with a strong rational profile based on the MBTI scores.
4. Draw a decision tree for the negotiators with an intuitive, feeling and judging style. Show the differences if the negotiator is extravert or introvert with these styles.

6.5 SUMMARY

This chapter started out with considerations of individual personality and how this affects negotiation behaviour. The Myers–Briggs types were introduced and explained. Negotiation styles derived from the individual perspective were added and then the professional backgrounds of negotiators considered, and specifically the impact this has on certain types of negotiations, namely legal, technical, entrepreneurial and sales negotiations, especially in relation to their particularities and how to circumvent difficulties. The differences between personalities, negotiation styles and professional backgrounds influence the negotiation process and outcome. The final section pulls together the differences of the negotiation parties by considering multiparty negotiations in which many negotiators try to cooperate, find coalitions and reach an outcome.

QUESTIONS

1. What are the four different types in the personality characterisation of Myers–Briggs? Why are they relevant for the classification of the 16 types? How are they relevant in negotiations?
2. Individual versus collective negotiation styles are a common source of conflict in international negotiations. How do they influence the negotiation process and outcomes?
3. Negotiations in multiparty settings have advantages and disadvantages. Discuss pros and cons and set up a negotiation scenario with multiple players.
4. How are BATNAs derived for dyad and multiparty negotiations? Explain BATNA and discuss.
5. Do different professions negotiate differently? Give examples of professions and their negotiation styles.
6. What other sales negotiation techniques have you found to be effective? Is there a correlation between personality type, negotiation style and the way salespeople negotiate? Discuss.

NOTES

1. Jung, C.G. (1921) *Personality Types*. Berlin, Springer; and (1971) *Collected Works of Personality Types*, Volume 6. Princeton, Princeton University Press.
2. The Myers and Briggs Foundation (2019) MBTI basics. Available from: https://www.myersbriggs.org/my-mbti-personality-type/mbti-basics/home.htm?bhcp=1.
3. The Economist (2018) The enduring appeal of personality types. 31 August.

4. Ahmed, M. (2016) Is Myers-Briggs up the job? *Financial Times*, 11 February.
5. Goldberg, E. (2019) Personality tests are the astrology of the office. *The New York Times*, 17 September.
6. Shonk, K. (2019) Managing a multiparty negotiation: expert advice on handling multiparty negotiation and the complications created by multiple parties. *Program on Negotiation*, 14 March.
7. Adapted from: PON staff (2019) Diagnose your negotiation technique and negotiation styles. *Program on Negotiation*, 22 January, https://www.pon.harvard.edu/daily/dispute-resolution/diagnose-your-negotiating-style/, which was adapted from: "Negotiating differences: how contrasting styles affect outcomes", by Laurie R. Weingart (2011), originally published in *Negotiation* newsletter, January 2007.
8. Weingart (2011) ibid.
9. Tinsley, C.H. and O'Connor, K.M. (2007) Looking for an edge? Cultivate an integrative reputation. *Negotiations, Program on Negotiation*, Harvard Law School.
10. McGinn, K.L. and Keros, A.T. (2002) Improvisation and the logic of exchange in socially embedded transactions. *Administrative Science Quarterly*. **47**(3), 442–73.
11. Weingart (2011) op. cit.
12. Cain, S. (2012) *Quiet: The Power of Introverts in a World that Can't Stop Talking*. London, Penguin.
13. Hofstede, G. and Usunier, J.-C. (2003) Hofstede's dimensions of culture and their influence on international business negotiations. In: Ghauri, P.N. and Usunier, J.-C. (eds) *International Business Negotiations*. 2nd ed. Oxford, Pergamon/Elsevier, pp. 173–54.
14. Inagaki, K., Campbell P., Lewis, L. and Keohane, D. (2019) Who can fix Nissan? *Financial Times*, 10 September.
15. Shonk, K. (2018) Sales negotiation techniques: our four sales negotiation techniques will help buyers and sellers alike. Try out these proven persuasion strategies and gain the advantage in your next business negotiation. *Program on Negotiation*, 2 July.
16. Lee, A.J. and Ames, D.R. (2017) "I can't pay more" versus "It's not worth more": divergent effects of constraint and disparagement rationales in negotiations. *Organizational Behavior and Human Decision Processes*. 141, 16–28.
17. Tversky, A. and Kahneman, D. (1979) Judgment under uncertainty: heuristics and biases. *Science*. **27**, 1124–31.
18. Malhotra, D. and Bazerman, M.H. (2007) *Negotiation Genius*. New York, Bantam.
19. Langer, E.J., Blank, A. and Chanowitz, B. (1978) The mindlessness of ostensibly thoughtful action: the role of "placebic" information in interpersonal interaction. *Journal of Personality and Social Psychology*. **36**(6), 635–42.
20. Maaravi, Y., Ganzach, Y. and Pazy, A. (2011) Negotiation as a form of persuasion: arguments in first offers. *Journal of Personality and Social Psychology*. **101**(2), 245–55.
21. "Incoterms®" is an acronym standing for international commercial terms. "Incoterms®" is a trademark of the International Chamber of Commerce, registered in several countries. The Incoterms® rules feature abbreviations for terms, like FOB ("Free on Board"), DAP ("Delivered at Place"), EXW ("Ex Works"), CIP ("Carriage and Insurance Paid To"), which all have very precise meanings for the sale of goods around the world.
22. Tjian, A. (2009) Four rules of effective negotiations. *Program on Negotiation*, 28 July.
23. Ott, U.F., Prowse, P., Fells, R. and Rogers, H. (2016) The DNA of negotiations. *Journal of Business Research*. **69**, 3561–71.
24. Susskind, L. (2016) The key to success: negotiation 101 for engineers, Viewpoint, *The Engineer*, 5 April. From *Good for You, Great for Me* (Public Affairs, 2014).
25. Susskind (2016) ibid.
26. Parker, V. (2003) Negotiating licensing agreements. In: Ghauri, P.N. and Usunier, J.-C. (eds) *International Business Negotiations*. 2nd ed. Oxford, Pergamon/Elsevier, pp. 243–74.

27. Artinger, S., Vulkan, N. and Shem-Tov, Y. (2015) Entrepreneurs' negotiation behavior, *Small Business Economics*. **44**, 737–57.
28. Lucas, L. (2019) Jack Ma retires from Alibaba. *Financial Times*, 10 September.

FURTHER READING

Emre, M. (2018) *The Personality Brokers: The Strange History of Myers-Briggs and the Birth of Personality Testing*. New York, Doubleday Books. (Published in Britain by William Collins as "What's Your Type?")

Jung, C.G. (1921) *Personality Types*. Berlin, Springer.

Jung, C.G. (1971) *Collected Works of Personality Types*, Volume 6. Princeton, Princeton University Press.

Malhotra, D. and Bazerman, M.H. (2007) *Negotiation Genius*. New York, Bantam.

End of Part II cases

CASE 1
ADANI AND THE CARMICHAEL MINE

In 2010, Adani Mining Pty Ltd (Adani), the Australian wholly-owned subsidiary of India's Adani Group, sought government approval for the development of the Carmichael coal mine and rail project.[1] Situated in Central Queensland, Australia, the Carmichael mine is expected to produce 60 million tonnes of coal a year, with Adani expecting to mine 2.3 billion tonnes over 60 years of operations. Adani planned to mine the coal and transport it from the mine to Hay Point and Abbot Point port areas via a railway line, from where it would be exported to India.

The project was initially expected to be worth $16 billion. Adani received approval from the Queensland state government, which also provided an initial grant for the project, with local banks expected to fund the remainder of the project. The initial negotiations were slow due to disagreements on the amount of royalty to be paid by Adani.[2] However, the events that followed were not planned for by the parties.

As the negotiations for the deal were being undertaken, there was protest by Greenpeace, the independent organisation that campaigns on the platform "for a green and peaceful future".[3] Greenpeace claimed that the Carmichael project threatened the future of the Great Barrier Reef and the local communities.[4] Part of the concern was that a large amount of fresh water would be diverted to the mining area, as well as the potential for waste material to be pumped into the reef. For the driest inhabited continent on the planet, the diversion of a large amount of water to the mine was a cause of concern. Another concern was that Australia, whose per capita carbon emission is one of the highest in the world, would be exporting a large amount of coal to another country.

As far as the local community was concerned, Adani claimed that not only would the project create thousands of local jobs, but the company would also invest in welfare and community projects that would benefit the local community and Queensland. However, the local indigenous population claimed that they were forced to negotiate the rights to use of their land or risked losing their native title.[5] This added to the negative perception that was being built against the project and Adani.

Then in 2017 came the news that due to public pressure, the local Australian banks had refused to fund the project. Without a financier, the project faced an uncertain future. Sensing an opportunity to get involved in the project, some Chinese banks proposed funding the project.[6] They too, like the local Australian banks, faced public criticism and threats of customers closing their accounts held with the Chinese-owned banks. The Chinese banks withdrew their offer to fund the project[7] and Adani was again left without a backer. To make matters worse, in February 2017, rail operator Aurizon, which was tasked with building a line linking the mine to the port, backed away from the project.[8]

The protests led by Greenpeace made the Carmichael project a central issue in the country's politics, with the #STOPADANI movement gathering pace around Australia. By mid-2018, members of the Australian government believed that the project was in limbo,[9] whereas Adani was still confident of securing a financial backer.[10] In September 2018, Adani was prosecuted over the release of coal-laden water into the Great Barrier Reef,[11] which according to the protestors was further evidence of the environmental dangers of the project.

Adani attempted to slash the cost of the project,[12] bringing it down to $2 billion. With financiers staying away from the project, it was decided that the Adani mine site would remain under native title until any progress was made.[13] With the federal election of 18 May 2019 looming, the State government of Queensland led by the Australian Labor Party decided to seek an extra review of the groundwater plans,[14] which threatened further to delay the project. Some critics claimed that the decision was made to win votes. However, the election results saw the Labor Party lose many seats to the incumbent federal government of the Liberals. Some obervers believe that the losses in Central Queensland can be attributed to the action against Adani as this threatened local jobs and community development.[15]

In June 2019, the Queensland government report showed support for the groundwater plans and subsequently the company received federal government approval.[16] Adani hopes that with the approvals now in place, financial institutions would be willing to fund the project and the company will be able to commence operations.

DISCUSSION QUESTIONS

1. Who are the key stakeholders in this case? How many of these would you consider to be third parties in the negotiations?
2. What (if anything) could Adani have done differently to convince the various stakeholders of the benefits of the deal?
3. Going forward, what can Adani do to reduce the threat of future protests against the project?

CASE 2
SHAW SPORTS: NEGOTIATING BEYOND NATIONAL BOUNDARIES

On 15 May 2019, Jason Shaw, Chief Executive Officer of Shaw Sports, waited in his Sydney office for a response to his phone messages from the company's supplier from India. Like many Australian sporting goods companies, Shaw Sports was outsourcing the manufacturing of its sports equipment to low-cost producers in Asia. Shaw Sports was expecting to receive a signed copy of the contract for the manufacturing of footballs and tennis racquets from the Indian supplier by mid-April, and with the football season scheduled to begin in a few months, Jason was worried about possible loss of sales and the negative impact the delay would have on the company's brand name.

SHAW SPORTS

Founded in 2006, Shaw Sports has experienced rapid growth and has developed a reputation as a quality manufacturer of sporting goods and fitness equipment in Australia. Jason Shaw, a former club football player, heads the company. After his retirement from football, Jason decided to establish Shaw Sports in Sydney, Australia. The company commenced its operations by acquiring a small local manufacturer of sporting goods and fitness equipment. Jason's knowledge and contacts with the local football clubs in Australia helped Shaw Sports achieve rapid sales within a matter of a few years. Encouraged by the success in Australia, Jason decided to enter the New Zealand market in 2012 where Shaw Sports's goods received an encouraging response from retailers and consumers.

Jason decided that in order to make further gains into the market, Shaw Sports would need to be more competitive in terms of price. Many of Shaw Sports's competitors were outsourcing their production to factories in South and South-East Asian countries. Jason started researching for suppliers of footballs and tennis racquets and came across Vijay Sports in India.

VIJAY SPORTS

Based in Mumbai, India, Vijay Sports is a manufacturer of sports equipment. Vijay is a Hindi name which means victory. The company was established in 1980 and sells its goods to major sports companies in India. The company has had some international experience as a contract manufacturer of junior cricket kits for small international retailers. Due to the lower wages of unskilled labour in India, the cost of manufacturing is around 40 per cent cheaper than Australia.

THE NEGOTIATIONS

On 10 January 2019, Jason contacted Vijay Sports in relation to the manufacturing of footballs and tennis racquets. After receiving a positive response, Jason started exchanging information pertaining to the transaction with Mr Raj Kumar - President of Vijay Sports. Both parties decided to discuss the details further, and Jason agreed to visit the factory in India in March 2019 to see the facilities and to meet Raj.

Jason had never visited India but was aware of the huge public following the game of cricket enjoyed in the country. Jason's past international travels included visits to the United States, Canada, New Zealand and England, so Jason was excited about his visit to a new destination. Jason hoped that the formalities of the deal would be agreed to in a few days, and he would be back in Sydney in about a week's time.

After arriving in Mumbai on 10 March, Jason took a taxi from the airport to his accommodation. On the way to the hotel, Jason noticed what he saw as gross violations of traffic rules by motorists. The smoke-filled air and the large number of people on the roads overwhelmed him. After reaching the hotel, Jason became more determined to complete the deal as soon as possible so he could return home.

The next day Jason visited the factory of Vijay Sports. He was greeted by Raj who showed him the manufacturing facilities. Jason was impressed by the size of the operation and was surprised to see many of the tasks being undertaken manually. Most of these tasks were automated in Shaw Sports's factory. After the tour of the factory, Raj invited Jason to a tour of the city, followed by lunch. Jason was keen to get down to business and did not want to stay longer than he had to. He declined the invitation and said: "*we can do that once we have discussed our proposals for the deal.*" With a smile on his face, Raj led Jason to his office.

As soon as they sat down, Jason took out a piece of paper with the Shaw Sports offer. He passed the paper to Raj and explained: "*This is our detailed proposal. You will find that the price we are offering is competitive and I have checked with others in the market to ensure that this is fair for both of us.*" Raj looked at the proposal briefly and replied: *"We can discuss the price later, let's talk a bit more about the design of the tennis racquets and the footballs you require."*

Jason seemed puzzled by Raj's response. Jason felt that the price he had offered was a bit higher than Vijay Sports could manage in the market, and had expected Raj to agree to it immediately. He also felt that the details of the sports equipment had not been discussed during the initial contact between the parties. As Jason started talking about the quality of the sports equipment required, Raj started discussing current football matches and the upcoming cricket world cup. Jason felt quite frustrated with the topic of the conversation as he felt that Raj was deviating away from the business at hand. At the end of the meeting, Jason went back to his hotel. He sat in his room frustrated as he had hoped that he would have been close to a deal but felt that they had not even commenced discussing any business activities. Jason re-read his proposal and felt that this was the best Vijay Sports could have asked for.

The next day Jason met Raj again at the factory. After exchanging pleasantries Jason asked Raj to look at the proposal: *"Raj, I am hoping that we can finalise some of the details today. I don't have much time left before I have to return to Australia. The sooner we can agree upon this, the sooner the contract can be drawn up. I need to have this sorted so that we meet the targets and complete orders before the football season."* Raj spent a few minutes reading the proposal and responded: *"Jason, thank you for drafting this offer. You've done well to prepare such a detailed proposal."* Jason was relieved. He felt that by being direct in his communication, he had forced Raj to discuss the deal and there seemed to be no issues anymore with the proposed offer.

Later that day Jason took up Raj's offer of seeing the city and spent the evening with Raj and some of the executives from Vijay Sports. Jason was happy that he had achieved his objective, and was looking forward to returning to Australia. As they spent the evening having dinner and discussing sports, Jason had a sense of accomplishment that he had managed to negotiate a good deal. The next day Jason visited Raj's office for the final time before he returned to Sydney. He informed Raj that the legal team in Australia would soon to draw up the agreement to be signed by Vijay Sports.

After spending the remaining few days visiting tourist attractions in Mumbai, Jason returned to Sydney and asked his legal team to draw up the agreement documents. The contract was sent to Raj for his approval at the end of March and was expected to be returned by third week of April.

By end of April Jason had not received any communication from Vijay Sports. Worried about the delay in signing the agreement, Jason tried contacting Raj. He was informed by Raj's personal assistant that due to family commitments, Raj would be away from the office until the middle of May and would contact Jason upon his return. As Jason awaited the call from Raj, he began to wonder why the deal was not yet finalised.

DISCUSSION QUESTIONS

1. What cultural factors could you observe during the negotiations between Shaw Sports and Vijay Sports?
2. How would you describe the communication styles followed by Jason and Raj?
3. What do you believe are the reasons for the delay in concluding the negotiations? How could these issues have been addressed?

CASE 3
ECG GROUP: FRAUD AND LIQUIDATION OF A JOINT VENTURE IN CHINA*

In 1994, US-based building-control systems specialist ECG US created a joint venture with China-based CIG Ltd, Realton JV, in order to manufacture and sell building-control system products, such as air-conditioning valves and fire-safety equipment, on the mainland. The joint venture was out of control from the beginning. Sales were weak, and, unbeknown to ECG US, the joint venture used other entities in order to gain contracts. With Realton unable to generate a profit, ECG US decided to dissolve the venture altogether by 2001. Nonetheless, the Chinese partner was adamant about continuing its operation, maintaining that Realton was profitable by Chinese accounting standards. As the two parties entered into negotiation, how should they have solved this quagmire while protecting their interests at the same time?

ECG GROUP

UK-based ECG Group was a multinational enterprise whose main business activity was comprised of the design, engineering, manufacturing and installation of building automation and intelligent control devices and systems for commercial and residential buildings as well as manufacturing plants and infrastructural projects worldwide. Its product portfolio included more than 13,000 products, including, but not limited to, sensors; thermostats; actuators; airconditioning valves; air, water and temperature controllers; and fire-safety equipment. ECG Group distributed these products through original equipment manufacturer partners, distributors and its own sales offices, which numbered more than 500 worldwide. ECG Group had two foreign subsidiaries, Illinois-based ECG US Ltd ("ECG US") and Singapore-based ECG Singapore Ltd ("ECG Singapore").

With a burgeoning property market and construction industry, China provided a lucrative opportunity for ECG Group in East Asia. In 1990, ECG Singapore established its presence in China by setting up a representative office in Shanghai to coordinate sales and engineering activities. The representative office played the role of a liaison between ECG Group and its customers in China, and ECG Group sent engineers to provide local engineers with product updates periodically. But with growing opportunities in China, it soon became apparent that the representative office was insufficient in supporting ECG Group's activities there. In 1994, ECG Group decided to expand its operation in China through a joint venture that would allow it to manufacture in China as well step up sales activities (see Exhibit 1).

Legal and Strategic Framework

The joint venture, Realton JV ("Realton"), was formed between ECG US and CIG Ltd ("CIG"). CIG was a Shanghai-based publicly listed company that specialised in the manufacture and distribution

---

* Grace Loo prepared this case under the supervision of Dr Neale O'Connor for class discussion. This case is not intended to show effective or ineffective handling of decision or business processes.

June 1994	1994–1998	1999	2000	2001
Establishment of joint venture	Manufacturing of control valves	Conversion to engineering co. to install control valves	Management fraud	Liquidation

Exhibit 1 Timeline for the development of the joint venture (Realton-Shanghai)

Exhibit 2 Partners in the joint venture

Partners	ECG US (60%)	CIG China Ltd (40%)
Core business	Building automation. Proven sales track record in the United States.	Temperature-control instruments. A Shanghai-listed company with strong sales in building automation products in China.
Origin	United States	China
Contribution	Contributed 75% of capital and supply technology and trained local engineers.	Contributed 25% of capital and marketed ECG Group's products.
Partner's strategic aim	To secure a profitable return on investment.	To share a stable return to complement its main business.

of automation devices, such as transmitters, actuators, valves and valve positioners, for the domestic and overseas markets. CIG also engaged in process design, system integration and instrument assembly for automation control systems. The industries it served ranged from railways and petrochemicals to thermal and nuclear power plants. ECG US and CIG had shareholdings in Realton of 60% and 40% respectively. Under the joint-venture agreement, ECG US would provide the technology for Realton to manufacture building-control system products - for instance, air-conditioning valves and firesafety equipment - and train local engineers, while CIG would handle the marketing of Realton's products (see Exhibit 2). Within Realton, the general manager was appointed by ECG US and the two assistant general managers were appointed by CIG (see Exhibit 3).

Loss of Control and Management Fraud

The joint venture was fraught with problems from the time it began operation in 1994. Sales were weak, and when orders were closed, customers complained about the products not meeting their specifications. By mid-1997, sales were so weak that the general manager suggested to ECG US that Realton should halt manufacturing altogether. In mid-1997, the US partner adopted the general manager's advice to stop manufacturing due to the lack of sales. In the following two years, the general manager recruited his own sales team to sell ECG products manufactured outside China, but he died of a heart attack in April 1999 and no new manager was appointed until September 1999.

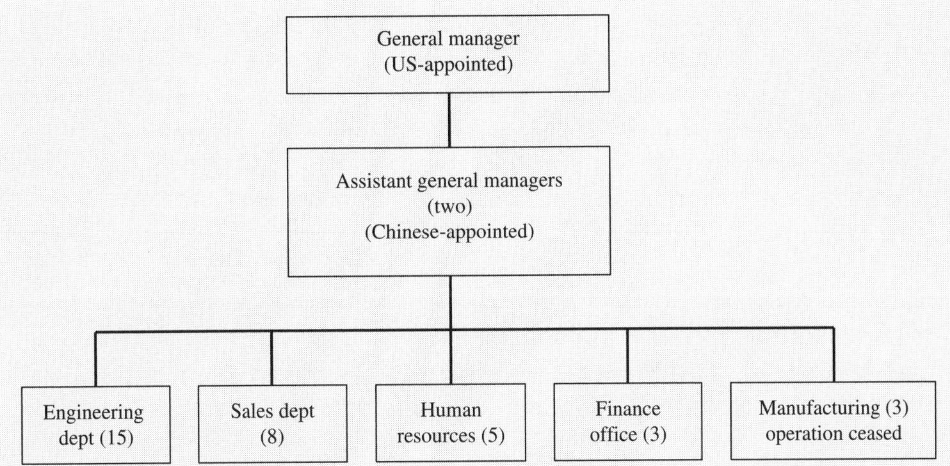

Exhibit 3 Organisational structure of Realton (Shanghai) JV LTD

Between April and September 1999, there was no financial reporting from Realton to ECG US. During this period, the sales manager originally appointed by the Chinese partner (CIG) started entering into contracts without any oversight. Companies in China used a contract common seal and a company common seal in place of authorised signatures for signing contracts, allowing individuals who held either of these seals to represent the company in official transactions. The sales manager closed consultancy contracts and placed orders for products and equipment with ECG US for the execution of these contracts. Though Realton paid for the purchases, the sales manager sent his own engineers to execute the projects and had the customers pay into his account; he pocketed all the revenues.

In January 2000, ECG Group's finance director for the Asia-Pacific region discovered that Realton had an unrecorded liability of US$560,000 and losses that amounted to US$690,000. Ninety per cent of the contracts signed by Realton with its customers were unprofitable even though they appeared otherwise on the books, because no consideration had been given to the shipping charges for the delivery of the products. Realton's finance manager, who was previously under the oversight of the general manager, failed to alert ECG US of the problem.

Independent auditors were subsequently brought in. The auditors found that, using ECG Group's technology and market information garnered through Realton, CIG had diverted Realton's most profitable contracts to parallel companies it had set up for this purpose.

> *In auditing the books and records of Realton JV, it has been discovered that Realton JV has been using a trading company controlled by CIG, Realton JV's Chinese parent company, to transact businesses. In addition to quasicontracts signed between customers and CIG, a service contract has also been signed between CIG and Realton JV. The purpose of the transaction is that a trading company is to handle the importation of foreign equipment while arranging disbursement of US dollars to ECG US. The trading company will receive renminbi or other currency at an inflated exchange rate to cover their service fee.*

The inter-company reconciliation between Realton JV and ECG US showed a balance of US$1.863 million due by Realton JV. Out of that amount, US$109,000 was owed by CIG/Yefa from customers who had not paid up. There was no contractual liability between ECG US and CIG/Yefa as Realton JV placed orders directly with ECG US and CIG would settle the amount when it received payment from customers.

Internal audit report by the Asia-Pacific Finance Director

Realton had discovered a high demand for the building-control systems and project-management services for the installation of such building-control systems. Nonetheless, Realton's business registration limited its scope of activities to manufacturing only, and engaging in the management of the building-control system installation projects involved importing foreign equipment, which would require Realton to apply for an import licence as well as foreign exchange. The Chinese government maintained control over foreign exchange, and even Chinese companies that collected their accounts receivables in foreign currencies had to surrender their foreign-exchange earnings to designated banks and buy foreign currency from these banks when they needed to pay overseas suppliers. To get around these restrictions, Realton turned to Yefa, a trading company in the CIG Group, for assistance in making payments for the purchases of products and equipment from ECG US or other sister companies in the ECG Group.

Contracts between Realton and its customers were denominated either in foreign currency or renminbi. When the contracts were denominated in renminbi, Realton would seek Yefa/CIG's assistance to remit foreign currency to ECG US for its purchases (see Exhibit 4). In cases where the customer was a foreign enterprise and the contract had to be denominated in a foreign currency, Realton would arrange for the contract to be signed between the customer and Yefa/CIG instead and had Yefa/CIG handle the importation and foreign exchange. The following summarised the transactions between the customer, Yefa/CIG and Realton for such contracts (see Exhibit 5):

- Realton arranged for a customer to sign a contract, which would be denominated in a foreign currency, with Yefa/CIG.

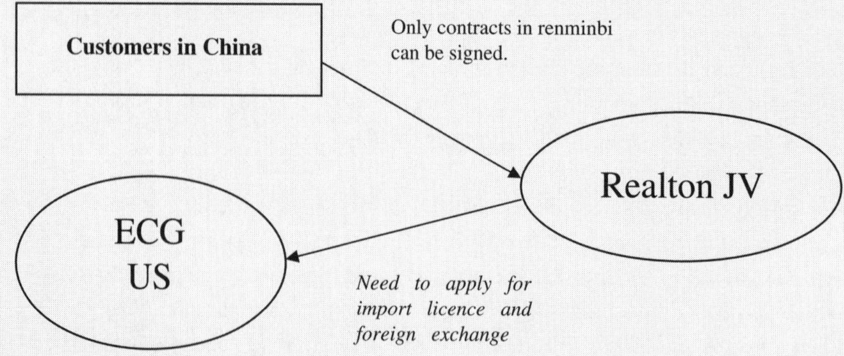

Exhibit 4 Transactions without a trading company

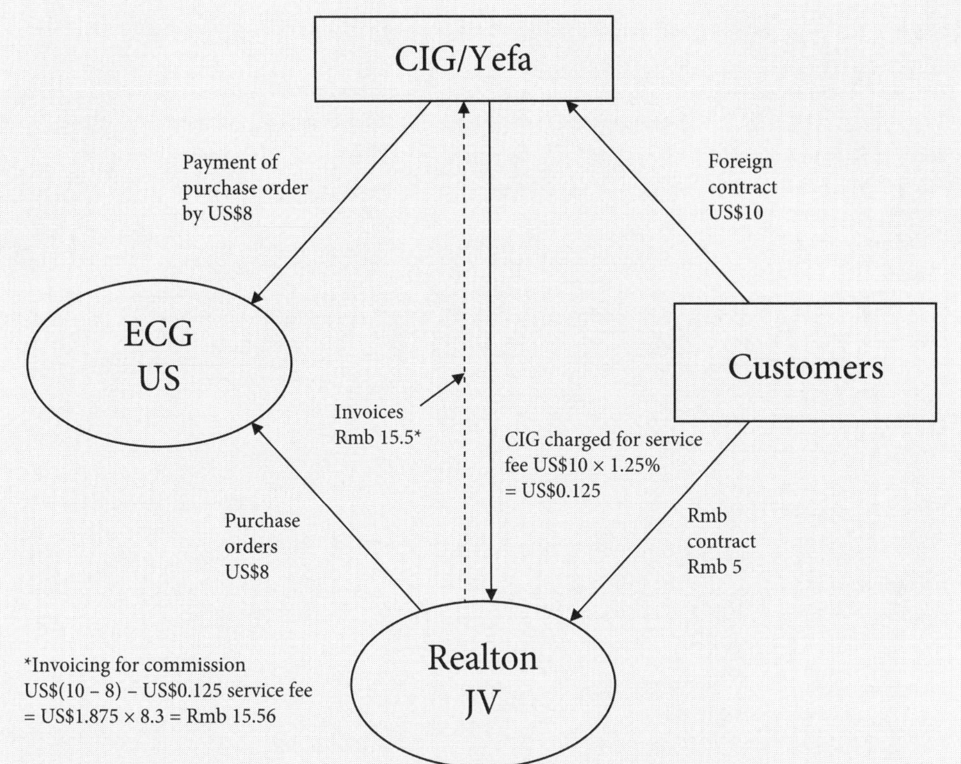

Exhibit 5 Contracts handled through trading company Yefa

- Realton would then sign a service agreement with Yefa/CIG, based on which it would purchase the equipment necessary for fulfilling the project from ECG US.
- When the customer paid Yefa/CIG in renminbi, Yefa/CIG would remit to ECG US to cover Realton's purchases from ECG US.
- Yefa/CIG charged Realton a service fee equivalent to a percentage of the contract amount for its part in handling the project.
- Since the contract was signed between Yefa/CIG and the customer, payment was made out to Yefa/CIG in foreign currency. Realton would issue an invoice to Yefa/CIG in order to collect its profit, and Yefa/CIG would pay Realton in renminbi. The invoice amount would be equivalent to the project contract amount minus the equipment purchase amount and Yefa/CIG's service fee.

The independent auditors formulated a summarised balance sheet for the best estimate of the carrying value of Realton based on the balance value as of 31 July 2001 and found other irregularities (see Exhibit 6):

- Up to Rmb 1.4 million[17] of imported equipment and Rmb 1.98 million of obsolete spare parts were not written off in accordance with normal accounting practices when Realton began to shift from a manufacturer to a project-management service provider.

Exhibit 6 Reconciliation from China GAAP to US GAAP (Realton JV, 31 July 2001)

	Mgt accounts YTD Rmb	Statutory Accounts Rmb	Adjustments (Estimated) Rmb	Estimated Value Rmb	(Dec.) Inc. %
Tangible assets	3,603,581	3,546,917	-1,982,372	1,564,545	-81%
Fixed assets	**3,603,581**	**3,546,917**	**-1,982,372**	**1,564,545**	**-81%**
Inventory	5,194,114	10,160,632	-4,369,072	5,791,560	-43%
Construction in progress		191,587	-191,587	-	
Organisational expenses		611,827	-611,827	-	
Other deferred expenses		257,177	-257,177	-	
Debtors - net trade	5,245,987	5,676,409	-567,641	5,108,768	-10%
Debtors - inter-company	430,423				
Advances to suppliers		225,367	-225,367	-	
Debtors - other	4,385,216	788,089	-39,405	748,685	-5%
Creditors - net trade	-1,721,147	-1,721,147		-1,721,147	
Creditors - intercompany	-11,103,472	-12,665,924	-	-12,665,924	
Creditors - other	-2,601,835	-222,029	-	-222,029	
Taxation	-134,433	-134,433	-	-134,433	
Net current assets	**-305,148**	**3,167,557**	**-6,262,076**	**-3,094,520**	**-198%**
Assets employed	**3,298,433**	**6,714,474**	**-8,244,448**	**-1,529,975**	**-123%**
Share capital					
Capital reserve	18,481,095	18,481,095	-	18,481,095	
Exchange variance	-165,837	-165,837	-	-165,837	
Reserves - revenue b/fwd	-10,839,298	-6,707,410	-	-6,707,410	
YTD transfers to revenue reserve	-850,939	-1,549,220	-	-1,549,220	
Asset written-down losses		-8,244,448	-8,244,448		
Total equity	**7,742,131**	**11,158,172**		**2,913,723**	**-74%**
Cash in hand and at bank	4,443,698	4,443,698	-	4,443,698	
Total debt	4,443,698	4,443,698		4,443,698	
Capital employed	**3,298,433**	**6,714,474**		**-1,529,975**	**-123%**

Note: In determining the estimate a prudent view is taken notwithstanding the disposable value in the fixed or current assets. No adjustment has been made for payable items because any error will end in a gain and that is not on par with the prudent view.

- Up to Rmb 568,000 of accounts receivables were unaccounted for due to invoices issued for the government tax on the import of equipment when the tax was already included in the customers' purchase invoices for the equipment.
- The depicted capital of Rmb 11 million should be reduced to Rmb 2.9 million, translating to 23.3% of the original share capital.
- The depicted net assets should be revised from Rmb 6.7 million to net liabilities of Rmb 1.5 million.
- Differences in accounting estimates for asset valuation led to historical costs being recorded for the non-use of manufacturing facilities, resulting in the write-off of US$1.38 million.

EPILOGUE

With all the financial irregularities uncovered by the independent auditors, ECG US decided to liquidate Realton. Under US liquidation law, ECG US had enough power to pass the resolution to dissolve Realton, as it was the majority shareholder. However, Chinese bankruptcy law required a consensus among all partners involved to dissolve a joint venture. CIG had been using Realton for its own gain and was more interested in maintaining those gains than in the health of the joint venture. It maintained that Realton's books were kept in accordance with Chinese Generally Accepted Accounting Principles ("GAAP") and the joint venture was profitable. ECG US was adamant about putting an end to this losing venture. How were the two parties to maintain their interests given the little common ground they shared?

NOTES

1. Queensland Government (2019) *Carmichael Coal Mine and Rail Project*. State Development, Manufacturing, Infrastructure and Planning. Available from: https://www.statedevelopment.qld.gov.au/coordinator-general/assessments-and-approvals/coordinated-projects/completed-projects/carmichael-coal-mine-and-rail-project.html.
2. Hinchliffe, J. (2017) Adani at odds over royalty negotiations for Australian coal mine. *Reuters*, 3 September.
3. Greenpeace Australia website: https://www.greenpeace.org.au.
4. Greenpeace (2017) Adani's Carmichael mine would be a disaster for communities and a death sentence for the Great Barrier Reef. Press Release, 5 June.
5. ABC News (2017) Traditional owners say they were forced to negotiate with Adani for fear of losing native title rights. 11 December.
6. Long, S. (2017) China will finance Adani mine, insiders say, but it will cost Australian jobs. *ABC News*, 23 November.
7. Reuters (2017) China's biggest bank says does not intend financing Adani's Carmichael coal mine. 4 December.
8. SBS News (2018) Adani dealt another blow to Qld coal mine. 9 February.
9. Energyworld (2018) Adani decision on Carmichael mine in limbo: Aus Consul General. 9 May.
10. Wolfe, N. (2018) Adani bosses confident they'll secure the money needed for their rail project. *News.com.au,* 18 July.
11. Horn, A. (2018) Adani prosecuted over release of coal-laden water near Great Barrier Reef. *ABC News*, 5 September.
12. Australian Financial Review (2018) Adani moves to slash costs to get Carmichael mine across line. 13 September.

13. Robertson, J. (2018) Adani mine site to remain under native title until finance confirmed, Minister says. *ABC News*, 15 September.
14. Ludlow, M. (2019) Adani mine faces potentially fatal blow. *Australian Financial Review*, 13 May.
15. Bermingham, K. (2019) Adani mine stance costly for Labor: Greens. *The Canberra Times*, 19 May.
16. BBC News (2019) Adani mine: Australia approves controversial coal project. 13 June.
17. US$1 = Rmb 8.28 on 30 July 1999.

PART III
NEGOTIATION PROCESS

7 Negotiation context

A negotiation in the simplest case is a means by which two parties come to a deal. It can happen in a relationship, social, political, legal and business context. Negotiations happen in a rich and complex context which influences how the parties communicate and how the process unfolds. The context of negotiations helps to structure the negotiation process and identify negotiation styles. The understanding of the negotiation context provides insights into the negotiating parties, processes and outcomes. The context of an international business negotiation can be relational, professional, social or cultural. The previous chapters highlighted the differences in cultural, social and professional context. As with many issues in negotiations, the questions are on how the parties have framed the context of the negotiation.[1]

Even more difficult than in dyad (two-party) or multiparty negotiation is the negotiation context for situations in which someone negotiates for someone else. This is when the role of the negotiator is to act as an agent, a mediator or a third party. This chapter introduces the basic negotiation context before the negotiation framework is dealt with in the next chapters. The first section deals with the negotiation context between countries and companies in bilateral negotiation contexts, then the chapter looks at the role of agents and third parties in negotiations before moving beyond the dyad context to look at negotiations that involve multiple parties, which adds another level of complexity to the discussions.

7.1 THE CONTEXT

Parties frame the context of the negotiation. Researchers of bilateral and multilateral international negotiations use the country perspective to highlight the complexity of negotiations. This is also a good starting point for studying international business negotiations. The country perspective adds complexity due to different geographical, economic, legal and societal frameworks.

There should be an understanding prior to the commencement of bilateral negotiations that the national government is to participate in negotiations with the subordinate group in order to move towards one of the following:[2]

1. Designing guarantees of "full participation" in governance and policy making for the subordinate group in the political country scenario. *The company perspective* uses subgroups within the company according to tasks (accounting, marketing, human

resources, research and development) and to country (regional hubs, geographical clusters).

2. Crafting a kind of consociation arrangement where the subordinate group is overrepresented, or has a veto, or both; *on the company level*: overrepresentation of functional areas for the benefit of the corporate identity.
3. Designing the form of "autonomy" which will be granted to a geographical area of the state or territory; *on the company level*: focus on subsidiaries with decision-making power and financial autonomy.
4. Devising the terms for a secession; *on the company level*: threats of secession in companies can be a strategy to achieving more focused goals.
5. Making arrangements for independence; *on the company level*: designing independent units and subsidiaries for bureaucratic, economic or political reasons.

Specifics of the country and company context are important for providing the basis of negotiations. Moving from the country level to the bilateral company level, the context now takes place in dyad negotiations concerning the provision of products and services. These negotiations relate to import–export contracts, but also joint venture and alliance formations mergers and acquisitions. The more parties that are included the more complicated are the preferences, interests, strategies and expectations.

Example 7.1 shows how intricate and complex the context in international companies has become and that many levels of interaction and negotiation are necessary in multinational companies.

EXAMPLE 7.1

PHILIP MORRIS AND ALTRIA WANT TO MERGE: INVESTORS ARE COOL ON THE DEAL TO CREATE A $210 BILLION TOBACCO TITAN

Altria, the producer of Marlboros, span off its non-American business, Philip Morris International (PMI), a decade ago. The reason for the split was both Altria's share price, which had been below its sum-of-parts value, and regulatory hounding of Big Tobacco over its role in causing cancer.

In 2016, American Tobacco made a bid for Reynolds American, maker of Camels. At that time an analyst at Wells Fargo (bank) urged PMI to reunite with its former parent. It took longer than expected. On 27 August the two said they were in talks to merge. Their combined market value just before the announcement was $210 billion.

The merger still makes sense for some bankers in the "global arms race" for "reduced-risk" products which use fewer harmful chemicals, given the benefits of scale and geographical reach.

Background information: In 2018 Altria spent $12.8 billion on 35 per cent of Juul Labs, a maker of popular high-nicotine vaporisers. It paid $1.8 billion for 45 per cent of Cronos Group, a cannabis company from Canada (which, along with some American states, has legalised pot). PMI has spent $6 billion over a decade to develop IQOS, a smoke-free device which heats tobacco and is expected to represent 40 per cent of its sales by 2025, up from 14 per cent in the previous year. In April it won approval from the Food and Drug Administration (FDA) to sell IQOS in America, starting from the next month (under an existing licensing agreement with Altria).

Source: Adapted from The Economist (2019).[3]

Discussion Point: Describe the negotiation context for Altria and PMI, given their history and company background. Discuss the complexities of multinational enterprises (MNEs) and countries in international negotiations and what needs to be considered when analysing the process and outcome of negotiations.

7.2 THE ROLE OF AGENTS

The negotiation context between two parties and between multiple parties is still considered direct, from both social and economic rationales, whereas adding agencies (especially in some countries, where this is a necessary condition for trading) and third parties requires the incorporation of more complex needs and preferences.

Agents bargain on behalf of someone else (the principal) with a third party.

Agents are used to prevent conflict arising between the negotiators. They are chosen based on their expertise, which should closely match that of the parties employing their skills.[4] Negotiating on behalf of others presents difficulties in itself. Negotiation agents are broadly defined as including legislators, diplomats, salespersons, consultants, lawyers, committee chairs – in fact anyone who represents others in a negotiation.

Agency negotiations in import–export relationships can occur on a governmental level. Particularly in some countries (Arab countries), the government uses agencies to negotiate on its behalf to facilitate import–export contracts. Figure 7.1 shows how the parties are aligned.

The agency relationship is important in easing negotiations due to the expertise of the agent regarding bureaucracy, regulations and the economic parameters of a particular country. Agency relationships are also important in negotiations for joint ventures or in other

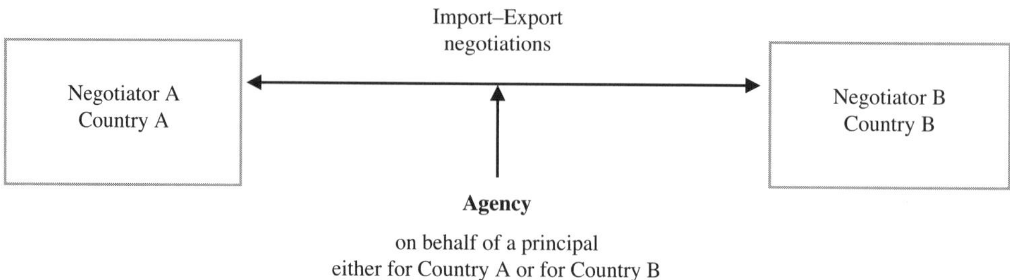

Figure 7.1 Agency relationship in import–export negotiations

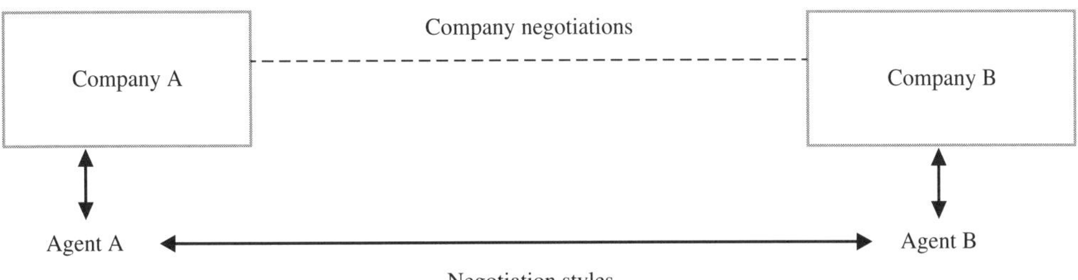

Figure 7.2 Agency relationship in company negotiations

corporate negotiations in which managers or expert negotiators act on behalf of the owners of the company (Figure 7.2).

Agents[5] often bargain with a third party on behalf of their principals. An agent faces uncertainty about the terms that are acceptable to the principal in relation to the minimum price level, which is called the principal's "reservation price". It could also be that the entire payoff function of the agent may be uncertain.

Increased uncertainty about the principal's reservation price and the payoff function, along with greater risk aversion, will increase the agent's minimum demands. This makes it difficult to reach an agreement between the agent and the third party, and therefore it is important to take into account the individual agent's behaviour in this scenario. The inherent uncertainty of agency bargaining can frequently make disagreement more likely. This is based on Axelrod's measure of the "conflict of interest"[6] in a game, optimal insistence prices in a one-shot bargaining situation, and two equilibrium concepts in a common commitment game. In many common negotiating situations, especially where *ex post* ratification of the agent's agreement is required (for example, union contracts, treaties), the use of an agent can also lead to an increase in the possibility of an impasse (see Example 7.2).

EXAMPLE 7.2
THE NEGOTIATION FOR DISTRIBUTORSHIP/AGENCY AGREEMENT[7]

Agency and especially distribution are embedded in a web of national and transnational laws. Competition policy and laws vary from country to country. It is therefore in the interest of anyone making one of these agreements to know the appropriate law. This allows, when circumstances permit, for this knowledge to be used as a negotiation counter.

In the United States contracts are surrounded by a complexity of laws stemming from the Sherman Act, which prohibits contracts that may lead to a monopoly. Agreements to restrict competition are not allowed. The granting exclusively to a distributor of a territory or product/brand is increasingly seen as violation of the law irrespective of its competitive effects.

In most Arab countries there are commercial codes in which provision is made for disputes to be taken before local courts, but it is normal for disputes to be referred to arbitration for quick settlement. This can either be at the International Court of Arbitration in Paris or locally. The local court has discretion to set aside arbitration according to certain rules.

Under EU law, agents are exempt from a general prohibition on agreements likely to affect trade between states. Where an agreement is not considered to affect trade between countries, then the law that is relied on in the event of dispute is the law agreed between the parties. In the United Kingdom the law of agency is weak; in France, Germany, the Netherlands and some other countries the law presumes the agent to be the weaker party and is considered entitled to compensation if an agent's services are terminated. It is therefore in the interest of a British agent to have an agreement with a French supplier under French law; for the French supplier, English or Scottish law provides an advantage should that supplier wish to terminate the agreement. In Belgium there is a law specific to distributorship which provides for compensation under specific rules for the goodwill which the distributor is assumed to have built up for the supplier.

7.3 THE ROLE OF THIRD PARTIES

Third-party interventions affect parties in a direct way. Interest-based mediators assist both sides in reaching a mutually satisfactory outcome.

There could be different reasons why an agent, a mediator or a third party is involved in negotiations. *Third-party intervention*[8] often affects the behaviour of negotiators in a direct way. The selling price will be higher when an agent is used than when no intermediary is involved. When a mediator is used, the selling price need not be affected.

The impact of third-party roles on negotiated outcomes is well established. The nature of the negotiated relationship between the "parties" can change if an agent is involved.

In a *dispute*,[9] it is often useful to seek out an interest-based mediator to assist both sides in reaching a mutually satisfactory conflict resolution. In these external negotiations, mediators meet with all the parties to get a sense of the interests underlying the negotiation and the objectives of the parties. For example, certain aspects of a new technology could be less important to the engineers than others and could be dropped if their more important objectives are protected. Once each party's core interests have been explored, the mediator can try out proposed trade-offs with each of the parties (shuttle diplomacy). After that, all negotiators can be brought together, and it will be established whether they could agree on an overall position. Knowledge of the key interests and possible trade-offs enables the mediator to propose an overall negotiation position that would protect the core interests. Reaching an overall agreement is then not difficult.

Shuttle diplomacy[10] is the practice of meeting separately with each disputant, and while widespread, is not without controversy. Critics have argued that these private sessions give the mediator too much power at the expense of the parties and that joint sessions improve the parties' understanding of each other. In highly contentious and emotional disputes, private meetings may be the only viable option for conflict resolution.

Caucusing[11] provides mediators with an important tool for addressing some of the mediation's most difficult dilemmas. Sometimes parties will never be willing to speak freely in front of each other. This is taken into account when mediators are used to bring a solution to a negotiation which is in deadlock or heading for a break-up.

In international negotiations, disputes and conflicts can easily arise due to the nature of complexity. The third party can give a sense of compromise to the parties to be able to reach an agreement. Not often is it the case that direct negotiations will lead to stalemate and the parties need to resolve all their differences. Therefore a third party who is in no way affiliated with the negotiating parties is paramount to help the parties find a solution. They do not always succeed, but even when they do, they are rarely credited or remembered for their contribution. Conversely, they are often subjected to great criticism when there is any failure. Even so, they act as a link and try to persuade the disputants; for instance, labour disputes, patent and trademark violation are common examples where the assistance of such third parties may be required.

Third parties can play different roles. The following four possibilities highlight the necessity and flexibility of third parties:

The *mediator* is a very commonly used neutral third party. The job of the mediator is to facilitate a negotiated solution through reasoning and persuasion, by suggesting alternatives to the involved parties. Mediators are common in labour-management conflicts and in civil court disputes.

The *arbitrator* negotiates as a third party having the authority to dictate an agreement between the parties. Arbitration can be requested by the negotiators or enforced on the parties by a court or contract. An arbitration, unlike a mediation, always results in a settlement. If one party is left overwhelmingly defeated, then the negotiator is very likely to be dissatisfied and it will be unlikely that they accept the arbitrator's decision. In that case, the conflict may reappear later. The rules set by the negotiators or set out in law influence the authority of the arbitrators.

The *conciliator* is also a third party entrusted with establishing an informal communication link between the negotiator and the counterpart. Conciliators are found in disputes which are largely international, labour, family and community conflicts. Conciliators are more than communication facilitators, since they also help in fact-finding, interpreting messages and persuading disputants to reach an agreement. Its effectiveness in comparison to mediation has proven difficult to establish because the two overlap a great deal.

Consultants are skilled and impartial third parties attempting to facilitate problem solving through communication and analysis. A consultant needs to have knowledge of conflict management. The consultant's role is needed to improve relations between the conflicting parties in order to reach a settlement by themselves. They should encourage the parties to learn about, understand and work with each other, rather than putting forward specific solutions. The consultant's approach pivots on a longer-term focus on building new and positive perceptions and attitudes between the conflicting parties.

Figure 7.3 gives an insight into the roles of third parties in negotiations.

Analyse in Exercise 7.1 the various options in relation to using a third party.

Example 7.3 set outs the case of a country–company international business negotiation regarding a contract between Nigeria and Royal Dutch Shell relating to oil production.

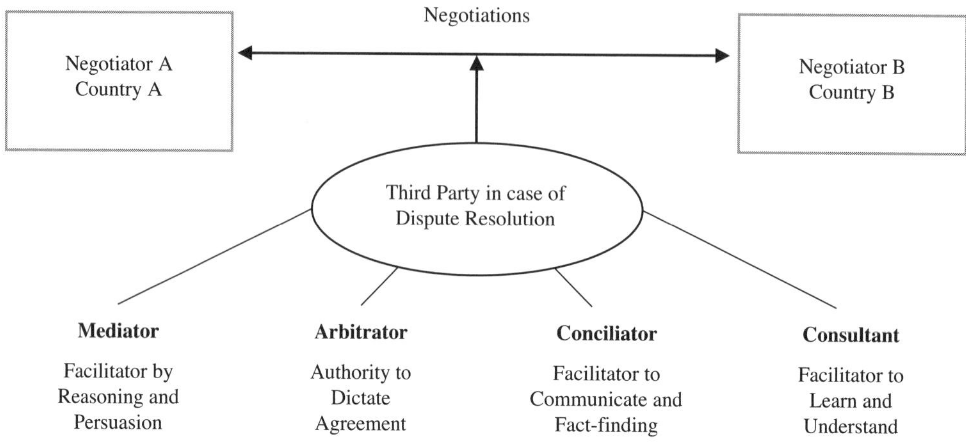

Figure 7.3 Third-party negotiations

EXERCISE 7.1
DEADLOCK SCENARIO

Consider a negotiation deadlock between two companies negotiating a contract for a long-term franchising agreement (famous examples in food and beverage or clothing are McDonalds, Coca Cola, Benetton). The negotiators intend to use either a mediator, conciliator, arbitrator or consultant. Outline the different approaches that the two parties are likely to take. Which type of third party should they choose and why?

Example 7.4 sets out the case of a joint venture international business negotiation between two companies, Clariant and Saudi Basic Industries Corporation.

EXAMPLE 7.3
NIGERIA AND ROYAL DUTCH SHELL BEGIN CONTRACT NEGOTIATIONS

Nigeria has begun renegotiating oil contracts with Royal Dutch Shell. The aim is for major energy companies to generate less in revenues from lucrative offshore blocks in Nigeria, Africa's largest oil producer. Nigeria has several types of contracts with major energy companies, including joint ventures for onshore blocks and production-sharing agreements for the deepwater ones. In the early 1990s, the state signed production-sharing contracts with companies including Shell, France's Total, Norway's Equinor, Italy's Eni and the United States' ExxonMobil. Nigeria produces 1.8 million barrels a day of oil, and the old agreements favour the foreign companies, giving them as much as 80 per cent of the oil against the 20 per cent for the state. The new contracts should start at 60 per cent or lower in the company's favour. The idea is that under the new contracts the companies take a greater share in the initial stages of operation, but the share gradually shifts in favour of the state as the companies recover their investments. The state energy company, the Nigeria National Petroleum Corporation, has already entered into renegotiations with Shell. Shell will see their existing contract expire in 2023. Others will expire by 2028. These renegotiations and the new terms arising from them will affect Shell's final investment decision on developing the new $10 billion Bonga Southwest deepwater project. The revised commercial framework will influence this project. For years, Nigeria has tried to overhaul these contracts and reconcile the huge revenue shortfall for the state of up to $28.6 billion over the decade to 2017. The original production-sharing contracts stipulated that they had to be renegotiated with more favourable terms for Nigeria when oil passed $20 a barrel, but this did not happen. Brent crude has exceeded this mark since the early 2000s. The government does not plan to collect that money from the oil companies. There are lawsuits between Nigeria, other countries and oil companies. There is leverage in settling lawsuits. The national assembly could soon pass reforms that are widely expected to bolster investment in the industry, and which are also thought to be key to negotiations over the production-sharing contracts.

Source: Adapted from Munshi and Raval (2019).[12]

Discussion Point: Using these parties (Shell and the Nigerian government as negotiators), describe the renegotiation of the joint venture or production-sharing contracts. Current terms are an 80:20 share of the oil in favour of Shell, with the government aiming to move towards a 60 to 40 relationship. Provide an analysis of the context, the conflict situation and whether the involvement of an agency or a third party is necessary. Many solution paths are possible.

EXAMPLE 7.4
CHEMICALS GROUP CLARIANT SUSPENDS SAUDI JOINT VENTURE NEGOTIATIONS

Swiss chemicals company Clariant has suspended negotiations with its key Saudi shareholder, Saudi Basic Industries Corporation, over the creation of a joint venture. This follows Clariant's announcement of challenging first half-year results on the day after its chief executive unexpectedly quit the company.

The Swiss and Saudi companies had been planning to create a joint venture to focus on higher-value speciality chemicals. After months of negotiations they have made the announcement that it is in the best interests of the shareholders of both companies to suspend the negotiations. The former chief executive, Ernesto Occhiello, quit the company after just ten months in the job. The announcement comes after Saudi Aramco agreed to buy Sabic for $69 billion, a company in which Occiello had been a senior manager previously. Unfavourable market conditions were mentioned as the reason for the suspension when the potential partnership had come under scrutiny after the Aramco deal. The suspension of the Saudi joint venture comes during a turbulent period for the Swiss company. It abandoned a plan for a $20 billion merger with Huntsman of the United States in 2017 following opposition from an activist investor group. The activists sold almost a quarter of their stake of the company to Sabic in 2018. The collapse of the Huntsman deal led Clariant to seek another partner that could allow it to achieve targets faster with an increase in profitability. Shares in Clariant have fallen 10 per cent in Zurich, and nearly 40 per cent since early 2018. The divestment of Clairant's pigment business continues. The group has also reported a net loss of SFr101 million (€910,000) and were weighed down by a SFr231 million (€2,080,000) provision for an ongoing competition law investigation by the European Commission.

Source: Adapted from Georgiadis and Raval (2019).[13]

Discussion Point: Position the negotiation context in this case. What are the parties' interests? In order to highlight the negotiation context, consider the stakes and strategies the parties might use as well. Set up the negotiations for the Swiss Clairant and the Saudi Basic Industries Group and use third parties for conflict resolution. Would they need mediators, arbitrators, conciliators or consultants for their negotiations? What would the joint venture negotiations look like if both companies were to use agents? Analyse the negotiation context with the respective parties and identify the relevant strategies and outcomes.

7.4 MULTIPARTY NEGOTIATION: TEAMS

Multiparty negotiations are different to dyad negotiations, since more actors, objectives and styles must be considered; on top of this, various coalitional solutions are an important feature.

What is a *multiparty negotiation*?[14] Multiparty negotiations involve three or more negotiation parties (countries, ministries, companies and their departments) with different goals, leading to trade-offs. For example, the 2016 amendment to the Montreal Protocol on Substances that Deplete the Ozone Layer involved negotiators from over 170 countries, who managed to find a legally binding accord to combat climate change. The deal is aimed at reducing the use of hydrofluorocarbons (HFCs), which is a chemical coolant found in air conditioners and refrigerators. Interestingly, it is often said that the outcome of the multiparty negotiation – held in Kigali, Rwanda – could be even more effective at combatting global warming than the higher-profile global climate change agreement reached in Paris in 2015. The Kigali multiparty negotiation is a compromise between rich and poor nations, and it took seven years to negotiate. Wealthier nations will freeze production of HFCs more quickly than poorer ones. The Kigali negotiations were intense and contentious. Big issues which affect many stakeholders are often multiparty negotiations to take into account the different interests of nations and cultures.

From a negotiation analytical perspective, most groups[15] initiate negotiations with a distributive phase and end them with an integrative phase. This means that at the start of negotiations there is greater conflict due to the efforts made to extract information; once this phase is over, the negotiators then adopt a simple rational approach to find a solution. The transitions between both strategic orientations (integration, distribution) and strategic functions (action, information) are difficult, but it can be said that the first transition is more likely to result in a change of orientation than of function and that negotiators are more likely to change either orientation or function (single transition) than to change both aspects of the negotiation simultaneously (double transition). Negotiators use process and closure strategies to interrupt distributive phases and redirect negotiations to an integrative phase.

Mathematically, there is a way of finding a solution to the multiparty negotiations. To compute the Pareto-optimal solution in multiparty negotiations,[16] the constraint proposal method is used. A neutral coordinator assists decision makers in finding Pareto-optimal solutions so that the elicitation of the decision makers' value functions is not required. The decision makers indicate their most preferred points on different sets of linear constraints. In the approximation to the Pareto frontier, a distributive negotiation among the efficient agreements can be carried out afterwards.

In many settings, multiparty negotiations are very common in international business negotiations. The composition of the teams, the leadership within the negotiating teams and the negotiation processes are matters of careful consideration. The following three issues show the complexity of multiparty negotiations compared to two-party talks:[17]

1. coalition formation,
2. process-management issues,
3. the fluctuating nature of each party's best alternative to a negotiated agreement (BATNA).

Coalitions – the choosing of members: The members in a multiparty negotiation can have difficulties getting heard, and so they try to find allies with similar ideas and by doing so can make demands which are stronger as they are presented by higher numbers of parties. A coalition with parties who share one or more of your goals is an important component in multiparty negotiations. Coalitions are powerful organisational tools that build on strength in numbers in multiparty negotiations. The building of alliances increases leverage without undermining the underlying relationship and allows members of the negotiation to reach across party lines to continue communicating even when it is difficult. Careful planning is important, particularly regarding how and when to meet with potential coalition partners. Before committing to a coalition, it is wise to discuss positions in order to avoid premature alliances. It is important to have sufficient flexibility to be able to move to another group at this stage.

Manage the process: Interactions in multiparty negotiations are more complicated than when there is just one party to deal with. For this reason, appointing a manager will help in organising the group. Putting together an agenda, setting rules, finding consensus among the parties and communicating the agreement to the stakeholders are important items to be dealt with by the manager of a multiparty negotiation. Creating a payoff matrix of the parties and their interests is an idea taken from a game theoretical approach discussed earlier. This will ease the way multiparty negotiations are dealt with among the parties, and the visualisation will bring clarity to the agendas. A payoff matrix[18] for multiparty negotiations can take the form of a spreadsheet that lists the names of the parties in rows, the issues to be discussed in columns, and the parties' priorities on those issues in the cells of the matrix created (Table 7.1). This spreadsheet is useful, since it can be updated during the negotiations and it allows the parties to see what has been achieved and how to proceed.

Table 7.1 Suggestions for payoff matrix for multiparty negotiations

	Negotiation issue				
	Pre-negotiation			Added during talks	
Parties	**Content**	**Sourcing**	**Length**	**Timing**	**Data retention**
HR					
Finance					
Marketing					
Sales					
IT					
Production					
Subsidiary 1					
Subsidiary 2					

Source: Adapted from Mannix (2006).[19]

In large multiparty negotiations it is useful to break into smaller working groups.[20] In these functional groups, preliminary proposals can be developed on elements of the overall agenda and differences can be bridged among members of different coalitions.

Calculate dynamic BATNAs: Like in two-party negotiation, a concrete idea of the BATNA, what will need to be done if a deal fails to materialise, should be articulated. The knowledge of the BATNA helps the party to stand firm in the face of offers that fall short of the goals. Similarly, along with all the above-mentioned items, it is necessary to analyse the BATNA of the other parties and coalitions at the table. Calculating the minimum offer to secure a commitment is relevant in multiparty negotiations. Determining each party's BATNA will be difficult, and sometimes impossible. It will be easier to identify each party's BATNA once discussions have begun, and with the payoff matrix it will be easier to determine.[21]

Example 7.5 provides a case of multiparty negotiations.

EXAMPLE 7.5

MULTIPARTY NEGOTIATIONS: LAWSUIT FILED AGAINST BOLLORÉ GROUP OVER CAMEROON PLANTATIONS – FRENCH INDUSTRIALIST'S FAMILY HOLDING COMPANY HAS STAKE IN AFRICAN PALM OIL GROUP

Sherpa, an organisation advocating for victims of economic crimes and leading a group of non-governmental organisations (NGOs) and unions, has filed a civil lawsuit against French industrialist Vincent Bolloré's company. They urge the group to improve working conditions at its palm oil[22] plantations in Cameroon. The civil lawsuit aims to force the Bolloré Group to comply with the commitments it made in 2013. These commitments are to the local communities and plantation workers of Socapalm, a Cameroonian palm oil company. This protection was supported by ten associations and unions of France, Cameroon, Switzerland and Belgium. The Bolloré Group owns 38.75 per cent of Socfin Group, a Luxembourg holding company, which itself owns a stake in Socapalm. The Socfin Group has a portfolio which focuses on the exploitation of more than 192,000 hectares of tropical palm oil and rubber plantations located in Africa and South East Asia. The lawsuit comes ahead of shareholder meetings for Socfin and the Bolloré Group. The Bolloré Group filed a complaint with the Organisation for Economic Co-operation and Development (OECD). After several months of mediation, the Bolloré Group and Sherpa agreed to put in place an action plan in Cameroon to improve the living and working conditions of the affected communities. Nevertheless, the Bolloré Group dropped this plan in December 2014. Bolloré Group's activities are concentrated across three business lines: transportation and logistics, communication, and electricity storage and solutions. It recorded €23 billion in revenues in 2018. Bolloré Group is also the largest shareholder in global media conglomerate Vivendi, which owns assets including Universal Music Group and Canal Plus.

Source: Adapted from Agnew (2019).[23]

Discussion Point: Set up a multiparty negotiation for the stakeholders in this negotiation scenario. Identify the negotiation parties, the possible strategies, the BATNAs and the coalitions. Highlight the trade-offs and possibilities to circumvent conflict. It might be useful to add negotiation styles from the previous chapter to come up with solutions to the multiparty negotiation scenario. Many solutions are possible. Analyse the multiparty negotiations between the business group, the Sherpa representatives and the Cameroon negotiators and draw a payoff matrix.

7.5 SUMMARY

This chapter deals with having more parties in negotiations than is the case with the dyad situations discussed in previous chapters. The complexity of decision making is increased with each new party that contributes to the negotiation. The agents, third parties and additional parties in multiparty negotiations add different preferences, objectives, styles and expected outcomes to the equation. The examples provided illustrate the different understandings of the parties and various ways of building cooperation and solving conflict.

QUESTIONS

1 What types of third-party negotiations are possible in international business negotiations?
2. How do the roles of agents and third parties differ in international business negotiations?
3. Discuss a case from the news and highlight the different influences the roles of the agent and third party would have had on the outcome.

NOTES

1. Harris, A.W. (1994) Negotiation context: an introductory essay. *Humboldt Journal of International Relations.* **20**(2), 1–25.
2. Harris (1994) ibid.
3. The Economist (2019) Philip Morris and Altria want to merge. 29 August.
4. Mnookin, R. and Susskind, L. (1999) *Negotiating on Behalf of Others: Advice to Lawyers, Business Executives, Sports Agents, Diplomats, Politicians, and Everybody Else.* Negotiation and Dispute Resolution. Thousand Oaks, SAGE.
5. Lax, D.A. and Sebenius, J.K. (1991) Negotiating through an agent. *Journal of Conflict Resolution.* **35**(3), 474–93.
6. Axelrod, R. (1984) *The Evolution of Cooperation.* New York, Basic Books, pp. 178–9.
7. McCall, J.B. (2003) Negotiating sales, export transactions and agency agreements. In: Ghauri, P.N. and Usunier, J.-C. (eds) *International Business Negotiations.* 2nd ed. Oxford, Pergamon/Elsevier, pp. 240–41.
8. Bazerman, M.H., Neale, M.A., Valley, K.L., Zajac, E.J. and Kim, Y.M. (1992) The effect of agents and mediators on the negotiation outcome. *Organizational Behavior and Human Decision Processes.* **53**, 55–73.
9. Goldberg, S.B. (2006) Beyond blame: choosing a mediator, *Negotiation* newsletter, January.
10. PON Staff (2019) Dispute resolution: the advantages of a neutral third-party mediator: shuttle diplomacy in mediation offers benefits to business negotiators seeking dispute resolution. *Program on Negotiation,* 19 March.
11. In the July 2011 issue of *Negotiation Journal*, mediator David Hoffman took a thoughtful look at the role of caucusing in mediation in an article entitled "Mediation and the art of shuttle diplomacy".
12. Munshi, N. and Raval, A. (2019) Nigeria and Royal Dutch Shell begin contract negotiations. *Financial Times*, 26 May.
13. Georgiadis, P. and Raval, A. (2019) Chemicals group Clariant suspends Saudi joint venture plan. *Financial Times*, 25 July.
14. Shonk, K. (2019) Managing a multiparty negotiation: expert advice on handling multiparty negotiation and the complications created by multiple parties. *Program on Negotiation*, 14 March.
15. Olekalns, M., Brett, J.M. and Weingart, L.R. (2003) Phases, transitions and interruptions: modeling processes in multi-party negotiations. *International Journal of Conflict Management.* **14**(3/4), 191–211.
16. Heiskanen, P., Raimo, H.E. and Hämäläinen, P. (2001) Constraint proposal method for computing Pareto solutions in multi-party negotiations. *European Journal of Operations Research.* **133**, 44–61.
17. Mnookin and Susskind (1999) op. cit.
18. Mannix, E. (2006) Three keys to navigating multi-party negotiations. *Negotiation* newsletter, February.
19. Mannix (2006) ibid.
20. Mnookin and Susskind (1999) op cit.
21. Mnookin and Susskind (1999) ibid.
22. The palm oil industry has a devastating impact throughout the world on health, pollution, deforestation and workers' rights, but no action seems to have succeeded so far in shaking up the practices of agribusiness giants.
23. Agnew, H. (2019) Activists file lawsuit against Bolloré Group. *Financial Times*, 27 May.

FURTHER READING

Bazerman, M.H., Neale, M.A., Valley, K.L., Zajac, E.J. and Kim, Y.M. (1992) The effect of agents and mediators on the negotiation outcome. *Organizational Behavior and Human Decision Processes*. **53**, 55–73.

Harris, A.W. (1994) Negotiation context: an introductory essay. *Humboldt Journal of International Relations*. **20**(2), 1–25.

Lax, D.A. and Sebenius, J.K. (1991) Negotiating through an agent. *Journal of Conflict Resolution*. **35**(3), 474–93.

8
The process of international business negotiations

Negotiating is a process whereby two or more parties who have their own individual objectives, demands and preferred outcomes discuss these in order to reach an agreement that satisfies the largest possible proportion of their mutual requirements. In all business relationships, including international business relationships, parties negotiate in the belief they are able to influence the process in such a way that they can get a better deal than simply accepting or rejecting what the other party is offering. International business negotiation is thus a voluntary process of reciprocity where both parties modify their own offers and expectations in order to converge on an outcome that satisfies both parties. The process of international business negotiation can be explained by dividing it up into stages and using a framework to identify the sets of variables and rationales that influence the process and the negotiated outcomes. In this chapter, we detail the stages of the negotiation process and introduce the negotiation framework. The negotiations are influenced by two sets of rationales: culture and strategy. We discussed the influence of culture on negotiations and communication in detail in Chapters 4 and 5.

The chapter begins by discussing the stages of the negotiation process. This is then followed by a detailed explanation of the international business negotiation framework before the chapter concludes by identifying key considerations when preparing for and managing the international business negotiation process.

8.1 THE STAGES OF THE NEGOTIATION PROCESS

The process of international business negotiations is divided into three separate stages, namely the pre-negotiation stage, the face-to-face negotiation stage and the post-negotiation stage.[1] Each stage represents a specific part of the negotiation process and includes all the communication that takes place and all the actions that the parties take for that specific part of the process. Once the objective of the stage is achieved, the parties move on to the next stage. Or in the case where the parties decide that further negotiations will not achieve their goals, they may abandon the process.

8.1.1 Stage I: pre-negotiation

Pre-negotiation stage: the first stage of the process where initial contact is made between parties to show interest in doing business together.

The *pre-negotiation stage* begins when the parties first make contact with one another and show an interest in doing business together. During this stage, the parties attempt to share some initial information that would act as the background for the negotiations in the next stage. Once the parties have agreed to have further discussions about the business venture, they proceed to collect as much information as they can about each other. This includes information about the other company's management, their current business partners, the size and positioning of the organisation in the industry, and potentially the individuals with whom they may negotiate.

The initial information helps the parties determine their relative power relationship and gives them the opportunity to seek any similarities between the organisations or the negotiators that could potentially assist them in breaking the ice when they ultimately meet. Since negotiations are undertaken to discuss issues and resolve problems that the initial proposals provided by the two sides may have raised, the problem must be defined jointly by the parties as it will determine and influence the direction of the negotiation process. In particular, the objectives and aims of the parties for the negotiations can be discussed during this stage as this can help achieve a favourable problem-solving situation.

The parties examine each other's position, and informal meetings are held to determine whether they should proceed to the next stage of the negotiation process. Failure at this stage can occur if the parties sense that the level of conflict may outweigh the level of cooperation between them or if the benefits from pursuing the business relationship would not meet their expectations. Therefore, the parties should try to cooperate honestly, examine whether achieving the objectives of both sides is a realistic expectation and identify what the obstacles are and how they will be addressed in order to achieve the objectives. One way to facilitate the cooperation between parties at this early stage is to start building interpersonal relations in an attempt to develop trust and goodwill. This is when the initial research about the management team of the other party can be useful, as negotiators will seek a shared interest or some commonality (perhaps a shared or similar experience, similar education background or professional culture) that can help act as a building block for the interpersonal relation and an ice-breaker for the first meeting.

A common expectation of the pre-negotiation stage is that the communication process is limited to written initial proposals or verbal communication through telephones. However, if deemed necessary, firms can invite individuals from the other party to visit their premises for informal meetings. Depending on the scale of the project, these visits may involve travelling to another country. The primary objective is to create goodwill and trust, which can help the parties create an environment that is conducive for formal negotiations.

8.1.2 Stage II: face-to-face negotiation

Face-to-face negotiation stage: when the parties meet to discuss the details of the proposed deal and to resolve disagreements and problems.

Once the parties move to the *face-to-face negotiation stage*, they send a signal suggesting that they can work together to find a solution to a joint problem. Both parties enter the negotiation process with their own objectives and goals and may have conflicting expectations for the outcome. As we discussed in Chapter 4, cultures have different expectations about the use of time. During this stage, it is important to understand what the other party's expectations are for the initial meetings. Will the emphasis in the first few meetings be on getting to know each other better and building interpersonal relations to develop trust, or will the parties move directly to discussing the task-related issues and the initially proposed offers made by the parties? It is challenging for parties to comprehend or adjust to each other's culture or traditions, but it is essential to be aware that these differences exist. In many emerging markets, social contacts developed between parties are far more significant than the technical and economic specifications. Negotiators from these countries take their time, avoid extremes, and are very careful not to cause offence or use strong words; and the expectation is the other party will follow suit.

The ability to control the negotiation process is linked to the relative power of the parties. The party with higher power would tend to set the agenda of the meeting and expect the other side to conform to their norms and expectations regarding the negotiation process and would also tend to make fewer concessions. However, to ensure that the level of cooperation is maintained, the negotiating parties should approach the face-to-face interaction with an open mind and show flexibility by having several feasible alternatives to how they would address the key concerns they have. These alternatives are discussed by the parties with the aim of finding some common ground and agreeing upon an outcome that is deemed to be mutually beneficial.

The start of the negotiation process and the topics to be discussed depend on the preferences of the negotiators. Some negotiators prefer to start negotiations by discussing and agreeing on the broad principles for the relationship. Another way to ensure success at this stage is to discuss conflicting issues as well as those of common interest. In particular, an initial discussion on items of common interest can create an atmosphere of cooperation between parties. The choice of strategy depends upon the customer or supplier with whom one is negotiating. It is helpful to anticipate the other party's strategy as early as possible and then choose a strategy to match or complement it.

8.1.3 Stage III: post-negotiation

Post-negotiation stage: the final stage where the final agreement between the parties is converted into a formal contract.

Once the parties have reached an agreement on the terms of the final proposal, they move to the *post-negotiation stage*. At this stage, all terms have been agreed, and the contract is being drawn up and is ready to be signed.[2] However, managing to reach the post-negotiation stage does not guarantee a successful outcome, and negotiations can break down even at this final stage. There are a number of reasons why failure could occur. If the negotiating parties are too eager to get to a deal and do not spend enough time discussing and agreeing the operational details, then many of these issues can be raised as concerns in the post-negotiation stage. Experienced negotiators realise that the agreement reached during the face-to-face negotiations needs to be carefully discussed and agreed upon so that when translated into a formal written contract there are fewer concerns. In particular, if the contextual background of the negotiating parties differs, then a considerable amount of time may be required to choose the wordings for the contract that convey the values and meanings that are acceptable to all the parties.

A related issue that can be encountered in this stage is linked to the issue of noise in communication, which we covered in Chapter 5. The negotiating parties may have agreed to what they believed are the terms, but when the contracts are drawn up by the legal departments/advisers, the terms may not seem accurate. The lawyers or experts who draw up the contracts share the same professional culture, and there is less ambiguity in the messages sent through the formal agreements. However, the negotiators may not have the tools to reduce the noise during the communication process, and the message may have become distorted and incorrectly decoded by the parties. At this stage, the parties may be required to return to the face-to-face negotiation stage to discuss the outstanding terms and conditions further. One way of addressing this concern would be through the use of the feedback loop. A technically accomplished negotiator will summarise and test the understanding of the other party by asking questions to reaffirm the agreement after each session. Example 8.1 highlights how a long-term deal between Starbucks and Kraft ended in an acrimonious dispute.

EXAMPLE 8.1
THE STARBUCKS-KRAFT AGREEMENT (AND DISAGREEMENT)

In 1998, Kraft began marketing and distributing bags of Starbucks coffee in supermarkets. The deal was seen as a way for Starbucks to start retailing their coffee to their existing and potentially new consumers through supermarkets, where Kraft had the supply chain connections and networks to maximise the distribution.

With increased competition from Nespresso and consumer preference for single-serve coffee pods, Starbucks felt it had to respond. The deal with Kraft limited Starbucks to only producing pods that worked in Kraft's Tassimo machines. In 2010, Starbucks offered Kraft $750 million to end their negotiated agreement, which Kraft declined. Despite the refusal, Starbucks broke the agreement and Kraft sought arbitration over the dispute. After a three-year dispute resolution process, the arbitrator ruled in favour of Kraft, and Starbucks was ordered to pay $2.76 billion for ending the agreement early.

This case highlights a number of issues. The initial negotiations to cooperate may have been held in the spirit of cooperation, but conflict is inherent in such relations. Had the companies put in provisions to renegotiate their deal at certain times, this dispute could have been resolved more amicably.

Sources: Adapted from Baertlein (2013);[3] and Shonk (2019).[4]

Discussion Point: Do you believe that the conflict between the parties could have been resolved without an arbitrator?

8.2 A FRAMEWORK FOR INTERNATIONAL BUSINESS NEGOTIATION

The general framework for analysing international business negotiations is composed of three sets of variables: background factors, atmosphere and process. It is then influenced by two sets of rationales: culture and strategy. Having covered the process of negotiation in detail, this section explores the variables in the background factors and the atmosphere. The international business negotiation framework is presented in Figure 8.1. We only provide a brief overview of the two sets of rationales here as they are covered in detail in Chapters 4, 5 and 9.

8.2.1 Atmosphere in international business negotiations

The atmosphere during the negotiations is linked with the relationship between the parties and interacts with the negotiation process at each stage. Atmosphere relates to how the parties regard one another, how they respond to each other's behaviour and how the properties of the process are dealt with. Different characteristics of the atmosphere can dominate from process to process. These characteristics are *conflict/cooperation*, *power/dependence* and *expectations*.

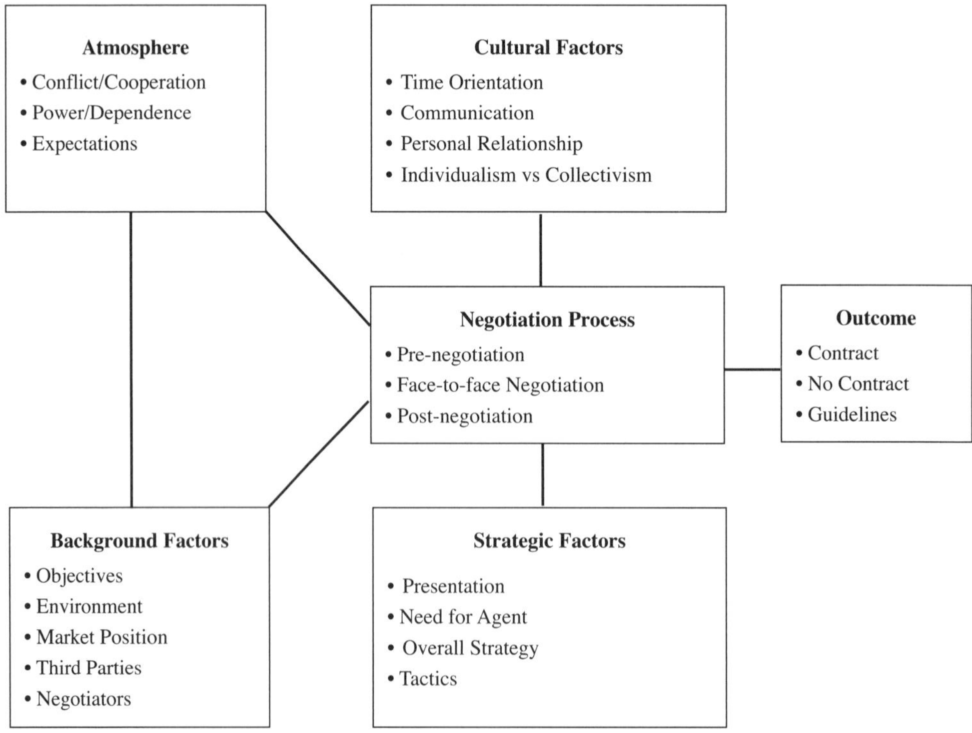

Source: Adapted from Ghauri (2003).[5]

Figure 8.1 The process of international business negotiation

The existence of both *conflict* and *cooperation* is central to international business negotiations. A common mistake made by inexperienced negotiators is to assume that any conflict during the negotiation process would mean the end of the deal. Both conflict and cooperation are the basis on which negotiations are held. If there is no level of cooperation observed in the first stage, then there is no reason to negotiate any further. And if there is no disagreement or conflicting interests, then again there is no need for negotiations as there are no issues to resolve. It is the level of conflict and cooperation that the parties need to control during the negotiation process to ensure a positive outcome.

There are a number of factors that influence the level of conflict/cooperation. If the negotiations are being held for the first time to establish a relationship, then the level of cooperation would be higher. But if the negotiations are being held to discuss an existing relationship, the level of conflict may be higher. Similarly, a higher level of cooperation is observed in the pre-negotiation stage and the chances of conflict increase during the face-to-face negotiations. Due to the various cultural and language differences that we covered previously, parties may perceive a higher level of conflict than what exists in the relationship, and this can affect the pace of the negotiations.

The *power/dependence* relation is another characteristic found in all negotiations. It is determined by how much one party depends on the other, and the availability of viable alternatives. In essence, power is determined by how much one party depends on the other. On account of this dependence, it is essential that both parties have an element of power and influence over the behaviour and actions of the other and are capable of exercising this efficiently. In most relationships one party is relatively more powerful than the other. Also, in most relationships the dependent party is aware of this imbalance but believes the other party will not exploit his/her power position.

This power is a property of the relationship and not an attribute of an actor. In fact, it is closely related to dependence. Therefore, the power relationship is balanced if both parties perceive equal power. The power relationship is unbalanced if one party perceives it is more powerful than the other, or if one party is highly dependent on the other (see Example 8.2).

The final element that contributes to the atmosphere variable concerns the types of expectations the negotiating parties have for the process. There are *short-term expectations* regarding prospects for the present deal, and there are *long-term expectations* regarding the possibilities and values of future business. Negotiators are more likely to make concessions during the negotiations if there is an expectation of a long-term recurring business opportunity. However, if the parties do not see any prospects for business beyond the current deal, then they may be more rigid in their approach to the negotiation process. The presence of expectations is therefore essential for the parties to continue negotiating. In other words, the higher the expectations of a deal or future deals, the more inclined the parties are to keep on negotiating and be flexible.

8.2.2 Background factors

The background factors are a set of variables that form and structure the context of a negotiation; as well as influencing the negotiation process itself, they influence the atmosphere of

EXAMPLE 8.2
WALMART: THE NON-NEGOTIABLE PARTNER

Walmart is the world's largest retailer and has built a strong empire based on its emphasis on keeping cost down and offering everyday low prices for its consumers. The company has expanded internationally, with a presence in 26 countries outside the United States. With over $500 billion in revenues, the company does not see the need to negotiate its terms of doing business. Suppliers who want to work with Walmart need to meet the company's objective of reducing costs and provide the lowest possible price for the quality expected by the organisation. The unbalanced power/dependency relationship that Walmart enjoys means that when the company's revenues fall, Walmart asks its suppliers to slash costs. The suppliers in turn have to find innovative ways to reduce their costs, knowing full well that failure to meet the terms would result in the termination of the agreement as a supplier.

Sources: Adapted from Hanna (2008);[6] and Roberts (2015).[7]

Discussion Point: Which other organisations do you believe have the market power to do deals without negotiating the terms? What risks (if any) do you see of deals where a party does not engage in any negotiations?

the negotiation. The effect of different variables on the process and its different stages varies in intensity. One of these variables may influence one stage positively and another negatively. A positive influence means that the process saves time and continues smoothly, while a negative influence causes delay and obstacles. Negotiation background factors include (1) objectives, (2) environment, (3) market position, (4) third parties and (5) negotiators.

1. *Objectives* refer to the final outcomes of the negotiations that the parties hope to achieve. These outcomes can be *common*, *conflicting* or *complementary*. The common interest between the parties is to have a successful transaction, and that is the reason the parties are negotiating. The conflict in the objectives occurs as the parties attempt to maximise their benefit, which can be at the cost of the other party's interest. Complementary objectives refer to the benefits that negotiating parties can gain as a result of the agreement. For example, when negotiating a joint venture, the motivation for one party may be to learn from the venture partner and gain technology, whereas the other party may be looking at gaining local market knowledge and supply chain access that they may be unable to get if they attempted to enter the market by themselves. Hence, the joint venture can complement the interests of the parties.
2. The *environment* consists of the political, social and structural factors relevant to both negotiating parties. Differences between the parties in respect to their environment often hinder the negotiation process in international business. For example, a publicly listed company from Germany may find negotiations with a French state-owned enterprise (SOE) to be bureaucratic. The differences in such a negotiation would be highlighted further in the expected outcomes. While commercial firms tend to look at return on assets and profitability as measures of success, for SOEs the attainment of the strategic goal set by the state would be of the highest priority. Changes in the

environment can be a source of disruption for organisations. A recent example of such an event is Brexit, where the United Kingdom has been deliberating its withdrawal from the European Union. We highlight this issue in Example 8.3.

EXAMPLE 8.3
BREXIT AND THE UK ECONOMY

On 23 June 2016, a referendum was held to decide whether the United Kingdom (UK) would remain as part of the European Union (EU) or leave and withdraw its membership. The referendum favoured the decision to withdraw from the EU, an act that came to be known as Brexit (a combination of the terms Britain and exit). Over the next three years the British government and the EU held multiple rounds of negotiations without reaching a conclusive outcome. This delay in Brexit was a source of concern for UK firms, who found it difficult to initiate new business ventures and conclude existing deals due to the uncertainty surrounding the post-Brexit operating environment. More than half the UK business executives surveyed identified Brexit among the top-three sources of uncertainty.

UK-based firms like the Indian-owned Jaguar Land Rover began shutting their manufacturing sites in the country due to falling sales, and a number of other firms started considering relocation to countries in the EU to continue receiving the benefits associated with operating in a member state. The Brexit example shows how the changes in the environment can affect the negotiation and business practices of organisations.

Sources: Adapted from Bloom et al. (2019);[8] Kollewe (2019);[9] and Ott and Ghauri (2019).[10]

The economic factors of a country, such as currency stability, level of unemployment and inflation, can also influence the bargaining power of the parties and, therefore, the negotiation process. If the outlook of a country's economy is weak, then the party from that country would be expected to give more concessions to secure a deal. We highlight this issue in Example 8.4.

3. The respective *market position* of the parties is a central factor influencing the negotiation process and bargaining power. The number of buyers and sellers in the market determines the number of alternatives available to each party, which, in turn, affects the amount of pressure imposed by its counterpart within the market. If a party has a monopoly in the market or industry, they will have much higher bargaining power when dealing with multiple sellers.
4. Most international business negotiations involve *third parties*. The third parties are the players other than the buyers and sellers and include groups and individuals such as governments, shareholders, labour unions, special interest groups, employees, consultants, subcontractors and agents. These parties may influence the negotiation process as they seek to protect their interests and objectives. Such a situation occurred when General Motors attempted to acquire Daewoo motors. Despite the support of the South Korean government, the deal was affected by the protests from the Daewoo workers' union (see Example 8.5).

EXAMPLE 8.4
THE GLOBAL FINANCIAL CRISIS 2008-09 AND THE CHINESE MANUFACTURING SECTOR

Due to China's domination of the global manufacturing sector, it is sometimes referred to as the World's Factory. This also means that the country's economy can be affected by external events. Such a situation occurred in the year 2008, when the global financial crisis affected many major economies, including those in Europe and North America. At that time, manufacturing accounted for 34 per cent of China's economy and manufacturing exports fell sharply. Many of the negotiated agreements with buyers in Western Europe and the United States could not be completed.

However, Chinese companies were able to find other buyers for their products and the Chinese economy still recorded an impressive 9 per cent growth. The example of Chinese manufacturing highlights the importance of being prepared for eventualities or "chance" events and having alternatives or a Plan B to continue operations.

Sources: Adapted from Priestley (2010);[11] and PWC (2015).[12]

EXAMPLE 8.5
GM-DAEWOO MOTORS NEGOTIATIONS

The 1997 Asian financial crisis slowed down the economies of many of the so-called Asian Tigers (countries in Asia that were growing at a fast rate). The South Korea model of growth had been led by large conglomerates such as Daewoo and Samsung. In the aftermath of the Asian financial crisis, companies like Daewoo were unable to sustain their diversified business activities. Daewoo, with the support of the South Korean government, sought to sell off the assets of their car manufacturing arm, Daewoo Motors. In November 2000, Daewoo entered receivership with $15 billion in debts.

General Motors (GM) showed an interest in acquiring the assets of Daewoo Motors and entered an initial bid in May 2001. The Korean car market was the second largest in Asia at the time and GM was keen to break into the market. The company had previously sold its 50 per cent stake in Daewoo in 1992 as a result of labour disputes.

Within a week of the bid being put in by GM, which was valued at up to $2 billion, Daewoo Motors' labour union started protesting against future restructuring and job losses. These protests were at times violent, and industry experts warned that GM may withdraw its bid. The company decided to strike a deal by reducing the amount of its bid and in exchange rehired staff that had been made redundant by Daewoo. Finally, in April 2002, the acquisition of Daewoo Motors by GM was completed. The case highlights the importance of flexibility and the role of third parties in the negotiation process.

Sources: Adapted from CNN (2001);[13] Sang-Hun (2006);[14] and Solomon (2001).[15]

Discussion Point: Do you believe GM and Daewoo underestimated the influence of the labour union on the negotiation process? How would you describe the outcome of the negotiations from the perspective of GM, Daewoo and the labour union?

Often, governments are involved and try to influence the buyers towards complementary objectives, such as infrastructure investments, employment opportunities, foreign exchange considerations and any other prospective relationship between the countries involved. However, governments can also intervene in the negotiations if they feel that the deal would be harmful to the interests of the domestic firms or consumers. For example, some industries are protected by national governments, and many proposed international mergers and alliances are blocked on the premise that they would create monopolies and harm competition (see Example 8.6).

EXAMPLE 8.6
PROTECTING THE AVIATION INDUSTRY

The increase in cross-border activities over the last four decades is in part credited to the opening up of new markets and improvements in the ease of doing business internationally. These developments have encouraged international alliances and merger and acquisition (M&A) activities. The global aviation industry is no exception, with major airlines joining forces as part of global alliances, such as Star Alliance and Oneworld, to provide better and flexible options for their customers to connect globally. Passengers today have more options to choose from when travelling internationally, and better connections mean that large distances are covered much faster. But while national governments are generally supportive of alliances, they tend to be less enthusiastic about M&As.

There are many instances in the global aviation industry where governments have blocked proposed M&As in the sector. For example, in 2013, the US Justice Department and US state attorneys general challenged a proposed merger between US Airways Group Inc. and AMR Corporation, the parent company of American Airlines. The government authorities feared that such a merger, which would have created the world's largest airline, would reduce competition and passengers would be forced into paying higher airfares and receiving less service.

For organisations, such actions by the government are a reminder of the power the institutions have, and the need to better engage with them in the initial stages of discussions between the parties.

Sources: Adapted from CBS News (2013);[16] and Mouawad (2013).[17]

Discussion Point: What arbitration options are available for organisations when national governments are involved in the negotiations?

5. And finally, as discussed earlier, the *negotiators* themselves influence the negotiation process due to their own experience and negotiating skills. Negotiators operate within two limits. First, they act to increase common interests and to expand cooperation among the parties. Second, they serve to maximise their own benefits and to ensure an agreement that is valuable to themselves. Such incidents are more observable in situations where an agent negotiates on behalf of the organisation.

The professional background and the personality of a negotiator also has an important role, mainly when information about the other party is in short supply and the negotiations are highly pressurised. A desirable personality for a negotiator is one that follows active listening, can show empathy, and can approach strangers with ease and confidence. However, the skills of negotiators are related to different objectives and motivations, pertaining to different people and professions. Negotiators with a technical background may be predisposed to placing more emphasis on technical issues, while those with a commercial history might have a more holistic approach and consider other items to be of equal or greater import.

8.2.3 Cultural and strategic variables that influence the negotiation process

As explained earlier, the face-to-face negotiation stage is influenced by cultural and strategic variables.[18] These variables influence both the process and the outcome of the negotiations. In particular, how *time* is used, a culture's preference for *individualism or collectivism*, the *patterns of communication* used and the *emphasis on personal relations* are issues that influence the process.

The strategic variables relating to the way *presentations* are made, the *strategic approach* of the negotiators, the *decision-making process* during the negotiations and the *use of agents or third parties* to conduct negotiations are issues that firms and organisations need to take into consideration when developing their strategy. We cover these variables in Chapter 9.

8.3 PLANNING AND MANAGING NEGOTIATIONS

A sound understanding of the stages and the variables that influence the negotiation process provides the context negotiators needs to analyse and understand international business negotiations. But how does one prepare for negotiations and manage the activities to ensure that a favourable outcome can be achieved for all parties involved? It all starts with the individual negotiators, who have to plan for the process. The best approach to take is to identify the objectives and outcomes that the parties hope to achieve through negotiations. Any attempts to achieve the goals through deceitful tactics, intimidation or fear is bound to fail in the end and can harm the reputation of the organisation and the individual negotiators.

Negotiators have to decide whether a deal can be structured that resolves the problem that the parties have to their mutual advantage. Such a deal requires patience, flexibility and clear lines of communication. If a deal cannot be achieved, then having no deal is better than having a bad deal. A bad deal cannot be sustained for long and would result in enormous problems. Experienced negotiators understand the importance of having realistic targets and do not chase after unrealistic goals.[19]

Previously, the ability to negotiate was considered to be an instinctive quality that individuals possess. But it is now regarded as a technique and the art of negotiation can be learned through experimental studies, empirical observations and sharing of knowledge by experienced negotiators. We discuss next how each stage of negotiations can be planned and managed.

8.3.1 Planning and managing negotiations Stage I: pre-negotiation

No matter how skilled and experienced a negotiator is, or how strong the market position and relative power of the organisation is, these attributes cannot overcome the shortcomings of poor preparation. With a problem-solving approach, this becomes even more important as both parties attempt to work together to do business with each other. In spite of this cooperative behaviour, negotiations involve trade-offs between individual and joint interests. Numerous authors have, therefore, stressed the importance of preparation and planning for negotiation.[20]

Identify the contents of the deal

All negotiations inherently have to deal with the issue of which party maximises their benefit. An early analysis of the objectives of each party and what they want to achieve as a maximum or minimum and what you want to achieve is necessary at this stage. Maximum and minimum should be established as illustrated in Figure 8.2. Scenarios A, B and C in the figure show visually different situations where there are areas for agreement. In the first scenario, scenario A, there is only a small overlap between the buyer's minimum outcome and the seller's minimum outcome. Both parties will have to work hard in order to reach a settlement and there may be many offers and counteroffers, but both sides can gain if they cooperate and are ready to graft. Scenario B shows a situation where there is much larger overlap between the buyer's and seller's minimum outcome. Both parties will not have to work too hard to reach a settlement, and thus the buyer and seller can negotiate comfortable in the knowledge that cooperating will be easy. In the final scenario, scenario C, there is no overlap between the buyer's and seller's minimum acceptable outcome. In this instance it is highly unlikely the two parties will reach a settlement, no matter how hard they try, as there is simply no intersection between the demands of the two parties.

Comparing one's own strengths and weaknesses to that of the other party is important. In international business negotiations, the other party does not just include the buyer or the party you are negotiating with, but also other competitors who have an interest in the same business. In most cases, a party's arguments or preferences are influenced by the offers their direct competitors have made. It has been known for negotiators to use professional investigators in order to acquire information on the other parties and to discover their weaknesses. In 1997 GM was paid $100 million by Volkswagen AG to settle a corporate espionage case.[21] More recently, Hilton Worldwide Inc. paid $75 million to Starwood Hotels and Resorts as part of a settlement agreement in a corporate espionage suit. A 1999 survey by the American Society for Industrial Security and PricewaterhouseCoopers estimated that Fortune 1000 companies had lost more than $45 billion from the theft of trade secrets; others however have estimated the cost at closer to $100 billion.[22] The information required to prepare and plan for negotiation should not be obtained through such unethical methods. It is relatively easy to acquire sufficient information from the annual accounts of the firms and through talking to their executives, customers and suppliers.

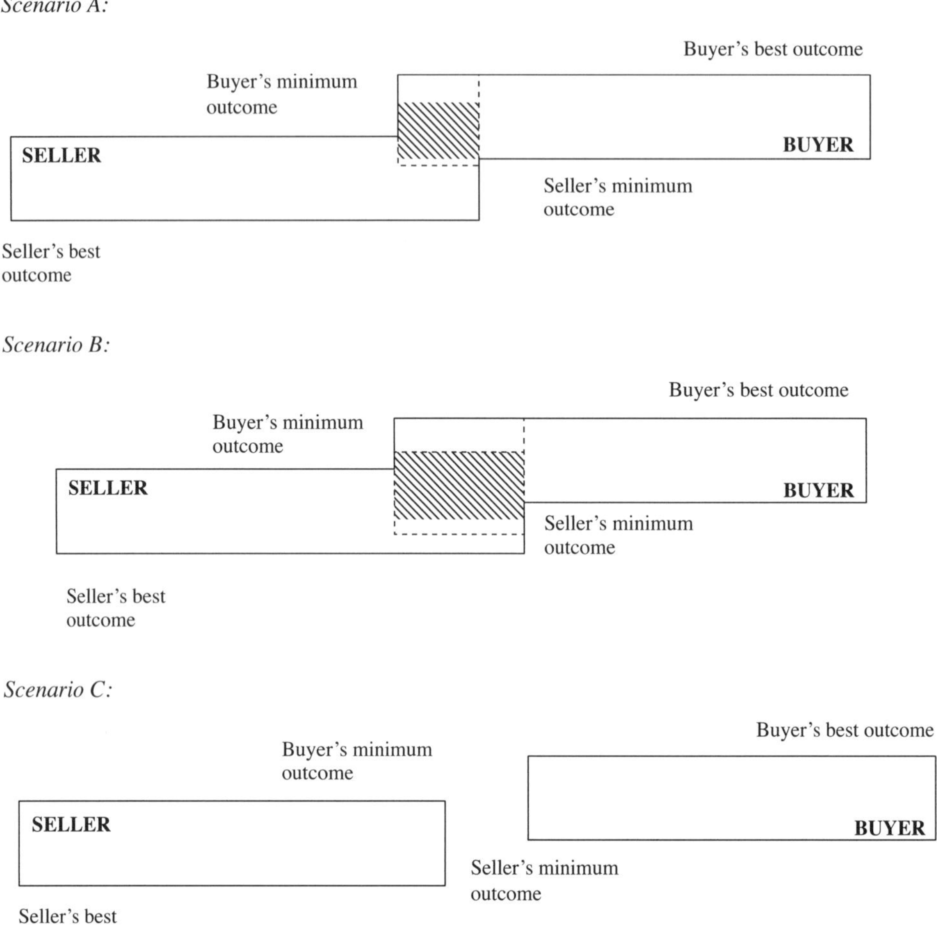

Figure 8.2 Initial analysis for negotiation

Create alternatives

An important aspect of the preparation process is to ensure that alternative options are created. There are several strategies by which the seller can pre-empt competitors, for example offering credit to the buyer, price reductions or long guarantee periods. Sellers must also allow for alternative solutions to conflicting issues. Question one's own position: "What if they do not accept this … ?"

Quite often, Western negotiators believe they have only three options: (1) persuasion, (2) threat or (3) concession. In fact, there are many alternative solutions to a problem. Different issues can be combined to produce numerous alternatives. If the customer demands a 5 per cent concession on the price, the other party can ask the customer to pay cash instead of the one-year credit proposed. In one case, the buyer demanded a 5 per cent concession on the contract price after everything else had been agreed upon. The seller instead proposed that he was willing to give a 10 per cent rebate on all the spare parts to be bought by the buyer during the next three years. This offer was accepted gladly by the buyer. One way of creating alternatives is to judge each conflicting issue based on the following scale: our ideal position–their ideal position. Here we should look for overlaps: is there any overlap of our and their position? If not, how can we create an overlap? What can be their minimum acceptable position? What is our minimum acceptable position? Can we move from there – perhaps give up on this issue and gain in another one which is not so sensitive to the other party but is equally important to us?

Identify yourself with the other party

It is important for parties to understand each other's position as this will help in trying to interpret and anticipate the other side's reactions to arguments. It is also suggested that attentively listening to what the other party has to say is critical to the success of the negotiation process. However, it is important to focus not just on what is being said, but also how it is said; that is, one should read between the lines.

Make the message appropriate

The other party must adjust the information exchanged for easy comprehension. Technical specifications and other material should be provided in the local language. Not only does this facilitate effective communication, but it also demonstrates respect for the local language and environment.

The problems of perception and language barriers often cause difficulties in the negotiation process. This is frustrating and places an added burden on all parties involved in the negotiating process. Different cultures interpret messages differently. An octopus is said to have several arms in the United States. It is said to have several legs in Japan. In Sweden, "next Sunday" does not mean the coming Sunday but the Sunday after. In India, "next Sunday" means the coming Sunday. "Nice weather" means sunshine in Europe. "Nice weather" means cloudy or rainy weather in Africa and many Asian countries. It is important that negotiators adopt appropriate behaviour for each negotiation. The chosen arguments should be tailored to the particular customer. One standard argument cannot be used throughout the world. Barriers to communication also arise from real or perceived differences in expectations, which create conflict instead of cooperation between parties.

In cross-cultural negotiations, non-verbal communication, in particular in the expression of emotions and the attitude of a negotiator towards the other party, is sometimes more important than the spoken language. Effective communication and understanding of people will assist you in adjusting your arguments to the moods and expectations of the other party. Negotiators may continue to hold out, not because the proposal from the other side is unacceptable, but because they want to avoid feelings of surrender. Sometimes simple rephrasing of the proposal or a different approach to the presentation can alleviate the problem.[23]

Accumulate relative power

Negotiators can determine who has the relative power advantage by gathering information about the other party, considering each party's position and developing different alternatives.

They can try to build their own relative power by developing arguments against the elements of power and improving their own position. In the negotiation process, this kind of power may be increased by repeatedly mentioning the weak points of the other party. The uncertainty regarding infrastructure and exchange rates must be handled here. Parties can agree on adjustments in the event of exchange rate variations. The party with greater information automatically acquires more power. The negotiator may have to work as a detective to ascertain the buyer's needs, his strong and weak points, and the strong and weak points of competitors. By being active in the negotiation process, an experienced negotiator can build up information in order to gain relative power. This can be done by asking the other party questions. It can also be done by giving conditional answers such as "If you agree to pay cash … then we can consider looking at our price", or "What if we agree to pay cash, perhaps then you can lower the price by 5 per cent?"

8.3.2 Planning and managing Stage II: the face-to-face negotiations

Who within the firm should negotiate?

A difficult question arises regarding who should conduct negotiations whenever a deal is to be made in a new market. Who is the most appropriate person to hammer out a particular deal? In fact, persons involved in international business negotiation can do more harm than good if they lack an integrated knowledge of their own firm and the objective of the deal. Whoever is selected for negotiations must have a good grasp of the deal's implications. This is especially true when long-term relationships are being discussed. One way to minimise this risk is to appoint a negotiation team, where the key members are selected from different departments.

Expendable person

Negotiating teams have to ensure that the people who negotiate on their behalf are expendable. The organisation's interest and the best outcomes are the primary concern, and in some instances this means replacing an individual to break a deadlock. This discussion gives rise to another question: from which level should the executives for the negotiations be chosen? In most countries, parties expect to negotiate with members of equal status. The managing director from one side expects to negotiate with his counterpart. It is advisable that firms match like with like.

Individuals versus teams

Parties need to consider not only who should represent the company but also the number of negotiators, that is, whether one goes for individual or team negotiations. Team negotiation affords marketers the opportunity to benefit from the advice and guidance of many participants. The choice of individual versus team depends on many factors, including the culture of the negotiating parties.

What makes a good negotiator?

A number of studies identify the characteristics of a good negotiator. Ikle defined a good negotiator as one having a "quick mind but unlimited patience, know how to dissemble without being a liar, inspire trust without trusting others, be modest but assertive, charm others without succumbing to their charm, and possess plenty of money and a beautiful wife while remaining indifferent to all temptations of riches and women."[24] This illustrates that a negotiator has a difficult task, that s/he must give the impression of being truthful and trustworthy. Also, that s/he demonstrates integrity. A marketer's personality and social behaviour are of equal importance to social contacts and formal negotiation in many emerging countries.

Depending upon their behaviour, negotiators are often grouped into different categories, such as bullies, avoiders or acceptors. Bullies want to threaten, push, demand or attack. Avoiders like to avoid conflicting situations and hide in fear of making a wrong decision or being held responsible. They will normally refer to their superiors for a final decision: "I have to call my head office ..." Acceptors always give a very positive answer and say "Yes" to almost anything, which makes it difficult to realise which "Yes" is "Yes" and which "Yes" is "Maybe", and whether they will be able to deliver what they are promising or not. The best way to handle these behaviour types is to first identify them and then confront them by drawing a limit, helping them feel safe and by asking them how and when they would be able to do what they are promising.

Patience

The complexity of the negotiation process means that it can be difficult for negotiators to establish who is the negotiating party and who has the final authority. One of the characteristics of a good negotiator is the ability to discover the timetable of the other party and allow plenty of time for the negotiation process. It is usually not feasible to expect to fly to a distant country, wrap things up and be home again in a week. Nor is it reasonable to coerce a party that is not ready to reach a decision. Negotiations with emerging market customers take a long time! Patience and time are the greatest assets a negotiator can have while negotiating with customers from these markets.

8.3.3 Planning and managing Stage III: post-negotiation

What is a good outcome?

A good agreement is one which leads to successful implementation. There are numerous instances where firms after concluding a negotiation have found themselves in difficulty because they have been unable to implement the contract conditions of a particular deal. In such cases, no agreement would have been a better negotiation outcome for the firm than the deal they agreed. A good outcome should benefit both parties symmetrically; it should not make one party feel as though it has a less advantageous contract than the other. Sometimes negotiators want to avoid specifying certain issues and deliberately want to build ambiguity into the arrangement. It is important to understand that ambiguity can lead to reopening of the conflict later on, in the implementation stage. On the other hand, if negotiators want to specify such issues explicitly, the negotiation process might be prolonged. Insistence on issues being unequivocally detailed may even prevent an agreement being reached. Thus, ambiguity is sometimes unintentional, whereas, on other occasions, it is intentionally deployed in order to speed up the process or to give the impression that a particular issue needs to be renegotiated.[25] Where possible there should be absolute clarity; ambiguous language and vague phrases open to a number of possible interpretations should be avoided at all costs.

It is normally considered that a good business deal is one that provides financial gains. But what were the objectives of the firm when it decided to enter into negotiations? Was it the present deal that was most important or was the future business opportunities? The outcome must be related to the firm's objectives. If the objectives have been met, then it is a good outcome. A successful negotiation is not a question of "win-lose" but a problem-solving approach to a "win-win" outcome.

Finally, negotiators should be aware that the main function of a contract is to avoid misunderstandings and circumvent problems in the future. The agreement should be the basis for the development of a relationship. As such, the agreement signed needs to be flexible enough to deal with either expected or unexpected future changes. The language and terminology used in the contract must be simple and clear. It should not be necessary to seek legal counsel every time the contract is consulted. Rather, good contracts should be documents that can be referred to regularly in order to provide guidance on how difficulties or "grey areas" can be overcome.

8.4 SUMMARY

In this chapter, we focused on the negotiation process and highlighted the three stages within it. The atmosphere and background factors that influence the process were presented in the negotiation framework. Although most research on negotiations tends to focus on the face-to-face negotiation stage, the other stages are equally important. The pre-negotiation stage lays the groundwork for the negotiations that are to follow. The initial exchange of proposals and information gathering help determine the bargaining power of the parties and the objectives they have for the negotiations.

The post-negotiation stage too is sometimes viewed as a mere formality. However, if the previous stages are not managed well or if the meaning of the messages communicated during the face-to-face negotiation stage is distorted, then the completion of the post-negotiation may be difficult. In some instances, resolving such issues may require a return to the negotiating table, or failing that, it may result in the deal being abandoned. Negotiators can prepare for the process by taking a realistic approach to the outcome to ensure that it is achievable.

In Chapter 9 we discuss the strategy variables that influence the negotiation process and outcome.

QUESTIONS

1. Explain the three stages of the negotiation process.
2. What role can third parties play in international business negotiations?

3. "The power/dependence relationship between the parties determines the level of cooperation and the emphasis on mutual benefits." Discuss this statement.
4. Research a recent international business negotiation that was affected by the environment. How did the environment influence the process and how did the parties respond to it?
5. How can negotiators prepare for the negotiation process?

NOTES

1. Ghauri, P.N. (2003) A framework for international business negotiations. In: Ghauri, P.N. and Usunier, J.-C. (eds) *International Business Negotiations*. 2nd ed. Oxford, Pergamon/Elsevier, pp. 3–22.
2. Roxenhall, T. and Ghauri, P. (2004) Use of the written contract in long-lasting business relationships. *Industrial Marketing Management*. **33**, 261–8.
3. Baertlein, L. (2013) Starbucks says $2.76 billion Kraft split was necessary. *Reuters*, 13 November.
4. Shonk, K. (2019) Examples of negotiating in business: Starbucks and Kraft's coffee conflict. *Program on Negotiation*, 16 September.
5. Ghauri (2003) op. cit.
6. Hanna, J. (2008) Negotiating with Wal-Mart. *Harvard Business School (HBS) Case*, 28 April.
7. Roberts, D. (2015) Walmart tells suppliers to slash prices. *Fortune*, 1 April.
8. Bloom, N., Bunn, P., Chen, S., Mizen, P., Smietanka, P. and Thwaites, G. (2019) Brexit is already affecting UK businesses – here's how. *Harvard Business Review*, 13 March.
9. Kollewe, J. (2019) Jaguar Land Rover begins Brexit shutdown as sales fall. *The Guardian*, 8 April.
10. Ott, U.F. and Ghauri, P.N. (2019) Brexit negotiations: from negotiation space to agreement zones. *Journal of International Business Studies*. **50**(1), 137–49.
11. Priestley, M. (2010) Australia, China and the global financial crisis. Parliament of Australia Library, Canberra. Accessed on 12 August 2019 from: https://www.aph.gov.au/About_Parliament/Parliamentary_Departments/Parliamentary_Library/pubs/BriefingBook43p/australiachinagfc.
12. PWC (2015) *People's Republic of China: Country Starter Pack*. Asia Link Business, Melbourne, Australia. Accessed on 20 August 2019 from: https://www.pwc.com.au/asia-practice/assets/china-country.pdf.
13. CNN (2001) Labor clashes threaten GM's Daewoo bid. 4 June.
14. Sang-Hun, C. (2006) In Daewoo, GM finds gold in overall gloom. *The New York Times*, 23 May.
15. Solomon, J. (2001) Daewoo staff rally to support takeover by General Motors. *The Wall Street Journal*, 14 June.
16. CBS News (2013) Government blocks US Airways, AA deal. 13 August.
17. Mouawad, J. (2013) U.S., filing suit, moves to block airline merger. *The New York Times*, 13 August.
18. Wilken, R., Jacob, F. and Prime, N. (2013) The ambiguous role of cultural moderators in intercultural business negotiations. *International Business Review*. **22**(4), 736–53.
19. Nadal, J. (1987) *Cracking the Global Market*. New York, Amacom.
20. Kuhn, R. (1988) *Deal Maker*. New York, John Wiley & Sons; Ghauri, P.N. (1986) Guidelines for international business negotiations. *International Marketing Review*. **3**(3), 72–82; Scott, B. (1981) *The Skills of Negotiating*. Brookfield, Gover; Sperber, P. (1981) *Fail-Safe Business Negotiations*. Englewood Cliffs, Prentice Hall.
21. Meredith, R. (1997) VW agrees to pay G.M. $100 million in espionage suit. *The New York Times*, 10 January; cf. Nasheri, H. (2004) *Economic Espionage and Industrial Spying*. Cambridge Studies in Criminology. Cambridge, Cambridge University Press.

22. Chan, M. (2003) Corporate espionage and workplace trust/distrust. *Journal of Business Ethics*. **24**(1), 45–58.
23. Fisher, R., Ury, W. and Patton, B. (1981) *Getting to Yes: Negotiating Agreement without Giving In*. New York, Penguin.
24. Ikle, F. (1964) *How Nations Negotiate*. New York, Praeger.
25. Ikle (1964) ibid.

FURTHER READING

Cavusgil, S.T., Ghauri, P.N. and Akcal, A.A. (2013) *Doing Business in Emerging Markets*. 2nd ed. Thousand Oaks, SAGE.

Ghauri, P.N. (2002) Negotiating international industrial projects: MNCs in emerging markets. In: Woodside, A.G. (ed.) *Advances in Business Marketing and Purchasing*. Stanford, JAI Press, pp. 187–201.

Reynolds, N., Simintiras, A. and Vlachou, E. (2003) International business negotiations. *International Marketing Review*. **20**(3), 236–61.

9
Strategies and tactics in international business negotiations

The negotiation process is influenced by the strategies used by the parties and the individual negotiators to gain a favourable outcome for the organisation and for themselves. We discussed in Chapters 4 and 5 that the cultural background of the negotiators influences their behaviour and communication during negotiations. In the case of strategy, we explain this as deliberate action taken by the negotiators during the face-to-face negotiations to maximise the benefits for one party. In this chapter, we discuss the variables that form the strategy used by negotiators and explain how they are used in international business negotiations. We begin by explaining the negotiators' strategic predisposition towards the negotiation process. The chapter then details the strategic factors that influence the negotiation process, and the section concludes by highlighting some strategic considerations during negotiations. In the next part of this chapter we take up and explain some tactical considerations that negotiators need to make while negotiating international business deals.

9.1 STRATEGIC PREDISPOSITION AND BARGAINING

Distributive bargaining: a win-lose mindset where the negotiator believes that the outcomes for their organisation can be achieved at the expense of the other party.

The strategic predisposition of the negotiators is determined by the way they view and approach the negotiation process. The terms "bargaining" and "negotiating" are used interchangeably in the literature even though in international business negotiation the two terms have very different meanings. The term bargaining suggests an activity in which the parties haggle to try to reduce the price or make concessions, resembling more bartering in a classic "bazaar-type" setting. Such an approach to business dealings is considered to be distributive in nature, with one side gaining at the expense of the other. Therefore, this *distributive bargaining* mindset leads to a win-lose approach to the deal. Such an approach to the negotiations can lead to conflict between the sides and ultimately is a zero-sum game as it can lead to failure. If both parties attempt to follow the win-lose approach, then a lose-lose outcome is more likely as neither party is willing to make concessions on their demands and ultimately neither party is able to achieve their objectives. The characteristics of a distributive bargaining approach include:

- Concealing information from or misleading the other party by making inaccurate claims.
- Displaying a rigid approach to the negotiations through an unwillingness to make concessions that would benefit the other party.
- Viewing the process as one where the negotiators have conflicting objectives.

This view of negotiations is thought of as being outdated. However, distributive bargaining continues to be part of business interaction, especially in labour-management negotiations.[1] In some countries, negotiations cannot be concluded unless a party feels that they have bargained a better deal during negotiations. This is a reality that negotiators need to be aware of and is central to the pricing strategy they use. We discuss this further in the next section when we look at some of the strategies applied in international business negotiation. The distributive bargaining approach is also applicable to certain professions. For example, military personnel are trained to achieve one outcome during a conflict, that is, victory. A win-win approach in battle and armed conflict is not an option in such situations. In some countries, government officials manage state-owned enterprises and their approach to negotiations can be robust during the process and rigid when it comes to outcomes. While in other countries, government officials are present in negotiations for big projects, even if the projects are to be purchased and managed by the private sector. Therefore, gathering information about the negotiators can help organisations prepare for the kind of bargaining approach the other party is likely to take.

Integrative bargaining: a win-win approach where involved parties work towards findings solutions that will help them achieve a beneficial outcome for all.

In contrast, parties can attempt to negotiate with the aim of achieving a positive outcome for all. Such an approach is seen as a win-win or a positive-sum game, with no party having to lose in order for another to gain. This approach is also referred to as *integrative bargaining*, and is based on the assumption that parties will be willing to make some concessions as long as the deal results in beneficial and attractive outcomes. In other words, everyone can win. This type of negotiation is associated with a problem-solving approach that relies on collaboration between the parties and honest and open discussion about expected goals and outcomes. If the parties are willing to identify the core problems jointly, then the negotiation can be seen as a process by which they can seek solutions to these problems. A recent example of such an approach was the acquisition of LinkedIn by Microsoft, which we detail in Example 9.1. However, if the collaboration between the parties is not handled properly, and the level of conflict increases due to lack of trust or other issues, then both parties can emerge with a jointly inferior deal. Many studies consider business negotiations to constitute this type of negotiation.[2] The characteristics of integrative negotiation, to which category international *business* negotiations belongs, include:

- Open information flow between the parties, with both sides sincerely disclosing their objectives and listening to the other party's objectives in order to find common ground.
- Understanding what the parties have in common as well as what are the conflicting objectives. Having identified the problem jointly, finding ways to pursue the common and complementary objective.

- Collaboratively attempting to find solutions that address the conflicting objectives of both parties.
- To achieve the above, both parties truly try to understand each other's point of view.

EXAMPLE 9.1
LINKEDIN ACQUISITION BY MICROSOFT

In February 2016, Microsoft CEO Satya Nadella met with LinkedIn CEO Jeff Weiner to discuss their ongoing relation, and the option of a business combination was raised. This proved to be the trigger for what eventually would be an acquisition of LinkedIn by Microsoft in June 2016. However, before the final deal was reached, a number of other companies, including Salesforce, expressed a strong interest in purchasing the shares of LinkedIn.

To pursue these initial expressions of interest, LinkedIn brought in a legal counsel, an investment banker and another adviser during March and April. The investment banker, Qatalyst Partners, reached out to other potential buyers to inform them that LinkedIn was on the market. In the end, two interested parties were left as potential buyers and started a bidding war for the company. LinkedIn asked the parties if either would pay $200 a share, which neither party agreed to. Salesforce made an initial bid of $171 per share and Microsoft immediately matched it, offering $172 per share. Ultimately, Microsoft increased its bid by 22 per cent, offering $196 a share in cash, which LinkedIn accepted.

So why did Microsoft increase its bid? And what did it hope to achieve through this acquisition? Microsoft has been slowly moving into new ventures as it plans for the change in consumer preference for cloud-based software leasing, which only a few years ago was dominated by Microsoft's Office Suite and Windows operating system. Microsoft saw LinkedIn as the ideal platform to offer its business solution and the acquisition would also include the online learning company Lynda.com that LinkedIn has acquired in 2015. Microsoft saw the objectives of the two sides as complementary and was willing to increase its bid to ensure that they did not miss out on this opportunity.

Microsoft's acquisition of LinkedIn has been termed a success as the company has managed to use the professional networking platform. Today, Microsoft offers executive training courses from Lynda.com to professionals on LinkedIn, as well as through their agreements with partner organisations like the airline Emirates, which offers complementary LinkedIn courses on board its flights.

Sources: Adapted from Parkhurst (2016);[3] Taylor (2016);[4] and Wingfield (2016).[5]

Discussion Point: Microsoft's offer was considered to be quite high. Do you believe the high price was justified at the time?

The characteristics of integrative bargaining are completely opposite to those that define distributive bargaining. Unlike the distributive bargaining approach, where the negotiation is seen as an opportunity to maximise one's own benefit at the cost of the other party, the integrative method takes a problem-solving approach where all can benefit. For longer-term relationships, the integrative approach is appropriate as parties work together to develop trust and solutions, which is lacking in a win-lose approach. It is important to note that the integrative bargaining approach to negotiations does not guarantee a successful outcome, and parties may move towards distributive bargaining during the negotiations due to changes in the organisation or influences from the external environment, such as change in government policies, economic conditions and so on. Experienced negotiators tend to respond to such changes by having contingency plans for different scenarios. We discuss these strategic approaches in the next section.

9.2 STRATEGIC FACTORS INFLUENCING NEGOTIATION

When negotiating in an international setting, parties have to prepare thoroughly, giving the right amount of care to issues such as how they should present things, which type of strategy should be used and what type of decision-making process is likely to be followed by the other party. Whether or not an agent or an outside consultant is required is also a strategic question.

9.2.1 Presentations

The presentation of a proposal needs to consider a number of issues:

- Should the negotiators present their proposal in a formal or informal manner?
- Will the presentation be made to individuals or to teams?
- What sort of content should be part of the presentations?

Negotiations are not confined to meetings in board rooms, and negotiators need to know whether the presentations they are going to make in relation to their proposal will be held in formal or informal settings. In countries like Japan and China, where interpersonal relationship-building is considered to be critical to the success of the negotiations, many informal meetings are held outside of the boardroom. These may include dinners or social meetings, and while business outcomes may not be formally discussed in these interactions, the exchange of information informally can be expected. Etiquettes around formal presentations in terms of introductions, exchange of name cards, acknowledgement of company information presented by the other party, the acknowledgement of authority and the non-verbal cues expressed during the presentation are all issues that negotiators need to plan and prepare for. Understanding when and how information can be exchanged and presented can make a difference to the actual outcome. Example 9.2 illustrates this issue in the case of Geely's acquisition of Volvo.

Another difference a negotiator may encounter is whether the presentations are made to teams or to individuals. In China and Eastern Europe, it is normal for teams to make presentations to other teams. Whereas in high power distance countries like India and parts of the Middle East, the presentation may be made to one individual, who is the decision maker. It is also important that the team decides who is best to present the information. Is it the most

EXAMPLE 9.2
GEELY'S ACQUISITION OF VOLVO

Geely Group, a Chinese automotive maker, wanted to expand their brand and products internationally but lacked the necessary technology, innovation and branding needed to achieve this goal. The company's founder, Li Shufu, set his sights on acquiring Volvo, the Swedish carmaker.

In 2007, Li sent a letter to Ford, Volvo's parent company, to express Geely's interest in purchasing Volvo. The letter received no response, and Li waited until 2008 to meet a senior Ford executive at the Detroit auto show to express his interest. He was again ignored. Instead of giving up on the idea, Li set up an acquisition team that included Rothschild and the then vice-president of Fiat China. Additionally, Li kept the Chinese regulators aware of his plans.

In the aftermath of the global financial crisis, Geely's proposed acquisition offer was taken seriously and negotiations commenced. A final agreement was reached in July 2010, with Geely acquiring Volvo for $1.5 billion. Throughout this process Li ensured that he kept all parties informed and communicated regularly during formal meetings and informal interactions to understand the concerns of the Volvo team about intellectual property protection and manufacturing operations. Geely assured Volvo that the production of the cars would continue to be in Sweden and the strong team Li had put together provided assurances about intellectual property protection.

Sources: Adapted from Chen and Ho (2009);[6] and Nueno and Lio (2011).[7]

Discussion Point: What assurances can organisations provide regarding protection of intellectual property rights?

senior member of the negotiating team or the person who is most knowledgeable about the project who will lead the presentation? In some instances, the information to be presented would need to be divided up into various sections, where the individual responsible for the specific area presents their ideas to their counterpart in the other team.

Finally, parties need to ensure that the content they present is relevant to the other team's requirements and expectations. The negotiators need to prepare for whether the other party expects the presentation to be filled with arguments detailing the advantages that the deal would present for them. Such presentations tend to focus on future scenarios and are not overly reliant on past and current data. Or is it more appropriate for the negotiator to present informative and factual information for the other party to draw their own conclusions from the data about what the deal may mean or their business? In many instances, negotiators are aware that they are not the only party presenting to the organisation, and may want to include in their presentation a comparison of what their firm can offer in terms of capabilities with what other competitors that are vying to win the organisation's business can offer.

So how can negotiators ensure that their style of presentation is appropriate? In addition to conducting research to prepare for the presentations, negotiators also have to be flexible. This may require them to prepare different versions of their presentations and choosing the one that is deemed to be most appropriate when the meeting commences.

9.2.2 Strategy

Tough strategy: a high initial demand, hoping for the other team to make the first concession.

There are several types of strategies in business negotiations. The appropriate use of the strategy depends on the context in which it is being applied and its effectiveness in delivering a beneficial outcome. The most important strategies are *tough, soft or intermediate*. A *tough strategy* involves a party making a very high initial demand and remaining resolute, hoping for the other party to make the first concession. This strategy may suit firms that have high bargaining power and command a strong market position. The other party may respond to this strategy by agreeing to their terms in order to work or continue working with them.

Soft strategy: start with lower demands and make concessions in the hope of reciprocity.

The *soft strategy* is the complete opposite of the tough strategy. In applying a soft strategy, a party does not start by making a very high initial demand, and is even willing to make the first concession in the hope that the other party will reciprocate. This strategy may be used by firms in response to the other party's tough strategy. It is also an appropriate strategy when an organisation wants to win the trust of the other side and hopes to build a long-term relationship that facilitates recurring business opportunities.

Intermediate strategy: start by making demands that match market conditions, and accept offer that meet expectations.

The *intermediate strategy* provides a balance between tough and soft strategies. When a party adopts an intermediate strategy, that party does not start by making a very high first demand, and as soon as an offer is made which meets its realistic expectations, it accepts it. This strategy is preferred by organisations that take a factual-based approach to negotiations, and their offer reflects the market realities (see Example 9.3).

EXAMPLE 9.3
TWITCH'S ACQUISITION BY AMAZON

Twitch is an online streaming video platform that is popular with gamers who live-stream their gameplay and share it with the gaming community. Initially launched by Justin Kan in 2007 as Justin.tv, which covered several categories, the popularity of the gaming category led to the creation of a spin-off in 2011 called Twitch. In 2014 Justin.tv was renamed Twitch Interactive. The growth of the company and popularity with gamers made it an attractive target for acquisition.

In 2014 it was reported that Google had reached a deal to acquire Twitch and integrate the gaming platform into its YouTube operations. The offer was purported to be worth $1 billion. However, the Google deal did not go through, with some industry experts citing concerns about antitrust regulations as the reason the bid was withdrawn.

Amazon saw this as an opportunity to put in its own bid for Twitch, which would complement its growing digital offerings, such as Prime Video and Amazon Music. Amazon made a bid for Twitch which was lower than that of Google's but closer to market expectations. In August 2014, Amazon officially acquired

Twitch Interactive for $970 million, a price that reflected Twitch's intermediate approach to strategy.

Sources: Adapted from Kim (2014);[8] Mac (2014);[9] and MacMillan and Bensinger (2014).[10]

Discussion Point: Based on the information about Amazon and Twitch, what do you believe is the relationship between the number of potential buyers and the strategic approach used by sellers?

Some negotiators may combine or switch between the strategies as a response to what the other party's expectations are. For example, in response to an offer made by a party that is displaying a distributive bargaining approach, the negotiators may start with a high demand and quickly make concessions to make the other party feel that they won, even though the concessions would not hurt their own objectives. This perception of a win may help the negotiator to move the negotiation from a win-lose to a win-win approach. Regardless of which strategy is used by the other party, it is important that the negotiators are prepared with their own counteroffer.

9.2.3 Decision making

Some information on the other party's overall decision-making pattern is necessary before entering into negotiations. Is that party more accustomed to using impulsive decision making? Or is the other party more likely to make decisions in a careful, rational way? Which negotiator will be the one who makes the decisions? Do the negotiators have the power to make final decisions or not?

When negotiators deal with parties that follow impulsive decision making, they may highlight superficial features of the product or deal that appeals to the other side. Negotiators may also create a sense of urgency to finalise a deal. On the other hand, if the negotiations are held with a party that makes decisions in a rational way, then the discussions would be around the details of the product or the agreement and would require the exchange of facts and information that can help inform the team's decision-making process. This use of impulsive or rational decision making is best understood by looking at the way salespeople have to adapt to the customer's approach. For example, a car salesperson dealing with a customer who seems to be an impulsive decision maker would be inclined to talk about the design of the car, the colour, the interior lining and other features, and highlight the limited number of such vehicles available on the market. Whereas the same salesperson would highlight the number of miles the car has done, its service history and the engine power when talking to customers who are rational decision makers. In Example 9.1, we highlighted the successful acquisition of LinkedIn by Microsoft. But not all of Microsoft's acquisitions have been that successful. Example 9.4 describes what can be seen as an impulsive and unsuccessful acquisition of Nokia.

Other issues related with decision making, some of which were briefly mentioned earlier, focus on whether the negotiating party follows collectivist or individualistic decision making, who within the negotiating team is the decision maker, and whether the negotiation party even has the authority to make the final decision. As discussed in Chapter 4, cultures can be

EXAMPLE 9.4
MICROSOFT'S FAILED NOKIA ACQUISITION

Nokia, the Finnish company that once dominated the market for mobile phones, was purchased by Microsoft in 2014 for a reported price of $7.9 billion. Within a year, Microsoft laid off 7,800 employees and had to write down nearly the full amount it paid for the company, indicating that the company had overpaid for the acquisition. The company finally ended up closing mobile phone manufacturing by writing down another $1 billion in losses in 2016.

So why did Microsoft make such an investment? Part of the reasoning was that Nokia accounted for 90 per cent of the Windows phone market and there had been rumours that Nokia was planning to move to the Android system. So a hasty decision to purchase Nokia was made to ensure that the phones continued to use the Windows operating system. Many within Microsoft were against the deal and could not see any benefit from the acquisition. The failure of the venture highlights the dangers of impulsive rather than rational decision making.

Sources: Adapted from Keizer (2015);[11] and Warren (2016).[12]

Discussion Point: It is often mentioned that higher returns are linked to higher risks. In this case, would the acquisition of Nokia be considered as risky?

individualistic or collectivist. In terms of decision making, individualistic societies would have a preference for decisions to be made by individuals, whereas in collectivist societies the decisions would tend to be made by the group. However, when negotiating with teams, it can be difficult in some cultures to understand the hierarchy of power. The titles used by the team members may not necessarily reflect the actual position of the individual in the team. This is particularly so in many countries in Asia and Africa, where titles like "president" or "chief executive" may not be reflective of the power that individuals with such titles may hold in the United States or Europe. It is therefore important for the negotiators to gather as much information before the negotiations and through observations during face-to-face meetings to ascertain who the decision maker in the team is. This allows the negotiators to pitch their presentation towards the decision maker and to reflect carefully on the messages that are being communicated by the individual.

9.2.4 The need for an agent or a third party

The presence of third parties can be observed in most negotiations. Their influence is limited to certain aspects and stages of the negotiations and may not even involve a physical presence at the negotiating table. When discussing the negotiation framework in Chapter 8, we highlighted the role of third parties. The involvement of third parties can also be a strategic decision by the firms to help them achieve their objectives. Third parties can include agents, interpreters, lawyers, conciliators/mediators/arbitrators, accrediting bodies, special interest groups and non-governmental organisations (NGOs), or even government agencies.

External organisations, such as the International Organization for Standardization (ISO), can validate the quality of a product or accredit the manufacturing or service delivery processes of an organisation. For parties negotiating for the first time, such quality assurances by external bodies can validate the seller's claims during the negotiations about their goods and services. The other task that third parties can undertake on behalf of the negotiating parties includes the valuation of property or assets that may be under discussion in the deal. Hence, the external parties can play the role of a facilitator that can help increase the clarity of the documents and validate any claims.

Owing to language barriers, *interpreters* may fulfil a critical role in the negotiation process by accurately transferring the meaning of the communication between the parties. Individual translators may be better equipped to translate the message from one language to another but not necessarily in the reverse direction. This issue can be addressed by employing multiple interpreters if the cost is justified by the necessity to secure substantiation and clarity. In their research, Sussman and Johnson have highlighted three major responsibilities for professional interpreters: to be an editor, to be a cultural coach, and to monitor and verify.[13] According to Sussman and Johnson, international executives should hire an interpreter with proven or accredited skills and try to avoid using multiple interpreters as this can lead to confused and protracted transactions. Organisations also need to plan in advance whether the interpreter will be a passive or an active participant.

In some instances, a negotiating party may opt for the services of an *agent* to either undertake the negotiations on behalf of the organisation or as a member of the negotiating team. One may question the need for an agent if an interpreter is available. For strategic reasons, it may be appropriate for agents to be used, especially in situations where the agent's networks and interpersonal relations could help the organisation achieve its goals. For example, in developing countries, the bureaucratic rules and policies can be difficult for outsiders to understand and manage. The process for seeking approval for business activities and relevant permits may be expedited if the organisation uses the services of a local agent for these activities.[14] Moreover, an agent can be useful to warn the negotiators about unethical issues and other irregularities if they expect these. A foreign firm cannot know or handle these issues on its own and does need some local assistance.

The need for *lawyers* in the negotiation process arises when the contract needs drafting and other legal aspects require fine-tuning. If lawyers are introduced by either party early on in the process, it may send a signal of mistrust to the other party, especially in countries that have a traditional culture and associate lawyers and legal issues with litigation. Lawyers may also be seen as disruptive and biased as their views are focused on the interests of the party they have been hired to represent and on potential conflicts instead of cooperation and joint benefits.

In situations where the conflict between the parties becomes so intense that they are unable to negotiate directly with one another, different sorts of third parties may be needed. These third parties include a conciliator, a mediator and an arbiter. A conciliator is the weakest form of third-party Alternative Dispute Resolution (ADR), and the process commences with the conciliator first meeting with both parties separately. They try to get the parties to start or resume a negotiation process when only one party is ready to negotiate. In an effort to resolve their conflict, the conciliator may discuss and suggest possible solutions. A mediator, on the other hand, actively assists the parties in negotiating a settlement to their dispute.

However, a mediator is not a judge and cannot impose a solution on the parties. Arbitration is a private out-of-court ADR. The disputing parties agree in advance that the process will lead to an award by the arbiter with which they agree to fully comply, even if it does not correspond with their expectations. Contrary to conciliation and meditation, which are used generally for domestic and small-size dispute resolution, arbitration is a well-established and widely used means to end disputes in international business. Clauses developed by arbitration bodies are often included in contracts negotiated at an international level. The most well-known arbitration body is the International Chamber of Commerce (ICC).[15] Since most countries have signed and ratified an international convention on the recognition of arbitration sentences by local courts, the enforcement of the decisions is not a concern.

There are a number of questions that need to be asked of a third party involved in international negations. In particular:

1. Who does the third party actually, not just formally, represent?
2. Are the interests of the third party really in line with the party they are supposed to represent?
3. Who is remunerating the third party? Is one or the other party paying them? Are the two parties sharing the cost of employing a third agent?
4. Is the third party biased, or susceptible to favouring their own interests over those of the party they are supposed to be representing?
5. How great is the risk of information leaking to undesirable parties (such as commercial competitors)? Are the confidential details of the negotiated material protected by a non-disclosure agreement or a confidentiality clause?

In the context of international business negotiations, these questions are especially meaningful, particularly in countries where the institutional environment is in its infancy and there is uncertainty in relation to the application of relevant laws.

9.3 TACTICAL CONSIDERATIONS DURING NEGOTIATIONS

The discussions in this chapter on the use of strategy have centred around the variables we first introduced in Chapter 8. In addition to these variables, there are a couple of strategic options that organisations have at their disposal. The first of these is *the location of the negotiation*. Where the negotiations are physically held can influence the negotiation process. Depending on the nature of the deal and/or the bargaining power, a party may insist that the negotiations take place in their home country. This gives the team the advantage of negotiating in home conditions, whereas the other party may face some of the challenges associated with travel, commuting and communicating in foreign conditions. Parties can hope to gain more concessions perhaps when the negotiations are being held on their terms, especially in instances where there is a large cultural distance between the host country and the other party's home country.

In many negotiations where the authors have been involved, it was observed that a foreign firm that is visiting a faraway country tries to negotiate in the hotel in which they are staying. This is considered to provide a home feeling, which means they do not feel like they are in a totally unknown environment.

The other related tactic that can be used by organisations is the *use of time*. We have previously discussed the issue of time as a cultural factor. However, during negotiations, time can be used as a tactical move. For example, the delaying of the progress of the negotiations can be a deliberate ploy to gain concessions. If the other party is seeking a quick deal or has travelled for the negotiations and is limited by the amount of time it has allocated for them, then slowing down the negotiations may prompt the other party to give some concessions in order to make progress. Negotiators need to be aware of such strategies and plan to either use the tactics if the opportunity presents itself or find ways to respond to these tactics if used by the other side. Example 9.5 discusses how Chinese negotiators have attempted to slow discussions in the China–US trade dispute in the hope of achieving a better outcome.

EXAMPLE 9.5
CHINA'S GO-SLOW TACTICS

The China-US trade dispute came to a head in 2018 when the United States imposed tariffs on Chinese imported goods. The United States claimed that unfair trade practices by China had resulted in a growing US trade deficit, the forced transfer of technology to China, and theft of US intellectual property. In response, China imposed its own set of tariffs against US goods.

In 2019 the two countries decided to resume talks to find a solution to the dispute and to restore trade relations. However, the US negotiators claimed that the slow pace at which the negotiations were progressing were a deliberate strategic ploy by the Chinese side, reflecting a new tactic of delaying the negotiations to seek a more favourable outcome. While the Chinese economy has been affected by the trade dispute, there is a belief in China that by not hurrying into an agreement, China can extract further concessions.

As the United States heads towards presidential elections in 2020, some experts believe that the slowing down of the US economy would harm President's Trump re-election prospects. The Chinese side is hoping that this fear of losing the popular vote may force the US side to cede further concessions.

Sources: Adapted from Deng (2019);[16] and Holland and Mason (2019).[17]

Discussion Point: What are the risks associated with using delay tactics in the negotiation process?

9.4 SUMMARY

The negotiation process can be seen as a partnership between teams that seek to build on the common objectives they share and find solutions to the conflicting issues. Such an approach is described as integrative bargaining, where all sides are attempting to achieve a positive outcome. On the other hand, some parties view the process like a game of chess, with each party making their move with the aim of winning the game by defeating the other player. Such a distributive bargaining approach is a zero-sum game where both parties can fail to achieve their objectives.

In this chapter we highlighted the differences in the strategic predisposition of the negotiators to explain how it influences the negotiation process. We also explained the factors influencing the strategy, including presentations, strategy, decision making and the need for agents and third parties. For negotiators, having a sound understanding of these strategic variables allows them to prepare themselves to defend against the strategy that the other party may attempt to use during negotiations and to draw up their own plans to counter it.

QUESTIONS

1. What are the key differences between distributive and integrative bargaining?
2. Explain how the formal/informal nature of a presentation can influence the exchange of information and the communication process.
3. The use of agents may provide some benefits for a company during negotiations. But there are also some limitations of using agents in international business negotiation. Identify and explain some of these limitations.
4. Explain the three main strategies of tough, soft and intermediate. How can negotiators respond to the use of these strategies?
5. In situations where the negotiating parties have ceased to communicate due to conflict, what dispute resolution options can be availed?

NOTES

1. Walton, R.E. and McKersie, R.B. (1965) *A Behavioural Theory of Labour Negotiations*. New York, McGraw-Hill.
2. See as representative of this point: Fisher, R., Ury, W. and Patton, B. (1981) *Getting to Yes: Negotiating Agreement without Giving In*. New York, Penguin; Ghauri, P.N. (1983) *Negotiating International Package Deals*. Uppsala, Almqvist and Wisell; Ghauri, P.N. (1986) Guidelines for international business negotiations. *International Marketing Review*. **3**(3), 72–82; Lewicki, R.J., Saunders, D.M., Minton, J.W. and Barry, B. (2003) *Negotiation: Readings, Exercises and Cases*. 4th ed. New York, McGraw-Hill; Pruitt, D.G. (1983) Strategic choice in negotiation. *American Behavioral Scientist*. **27**(2), 167–94.
3. Parkhurst, E. (2016) Bill Gates helped negotiate Microsoft-LinkedIn deal after Salesforce started bidding war. *Puget Sound Business Journal*, 6 July.
4. Taylor, H. (2016) Why Microsoft beat Salesforce to acquire LinkedIn. *CNBC*, 15 November.
5. Wingfield, N. (2016) Microsoft buys LinkedIn for $26.2 billion, reasserting its muscle. *The New York Times*, 13 June.
6. Chen, G. and Ho, P. (2009) Geely taps China banks to back $1.8 billion Volvo deal. *Reuters*, 1 December.
7. Nueno, P. and Liu, G. (2011) How Geely waited for Volvo. *Financial Times*, 20 December.
8. Kim, E. (2014) Amazon buys Twitch for $US970 million in cash. *Business Insider Australia*, 26 August.
9. Mac, R. (2014) Amazon pounces on Twitch after Google baulks due to antitrust concerns. *Forbes*, 25 August.

10. MacMillan, D. and Bensinger, G. (2014) Amazon to buy video site Twitch for $970 million. *The Wall Street Journal*, 26 August.
11. Keizer, G. (2015) Microsoft writes off $7.6B, admits failure of Nokia acquisition. *Computerworld*, 8 July.
12. Warren, T. (2016) Microsoft wasted at least $8 billion on its failed Nokia experiment. *The Verge*, 25 May.
13. Sussman, L. and Johnson, D. (1996) Dynamics of the interpreter's role: implications for international executives. *Journal of Language for International Business*. **7**(2), 1–14.
14. Rammal, H.G. (2005) International business negotiations: the case of Pakistan. *International Journal of Commerce and Management*. **15**(2), 129–40.
15. For ICC standard arbitration clauses, see: http://www.iccwbo.org/products-and-services/arbitration-and-adr/arbitration/standard-icc-arbitration-clauses/.
16. Deng, C. (2019) Slow progress in trade talks is partly a result of China's new tactic to wait. *The Wall Street Journal*, 31 July.
17. Holland, S. and Mason, J. (2019) Trump says China may try to delay trade deal until 2020 election. *Reuters*, 27 July.

FURTHER READING

Aslani, S., Ramirez-Marin, J., Brett, J., Yao, J., Semnani-Azad, Z., Zhang, Z.-X., Tinsley, C., Weingart, L. and Adair, W. (2016) Dignity, face, and honor cultures: a study of negotiation strategy and outcomes in three cultures. *Journal of Organizational Behavior*. **37**(8), 1178–201.

Geiger, I. (2017) A model of negotiation issue-based tactics in business-to-business sales negotiations. *Industrial Marketing Management*. **64**, 91–106.

Rao, A. and Schmidt, S.M. (1999) A behavioural perspective on negotiating international alliance. *Journal of International Business Studies*. **29**(4), 665–94.

Saorín-Iborra, M.C. and Cubillo, G. (2016) Influence of time pressure on the outcome of intercultural commercial negotiations. *Journal of Promotion Management*. **22**(4), 511–25.

10 Ethics in international business negotiations

In recent years, the topic of ethics has attracted increasing attention in almost every function of a firm from marketing to accounting and new product development. It has also become an integral part of academic research and teaching. We believe that it is particularly important in negotiations, as almost all negotiations involve some ethical dilemmas that need to be considered or dealt with.

We begin this chapter by identifying ethical issues in international business negotiations. We then explain the ethical and unethical positions that negotiators can take and discuss the universal or relative application of ethical norms and beliefs. Finally, we discuss the psychological perspective on unethical negotiating.

10.1 WHAT ARE ETHICS IN INTERNATIONAL BUSINESS NEGOTIATIONS?

Ethical considerations are inherent in international business negotiations as companies do business in different countries where norms and legal standards of ethics may be different from one's home market. Even within Europe, rules and regulations regarding consumer protection, selling harmful products or pollution limits can be different. Moreover, attitudes towards work ethics, leisure and customer welfare are different in different countries.

In emerging markets these regulations are definitely different; as a consequence, some multinational enterprises believe that they do not have to follow the same standards in every market. In this chapter we will discuss the ethical issues and dilemmas that most commonly arise in international business negotiations, but first the following example looks at a simpler, single-transaction scenario relating to the sale of a car. When selling a car, a question that could be asked is "whether it is ethical not to tell the potential buyer that you are selling the car because you have had several problems with its gearbox and that your car mechanic advised you to have it replaced? In another scenario for the same car, when your neighbour hears that you are selling the car, he tells you that one of his colleagues at work is looking for such a car and that he can help you to sell it to him. Being your neighbour, he also knows that you have had a lot of problems with the gearbox and that you do not want to get it repaired as it would cost around €1,000. At that point the neighbour suggests to you that if you pay him €400, he can convince his colleague to buy your call without telling him about the problem. Now, would you do that? Do you think that it is ethical? Let's look at another scenario: you say to your mechanic that you do not want to undertake the repair and would like instead to sell the car. Your mechanic offers to help you sell the car from his workshop at the price you want but then will charge you €500 as a commission. Now, would you do that? Do you think it is ethical?

As we can see from above example, even in a simple transactional negotiation there are often ethical considerations to be made. Negotiators are thus often confronted with ethical dilemmas such as whether they should aim to achieve their objectives without worrying about the ethical issues. In international business negotiations, negotiators are aware that the standards and norms are different in different countries, and they are faced with the dilemma of whether they should follow their own standards or can be flexible when they are in a different country where some questionable practices, according to their standards, are tolerated.

Ethics are generally accepted standards about what is right and what is wrong while doing business.[1] Ethics are, thus, broadly applied social norms and rules about what is right or wrong that enable societies to function harmoniously. These norms and rules are different for different situations. Norms are different when you are doing business to when you perform your day-to-day work. This means that ethics in negotiations are rather specific and should be considered when we do business. Ethics in negotiations means that when we are agreeing on economic or other benefits to be awarded to one or more parties we have to ensure that these benefits are not contradictory to established norms and rules in that situation. Several scholars have suggested that when we face an ethical dilemma/situation, we use one of the following approaches:[2]

1. End-result approach: Stick to our objectives and normal ways to achieve these objectives and evaluate rightness by evaluating its consequences.
2. Duty approach: Stick to the rules and regulations. Our obligation is to follow the rule of law and our universal standards.
3. Social contract approach: Stick to the norms and values of our organisation or community, as we want to be a good member of the community and follow its rules.
4. Personal ethics approach: Stick to our own conscience and personal conviction. We follow our own moral standards.

These four approaches to ethical situations are further explained in Table 10.1.

10.2 ETHICAL AND UNETHICAL POSITIONS

In negotiations it is not always a question of being ethical versus unethical; quite often some tactics are ethically ambiguous, in that it is doubtful or uncertain whether a certain tactic/action is ethical or not. As mentioned earlier, the behaviour of people depends upon their logical standpoint. For example, in international business negotiations is it unethical to make an inflated first offer or not to disclose your walk-away point to the other party? Is it unethical to spread rumours about your competitors? Is it unethical to bluff (exaggerated

Table 10.1 Four approaches to tackle ethical dilemmas

1. End-result logic	The consequences of the action should be considered. Actions are right if they promote collective happiness, although it is difficult to define a collective happiness and we should also consider short-term versus long-term happiness. In negotiations one does whatever is needed to get the best possible outcome.
2. Duty logic	Actions should follow moral principles and not feelings of pleasure. In negotiations one is obliged not to engage in untruthful actions that are against the rules.
3. Social contract logic	Actions should be taken in a social context. Communities determine rules of action. What is best for the common good is good and morality determines what is right or wrong. Thus, follow the rules of your community and if others lie in a certain situation, you can also lie.
4. Personal ethics logic	Each individual's conscience guides her/him about what is right or wrong. There are no set rules; each person has her/his standards according to her/his beliefs. This means that it is difficult to achieve a collective definition of ethics and this makes it difficult to have a uniform ethical approach. Thus, if your conscience allows you to be untruthful then it is fine.

Source: Adapted from Hitt (1990).[3]

threat or promise)? Is it unethical not to tell the whole truth about your financial strength/weaknesses? Is it unethical to spy on the other party or your competitors? All these tactics are grouped under ethically ambiguous tactics. In the international setting, in some countries many of these might just be the normal way of doing business, whereas in others these might be considered unethical or immoral.[4]

EXAMPLE 10.1
UNDUE INFLUENCE?

Lobbying takes its name from the hallways in Parliament, where constituents and campaigners have traditionally made their case to legislators. Yet those who practise it seldom attract the attention in Britain that they do in America. There, presidential candidates earn cheers for lamenting the grip on Washington of political consultants who seek to influence government in favour of their clients. A whole television series was devoted to the theme.

The last time lobbying in Britain received anything like the same coverage was in the 1990s: MPs were found to be taking cash in exchange for asking useful parliamentary questions, and then a former Labour adviser-turned-lobbyist was caught boasting of his access to ministers. Now it is edging back into the news.

In 2008 the House of Lords committee on members' privileges met to discuss whether an inquiry could be launched into the allegation that Lord Hoyle, a former Labour frontbencher, was paid in 2005 to introduce an arms lobbyist to Lord Drayson, then defence-procurement minister. This is not illegal but it is frowned on: Lord Hoyle should have declared to Lord Drayson that he was being paid, something he cannot remember doing. A subcommittee has been charged with investigating complaints about peers since 2002, but its five members, whose average age is 77, have yet to be tested.

In the Commons, meanwhile, the public-administration committee (PAC) has been looking since last June into the impact of lobbying on government decisions. If it decides the line between rightfully conveying constituents' views and unduly influencing those in authority is regularly breached, it may conclude that there is a case for external regulation, as in America.

Lobbyists insist that theirs is a respectable business. One reason is that the cash-for-questions affair gave rise in 1994 to a self-regulatory body, the Association of Professional Political Consultants (APPC). It forbids practices such as employing serving politicians and requires lobby firms to disclose the names of their clients and consultants. The APPC's 55 members account for four-fifths of industry turnover.

Another reason is that personal contacts in government are less important than they were. Lobby firms maintain that ministers will often meet them in their own right if they can provide expertise on a particular subject and mobilise key players.

Source: Adapted from The Economist (2008).[5]

Discussion Point: Lobbying is one way that large organisations in particular can attempt to influence policies and build a positive reputation. Do you believe that lobbying is an ethical business practice?

However, some strategies and tactics are clearly considered as unethical in most countries. These include:

- Use of *untruthful information* about the product, technology or investment to mislead the other party.
- *Buy the influence* of a negotiation team member from the other side.
- *Bribery* and exchange of large gifts.
- *Pay a member of the other party* to disclose some sensitive information about the other party or a competitor's offer.
- *Negotiate and agree to unrealistic terms* knowing that these will not be fulfilled.
- *Doing or receiving favours* for/from the other side to influence the course of negotiations.[6]

The cultural background of the negotiators also influences their perception of what is ethical or unethical. For example, face-saving is important in China as it helps protect an individual's position in the *guanxi* network and their social status. Hence, the use of "white lies" to protect the individual's reputation may be considered to be acceptable. These "white lies" can be seen as emotion management tactics, compared to "lies" that are focused on cognitive tactics.[7] Emotional-appeal strategies employ persuasive language to appeal to the emotions of the other party rather than facts to build a valid logic. Lying may provide a short-term benefit to a negotiating party, but if the lie fails, it can threaten to damage the established relations between the negotiating parties, or may even move the bargaining power away from the lying party.[8] Do you consider such emotion management techniques to be ethical? In some instances, the answer to whether a certain act is ethical may not be that easy. Example 10.1 poses such a question about ethical behaviour.

EXAMPLE 10.2
INFRINGING PATENTS TO PRODUCE GENERIC DRUGS

In 2005, the World Trade Organization's agreement on Trade-Related Aspects of Intellectual Property Rights (TRIPS) came into effect. Prior to TRIPS, governments would decide whether they would grant patent rights to pharmaceutical firms, thereby allowing generic drug producers to copy life-saving drugs and produce them at an affordable price. However, with the introduction of TRIPS, pharmaceutical firms could register their patent and stop generic drug producers from selling lower-cost products. Such a case occurred in India, one of the world's largest generic drug producers, when Novartis attempted to register a patent for its "new" leukaemia drug Glivec. Novartis argued that it had made minor changes to the product and, therefore, it deserved to be registered as a new patent. The Supreme Court of India ruled against Novartis and allowed locally produced generic drugs to be sold at a lower cost. The decision was supported by many not-for-profit organisations, including Doctors Without Borders. Firms like Novartis argue that the research and development (R&D) cost of producing these life-saving drugs is quite high and requires a substantial amount of time as well. Do you believe big pharmaceutical firms are acting ethically by patenting life-saving drugs and selling them at a high price?

Over time, the enforcement of TRIPS has improved and governments are less willing to allow any perceived breach of patents. In early 2017, Novartis successfully sued Indian drug manufacturer Cipla for breaching its copyright for the respiratory drug Onbrez. After the verdict was handed down, Novartis was concerned that not only would they face criticism but their brand reputation would also be damaged. The company therefore decided to work with Cipla to manufacture and market drugs. At the end of the day, the opportunity to work together for a win-win outcome outweighed the short-term advantages of a win-lose approach.

Sources: Adapted from Blackstone (2012);[9] Shah and Rajagopal (2017);[10] Sharma (2014);[11] and Smedley (2013).[12]

Discussion Point: Pharmaceutical firms argue that the price of life-saving drugs reflects the cost of research. Is it then ethical for other firms to reverse engineer and produce a replica generic drug without compensating the pharmaceutical firm that develop the drug initially?

In international business negotiations, bribery is considered the most common unethical concern. In fact, the bigger the deal in value, the higher the risk that some bribery or other type of illegal payment or favour will be involved. This can range from smaller gifts such as a Rolex watch to a fully paid vacation, sometimes with hostesses, for a member or members of the opposite negotiation team. Quite often a bribe is paid in cash to a member or influencer of the other team as a percentage of the contract value. This cash can reach a value of millions of euros. A big contract can easily be worth €300–500 million and a 5 per cent bribe/commission for such a contract can easily reach €15–25 million.

EXAMPLE 10.3
HOT, GREASY POTATO

The implementation of a new anti-bribery law has been delayed, again. When Tony Blair intervened in 2006 to call off a police inquiry into allegations that BAE Systems, an armaments firm and Britain's biggest manufacturer, had paid bribes to secure a decades-long £43 billion ($70 billion) arms deal with Saudi Arabia, he cited national-security grounds. Anti-corruption campaigners decried the move as further evidence of Britain's laxity over allegations of corporate misbehaviour. In 2008, in a bid to restore the country's tarnished reputation, the previous Labour government began drafting a new law intended to clamp down decisively on backhanders.

Both the Liberal Democrats and the Conservatives backed the bill in opposition; it duly became law with cross-party support last year. The act was due to come into force in April, after the publication in January of guidelines on how it should be interpreted. It will impose stiff penalties on companies convicted of paying bungs, such as unlimited fines and, in some circumstances, prison sentences for directors.

Yet the Ministry of Justice said it had decided to postpone the act's implementation. The rules will now not come into force until at least three months after the department publishes a new, revised set of guidelines - but it has said nothing about when that might be.

The delay is a relief to business groups such as the Confederation of British Industry, which frets about how the law will work and has lobbied for more clarity than the original guidelines provided. Its critics do not want to look like they are saying that the law will make it harder for us to pay bribes and so will be bad for business (although it might be). Instead they have focused on the alleged fuzziness of the rules.

Another sticking point concerns so-called "facilitation payments", a phrase that is sometimes a euphemism for bribes but can also refer to small, unofficial payments that are seen as customary in some countries. America's Foreign Corrupt Practices Act - generally reckoned to be fairly strict - allows such handouts, popularly referred to as "grease payments", in some circumstances. In theory, Britain's new law forbids them, though the government has said cryptically that "non-criminal" cases would probably not be prosecuted.

Where business sees a welcome rethink, anti-corruption campaigners see a climb-down, the latest in a long saga of delays and foot-dragging by British governments of every stripe.

Source: Adapted from The Economist (2011).[13]

Discussion Point: What should negotiators do if an informal approach for a facilitation payment is made during negotiations? Do you believe that the current definition used in business for corruption covers all types of illegal activities?

There are two extreme positions for handling ethical situations: universal versus relative. In the case of *universal position*, we should follow a moral position that is universal and

Universal position: follow a moral position that is universal.

Relative position: belief that norms and rules are local and vary across countries.

wherever we are we should follow our moral principles. In the case of *relative position*, we believe that norms and rules are local and different in different communities/countries. This means that wherever we go to do business we should follow local rules and norms. In this respect actions can be judged on the basis of legality, that is, whether an action is legal or illegal, or on the basis of legitimacy, that is, whether an action is acceptable or not. This also means that certain activities might be acceptable in one culture but not in another one. Activities can thus be divided into four categories:[14]

1. *Normal activities* that are within the limits of the law and are also acceptable and thus legitimate.
2. *Informal activities* that are not considered legal but are acceptable. For example, the grey economic sector in many countries.
3. *Criminal activities* that are clearly illegal and are not acceptable and thus illegitimate.
4. *Legally violent activities* that are within the limit of the law but are outside the limit of the acceptable activity. Usunier and Verna believe that export of toxic waste to developing countries falls under this type of activity.[15]

The above activities are listed in Figure 10.1.

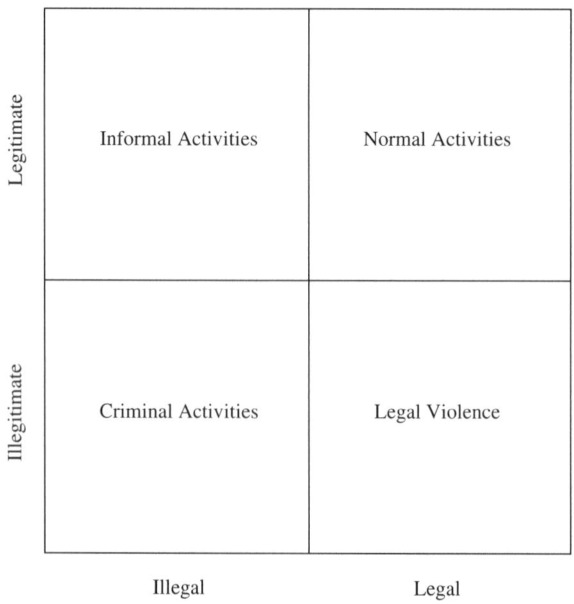

Sources: Adapted from Usunier and Verna (1994);[16] and Usunier (2003).[17]

Figure 10.1 Understanding the relevant ethical issues

10.3 UNIVERSALISM VERSUS RELATIVISM

Ethical universalism: ethical principles that are universal and are applied in the same manner worldwide.

Ethical relativism: what is right or wrong depends on interpretations by the local culture and norms.

For international business negotiations, we need to decide our standpoint on ethical matters: do we practise universalism or relativism? *Ethical universalism* means that ethical principles are universal and should be applied in the same manner irrespective of where we do business. The Foreign Corrupt Practices Act (FCPA) of 1977 and 1988 in the United States is a good example. The FCPA demands that American firms doing business anywhere should apply the same ethical rules and standards as at home. *Ethical relativism* means that what is right or wrong depends upon how it is interpreted by the local culture and norms, as rules are local and should be followed by anyone doing business in that country. This is contrary to the FCPA that is practised in the United States and should be followed by American firms wherever they do business. Several European companies and countries, however, follow ethical relativism: "When in Rome do as Romans do." Sweden, Switzerland, France and Germany are examples of countries that follow this.[18]

In practice, however, many firms, American as well as European, do engage in unethical activities such as bribery while doing business abroad. Some of these companies perform these activities through their agents, who are independent companies and are responsible for their own activities.

10.4 THE INEVITABILITY OF UNETHICAL NEGOTIATING – FROM A PSYCHOLOGICAL PERSPECTIVE

Causes and consequences are explored in a symposium directed by Gunia.[19] The causal side of unethical negotiation behaviour focuses on factors which include moral character, ethical fading and environmental cues that lie outside the negotiators' awareness. There is an assumption that unethical behaviour and negotiation go hand in hand. The previous sections have shown that unethical behaviour crosses cultural borders. There is also an assumption that unethical negotiation is uniformly harmful and ethical negotiation is inherently desired. The consequences of unethical negotiations and deception often harm the deceivers and their trustworthiness, encouraging their counterpart to retaliate thus leading to poorer economic outcomes. Similarly, the deceived party performs worse. There are questions as to whether unethical negotiations could also lead to pro-social behaviour. In organisational decision-making contexts, environmental cues can influence interdependent individuals' deception. In international business negotiations, there are situations in which unethical behaviour can lead to better outcomes.

A recent example of unethical behaviour concerns the ousting of the CEO of Renault–Nissan Carlos Ghosn and the implications this had for his successor. International business negotiations are harmed by unethical behaviour, with future consequences for trust, as

EXAMPLE 10.4
WHO CAN FIX NISSAN?

For almost a year, Hiroto Saikawa defied gravity. Against expectations, Nissan's chief executive survived the ousting of Carlos Ghosn, a damning corporate governance probe, accusations that he signed off falsified documents, a collapse in investor support and a 95 per cent plunge in quarterly profit at the Japanese carmaker. But Mr Saikawa's admission last week that he was improperly overpaid finally tipped the scales. The board unanimously agreed on Monday to remove him in a week's time, ending a two-and-a-half-year tenure overshadowed by quality scandals and persistent doubt about his management capability following the arrest of Mr Ghosn. Mr Saikawa's forced departure and the search for a new chief are pivotal events for the company and for its alliance with France's Renault. His exit leaves Nissan looking for a leader who can pull off the triple feat of resuscitating a Japanese icon, navigating a potential four-way global merger and making a clear break with the Ghosn era.

Source: Inagaki et al. (2019).[20]

Discussion Point: In which category did Ghosn's unethical behaviour fall? Find more examples of the unethical negotiation behaviour of CEOs.

demonstrated by the Nissan case in Example 10.4, an extract from an article in the *Financial Times* that shows the implications of unethical negotiation behaviour.

As it is unlikely that deception, bribing and bluffing can be eliminated, it is important to take steps to build up trust to avoid unethical negotiation behaviour.[21]

1. Build mutual benevolence.
2. Create opportunities for displaying trust.
3. Demonstrate trustworthiness.
4. Place the negotiation in a longer-term context.
5. Bring in mutually respected intermediaries.

10.5 SUMMARY

Conducting discussions in an ethical and transparent manner should form the basis of any international business negotiations. However, what is considered to be ethical or unethical behaviour can vary across institutional and cultural contexts. In this chapter we identify some of the ethical dilemmas that negotiators can face and make suggestions for how to address them. The chapter also discusses which ethical values and norms are universal and which ones are specific to individual countries and contexts. Preparing well for the negotiations should ensure that individuals are aware of the legal requirements and limitations to what can be offered during negotiations. Negotiators also need to make judgements about what strategies they should, or the other party could, employ during negotiations, and whether these are ethically and morally acceptable.

QUESTIONS

1. Describe the four approaches to tackling ethical dilemmas.
2. What are the advantages and disadvantages of using universal or relative positions to handle ethical situations?
3. "When negotiating a deal with a party from an emerging economy, it is important that Western negotiators do not attempt to impose their own expectations about what is right and wrong. Instead, by following local norms and practices, negotiators can minimise the challenges associated with the introduction of 'foreign' business practices." Discuss this statement and identify the pros and cons of negotiators following the notion of ethical relativism during the negotiation process.

NOTES

1. Lewicki, R.J., Barry, B. and Saunders, D.M. (2007) *Essentials of Negotiation*. 4th ed. New York, McGraw-Hill.
2. Hitt, W. (1990) *Ethics and Leadership: Putting Theory into Practice*. Columbus, Battelle Press; Hosmer, L.T. (2003) *The Ethics of Management*. 4th ed. New York, McGraw-Hill.
3. Hitt (1990) ibid.
4. Lewicki et al. (2007) op. cit.
5. The Economist (2008) Britain: undue influence? 3 April.
6. Usunier, J.-C. (2003) Ethical aspects of international business negotiations. In: Ghauri, P.N. and Usunier, J.-C. (eds) *International Business Negotiations*. 2nd ed. Oxford, Pergamon/Elsevier, pp. 437–60.
7. Chan, S.H. and Ng, T.S. (2016) Ethical negotiation values of Chinese negotiators. *Journal of Business Research*. **69**(2), 823–30.
8. Wetlaufer, G.B. (1990) The ethics of lying in negotiations. *Iowa Law Review*. **75**, 1219–73.
9. Blackstone, S. (2012) This Indian pharmaceutical tycoon is exploiting a patent loophole to cut the costs of cancer drugs by 75%. *Business Insider Australia*, 19 June.
10. Shah, S. and Rajagopal, D. (2017) Cipla, Novartis explore marketing tie-up. *The Economic Times*, 14 July.
11. Sharma, E.K. (2014) Novartis-Cipla battle shakes up Indian pharma industry. *Business Today*, 18 December.
12. Smedley, T. (2013) Patent wars: has India taken on Big Pharma and won? *The Guardian*, 15 May.
13. The Economist (2011) Hot, greasy potato. 3 February.
14. Usunier (2003) op. cit.
15. Usunier, J.-C. and Verna, G. (1994) Ethique des Affaires et Relativite Culturelle. *Revue Francaise de Gestion*. **99**, 23–40.
16. Usunier and Verna (1994) ibid.
17. Usunier (2003) op. cit.
18. Usunier and Verna (1994) op. cit.
19. Gunia, B.C. (2019) Ethics in negotiations: causes and consequences. *Academy of Management Perspective*. **33**(1): 3–11.
20. Inagaki, S.K., Campbell, P., Lewis, L. and Keohane, D. (2019) Who can fix Nissan? *Financial Times*, 10 September.
21. Cramton, P.C. and Dees, J.G. (1993) Promoting honesty in negotiations: an exercise in practical ethics. *Business Ethics Quarterly*. **3**, 1–23.

FURTHER READING

Al-Khatib, J., Rawwas, M.Y.A., Swaidan, Z. and Rexeisen, R.J. (2005) The ethical challenges of global business-to-business negotiations: an empirical investigation of developing countries' marketing managers. *Journal of Marketing Theory and Practice.* **13**(4), 46–60.

Fulmer, I.S., Barry, B. and Long, A. (2009) Lying and smiling: informational and emotional deception in negotiation. *Journal of Business Ethics.* **88**, 691–709.

Lytle, A. and Rivers, C. (2007) Lying, cheating foreigners!! Negotiation ethics across cultures. *International Negotiation.* **12**(1), 1–28.

Wood, G. (1995) Ethics at the purchasing and sale interface: an international perspective. *International Marketing Review.* **12**(4), 7–19.

11 Negotiating different types of contract

This chapter describes various types of contracts that are common in international business. Dissimilarities in the nature of commercial contracts, such as an agent/distributor contract, a licensing/franchising contract, a contract for a joint venture, a contract for mergers and acquisitions, and a contract for a turnkey project, all entail a different type of negotiation process. Equally, each contract also offers a variety of opportunities. At the same time, different markets pose different challenges due to the distinctive nature of each nation's economic environment, infrastructure, and political and cultural environment. Every contract, therefore, has its own characteristics and peculiarities that need to be judiciously weighed and considered. Once a company has aligned the form its international business operations will take with its existing activities and decided what type of operation is most suited to its present ones, it then needs to decide what type of contract it needs to negotiate. Theories of the multinational enterprise suggest that when the costs of transacting through a market are higher than the costs of conducting the transaction through the firm, negotiations will occur.[1] The chapter begins by discussing the most common types of contract that are negotiated in order to enable a company to conduct overseas ventures.

11.1 AGENT/DISTRIBUTOR CONTRACT

When a firm is negotiating with a potential agent or a distributor over a contract relating to a foreign market the firm has to be particularly concerned about the following issues:

- It has to allow an agent or distributor partial or full control over the marketing function in the host market.
- It has to ensure that the agent/distributor will provide the right level of commitment to its business.
- It has to ensure that its patents, trademarks and goodwill be properly protected.
- It has to ensure that it will get proper and quick feedback on its business from the market.
- It has to ensure that the legal system in the host market allows it to enforce the contract it will agree on.

Marketing products and services through agents or distributors involves low levels of risk in international operations and provides a good opportunity for a company to learn while making a profit. An agent/distributor relationship is frequently characterised by asymmetrical power: one of the parties enjoys greater levels of power and influence over the other. The party that has greater power naturally has an advantage that it can exploit if it chooses to do so. In negotiations over distribution rights, there is a great temptation for the party with the greater level of power to exercise it over the other one, and this temptation needs to be controlled. This means that the selection of a suitable agent or distributing partner is of critical importance, and therefore is a crucial decision, as the success of the product, or products, in the foreign market is entirely dependent on that distributor. If the supplier is in a stronger, more powerful position and puts forward unrealistic demands, this will actually be against the supplier's own interests as both parties should achieve their goals through mutual collaboration. Collaborative behaviour in different channels of distribution is a result of a deliberate choice or achieved through careful management of the relationship by one of the parties. Cooperation between parties in an agent/distributor negotiation is most important when the transaction is not one that is purely market based, but one where parties have an exchange history and where there are prospects for future value-adding activities.[2] When a firm is starting to negotiate the export of its product for the first time, it needs to locate a distributor or agent who has the best relationship with the most important customers in the market that it wants to serve. Once the exporting company has designated which its preferred distribution partner is, it then needs to evaluate who has greater power. Where the greater power resides depends on the strength of the relationship the distributor or agent has with its customers, and if the product being supplied is protected by intellectual property rights.[3]

The outcome of the initial agreement between a supplier and distributor does not mark the end of the deal; nor does it mark the end of the negotiations. Rather, it is the first in a series of negotiations that are now characterised by mutual dependence. As the relationship evolves, conflicts can arise if, for example, the agent is not working aggressively enough to promote the company's products or the principal does not deliver their product on time.[4] These and other problems that may arise mean that the two parties have to renegotiate their original agreement. There are also external pressures that may arise, such as a recession in the host or home country, or a change in import tariffs that means it is necessary for one or both parties to renegotiate. Finally, the successful reception of an exporting company's product in a foreign market may lead it to explore the option of establishing its own sales representative or marketing subsidiary.[5] This changes the power dynamic and the level of interdependence between the two parties and is again a cause to revisit and renegotiate previous commitments. Once the two parties have been operating together for a while, during which time they have built up an exchange history, each has more information on which to base its decision about whether there are good prospects for future value-added activities.

When considering a renewal of terms, a company should ask itself whether it is still getting what it needs from the relationship, whether the relationship is functioning as efficiently as the best realistic alternative, whether the cost is the lowest it can be and what changes have occurred in the world that require amendments to be made. Moreover, when negotiating the initial contract it will have been impossible for both parties to specify all possible and relevant contingencies.[6] Thus, it is natural for discussions about any future agreement to focus on short-term business arrangements given the likelihood that further change will require further negotiation. The focus of such discussions should be to revisit issues such as product quality, price and commitment to the market.[7]

No matter how successful, long and productive a relationship between a principal and their agent has been, there comes a time when all such relationships must end; indeed, in some cases it may be necessary to terminate the agreement earlier than was initially envisaged, because it is no longer able to support the common objectives on which it was originally based or because of feelings of dissatisfaction.[8] When terminating an agency or distribution agreement, an adequate notice period should be given. Early termination of a contract will lead to fundamental changes in either the business of the distributor or the employment and income of an agent. Negotiation is a means of resolving such uncertainty and assisting the other party during a period of upheaval through open communication.[9] If, however, a serious breach of contract has occurred, then the other party may be unwilling to offer such support and assistance.

This raises the point that agency and distribution contracts are made under a legal framework of national, international and supranational (such as EU) laws. Being fully informed about what laws are relevant to the agent/distributor contract and what the implications of these laws are constitutes a central element of a negotiation preparation. It is incumbent upon a business undertaking overseas operations to be aware that in an international setting there are multiple sovereigns, meaning that one party cannot necessarily enforce its property rights because there might not be a readily applicable international law.[10] Businesses must therefore take precautionary measures to protect themselves.

While negotiating with distributors, the most important dimensions of the deal include their level of commitment, marketing skills and financial strength. A highly committed distributor is crucial for the success of a product or service in a market. It is important to check the turnover rate of a distributor's product portfolio; a stable portfolio indicates a high commitment to the business the distributor takes on. To gain full commitment from a distributor, it is important to make sure they have a complete understanding of your objectives. In negotiations, demanding a minimal sales level is a good way of guaranteeing a minimum level of commitment.[11]

For marketing skills, thoroughly checking a distributor's marketing capability is good practice. This can be done by assessing the type of advertisement and promotional activities the distributor can perform and for what activities they will need support from the principal firm. Depending upon the product type, it is important to check their marketing methods: participation in trade fairs and exhibitions along with size and quality of sales all feed into the decision over whether it will be necessary to provide the distributor with training.

A proper understanding of the market demographic that the firm wants to tap into is important for future success. A distributor's experience with local marketing channels and the scope of their activities will dictate whether sole distribution rights should be granted. The extent of existing market coverage and experience are good indicators of the scale, national and regional, the distributor can handle. The distributor's existing market share can reveal their status in the market. If it is necessary to train or upskill the marketing team or salesforce of the distributor, it is critical to evaluate whether existing employees are capable of taking this on board or whether taking on new employees specialising in the particular product or service that is to be sold would be a better option. The cost of the training programme should be discussed in the negotiations, as well as who should bear this cost: the manufacturer, the distributor, or both through cost sharing.

Checking the financial strength of the potential agent or distributor is one of the most important criteria when negotiating an agent/distributor contract. The agents or distributors will need financing to maintain an inventory, to run their operations and to effectively market the product or service. A full, comprehensive check of the agent's or distributor's financial accounts and statements is a good starting point for this exercise. Additional investment may be needed if the agent or distributor is to take on new business. It is not, therefore, just the current financial situation of an agent or distributor that needs to be established, but their future financial position if they are to sell the new product in the market. Knowledge of the agent's or distributor's financial strengths and weaknesses means that the principal can better respond to requests for financial assistance if they are made. If the product or service requires technical support, a commitment of human and physical resources may not be sufficient; financial investment may also have to be made.

11.2 NEGOTIATING LICENSING AND FRANCHISING

Many firms decide they want to do business in a foreign market without making a major investment. In order to operate overseas in this way, the firm (licensor) makes it knowledge, trademarks, patents and name available to a foreign firm in exchange for royalties or other forms of payment. It is a quick, less problematic way of doing international business. Companies, however, need to be aware of the following issues:

- Royalties to be received are easy to audit and are guaranteed payments on a regular basis.
- A company has to ensure that any product or business development done by a licensee is reported back to the licensor.
- The agreement should only be made for a fixed period of time, because if the product is successful, the licensor may want to start selling or producing the product in that market on its own.
- The licensor has to be aware of the cost of regulating so that it may ensure that the licensee is fulfilling all the terms and conditions specified in the contract.

The *licensing* agreement varies from contract to contract but often includes:[12]

1. Specification of the product being licensed.
2. Potential development of the licensed product.
3. Exclusivity.

Franchising is similar to licensing but means that a company allows its franchisee to use not just its proprietary rights in a particular foreign market but also its business model. The franchisor secures a fee, royalties or other compensation while specifying the terms and conditions that the franchisee has to follow. In this case, the franchisor firm needs to be particularly concerned about the following:

- That the franchisee is fully motivated and committed.
- That the franchisee protects and respects the brand and image of the franchisor.
- How to ensure control over and audit of franchisees activities.

This type of international business is particularly suitable when a company has a product that is difficult or costly to export and it does not want or have the ability to make the investment that is required to do business in an overseas market by itself.

It is possible to identify various issues prospective licensors and licensees should consider before starting to negotiate a particular licensing agreement. These include making sure high levels of preparation, such as making preliminary enquiries and evaluations of the business impact and competitive consequences, have been carried out. Further, when the formal negotiations commence, a demonstration of thorough preparation by each of the parties will reflect well on them and facilitate the process. Early questions in the minds of negotiations generally include "how serious are these guys?" and "are we genuinely convinced that we can do business with them?"

Patent: the exclusive right to sole ownership and use of technology for a period of time.

When a technology is being licensed, the most important intellectual property right is the patent. A *patent* is an exclusivity right that allows the owner of the patent the sole ownership and use of the technology for a period of time within a defined technical area. This technical area will be new, previously unknown, and applicable to industry. Patent documentation must describe fully the newness of the technology and what its applied effectiveness is. Once the patent has expired, the technology may be exploited freely by anybody who wants to use it. When a negotiation takes place over the licensing of a technology, the agreement can therefore only be a temporary one, but it does entail a monopoly on the use of the technology being created. It also means that, through the terms of the contract, the licensee has to be prevented by the licensor from revealing information about the technology.[13]

A good analogy for the issues that have to be dealt with in a negotiation between a licensor and licensee comes from the relationship between an architect and a client. An architect and their client will agree the shape and form of the building that the architect will design. The design must meet the client's requirements for the building and will draw on the architect's skills and experience while taking into account the environmental circumstances and the necessary planning permissions and building regulations. The detailed design that is ultimately presented to the builder will be the aggregate of all the component elements. It is a design that will specify materials of construction and detailed designs for each individual area that are well established as suitable for their role in the overall design. It will reflect the architect and client's agreements on details and their personal preferences. It will conform to the requirements of the various regulatory authorities. Aside from the design and the legal/regulatory framework, there are other aspects of the relationship between the architect and the client that have counterparts in a licensing agreement between a licensor and a licensee.

Thus, the architect will be paid a fee for his services that will reflect the quality and value of his product. The licensing agreement will similarly specify what the licensor is to be paid both for his services and for the value to the licensee of the transferred technology and rights in the form of licence fees or royalties. The architect will accept responsibility and liability (at least to an extent) if his product is not fit for the agreed purposes, does not meet regulatory requirements, or infringes the rights of third parties.[14]

In summary, a licensing agreement must specify:

1. What the licensor allows the licensee to do.
2. How and when the licensee is to do these things.
3. How licence fees (or royalties proportional to the extent of use of the licensed technology) are calculated.
4. The capacity of the licence and the use of the licensor's "proprietary" information. It must cover what will happen if the performance of the licence agreement, or the licensed technology, does not turn out as agreed or expected.

There is a range of possible agreements, varying in type and complexity. At one end of the spectrum is a simple non-exclusive patent/design/software licence. At the other end there are major production technology licences that envisage multinational investment, global sales, and design, engineering and training services. The most commonly used types of licensing agreement in international business can be identified as:

1. *A patents licence:* Patents are a spin-off from research and development (R&D) activities. The owner of the patent may be a university, a research institute or an individual. Hence, a patent acquisition strategy must be devised that balances financial risk with the realistic prospects of interesting potential licensee enterprises. It is rare in international business for inventions to go to market after being developed and commercialised only by the innovator. More commonly, the innovator will seek a partner from a commercial enterprise already established in the relevant area or market to help them develop the product.

   In this scenario the innovator should maintain an up-to-date schedule of the patent portfolio for the invention. In this way, the innovator maintains the patent by making stipendiary payments. Once a patent has expired, it is difficult and expensive to recover, if it is possible to recover at all. The interest of the commercial partner will be to control the patent portfolio and its use to serve its business interests.

   In contrast to the partnership between an innovator and a commercial enterprise, a manufacturing company that is not well positioned to exploit the market potential of a patented innovation will develop a different patent licensing strategy which could be offensive, defensive or opportunistic. The difference in this scenario is that the licensor knows the relevant product/service field. The patents the commercial enterprise will be seeking to license will be relevant to their current business operations, rather than being of potential value at some unspecified point in the future. It commonly takes a minimum of five to eight years to prove the commercial applicability of an invention, which has to pass development and market tests.

Opportunistic, revenue-generating patent licensing by companies only makes sense when a thorough assessment of the competitive impact of such licensing has been undertaken and is shown to be non-threatening. Opportunistic patent licensing is a feature of mature industries and markets. Licensing revenue is mostly extra profit: licence fees paid buy into the fruits of creative R&D at a price usually much less than the true cost of developing equivalents. The patent owner would ordinarily indicate his realistic terms for a licence, as a basis for negotiation.

In any patent licensing the issue of whether the licence should be exclusive or not always arises. The issue hinges on whether the licensee should have sole use of the technology or whether other companies should also have use of the technology. There are a number of possible combinations and alternatives such as manufacturing licences and sales licences. Before negotiations begin in earnest for a licence, the parties need to assess what their aspirations and objectives are, and what they could accept. It is essential that a patent owner recognises that *any* licence awarded to a major player in a market *may* in effect be exclusive and no other person or company may access the technology because the agreement exhausts any further opportunity to licence, export or invest directly in that market.

Once the negotiations have been successfully completed, execution copies of the licence agreement have to be prepared and signed by both parties. The agreement may become binding at that time or it may first need to be approved or "taken on record" by the relevant authorities. The agreement will anticipate such conditions precedent and will usually set a time limit for achieving them. Unless a fully paid up licence is bought by a lump-sum payment (or through phased instalments), the agreement will specify the licensee's obligations to report the extent of the working of the licensed patent and pay the stipulated royalties, and perhaps to pay at least certain annual sums to keep the licence.

Finally, another necessary agreement provision will be one setting out respective rights of termination of the licence unilaterally, either from choice or for a specified cause such as an uncured breach of a condition of the licence.

2. *A knowhow licence:* The situation is very different in the case of a knowhow licence. This knowhow is concealed within the product, held in confidence by employees under the conditions of their employment and recorded in company reports, access to which is regulated. The presence of knowhow is merely suggested to other companies in the same industry by the quality of the company's products and their competitiveness. Unless an exchange of knowhow is proposed, the seeker of a licence would not be expected to be in direct competition with the company that holds the sought-after knowhow. When knowhow is exchanged (via a cross-licence agreement) there might be an exchange of

R&D information. The benefit to the seeker of the licence for such knowhow would be the expected economic impact on their business.

A factor in any consideration of whether to seek the acquisition of knowhow is the added time element implicit in an alternative. Undertaking R&D is uncertain and costly. An additional consideration in the markets of different countries is the impact any anti-competition legislation might have and whether there are restrictive conditions attached to the licence. It is possible to relinquish a patent licence and know exactly what position the company is in, but it is impossible to unlearn confidential knowhow.

As the best method of keeping something secret is not to tell anybody, the owner company will try very hard not to reveal the nature of the information in their possession. A strategy therefore has to be devised which can unite the parties in a confidential deal, in the belief that it is the right thing to do.

When an initial indication of interest in its knowhow has been received, the target company will first satisfy itself that the enquiry concerns knowhow which it is prepared to licence and, further, that it is willing, in principle, to licence this to the company. The next step will be to put in place a non-disclosure agreement to structure and control the information flow so that it answers the question "is there a fit between the knowhow that can be offered and the realistic needs of the enquiring company?" The evaluation phase to which the non-disclosure agreement applies may involve a two-way flow of confidential information.

The company possessing the targeted knowhow will strive to accomplish the evaluation without revealing too much of what its knowhow is, while being forthright about what its knowhow could achieve for the enquirer.

The enquirer company must ensure that its present knowledge is suitably fully recorded as of a date prior to receipt of confidential information from the target company. This knowledge comprises that which is being used commercially, that which is included in R&D reports, and that which describes plans, targets, approaches and methodology for R&D programmes. This is a major exercise, but also a vital one, as it is possible that the target knowhow will be found not to be significantly different. A recommended practice is to deposit a sealed and dated package of the significant already-possessed knowledge with a reputable outside body.

No matter how close or far apart the technology "tool kits" of the two companies are, this record will be relevant to the effect of the confidentiality obligations accepted by the enquiry company both at the enquiry stage and after the knowhow package has been agreed.

Sometimes the agreement merely recognises that the prospective licensor will be supplying information of a certain class, without legally compelling them to do so. More usually, the prospective licensor undertakes to supply information of a certain class but only that which will be sufficient to enable the recipient party to make a preliminary assessment of the technology and to determine his interest in it. Even when the information has no practical utility, it is still relevant for the decision-making process. The prospective licensee's non-disclosure obligations will consist of an undertaking not to disclose knowhow to other persons. There may be an obligation to confine received information to those regular employees, managers and directors who reasonably need to have it for the purpose of the evaluation.

There is a need at the evaluation stage for the parties to feel comfortable that third-party patents will not be a problem. Patents are national, and national bodies of patents differ from one country to another, as different patentees have different patenting policies, some choosing to patent process technologies, others preferring to rely on secrecy and a local "right to work". This local "right to work" is not licensable or transferable, except with the transfer of an entire business. The potential licensor should assure himself that the territory into which his knowhow may pass for commercial use is indeed as patent-free as his own. The prospective licensee may have done a general patent search and may seek specific assurances, but this is not a substitute for a clear general assurance from the prospective licensor based on an understanding of what knowhow is under consideration.

At this stage it is helpful if the parties give consideration to the tax regimes they are subject to for an international transaction. Certainly, during the negotiations these issues will need to be clear and provided for. It will be possible at the evaluation stage for the prospective licensor to indicate the fee he would seek to charge for assembling and transferring a defined package. This fee would include compensation for the effort involved in assembling the package and would reward the disclosure of useful knowhow to another with an option to use it. It would not reward the value of the knowhow package to a prospective licensee. That value is difficult to quantify at this stage and must be left to the detailed licence negotiation stage when an objective (or at least a sensible pragmatic) basis of determination will emerge as the relative capabilities of the two technology positions can be economically compared.

A possible distorting influence on the negotiation of licence fees arises when the prospective licensor has already licensed essentially the same technology or intellectual property rights to another on terms such that if more favourable terms should be offered to a later licensee in equivalent circumstances, those more favourable terms must be offered to the existing licensee.

3. *A combined patents/knowhow licence:* A company seeking to license its technology will shortlist types and sources of appropriate technologies from which a final choice will be made concerning what to license. This is an activity that consumes resources and consideration should therefore be given to whether a consulting firm should be hired to make these enquires on the company's behalf. A licensor company that is itself in the same product business may examine its licensing policy in order to dissuade prospective licensees from making an investment because it perceives there would be a threat from the ensuing competition. However, if the licensor company becomes convinced that the prospective licensee is determined to invest, no matter what, it may prefer to license its own technology rather than see the technology of a competitor being used. A licensor inevitably knows the scale and technology basis of their licensee's plant. The licensor controls the extent to which the licensed technology may be used

for expansions and/or in additional plants, and where those plants will be located. The licensor may also impose a requirement for feedback on (or exchange of) operational improvements, even on advances made in R&D, by their licensee. All these benefits will have an impact on relative industry competitiveness.

If the prospective licensor is not itself an operating company, even though it may have apparently successfully licensed its technology, there are significant risks to a potential licensee. First, the licensor's knowledge of precisely what their licensees have done, for example to solve problems inherent in the technology supplied to them, may be limited. Second, such licensors use new licensees as test beds for technology or design variants that have not been proven at the commercial scale. Licensees may have little contractual freedom and may not have the knowledge and skills to solve the problems they encounter.

A prospective licensee should look to receive a package comprising a basic process and outline engineering design together with a clear licence option in which all the essential provisions are spelled out. The package will be supplied only on strict confidentiality terms and will cost money. However, it does enable the licensee to evaluate and cost the technology; to have an informed negotiation with the licensor and consider alternatives; to assess the patent position thoroughly; to visit other licensees and see how the technology has been implemented by them; to confirm that the licensor can transfer the technology effectively; to confirm capital cost estimates; to confirm suitability of other sources of raw materials; to confirm that the product will sell; and to establish effluent and emissions standards.

During the enquiry phase, the prospective licensor and potential licensee must discuss the extent to which the licensed production technology might be used to establish further production plants and where these might be located. Similarly, the potential licensee will have clarified where export sales of product will be allowed. A number of distinct aspects of this topic need to be considered. First, a right to use knowhow supplied as a design package of a first plant for the design of further plants is an empty right if the licensee does not have the competence to design such plants. So, a potential licensee should ensure that he will acquire from the licensor not merely an instruction kit to engineer, build and operate a particular plant but also an insight into the basis of its design. The licence agreement should clarify and define this service and also address the question of whether the new design will embody improvements that have been subsequently developed by the licensee and/or licensor and on what terms. A licensee would be expected to implement R&D for any technology underpinning a core business activity. Second, licensors may seek to prevent product sales in given territories or outside a defined licensed area. The legality and enforceability of such impositions will need to be researched before they can be agreed. It is legitimate for licensors to reserve the right to enforce their patents in territories where they wish to prevent the sale of the same products imported from other territories, so far as their patents allow them to do so. It may be agreed that the potential licensee will purchase products from the prospective licensor or one of his licensees to ensure that the products will be suitable for the intended market or downstream consuming units.

The financial provisions of a licence agreement receive much attention during the negotiation process. The size of service fees and of licence payments on a present worth basis will be set by finally reaching congruence between what the respective parties feel they can impose or afford in each particular circumstance. External influences (such as government intervention in the approvals process or any prior undertakings to other licensees) may constrain the choices available. The sums that the licensee has to pay for exploitation of their licence may be definite in amount and timing (licence fees) or they may be periodic payments based on the measured extent of use (royalties). The taxation effect and the degree of risk will be different in the two cases. The method to calculate the sums due to the licensor, how they are paid (the timing and currency of payments), and how tax withholdings are treated should be specified in detail. The existence of a double taxation treaty or legislation granting credit unilaterally will be significant. Additionally, for tax reasons, or because of the particular contributions made to the value of the licence by patents, it may be important for either party to deal with the financial provisions of the patent licence separately from those for the knowhow licence.

Neither negotiating party should make any commitments that are legally enforceable except in specific agreed respects where it is absolutely necessary for both parties to establish whether a basis for an effective technology licence or intellectual property rights exists. No warranties of guarantees should be given during the negotiation. The executed contract should contain what is going to be supplied, when it is going to be supplied, the scope and form of technology being transferred and any restrictions or limitations of use of the intellectual property. The executed licence agreement should also set forth issues of responsibility and liability for the performance of the product, and what will happen if these criteria are not met. Finally, the final licensing contract should state the financial terms of service, future options and contingencies, and the limits to which the licence can be exploited. It is in fact normal for licence agreements to be as complete as is possible, stating all terms and schedules agreed upon by both parties, with the possible exception of confidential agreements. After this contract has been signed, all prior commitments will be of relevance.

Both of the negotiating parties will want to be assured that those who are acting on behalf of the other party have the capacity and authority to negotiate in good faith. This can be achieved through initial face-to-face meetings between the parties, when a senior corporate or business general manager from each side is present. Typically, the negotiating team would consist of a Project Manager or Licensing Manager, who will have a technical and business background. Technical, engineering, legal and intellectual property specialists may support this individual, as is appropriate for the demands of the negotiations.

The majority of the negotiations should be face-to-face to ensure that misunderstandings are aired openly and to maintain momentum. At a certain stage the licensor will present an outline licence agreement for consideration. This is simply one party's view of the matter. Depending on the progress made over the course of the negotiations, this draft licence agreement will be revised by both parties, usually by their legal/

intellectual property specialists, and the drafts exchanged. These drafts should deal with uncontentious issues, for example reporting and payment routings for fees and royalties, currency exchange calculations, tax withholdings and certificates, the effective date of the agreement, any necessary government or central bank procedures and approvals, and choice of law contract.

11.3 JOINT VENTURES

Joint ventures have been a popular way of doing business abroad, particularly when there is a very attractive market, but a firm faces high levels of uncertainty or does not have enough knowledge and is therefore reluctant to invest on its own. In some instances, local governments demand that a foreign firm take a local partner if they want to do business in their country. This is however changing, and now many countries do not demand this from foreign firms. In this type of business, equity is shared and both a foreign and a local company own the business jointly. This creates a mutually beneficial relationship for both parties. Parties share the risk and benefit from one another's strengths. In some cases, there may be more than two partners.[15]

In joint venture negotiations parties need to be particularly concerned about the following issues:

- Choosing the right partner is particularly crucial in a joint venture contract. It is therefore important that companies are clear about what type of partner they want. Joint ventures, like marriages, often have problems and end up with separation or divorce. A firm that is looking for a joint venture should first draw up a list of potential partners in the particular market and compare their profile with the objectives of the firm. What type of partner do they want? Who has the complementary resources or skills they need to make the project a success? Any potential partner must have the requisite skills or knowledge that is wanted. A joint venture requires investment from both parties, and it is imperative to establish whether the potential partner has the capacity and desire to invest. Otherwise, the local partner would only want to contribute local knowledge, and it will be incumbent on the foreign partner to make all the investment. This was the case in many joint ventures that were signed with Chinese firms in the 1990s, most of which encountered difficulties and ended up failing. In the case where a foreign firm wants a local partner to handle a difficult political and regulatory situation, it is not easy to assess the strengths and weaknesses of potential partners and decide which potential partner is most suitable. Each potential partner will claim that they are the most suitable proposition, have the right connections in the public and private sector, have access to ministers and the knowhow to influence the country's government. This has proved to be particularly true in India. It is not advisable to select a partner who is known to be very close to one particular political party. The firm may face challenges in the implementation of the contract if this selected political party is not in government, or if the party is in government but loses power in elections that follow shortly after the contract has been signed. Choosing the right partner in a foreign market is a crucial decision and it is very important that the assessment of potential candidates be extremely rigorous.

- In order to be clear about what type of partner a firm is looking for, the firm should have well-defined ideas about what business it wants to do in a particular market. Firms enter foreign markets for a variety of different reasons. Sometimes foreign expansion is a means of growth; other times a firm is searching for efficiencies or skilled labour. A firm's decision to expand overseas can also be motivated by the need to secure reliable and consistent sources of supply and components. Depending upon the objectives, different sorts of partners are needed. This is why before a firm initiates the search for a partner it first needs to be clear about the reasons for its entry into a foreign market, and about what type of partner is going to be the most suitable for it.
- Complementarity of resources and strengths are important, as each party wants to benefit from the other's strength. When choosing a partner, it is not a good idea to select a firm that has similar capabilities as your own firm. A partner can only be good if it complements your capabilities, whether it is dealing with the local legislative institutions, making the manufacturing process more efficient or providing superior marketing expertise in a specific market.
- In joint ventures parties may take an equal, 50/50 stake or one party may have a majority stake, such as 60/40 or 70/30. However, it is important to be clear which of the parties will have overall control and which of the parties is going to be responsible for making decisions on different parts of the operation. The risk of losing control of their product, technology or brand is one of the most common problems firms face in foreign market joint ventures. First, it is difficult to decide how much control should be handed over to a local partner and how much should be kept. Second, once a firm has decided how control should be kept in order for them to achieve their objectives in the market, difficulties during implementation arise as local partners are in a stronger position. To manage this complex scenario, many firms want to have a majority equity share as they believe that this will help them retain the levels of control they desire. This has not, however, proven to be an effective measure in many cases. Some companies want to keep control of the technology if possible, because it will make the local partner dependent on the foreign partner's input in the joint venture. In such cases control over local operations and marketing is delegated to local partners.
- Negotiations for joint ventures are different from negotiating an agent or distributor contract. The subsequent success of the joint venture depends upon effective and careful negotiations. One of the most delicate tasks when negotiating a joint venture in a foreign market is deciding on and evaluating each partner's particular contribution. Not all the contributions a partner may make are observable and tangible; nor are all contributions easy to evaluate in monetary terms. For example, it is difficult to put a price on the value of knowledge in a local market offered by a local partner. Similarly, how much is access to the local partner's network worth? How much their reputation? How much their marketing expertise?

It is imperative to be cognisant of the role of government and the regulations that exist around local/foreign joint ventures. Are there any restrictions on equity ownership for a foreign partner? Although such restrictions for foreign partners have been abolished in many markets, local partners may use the shadow of such restraints during a negotiation to demand the majority share. In this respect it is important to check the capital inflow into the joint venture. Who will be losing how much, and in the case where some capital is to be borrowed, which party will offer guarantees to the banks? Are there any subsidies available from the government? The future capital increase/decrease and terms around this should also be negotiated. How should the shares in the joint venture be divided among the partners, and should there be a limit (maximum/minimum) on each partner's shareholding?

Another delicate issue, but one that is similarly important in any negotiation, is the appointment and composition of the board of directors and senior managers. In some countries local partners are often accused of nepotism in order to gain control or exclude foreign partners from important decisions. Arrangements concerning production facilities, operations, quality control and other related issues should be negotiated and agreed upon in order to prevent future conflict or disagreements. The same approach should be adopted for marketing activities such as new product development, R&D and branding. It is advisable to agree on which partner will exercise decision-making power on which issue.

Finally, it is important to have an understanding of the regulating laws and the legal implications of these for a joint venture. It can be highly damaging if the negotiations are concluded with an agreement without having agreed under which jurisdiction the contract is to be governed. Frequently, the contract is governed by local law. Example 11.1 shows how McDonald's used such an agreement to expand its operations in China.

EXAMPLE 11.1
MCDONALD'S 20-YEAR NEGOTIATED DEAL WITH SINOPEC IN CHINA

What can an organisation do to rapidly increase its retail outlets in a foreign market to remain competitive? Such a scenario was faced by McDonald's when it entered the Chinese market. McDonald's opened its first restaurant in China in 1990, three years after KFC entered the market. McDonald's growth in China was slower than that of KFC, which as the first Western fast food restaurant had established strong brand recognition and by 2007 was opening one store a day and had 1,700 stores in China. In contrast, McDonald's had 780 restaurants.

For both companies, rapid growth in the country was important, especially before the Olympic Games to be held in Beijing in 2008. Beyond the Olympics, McDonald's wanted to cash in on the increasing ownership of automobiles in China and build more drive-thrus. However, building new restaurants required approvals and finding prime real-estate locations, activities that took time that McDonald's did not have. Instead, the company decided to negotiate with Sinopec, the Chinese oil giant. McDonald's chose Sinopec as they had a network of 30,000 petrol stations in China.

Seeking a long-term relationship, the companies agreed on a 20-year deal that saw McDonald's increase their presence by another 1,000 stores before the 2008 Olympics, with plans for 100 stores to be opened every year. In 2017, as part of McDonald's global restructuring, the company sold the controlling stake of its operations in the country to China-based company Citic Ltd, in a deal worth $2.1 billion. McDonald's retained 20 per cent of the ownership. In mid-2017, McDonald's announced that it would nearly double the number of restaurants from 2,500 to 4,500 within a time span of five years. This would make China the second biggest market for McDonald's outside of the United States.

McDonald's success in China highlights the importance of negotiating alliances with partners that have a large physical presence in the country along with social networks. By doing so, McDonald's was able to lay the foundations for growth in China, which the company is continuing to experience.

Sources: Adapted from Chan (2017);[16] Chien (2007);[17] China Daily (2007);[18] Ng (2006);[19] and Pisani (2017).[20]

Discussion Point: What are the advantages for a globally recognised company like McDonald's to form alliances with local firms? What are some of the risks associated with this strategy?

In summary, companies should be clear about the distinction between partner-related and task-related issues, both of which are essential to negotiating an international joint venture contract. Partner-related issues include whether the partner is suitably qualified and has appropriate characteristics. Qualifications and characteristics can range from personality, reliability, commitment and guaranteed intellectual property protection to reputation, experience within the particular sector and the extent of firm complementarity. Task-related issues refer to the operational capabilities of the potential partner, the specific skills that are required such as marketing or after-sales service, and the partner's financial resources. In the case where the partner does not have the required finances, is that partner able to access the funds through the market? The issue then becomes whether the partner has sufficient finance-raising capabilities.[21]

11.4 NEGOTIATING INTERNATIONAL MERGERS AND ACQUISITIONS

Mergers and acquisitions (M&As) have been on the rise for the last three decades. However, many of these M&As fail to achieve the objectives that the parties involved want to reach. This failure to achieve objectives often leads to the combined value of the companies decreasing. The overall research on M&As reveal that in most deals at least one party, usually the purchasing company, ends up with a lower value than before.[22] This is particularly true for international deals that involve complicated institutional, legal, cultural and commercial factors. Many of these failures and complications can be avoided if a proper negotiation process is followed.

M&As are perhaps the most important decision a company will make. In a single transaction the course of the company and the careers of its managers and staff can be changed; value for shareholders can be created or destroyed. Following the $38 billion merger of car manufacturers Daimler and Chrysler announced in May 1998, the merged company lost 40 per cent of its share value in the period to December 2000.[23]

In a merger the assets of two companies are combined to form a new legal entity. In an acquisition, control of the assets of one of the companies is transferred to the acquirer and the taken-over firm ceases to exist. In reality, the merging of two equals is rare, with most deals resulting in one company taking over another.[24] Mergers can be horizontal between two competing firms; vertical between buyer and supplier; and conglomerate, where the companies involved are unrelated.

Preparations for M&A negotiations are very different from those of other deals, as quite often the parties do not want to reveal that a merger or acquisition between the two companies is going to take place, as if revealed too early, the market value, share price or reputation of one or both companies will be negatively affected and lead to speculations. Most information gathering is done secretly and the companies have to trust the information they collect. This is, however, particularly difficult in cross-border M&As as both companies exist in different legal and cultural structures. Differences in local accounting and auditing procedures and regulation may show a company to be in good health and profitable, but when evaluated using other standards of accounting, the company might actually be unprofitable and should thus be purchased for a lower amount. Differences such as these do exist within Europe and the United States. In spite of International Accounting Standards, the systems followed in different countries are different. Moreover, taxation rules are different in different countries, such as between the United Kingdom and Ireland and between the United Kingdom and France, and is this particularly the case in emerging market countries. Some countries, such as Sweden and Norway, have transparent annual accounting and financial statements which are publicly accessible, while in other countries these accounts are closed and not publicly available, such as in Japan, Germany and China.[25]

While preparing for negotiations, conducting an accounting and financial audit, particularly of the firm that is to be acquired, is crucial. Regarding commercial scrutiny, turnover and profits should be checked for the past five years. Furthermore, it is important to examine creditors and debtors. A clear picture of assets and liabilities is imperative when assigning value to a company. In many cases the size of a pension fund or liabilities may make or break the deal. The manner in which pension contributions are calculated and the size of the fund are different in different countries and for different companies. Knowledge of these issues will facilitate understanding about why a company is enthusiastic about a potential takeover. The underlying motives may differ from those that are expressed publicly through official channels.

The negotiation process will be smooth and efficient when the negotiators are fully aware of the underlying reasons and motives. An integrative approach and a positive atmosphere are important for a positive relationship to flourish during and after the negotiations. Focusing on future benefits will enable this to come about.[26] When negotiators express and display cooperative behaviour during negotiations this leads to a smooth integration once the contract has been signed. In fact, the integration of the two companies begins even before the M&A agreement comes into effect. Cultural integration in such cases can be the biggest constraint, but it is also possible to manage this integration effectively.[27]

11.5 NEGOTIATING TURNKEY PROJECTS

Turnkey projects: type of contract where the foreign firm takes the responsibility of building a facility and when completed hands it over to the buyer to operate.

In these types of contracts/projects the foreign firm takes the responsibility of building a production facility such as a factory, a service facility such as a hospital, or an infrastructure facility such as power plant that the buyer can operate once construction has been completed and it is ready to be handed over. To enable the buyer to operate the facility, these contracts often include training management and local staff after the project has been completed. *Turnkey projects* are often big projects worth vast sums of money.[28] Projects that include building, technology, knowhow and training of local staff are still very common, particularly in emerging markets.

Selling firms should be particularly careful about the following issues in package deals and turnkey projects:

- The financial arrangements/position of the buyer. As these projects often entail large amounts of money, it is useful to know how the buyer intends to the finance their purchase and whether a third party will be involved. If a third party, such as the World Bank, is involved, the firm needs to look at the conditions that have been stipulated by the World Bank in order to fund this.
- A clear understanding of who is doing what, when. Is the local party going to help clear the material and machinery through customs? In many countries, getting goods cleared through customs and other parts of regulations is a long and tedious process that can cause unnecessary delays. Do the engineers/workers need to have work permits in order work? If yes, is the local party going to facilitate that? Many countries do not allow foreign workers to work/install machinery on the site without a proper work permit. Applying for and receiving the permit can be a lengthy process.
- A clear understanding of taxation rules and regulations.
- Are training costs for the local staff going to be included in the price or are they going to be invoiced separately?
- The unique characteristics of each project. Normally it is not possible to use a standard contract for these projects, as each project is different in scope, size and nature. Plant and equipment supplied to each project varies depending on the price, environment and responsibility assigned to each party.
- The role of governments. Quite often these projects are sold to governments or the government is involved even if the project is private or semi-private. In negotiations, therefore, a number of the issues discussed above, such as work permits, customs clearance and taxation, can be negotiated directly with government representatives.
- The involvement of governments also creates an element of risk, as if the government changes before the project is completed then the project can encounter serious problems, as has been the case with changes of government in India and Brazil.

Example 11.2 identifies some of the advantages of turnkey projects for firms.

EXAMPLE 11.2
USING ORGANISATIONAL KNOWLEDGE TO NEGOTIATE TURNKEY AGREEMENTS

Turnkey projects provide opportunities for organisations to work with other firms and to use their existing tacit and explicit knowledge to expand their operations internationally. This is especially important for firms who may have limited opportunities in their own markets. For example, many Australian engineering and architecture firms seek opportunities internationally for the construction of new stadiums and other major projects. Australia is a young country with a relatively small population compared to the total area of the country, and there are few new mega construction project opportunities for the firms to be part of. By joining other international firms, Australian companies have been able to be part of turnkey projects, such as the construction or refurbishment of sporting stadiums, including Wembley Stadium in the United Kingdom.

Similarly, Japanese firms like Hitachi have been taking advantage of the economic growth of countries like Singapore and have become part of turnkey projects to construct industrial plants.

Sources: Adapted from Kermode (2018);[29] Kimoto et al. (2013).[30]

Discussion Point: How can organisations become part of international consortiums to bid for turnkey projects? What are the potential challenges associated with negotiating such deals?

11.6 SUMMARY

There are different types of deals that are negotiated in international business. These deals require a sound understanding of the internal and external environments as they influence the negotiation deals. In this chapter, we identify the key issues and influences that affect the negotiations related to agent/distributor contracts, licensing and franchising agreements, joint ventures, mergers and acquisitions, and turnkey projects.

QUESTIONS

1. What are the most important dimensions of the deal when carrying out negotiations with distributors?
2. How can firms protect the ownership and use of their technology when negotiating a licensing arrangement?
3. What are some of the issues that parties need to be concerned about in a joint venture agreement?
4. In what ways are preparations for mergers and acquisitions (M&As) negotiations different from other deals?
5. What are some of the risks associated with negotiating a turnkey project?

NOTES

1. Kogut, B. (1986) Designing contracts to guarantee enforceability: theory and evidence from East–West trade. *Journal of International Business Studies.* **17**(1), 47–61.
2. Weitz, B.A. and Jap, S.D. (1995) Relationship marketing and distribution channels. *Journal of the Academy of Marketing Science.* **23**(4), 305–20.
3. McCall, J.B. (2003) Negotiating sales, export transactions and agency agreements. In: Ghauri, P.N. and Usunier, J.-C. (eds) *International Business Negotiations.* 2nd ed. Oxford, Pergamon/Elsevier, pp. 223–41.
4. Cavusgil, S.T. and Ghauri, P.N. (1990) *Doing Business in Developing Countries: Entry and Negotiation Strategies.* London, Routledge, pp. 95–9.
5. Rugman, A., Lecraw, D.J. and Booth, L.D. (1985) *International Business: Firm and Environment.* New York: McGraw-Hill, p. 91.
6. Hart, O. and Moore, J. (1988) Incomplete contracts and renegotiation. *Econometrica.* **56**(4), 755–85.
7. Edlin, A.S. and Hermalin, B.E. (2000) Contract renegotiation and options in agency problems. *Journal of Law, Economics, and Organization.* **16**(2), 395–423.
8. McCall (2003) op. cit.
9. Puelinckx, A.H. and Tieleman, H.A. (1981) The termination of agency and distributorship agreements: a comparative survey. *Northwestern Journal of International Law and Business.* **3**(2), 452–95.
10. Boddewyn, J.J. and Brewer, T.L. (1994) International-business political behaviour: new theoretical directions. *The Academy of Management Review.* **19**(1), 119–43.
11. Cavusgil, T., Ghauri, P.N. and Agarwal, A. (2002) *Doing Business with Emerging Markets: Entry and Negotiation Strategies.* Thousand Oaks, SAGE.
12. Anand, B.N. and Khanna, T. (2000) The structure of licensing contracts. *Journal of Industrial Economics.* **48**(1), 103–35.
13. Parker, V. (2003) Negotiating licensing agreements. In: Ghauri, P.N. and Usunier, J.-C. (eds) *International Business Negotiations*, 2nd ed. Oxford, Pergamon/Elsevier, pp. 243–73.
14. This analogy comes from Parker (2003) ibid.
15. Hyder, A. and Ghauri, P. (2000) Managing international joint venture relationships: a longitudinal perspective. *Industrial Marketing Management.* **29**(3), 205–18.
16. Chan, K. (2017) McDonald's sells China business in deal worth up to $2.1B. *Associated Press News*, 10 January.
17. Chien, K. (2007) McDonald's, Sinopec sign 20-year drive-thru deal. *Reuters*, 19 January.
18. China Daily (2007) Joint agreements the best choice for multinationals. 8 May.
19. Ng, E. (2006) Sinopec in deal with McDonald's on drive-in outlets at petrol stations. *South China Morning Post*, 21 June.
20. Pisani, J. (2017) McDonald's plans to nearly double restaurants in China. *USA Today*, 8 August.
21. Cavusgil, T., Akcal, A. and Ghauri, P. (2013) *Doing Business in Emerging Markets.* 2nd ed. Thousand Oaks, SAGE.
22. Buckley, P. and Ghauri, P. (2002) *International Mergers and Acquisitions.* London, Thomson.
23. The Financial Times (2007) Timeline: from global merger to sale. 14 May.
24. UNCTAD (2000) *World Investment Report 2000.* New York and Geneva, UNCTAD.
25. De Beaufort, V. and Lampereur, A. (2003) Negotiating mergers and acquisitions in the European Union. In: Ghauri, P.N. and Usunier, J.-C. (eds) *International Business Negotiations.* 2nd ed. Oxford, Pergamon/Elsevier, pp. 291–324.
26. Fisher, R. and Ertel, D. (1995) *Getting Ready to Negotiate.* New York, Penguin.

27. Zueva, A., Fotaki, M. and Ghauri, P.N. (2012) Cultural evaluation and subjectivity in mergers & acquisitions. *British Journal of Management*. **23**(2), 272–90.
28. Ghauri, P. (1986) Guidelines for international business negotiations. *International Marketing Review*. **3**(3), 72–82.
29. Kermode, P. (2018) Multiplex still building post buyout. *Business News Western Australia*, 16 November.
30. Kimoto, Y., Chang, J.Q. and Sugiura, T. (2013) Turnkey construction of factories in Asia. *Hitachi Review*. **62**(4), 244–9.

FURTHER READING

Anwar, S.T. (2019) Kraft's acquisition of Cadbury: was it an amicable transatlantic merger or a hostile takeover? *Thunderbird International Business Review*. **61**(2), 439–51.

Hartmann, A.M. (2019) Negotiating for strategic alliances. In: Khan, M. and Ebner N. (eds) *The Palgrave Handbook of Cross-Cultural Business Negotiation*. London, Palgrave Macmillan, pp. 53–70.

Lee, K.H. (2018) Cross-border mergers and acquisitions amid political uncertainty: a bargaining perspective. *Strategic Management Journal*. **39**(11), 2992–3005.

Salacuse, J.W. (1998) So, what is the deal anyway? Contracts and relationships as negotiating goals. *Negotiation Journal*. **14**(1), 5–12.

End of Part III cases

CASE 1
ETHICAL DILEMMA WHILE NEGOTIATING[1]

Lead-Excel is a well-known Canadian fashion label that has decided to outsource its manufacturing to Bangladesh to take advantage of low-cost labour. Bangladesh is one of the largest manufacturers of ready-made garments, and the sector contributes about 80 per cent of the country's exports.[2] The company received quotes from manufacturers in Bangladesh and identified a potential partner, Dhaka Garments. In the wake of the Rana Plaza incident, Lead-Excel was understandably cautious in choosing the right manufacturing partner and decided to send a team of managers to audit the manufacturing facilities of the potential partner and to negotiate an agreement. In particular, the focus of the audit was to ensure that working conditions in the contracted factory were safe, and Lead-Excel's products would be manufactured without the use of child labour.

A day after arriving in Dhaka, Bangladesh, the negotiating team of Lead-Excel, led by Sarah Williams, visited the factory of Dhaka Garments. They were pleasantly surprised to find that the factory has stringent safety requirements. However, Sarah noticed that 80 per cent of the factory's workers were women. She investigated this further and found that women were paid 15 per cent less than their male counterparts for doing the same work in the factory. Bangladesh has a minimum wage award, which is one of the lowest in the world for manufacturers of ready-made garments. While the men were paid slightly more than the minimum wage, the women working at Dhaka Textile were not. Sarah also discovered that some claims of use of child labour in the factory had been raised, but these were not found in any reports produced by the government work safety audit. She suspected that this may in part be due to high levels of corruption in the country. Both parties decided to meet in a couple of days to discuss details of the deal.

At a social gathering of expatriates that evening, Sarah expressed her concerns about women being underpaid and possible use of child labour and suggested that she will be raising this as an issue with the head office in Canada and with the management of Dhaka Garments during negotiations. A fellow Canadian expatriate, Jim Brown, who has been working in Bangladesh for five years, was also in attendance at the event. After hearing about Sarah's concerns, he approached her and explained that the practice of paying women less than men was not illegal in the country. According to Jim, the work in the factory allows the women to contribute to the family's budget and helps them educate and feed their children. If these women were not employed by the factories, then it would add to the social problems in the country. So even though the factory was paying the women workers less than the men, not being employed would be a bigger problem for the women and their families. Jim suggested that it would be insensitive of Sarah to attempt to force her own beliefs and values when operating in Bangladesh. Jim also suggested that her company's decision to move the manufacturing to Bangladesh was to take advantage of the low cost of manufacturing, and her managers are unlikely to take any action on any unproven claims of child labour that may result in higher wages. Sarah, however, feels that the practices are unethical and is determined to raise these issues.

DISCUSSION QUESTIONS

1. The case highlights that nothing illegal has been proven about the operations in Bangladesh. Should Sarah Williams still raise these issues with Dhaka Garments during negotiations and inform the head office in Canada? Explain the reasons for your answer.
2. Jim Brown suggested that Sarah would be imposing her own beliefs and views (or using self-reference criteria) when analysing the labour management issues in Bangladesh. However, if Sarah does not do anything, then she could be accused of following ethical relativism or following the local norms and practices. How can she balance these two issues?

CASE 2
AIRBUS AND BOEING: WILL NEGOTIATIONS BRING AN END TO A 15-YEAR-OLD DISPUTE?[3]

Boeing and Airbus are the world's largest commercial airline manufacturers. Both companies claim that the other receives unfair government advantage through subsidies, soft loans, or grants for research. This conflict between Boeing from the United States and Airbus, a European multinational, dates back to 2004.

THE ISSUES AND THE NEGOTIATION PROCESS

For Airbus and Boeing, the direct and indirect involvement of the government and the size of their operations meant that much of the negotiations and communication between the parties was undertaken at the government-to-government level. In 2004, Boeing lobbied the US government to approach the European Union (EU) to seek talks to discuss the issue of alleged subsidies that Airbus was receiving via government loans. The US government cancelled the US–EU agreement that covered support for Boeing and Airbus. The EU, in response, filed a complaint with the World Trade Organization (WTO) against the US government for providing aid to Boeing.

The WTO asked both parties to resolve the outstanding issues bilaterally. These negotiations failed, and in 2005 the WTO became actively involved in resolving the dispute. Between 2009 and 2011, the WTO ruled that both the EU and the US governments had provided unfair support to Airbus and Boeing. This ruling was challenged by both parties, who claimed that the WTO's ruling did not cover the scope of the issue sufficiently, and appeals were lodged.

In 2012, the parties claimed that they were complying with the WTO rulings while accusing the other party of failing to do the same. By 2017, the WTO had ruled that the EU had failed to comply with its ruling while reversing some of its previous decisions made against the US. As organisations cannot directly take their case to the WTO, they rely on their governments to take action on their behalf. However, the risk of this approach is that the issue can become linked to other trade and investment issues. By 2018, the Airbus and Boeing issues had morphed into threats of countervailing duties and sanctions to be applied to other goods and services entering the boundaries of the two economies. The two parties agreed to WTO arbitration the same year to determine the scope of the tariffs.

In 2019, the WTO continued to rule on the appeals and counter-appeals filed by both parties. By June 2019, both sides acknowledged that the WTO rulings against them, and the subsequent appeals, did not seem to resolve the issue, with the US side suggesting that they were open to bilateral negotiations with the European side that would allow Airbus to receive some government funding on commercial terms. However, in public, both sides accused each other of refusing to negotiate an outcome.

In September 2019, with news of an imminent WTO ruling, Airbus urged a negotiated settlement of the issue that had morphed into a major trade battle between the US and Europe. Finally, in October 2019, the WTO ruled in favour of the US, deciding that Boeing had sustained significant losses due to the subsidies received by Airbus. The award of $7.5 billion annually in favour of the US can be recovered by applying countervailing measures against goods entering its market from the EU. The WTO is expected to announce its decision on the EU's counter-tariff. As the dispute enters its 16th year, an amicable end to the dispute remains a distant reality.

DISCUSSION QUESTIONS

1. What were the benefits (and limitations) of involving the World Trade Organization (WTO) as arbitrator of the dispute?
2. Using the negotiation process, analyse the tactics used by the two parties to resolve the dispute.

CASE 3
T-BLADE: SKATING INTO THE NORTH AMERICAN MARKET*

It was a rainy afternoon in March 2003. Dr. Mathias Kunz, CEO of t-blade GmbH, was just about to board his Lufthansa flight from Calgary, Canada, back to Frankfurt, Germany. He was returning home from a meeting with his business partner, Graf Canada CEO Mike Hill. Graf Canada was one of the largest hockey equipment manufacturers in the world. Kunz had a few minutes left until boarding

---

* Patrizia Feicht, Ingo Petersen, Sebastian Rummier and Hannah Wehling prepared this case under the supervision of Professor Lutz Kaufmann and Alex Michel to provide material for class discussion. The authors do not intend to illustrate either effective or ineffective handling of a managerial situation. The authors may have disguised certain names and other identifying information to protect confidentiality The authors would like to thank Dr. Mathias Kunz for his outstanding support.

We continuously want to improve our case development process and ask you to share your experience with us. For feedback please contact Lutz Kaufmann at Kaufmann@whu.edu.

time, and so he sat in the waiting room gazing through the large windows at the waiting planes outside. Suddenly, he flashed back to a moment 2½ years ago, when he had been sitting staring through the exact same window into a future then so unclear and uncertain, yet with so much excitement and admittedly naiveté. He had yet had to learn a few lessons when the adventure of the North American market began for t-blade on that cloudy night in November 2000. The excitement had not vanished, but had accompanied him on every single one of his now-common trips to Calgary, Canada, where the headquarters of Graf Canada was situated. The short time Graf Canada and t-blade GmbH had been working together on introducing and promoting the revolutionary t-blade technology had been filled with exciting events, a lot of work, and rewarding results. But now had come the point when they both had to decide on the future of their partnership as The Hockey Company (THC), the second largest ice skating equipment manufacturer worldwide, had been approaching them repeatedly with a serious request to join them in their efforts to turn the t-blade technology into a globally-accepted standard. THC's offer sounded promising, yet Kunz and Hill both were also aware of the risks that including a large company such as THC in their circle would bring. A ten-hour flight lay ahead of Kunz, which was sufficient time to think and re-think over all the pros and cons that he and Hill had discussed during the past two days. One thing was for sure: this decision would not be an easy one.

HISTORY OF T-BLADE GMBH

The product and its development

The beginning of the t-blades dates back to the late 1980s when Holger Würthner, a technical engineer with two ice hockey-fanatic sons, decided to tackle the problem of quickly blunting blades that hockey users all over the world complained about. He realized that the technique of mechanically sharpening the steel blades basically had not changed since the introduction of hockey skates, and set out to revolutionize hockey blades. It took him more than ten years of hard work, during which he reached all levels of emotion between thrilled excitement and complete devastation. However, at the end he managed to invent a new generation of blades (see Exhibit 1).

Before 1980:
Solid steel skate and holder

From 1980 to present:
Solid steel skate and plastic holder – TUUK standard

Future of ice skates:
t-blade system

Exhibit 1 Evolution of ice skates

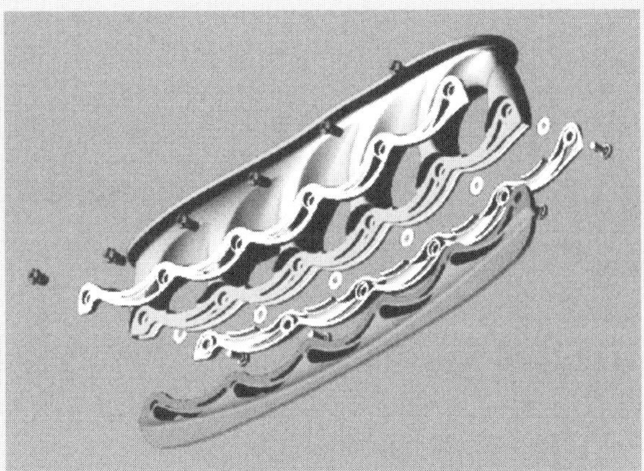

Source: t-blade.

Exhibit 2 t-blade system (blade with runner, stabilizer and holder)

These blades consisted of three parts (see Exhibit 2): one fixed to the shoe (the holder), the second containing the actual blade (the runner), and the third connecting the first two (the stabilizer). Using this system, blunt blades could be replaced quickly with new ones by the user himself and no sharpening was required at all. This development was already a big step forward, but the real revolution was the blade itself. In the past, blades were simply a piece of steel attached to the skating boot through a plastic holder. This steel blade blunted at varying rates, according to the intensity of use. While recreational users had to sharpen their blades on average once a month, professional ice hockey players stated that their blades were often blunt after the first or second third of the game, making quick turns and directional changes more and more difficult and less exact and controlled. The sharpening of the blades had to be done by a professional with a specialized machine, which took some time. Besides, it was hard to control the way the blades were shaped afterwards so the boot sometimes leaned more to the one side or the other afterwards, so that the skater had to adapt each time to a new skating "feel" on the ice. Würthner developed a blade that sought to overcome these obstacles: his blade was merely a thin stripe of two metals molded together and attached to the plastic runner. The combination of these two metals made the blade strong; it blunted 4-5 times slower than traditional blades. Once blunt, the blade could easily be replaced by the skater himself. In addition, the blade also had positive side effects: the friction of the blade on the ice created heat that usually led through the steel blade and vanished unused into the air (see Exhibits 3 and 4). However, since Würthner's blade was only a small metal band held by plastic all around the heat remained concentrated to the actual edge of the blade and could not vanish into the large part of steel, as it was the case with conventional blades. The concentrated heat thus could melt the ice underneath better and improved the gliding properties of the skate on the thin water film, the underlying physical principle of ice skating. This enabled the skater to glide much faster and made his turns and changes in direction a lot quicker. Because of this effect, Würthner called his blade "thermo-blade" or "t-blade" for short. Another positive effect of the t-blades was that the plastic construction was more flexible than the steel blades and thus proved to be more gentle on bones and joints. (For more details on performance measurements, see Exhibit 5.)

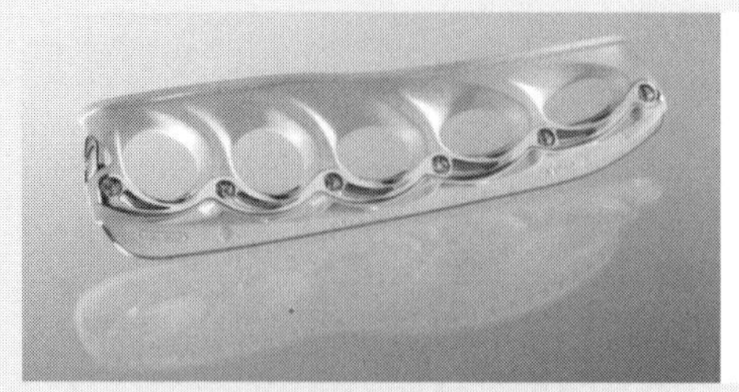
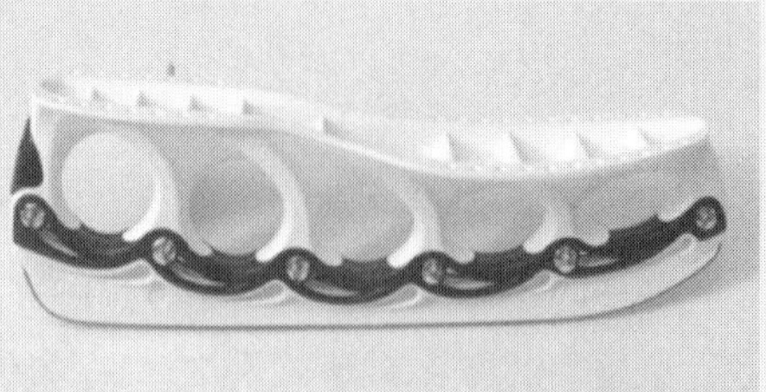

Source: t-blade.

Exhibit 3 t-blade skates design

Source: t-blade.

Exhibit 4 t-blade in action

In 1994, Würthner filed patent for his t-blade technology, and succeeded in obtaining a very broad patent that included every composite blade in the winter sporting goods sector, which was granted in 1996. Würthner was sure that his t-blade was going to be a success: with the typical view of an engineer, he thought consumers would buy his product just because of its superior qualities. He had spent a huge amount of time and money in the development process and now expected to earn the fruits of his labor. However, he came to realize that dealers were as unwilling to sell his blades as much as customers were unwilling to buy them. The few brave enough to test the invention had found teething problems: for example, the plastic was not strong enough to hold under extreme conditions but was bending instead, preventing the skater from keeping his foot in the normal skating position. Thus, Würthner's invention was not received with the open arms he had imagined. But he did not lose faith and set out to test and improve his invention, spending even more money in the process. By the end of 1999, his resources were exhausted: he had spent two million euros belonging to his family

Ultra Light

The use of the special glass fibre constructed holder and the glass fibre steel constructed runner results in a 19% reduction in weight in comparison to other skate blades. This weight reduction results in quicker acceleration and in increase in maneuverability. Users have noticed a remarkable increase in stamina in the third period.

Super Speed

The blade surface itself is extremely smooth. Due to the glass fibre steel construction, the steel portion of the blade retains heat better than conventional blades while skating. Higher blade temperature immediately provides a water film for gliding and reduces gliding friction by 40%. This has been verified by several independent tests conducted by a respected university.

Forget Sharpening

No sharpening necessary, the blades are simply replaced. Since they are made of a special glass fibre, with just a thin metal gliding surface, they are more economical than sharpening. Moreover, the unprediictability of poor sharpening is avoided. Thanks to the ultra hard steel alloy, the edges are much sharper and the surface much smoother.

Always Optimal Blade

Blades can be changed very easily to adlapt to ice temperature, player weight and preference. Three different rockers can be combined with five different hollow radii. And, if one loses an edge during a game, it can easily be changed without missing several shifts.

Narrowest Turning Radius

The elasticity of the system allows players to achieve a narrower turning radius without decrease in stability.

Source: Press Release CCM; 2003.

Exhibit 5 Performance features of t-blade

and friends, he had sold the turning shop his parents had left him, and he was deeply in debt. When the banks finally decided not to provide any additional loans, Holger Würthner did not know where he could turn anymore. There was no one left willing to lend him any money, whether banks, private investors, or friends.

The foundation of t-blade GmbH

Würthner's last desperate cry for help reached Mathias Kunz, the brother of Würthner's daughter-in-law, who was at that time working for a leading consulting company. As his special field of activity was start-ups, Kunz promised to look into the matter out of a sense of family responsibility. But family responsibility soon turned into real interest, which then turned into excitement and ended in a brave decision. Kunz quit his safe job as a consultant and plunged into market research. He made great efforts and raised new capital to keep Würthner's company up and running. In 2000, he and Würthner became equal partners in the new t-blade GmbH. Under Kunz's guidance, Würthner managed to get rid of the teething problems that plagued the t-blade system. Meanwhile, Kunz realized that skate manufacturers would not take the risk to incorporate the new t-blades in their product. The only way to get consumers to test their blades and to create demand was thus to sell the complete package of blade and boot.

Kunz managed to establish production of small quantities of boots in China. These were low-quality compared to the ones then offered in the market, but they did incorporate the t-blade system. Before the introduction of t-blade, the quality of skates was determined only by the quality of the boot, as the blades incorporated in the skates were all the same. While t-blade entered the market with boots of inferior quality, the t-blade system attached to them was far superior to all other blades. It was now a question of whether consumers would learn to distinguish skates according to the blades attached to them. t-blade skates were supposed to be introduced at a fairly high price level, priced only slightly below expensive professional skates. Having learned from Würthner's mistakes Kunz knew that the crucial point was to get pro shops and specialized sporting goods retailers to sell their skates. He also knew that neither his nor Würthner's connections were sufficient for that. Thus, he hired an old ice hockey sales representative who used his existing contacts all over Germany to get the t-blade skates in the stores.

The entry in the German market

The success of t-blade skates was overwhelming in the German market. Seemingly out of nowhere, the new skates became the top sellers in their price segment in no time. This caused THC, the world's second largest skates manufacturer, to incur a serious drop in sales within that segment. Teenagers from 12 to 16 years old were most responsible for t-blade's success in Germany. They were attracted mainly by the new, different, and stylish design of t-blade skates and soon the skates became *the* skates to have in Germany. Besides, professional players were more and more inclined to use t-blades, realizing that the blade gave them a clear advantage over other players. Soon, a number of professional players in the German ice hockey league used t-blades and, even more important, a couple of NHL players had taken notice of the t-blades and started to use them as well. Kunz and Würthner were thrilled about the success, but Kunz knew that this was only the beginning. He had done his market research well and aimed far beyond the German market. His goal was to become a global blade supplier and to establish t-blade as a new standard for hockey blades.

THE HOCKEY EQUIPMENT INDUSTRY

The market

Becoming a global player instead of only focusing on the German or the European market was very important, given the fact that the most important markets were somewhere else. The size and potential of a market were limited by the number of ice skating centers where it was possible to skate year-round. While Germany only had 200 such skating centers and only around 30,000 registered hockey players (that is, players who were members of a hockey club), Canada had around 3,000 skating centers and almost 1 million ice hockey players (including 400,000 registered[4] players), making it the largest and most developed market. Other European countries such as Sweden, Finland, or the Czech Republic, where hockey was one of the most popular sports, only counted around 60,000 registered players and only several hundred skating centers.[5] The USA had 1,500 skating centers

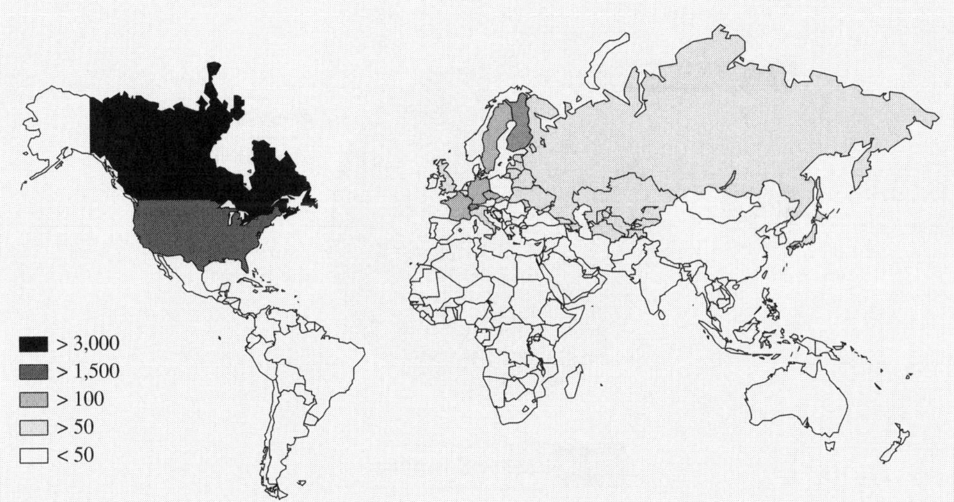

Source: The Swedish Ice-hockey Association, 1999.

Exhibit 6 Worldwide distribution of ice skating centers

and almost 400,000 registered hockey players with more than 1 million unregistered ones, who only played hockey occasionally in their free time. Thus, the USA was the second most important market (see Exhibit 6).

The hockey equipment manufacturers

It was thus not surprising that the dominant hockey equipment manufacturers in the industry were either located in Canada or the USA. The market for hockey equipment was therefore highly concentrated. The worldwide market size for ice hockey skates was estimated to be around 680 million USD. The top two players, Bauer Nike (a wholly owned subsidiary of Nike Inc.) and THC, had a combined market share of around 70%. Although Bauer Nike and THC both had a turnover of around 220 million USD, Bauer Nike was the larger player in terms of units sold, and had the more powerful parent company. The third and fourth largest players, Graf Canada and Easton Sports, accounted for most of the remaining 30%, with sales figures in the lower two-digit-million area (see Exhibits 7 and 8). Graf Canada exclusively focused on ice skating equipment, whereas Easton Sports was also active in baseball, cycling, and archery.

The value-chain of ice-skates' production

Ice-skates manufacturers usually were only the final assemblers of the different parts of the skate. The production of the boot was commonly outsourced to low-labor-cost countries such as China who, over time, had gained expertise in mass-producing highquality boots. The other part of ice skates, the blade, was perceived by the industry as a commodity good. Companies all over the world were producing simple steel blades as one of many other commodity steel products. Each skate manufacturer typically made use of two or three specific blade suppliers to avoid total dependency on one supplier,

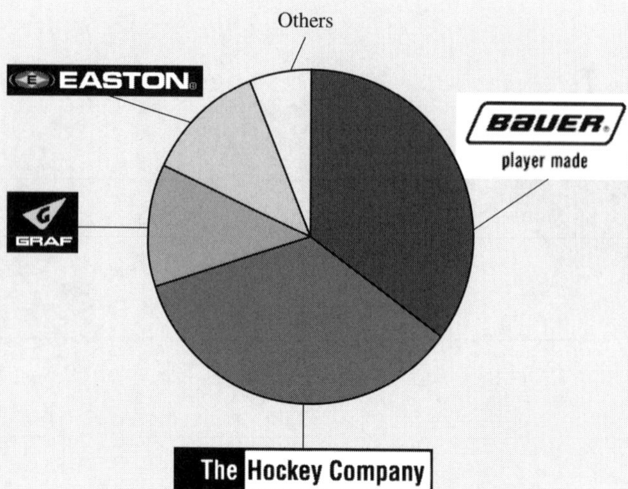

Source: t-blade information material.

Note: The graph represents the market situation, but actual market shares are disguised.

Exhibit 7 Worldwide market share for hockey skates

yet the suppliers were basically easily interchangeable. The estimated number of blades sold per year was around 15 million pairs.

T-BLADE'S ENTRY IN THE NORTH AMERICAN MARKET

The first steps in the market

When Kunz quit his job and decided to dedicate himself to t-blade, he had a vision. Kunz did not want to compete directly with the big players in the ice hockey industry. He realized that establishing t-blade GmbH as a real ice-skate manufacturer would be impossible in the long run as they lacked the knowledge and expertise to produce boots. He felt that it would be best for t-blade to concentrate on its core competency: the blade system. The technology was proven to be superior and in addition it was not easy to imitate, since it was very well protected by the patent. He felt that the ultimate goal for t-blade should be to become a branded supplier and as such create and set a new standard for the blades of hockey skates. But Kunz also recognized the importance of the North American market. If t-blade wanted to become a global blade supplier, they had to be present in this market. Consequently, the next step for Kunz was the market entry into North America.

His strategy for the entry was simple: be present, make as many contacts as possible, and close deals. The best way to have a presence in the ice hockey industry was through ice hockey trade fairs, especially the three most important ones: the European "ESPORT", the "Canadian Sporting Goods Association" (CSGA) in Toronto, and the "Let's Play Hockey" (LPH) in Las Vegas. Thus, Kunz and a small team tried to demonstrate their presence at these trade fairs. They presented their t-blade at a small stand trying to make contacts and connections in the ice hockey world. Competitors, manufacturers, sellers, and athletes passed their stand – but the reaction was not the one Kunz had hoped for. Most people had not much more than a "oh, another blade" reaction for the t-blade system. There

Bauer Nike

Bauer Nike is a wholly owned subsidiary of Nike, Inc. It is one of the world's leading and most-recognized manufacturers of hockey equipment, fitness and recreational skates. The global headquarters is in Greenland, New Hampshire. The Canadian headquarters is in Mississauga, Ontario. European headquarters are in Munich, Germany and its research, design and development headquarters is in St. Jerome, Quebec. Bauer Nike sells products in over 9,000 stores in more than 35 countries worldwide. Its equipment is extensively used by NHL players. More than 60% of players wear Bauer or Nike skates.

The Hockey Company

The Hockey Company

Through its subsidiaries, The Hockey Company, headquartered in Montreal, Canada, is the world's largest marketer and manufacturer of hockey equipment and apparel, as well as National Hockey League authentic and replica jerseys. The company manufactures and markets products under the CCM, KOHO and JOFA brand names. The CCM, HEATON, and KOHO brands of goalie equipment are now prominent in the world market, while the JOFA brand is the protective equipment of choice among 99% of NHL professional ice hockey players.

Graf Canada

The Swiss family enterprise was founded in 1921. 17 years later, the company produced its first hockey skates with assembled blades. Until the mid 1970s Graf produced a full line of sport shoes. Since then, Graf had changed its strategy and concentrated primarily on the manufacturing of hockey and figure skates. In order to strengthen its presence in the North American market, Graf opened a manufacturing facility in Calgary, Canada.

Easton Sports

Easton Sports Inc. with its headquarters in Van Nuys, California is the primary innovator of the aluminium baseball bat. Along with baseball bats, Easton also makes other high performance baseball equipment, softball, hockey, and archery equipment, as well as bicycle frame tubing and components and tent tubes. Many professional athletes use the company's products including Luis Gonzalez and Bobby Abreu (baseball) and Steve Yzerman and Paul Kariya (hockey). Doug Easton founded the company in 1922 as a maker of custom wood bows and cedar arrows.

Exhibit 8 Mission statements of hockey skate OEMs

were only very few vague offers for deals which for the most part included manufacturers wanting to buy the technology and the patent.

Kunz was disaffected quickly and harshly brought back to reality: he had to admit that things were not as easy as he had thought This last step might have been just a little too big for t-blade. Yet he was far from being discouraged and giving up never had been an option for him. Maybe he could not elevate his technology to a new standard himself. The solution, he thought, would be a strong partner already established in the market who would use only t-blades for his skates. These skates would simply prove to be better than the products of competitors and, soon enough, all of them would switch to incorporate only t-blades in their skates. To achieve this keen goal, he had to be careful in choosing his partner. The number one in the market, Kunz thought, would be powerful enough to force him into exclusively selling t-blades to them, thereby enforcing their own competitive position. This, however, would not suffice to make the t-blade system the new standard blade. The number two competitor, on the other hand, would certainly use him to beat the number one once again forcing him into an exclusive selling agreement. The only possible partners, Kunz realized, were thus number three Graf Canada and number four Easton Sports, the only players in the markets who were large enough to be able to support the t-blade, but who would realize that it would not be possible to keep the technology only to themselves in the long run.

Ultima ratio: the bluffed threat

Yet it was another thing to call their attention to his product and the company. Kunz knew that once one of the top four competitors showed interest in his technology all the others would follow quickly so he needed to convince any of them to recognize and acknowledge the t-blade technology at some point. He thus began to enforce his presence on the trade fairs. He started to choose the spots for his stands strategically: right in front of THC or side by side with Graf Canada - he made sure that he was seen and noticed. It was important that all four competitors saw the traffic of sellers and athletes at his stand and even more important that they could all see the moment someone made a move to approach him. To him it seemed as if everyone was watching him closely yet none of them made that crucial first move. He sent samples of his products, prototypes of the newest t-blade model, and invitations to come see his production and development process to prove that his products were trustworthy and reliable. These actions again resulted in offers to buy his technology, but when he mentioned the idea of a partnership, heads shook disapprovingly and doors shut. Kunz had to realize that none of them was taking him seriously; they did not feel that his new t-blade could become a threat to the conventional TUUK standard (see Exhibit 1) they used for their blades. It seemed as if they wanted to sit it out and wait and see how long he could go on like this. He could only hope that they were not aware of how delicate the situation was for t-blade: investors at home wanted to see results, as Kunz had already spent a lot of money on his entry strategy - all these fees for stands at the trade fairs and the costs of the material he had sent out were expensive for a small company like his. But Kunz knew that right now was the only chance for t-blade - if he did not find a partner to help him establish his technology in the market now he would probably never be able to enter.

He decided to play his last ace in the hand: he knew that all skate manufacturers had at least recognized his triumph in the German market. He had built up a sales network out of nowhere and t-blade skates had become the best selling skates in no time. How did the manufacturers know that he was not going to do the exact same thing here in North America and compete with them in their most important market? Kunz was aware that his idea was nothing but a huge bluff: although the t-blade system was far superior to the other blades, the quality of the boots was in all ways inferior. More importantly, all manufacturers had carefully built huge sales networks over time to reach their final customers. To build an only slightly comparable network from scratch would require money in dimensions that he did not even want to think of. He was looking for a partnership where he could act as a branded supplier; it had never been his intention to compete directly with skate manufacturers. However, he never would have the resources to face this competition. Yet none of the skate manufacturers could know about his financial situation. He might have an investor back home with deep pockets who would supply him with all the capital needed. The plan was thus as simple as it was risky: t-blade would scare the manufacturers into a partnership, or at least threaten them enough to realize t-blade was a player that one had better have on one's side, a partner worth having.

Building t-blade's distribution network

The main problem in building the sales network was finding the right sales representatives with the right contacts and connections. Most top sales representatives were of course employed by the four biggest skate producers and with exclusive contracts unfortunately being the norm, representatives were deterred from including alternative products or brands in their sales portfolio. Kunz thus hired his good friend Scott Myers, a retired ice hockey pro who had grown up in the same region as Kunz, once played in the NHL, and was still in touch with other athletes and pro shops. Scott became the head of t-blade's new sales organization, which he basically founded in his garage. He included his friend Rob Harrolds, who was running an entrepot in Winnipeg, Canada, from which he supplied pro shops with equipment. Rob could provide the logistics necessary to supply pro shops and retailers with t-blade products. Kunz sent his t-blade products to the warehouse in Winnipeg from which they were distributed by Rob to the pro shops and retailers that Scott had convinced to take t-blade skates into their assortment. It was admittedly a very basic sales organization, yet Kunz felt that his every move was being watched and his actions would be interpreted as the first step of a carefully planned market entry. The date of the Las Vegas trade fair (LPH) was fast approaching and Kunz knew this would either be the date of t-blade's demise or a new beginning.

Choosing a partner

The decisive moment finally came on the second day of the Las Vegas trade fair in January 2001. Kunz had positioned his stand as close as possible to the Graf Canada booth. It was a busy day, as the t-blade system was now often the center of attention. Looking up, Kunz recognized Mike Hill, president and CEO of Graf Canada casually walking over to the t-blade stand. Just as casually the two men started a conversation - yet it was far from centering on blades. Instead, they discovered that they had far more in common than just ice hockey equipment: their interest in mechanical clocks that were built in Kunz's home town, their love for steak and, most importantly, a natural liking of each other. When Hill discovered that Kunz was staying at the same hotel, he casually asked to join him for breakfast the next morning. The breakfast turned out to be just as enjoyable as their encounter the day before. This time they found out that not only did they enjoy each other's company, but they both had a similar understanding of their business and thus might enjoy doing business as well. For the duration of the trade fair, they continued to have breakfast together and developed their ideas of what a potential partnership of their companies might look litke, which were sketched on a napkin at the breakfast table.

To Kunz, these breakfasts with Mike Hill had another very welcome side effect: everyone could watch him spending time with the CEO of one of the largest skate manufacturers, and when they made their entrance into the trade fair hall together, their harmonic interaction and growing familiarity was visible to competitors, sellers, and athletes.

This was the signal Kunz had been longing for and it did not miss its mark: almost immediately, Easton approached Kunz and offered to figure out a way to work together. Kunz had already chosen Graf Canada as his favorite, yet a bird in the hand is worth two in the bush, so he was keen on keeping up the relations with Easton in case he would not get his way with Graf Canada. With this in mind, Kunz entered into a discussion with Easton while still having his meetings with Hill. Kunz also hoped to be able to exert more pressure on Hill by having Easton up his sleeve. During one of their conversations at the t-blade booth, Kunz carefully mentioned his recent encounters with Easton. Turning abruptly to his assistants, Hill said, "Come on, boys, that's it, we're leaving!", grabbed his leather jacket and walked off without another word. Kunz worried for a second that he might have gone too far and stretched the thin band of trust between them a bit too far, yet he told himself that now was not the time to get nervous. The next morning, Hill awaited Kunz at their usual breakfast table as if nothing had happened. Kunz knew that they had just entered a new phase in their relationship.

NEGOTIATING WITH GRAF CANADA

Preparing for the negotiations

As soon as Kunz got back to Germany, he began to transcribe the ideas that he and Hill had collected on a napkin into a draft for their partnership contract. He was very eager to quickly reach a stage where they could start concrete negotiations. From his work experience in Germany Kunz was used to quick responses and in particular concrete actions. Yet Graf Canada took its time. Kunz was invited several times to visit production facilities and meet managers and employees as well as sellers who were part of the distribution network. But for a long time, Hill and Graf Canada avoided specifically touching the issue of their potential partnership. Kunz finally got impatient and casually mentioned during one of his visits that the alternative of working with Easton was still on the table. Graf Canada's reaction came very fast this time, and the date for the beginning of the negotiations was fixed for the beginning of September 2001.

Kunz made extensive preparations for these negotiations, which would decide the future of t-blade. He started by carefully assessing t-blade's negotiation position and their alternatives in case they did not reach an agreement, but also tried to imagine the way Graf Canada would see the situation. Graf Canada seemed to be a perfect strategic fit: the company put great emphasis on the quality and innovativeness of its products as a selling point. To keep this image, Graf Canada needed frequent innovations and also needed to be the first to introduce and adopt new technologies and standards. As a consequence, the entire structure of Graf Canada was very open towards the incorporation of new technologies even if they had not been developed by Graf. There did not exist anything such as a "not invented here" problem which would have been disruptive to the acceptance of the t-blade technology within the company. Kunz knew the company was not only interested in incorporating the t-blade technology in their blades, but that they also wanted to act as the sole distributor of the replacement parts for the t-blades. He also knew that he could not let them get their way in this point. As soon as the t-blade system reached a certain level of acceptance in the market, the business of blade replacements would become very important because margins on the replacement parts were comparatively high in relation to the rest of the hockey equipment. Whoever distributed these t-blade replacements would be nearest to the final customer and thus had the power. Kunz had to keep a say in this matter, yet he wondered how far he could go. Graf Canada did not seem to have other plausible alternatives to the t-blade technology. Mike Hill had mentioned to him that there were a few other revolutionary blade technologies out there but as far as Kunz had seen none of them had been tested successfully yet and he suspected it would take them a while to reach a state where they could actually be used. Thus if they did not reach an agreement Graf would probably just wait and hope that t-blades would not find anyone else to promote its blades until Graf's own new technology was ready. From Kunz's point of view, Graf Canada was the ideal partner. The connections he had made with Easton were only very loose; he doubted that they could reach a state in which serious negotiations were possible any time soon. It also had yet to be proven that t-blade could work together with Easton as well as this seemed to be the case with Graf Canada. In any case, this would put an enormous strain on t-blade's financial resources. As long as t-blade did not have a partner, it needed to keep investing heavily in building a t-blade distribution network in order to keep the threat of a "standalone" market entry credible. Kunz decided that it would be best to include Scott and Rob in his negotiation team as they knew the North American market far better than he did. He felt that it was important to him that they continued to be a part of t-blade in the future. Together, the three spent many sleepless nights discussing their negotiation strategy and preparing for the long rounds of negotiation that lay ahead of them.

The negotiations

The important day came at last. Mathias Kunz, Scott and Rob arrived together at the headquarters of Graf Canada in Calgary, Canada. The woman behind the desk at the entrance greeted them cheerily as she remembered Kunz from his earlier visits very well. She offered to show them the way to the meeting room which Kunz politely declined. He had been here often enough to know his way around. After a short walk through the building, during which Kunz was recognized and greeted by many employees, they reached the meeting room. They were a bit early, but Mike Hill was already awaiting them together with his team, consisting of Graf Canada's chief operating officer and chief financial officer. The room was dominated by the large negotiation table on the one side of which the Graf Canada team had taken their seats. Large windows let in the bright rays from the early sun and gave the room a friendly atmosphere. The walls were covered with posters of NHL stars wearing Graf Canada equipment, and several display cases displayed the most recent and most popular Graf Canada products. These "sporty" surroundings took away the formal stiffness often present in such large meeting rooms. It almost felt as if they had come together to watch the final game of the Stanley Cup on the large flat screen at the one end of the room. The Graf Canada team welcomed Kunz and his team warmly, and Kunz and Hill introduced their team members to the other side by their names and positions within the company. Hill had organized coffee and breakfast for the entire group. They talked about the weather, the recent developments in the NHL, and Hill and Kunz entertained the whole group with stories from all the breakfasts they had had together in the past year. Conversation turned then to t-blade and almost unnoticeably the two teams entered their negotiation. The atmosphere changed quite a bit, however. Steve Hyke, the COO of Graf Canada, especially showed a great deal of skepticism towards the t-blade team and the t-blade technology. Several times, he expressed serious doubts and stressed the fact that there were indeed other options for Graf Canada than a collaboration with t-blade. Even though Hill made efforts to smooth the situation, the atmosphere grew tense. Voices grew louder and the stress level peaked. The t-blade team stuck together. They had discussed in detail and agreed which were the most important points in which they could not give in. Thus they stood strong and unintimidated and refused to let Steve Hyke talk or threaten them into letting Graf Canada take over the further development of the t-blade technology. At the end of the day everyone was exhausted, and they seemed not to have gotten one step closer to an agreement of any sort. The draft with Hill's and Kunz's ideas lay untouched on the table – none of the Graf Canada team members seemed to acknowledge its presence.

Remembering that Kunz shared his love for steaks, Hill invited him to have dinner at his favorite steakhouse. Sitting together in front of their filled plates at a table in a cozy niche of the restaurant, they started talking about t-blade again and once again realized that the vision they had was the same: they wanted to establish t-blades as the standard ice skating blade and change the industry. They both agreed that this was only possible if they really worked together. Once again they made use of their napkins to jot down their thoughts and slowly emerged the idea of what would later be called "t-blade Inc.", a company founded for distribution purposes only, in which t-blade and Graf Canada would be equal partners and owners. The same night Kunz and Hill decided about the main duties and responsibilities each partner would have: t-blade GmbH became OEM supplier of Graf Canada, t-blade Inc. would handle all flows of material needed to supply replacement parts. Graf Canada's existing distribution network would be used and Graf Canada would thus take over the day-to-day handling of the distribution. In addition, both of them agreed that their partnership could not be exclusive. At some point in time, they would have to include other strategic partners in their company and they were both willing to do so. When Kunz and Hill separated late at night to catch a few hours of sleep before negotiations restarted the next morning, they did so with the good feeling that they had reached a mutual understanding and were heading in the same direction.

The next morning the two teams got back together to take things up where they left them. However, before anyone could open the negotiation Mike Hill rose and stated matter-of-factly that there was no question about whether a partnership between t-blade and Graf Canada made sense. He was convinced of t-blade's technology and glad to work on a level of equal partners with them. Kunz and Hill presented the way they envisioned their future cooperation and only a few doubts were uttered on either side of the table. In the end, their solution was jointly accepted. It took a couple more meetings also including lawyers to clarify some of the minor legal issues. Shortly afterward, t-blade Inc. was born, a company that issued two shares each at the price of one Canadian dollar – one of which was held by Graf Canada and the other by t-blade GmbH. The articles of association of t-blade Inc. remained exactly as Kunz and Hill had envisioned it during their dinner and no lawyer could convince them to change it in any way.

The outcome of the negotiations

Looking back Kunz could say proudly to himself that he had been able to realize 80% of the goals he had identified before the negotiation. Yet one of his aims had not been fulfilled and it was one that left a bitter aftertaste: Kunz had always envisioned for Scott and Rob, who had started to build a distribution network for t-blade, to find their place in the distribution network of Graf Canada – he had silently hoped that it would be possible to simply merge the two networks. However, Hill was very unwilling to sign the contracts of employment for both of them and, in the end, Kunz and his team realized that this was a compromise they had to make in order for the vision of t-blade to stay alive. Even though Kunz felt a personal loss in not being able to employ Rob and Scott any longer, all three of them knew that he had to let them go for the sake of t-blade's future.

t-blade Inc. was founded in 2002 and was profitable from the start. t-blade GmbH could also claim very satisfying revenues as the sole OEM supplier. The t-blade technology was used and desired by an increasing number of players. It was only a couple of months later when THC started to become more and more interested in the technology, as it could not overlook the very present demand for t-blades any longer. Kunz and Hill both had expected to gain some interest from the biggest players. While they both agreed that they were absolutely open to new partners, they also agreed on the fact that they would not let anyone gain too much influence and take control out of their hands. Thus they reacted amiably but very carefully to THC's approaches (see Exhibit 9).

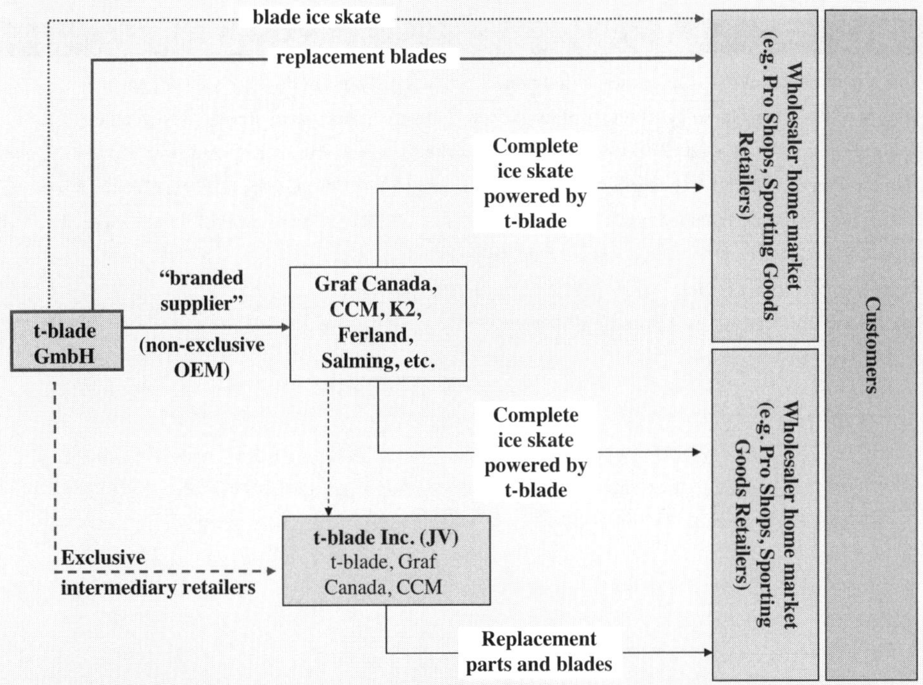

Exhibit 9 The t-blade business model

When Kunz stepped off the plane in Frankfurt, thoughts were still whirling around in his head. He knew that if they considered THC as a partner, long hours of negotiation lay before them. He could not help but compare this situation to the one he had to face before the negotiation with Graf Canada. He remembered how uncertain he had felt back then, knowing that the whole future of the t-blade technology depended on the outcome of that negotiation. He was surprised how much a situation could change in such a short period of time. Now he was neither intimidated nor scared by the possibility of facing the second largest global ice-skate manufacturer in a negotiation, nor did he fear for the future of t-blade anymore. Yet he knew that other problems would come up, new contingencies would have to be taken into account. In his head he started already to assess his alternatives and THC's other options ...

DISCUSSION QUESTIONS

1. How would you evaluate Kunz's approach to finding a partner in North America?
2. How did the relations between Matthias Kunz and Mike Hill influence the negotiations between the two sides?
3. Based on the negotiations described in the case, what potential challenges could Kunz face if they proceed to negotiate a partnership agreement with THC?

NOTES

1. This is a hypothetical case. The names of individuals and organisations in this case are fictional.
2. Obe, M. (2018) Bangladesh fights future of its garment industry. *Nikkei Asian Review*, 4 November.
3. Sourced from: Ekblom, J. (2019) Timeline: highlights of the 15-year Airbus, Boeing trade war. *Reuters*, 2 October; Hemmerdinger, J. (2019) Airbus calls for negotiations to settle US–EU trade dispute. *Flight Global*, 18 September; Boeing (2019) Boeing statement on WTO ruling. 28 March; USTR (2019) U.S. wins $7.5 billion award in Airbus subsidies case. Office of the United States Trade Representative, 2 October.
4. Registered players are players that skate at least three times per week.
5. See The Swedish Ice Hockey Association, 1999.

PART IV

NEGOTIATING EFFECTIVELY

12
Negotiating around the world

The institution-based approach to analysing business negotiation processes and activities in a country focuses on two elements: formal institutions and informal institutions. Formal institutions consist of rules of the game, policies, laws and regulations that are enforced by institutions. Informal institutions refer to personal networks and culture that is prevalent in the country. In developed countries, the formal institutions dictate how business activities are to be conducted and there is much clarity about the roles of the institutions and the obligations of organisations operating in the national territory. However, in emerging and transitioning economies, the institutional environment, although in place, is not followed in a rigorous manner and thus there are implementation gaps. In such an environment, policies and rules may not be applied as stringently, and informal institutions take their place to fill the void and to provide assurances that enable business activities to continue. In addition to institutions, the range of variables that influence negotiations vary from one country to the next. They include market size, whether the country is a prime location for outsourcing or not, whether the country is an emerging market economy or not, and a whole host of other factors. In this chapter, we discuss how these factors influence the negotiation process around the world. In particular, this chapter attempts to describe and assess the individual strategies and tactics that are required to successfully negotiate business transactions in countries and regions around the world.

The next section presents information about negotiations in Asia, with a particular emphasis on China and India. This is followed by discussions about negotiations in the Arab world and Russia. The chapter concludes by discussing some guidelines for international negotiators.

12.1 NEGOTIATING IN ASIA

Asia is home to nearly 60 per cent of the world's population.[1] It is, therefore, an important global market and hosts some of the world's largest multinational enterprises (MNEs). In this section, we detail the business environment and negotiation behaviour found in China and India and provide a summary of the negotiation issues in India's neighbouring South Asian countries of Bangladesh and Pakistan. These countries represent two major emerging markets, each having almost 200 million inhabitants, and unlike India and China, have always been open for Western MNEs. As a result, most of the Western MNEs have been doing business there for more than 50 years. Most of the earlier research, however, in addition to China and India, has been focused on Japan and South Korea,[2] but we will not discuss these countries in this chapter.

12.1.1 China

The world's most populous country,[3] China, is also its second largest economy. Located in East Asia, China shares some of the same cultural values of collectivism, hierarchy and respect for authority and seniority with its regional neighbours. China's transition from a manufacturer of cheap goods to a high-tech manufacturer mirrors the experiences of Japan and South Korea, who undertook a similar journey. The "Made in China" programme aimed at transforming the country into a global technology hub and the Belt and Road Initiative aimed at creating tariff-free corridors for Chinese enterprises are some of the ambitious programmes that the government has embarked on.

China follows a socialist market economic system, transitioning from a planned to market-based economy. The institutional environment in China is rather strong, as the country became a member of the World Trade Organization (WTO) in 2001, and some laws that were enacted to facilitate trade and investment are being enforced. Historically, international firms could only enter the Chinese market in a joint venture with a local partner. The expectation of a joint venture has been relaxed in most industries, but many foreign firms prefer to continue working with a Chinese partner. This is in part due to the unfamiliar institutional environment, but working with local firms also provides local knowledge and networks that foreign firms lack.

Based on previous studies on China,[4] some recommended guidelines for conducting effective negotiations are presented below. The recommendations are organised by the four P's: Priority, Patience, Price and People.

1. *Priority:* Chinese state-owned enterprises (SOEs) are ranked among the top organisations in the world based on their global revenue.[5] The Chinese government prioritises the growth of certain industries and sets goals, and Chinese SOEs do business according to the government's priorities, policies and plans. Research suggests that when negotiating large industrial projects, foreign firms should make a careful study of the Chinese government's priorities and implementation policies. These priorities are also important indicators of what the Chinese want to spend their foreign exchange on. It is important, therefore, for a company to determine whether the project they are offering falls under the priority project category. If the project is included in one of China's priority categories, then it will be of interest and negotiations should proceed relatively smoothly.
2. *Patience:* Negotiating in China takes time because different Chinese organisations and different departments within one organisation tend to be involved in negotiation processes. Further, the formal institutional environment is rather difficult to comprehend, and decision making within the Chinese bureaucracy is slow and takes time. From a cultural perspective, the Chinese will not rush into any serious meetings with someone

they do not know or trust, and a certain feeling of closeness must be established before negotiation can begin. The Confucian notions of good relationships, face, etiquette and harmony are all time-consuming qualifications that require patience, and international negotiators need to invest much time in demonstrating their long-term commitment to doing business in the country. Example 12.1 highlights the importance of patience in China.

EXAMPLE 12.1

LENOVO'S ACQUISITION OF IBM

IBM was a pioneer of personal computer (PC) manufacturing, having launched the business in 1981. By the early 2000s, the company was looking to withdraw from the market. Lenovo, China's largest PC manufacturer, showed its interest in acquiring IBM assets and negotiations commenced in the year 2003. The negotiating progressed at a slow pace as the parties attempted to negotiate a favourable deal for all sides. However, there were other concerns that were slowing down the deal. Questions about American national security being compromised were raised during this period. However, the parties continued to work together. After a period of 13 months, the deal was finally reached, and Lenovo bought IBM and its brands such as Thinkpad for a price of $1.25 billion.

Sources: Adapted from China Daily (2004);[6] Spooner (2004);[7] and Wright (2004).[8]

Discussion Point: What long-term guarantees can negotiators provide for deals that seem to raise national security issues, especially in the area of information and communication technology (ICT)?

3. *Price:* The issue of price is a sensitive one in China due to the political philosophy followed in the country. Chinese negotiators value trust and sincerity and would be suspicious if a party reduced its price drastically and/or too early. Hence, while a strategy that attempts an exaggerated soft strategy of bargaining and making huge concessions may be attractive for impulsive decision makers, it would have limited appeal for rational decision makers like Chinese negotiators. On the other hand, the Chinese are extremely face-conscious. If a foreign company rejects a request for a price discount, the Chinese client will probably feel insulted. If it is discovered, however, that a foreign company is "giving face", then it is likely the Chinese side will adjust accordingly and be more helpful and friendly in the later rounds of negotiations. It is recommended, therefore, that firms calculate price and bargaining limits carefully, and *always* reserve certain margins that allow Chinese negotiators to gain face.
4. *People:* As discussed earlier, in countries where the formal institutions are less important, people rely on informal institutions such as local traditions, customs, culture and interpersonal relations to provide assurances on the basis of which business and other important activities can be undertaken. Because of the deep Confucian aversion to legal procedure, Chinese society and businesses believe more in people than in contracts. International firms should, therefore, take a people-oriented approach to establish a high level of trust with their Chinese partners. The level of exchange of information in

China depends on whether people are seen as members of the in-group or out-group. Foreign firms and international negotiators are, by default, seen as outsiders and face the liability of outsidership. To overcome this liability, firms need to develop *guanxi* (or business networks). These networks cannot be built immediately, and it may require the help of third parties or members from an existing network to initiate the process of introducing the parties to each other. These relationships and trust are developed during the informal meetings and sessions in between the formal negotiations, such as during lunches and dinners. Firms that feel that they are unable to develop such relations may use the services of an agent for the negotiation process. However, this has a limited appeal, as in the long run the interpersonal relations are built between the agent and the other party, making it difficult for the company to replace the agent.

The strategies employed by Chinese negotiators are in part influenced by the *Chinese stratagems*, or *Ji* in Chinese. The stratagems refer to the long-standing Chinese cultural tradition that shapes the strategic behaviour of Chinese people in general and in business. The word *Ji* is found in the *Art of War*, written 2,300 years ago by the famous Chinese military strategist Sun Tzu. The Chinese stratagems are carefully devised plans that help individuals or groups deal with various kinds of situations. The plans are meant to provide psychological and material advantage over one's adversary. A variety of Chinese stratagems can be found in the *Art of War*, such as deception, conquering by strategy, creating a situation, focus, espionage, benchmarking, shared vision, extraordinary troops, flanking, prudence, flexibility, leadership.

The Chinese stratagems have been summarised into a compendium titled *The Thirty-Six Stratagems* (The 36 *Ji's*) (see Table 12.1). The thirty-six are theoretically grouped into six categories: Nos. 1–6 are to be used when a person is in a position of superiority; Nos. 7–12 are expected to be used during a confrontation; Nos. 13–18 are for offensive action; Nos. 19–24 for when the situation is unclear; Nos. 25–30 suggests how to gain ground; and Nos. 31–36 are to be used when faced with a defensive position. In practice, however, all of the stratagems may be flexibly used in any possible situation.[9] The Chinese may subconsciously use the stratagems during negotiations as they are entrenched in Chinese social values and culture.[10]

Chinese managers view the marketplace as a battlefield. Therefore, military stratagems lend themselves favourably to negotiating practices. This link has been found in the literature on the patterns of Chinese negotiating practices, such as Attacking the opponent's vulnerabilities – Stratagem 2 ("Besiege Wei to rescue Zhao"); Playing home court or home advantage – Stratagem 4 ("Await leisurely the exhausted enemy"); Manipulating emotional-appeal tactics by emphasising friendship and hospitality – Stratagem 10 ("Hide a knife in a smile"); Stratagem 31 ("The beautiful woman stratagem"); and Playing the competitors against each other – Stratagem 3 ("Kill with a borrowed knife"). The Chinese negotiator prefers to create a favourable situation in which they can use their strategic manipulation to influence the other party to conduct business in the way they want to conduct business.

The Chinese aim to get to know the other party in initial informal meetings. In these meetings they particularly want to ascertain whether the other party has the technology

Table 12.1 The thirty-six ancient Chinese stratagems

1. Cross the sea without Heaven's knowledge – Man Tian Guo Hai	19. Remove the firewood from under the cooking pot – Fu Di Chou Xin
2. Besiege Wei to rescue Zhao – Wei Wei Jiu Zhao	20. Muddle the water to catch the fish – Hun Shui Mo Yu
3. Kill with a borrowed knife – Jie Dao Sha Ren	21. The golden cicada sheds its shell – Jin Chan Tuo Qiao
4. Await leisurely the exhausted enemy – Yi Yi Dai Lao	22. Shut the door to catch the thief – Guan Men Zhuo Zei
5. Loot a burning house – Chen Huo Da Jie	23. Befriend the distant states while attacking the nearby ones – Yuan Jiao Jin Gong
6. Clamour in the east but attack in the west – Sheng Dong Ji	24. Borrow the road to conquer Guo – Jia Dao Fa Guo
7. Create something out of nothing – Wu Zhong Sheng You	25. Steal the beams and change the pillars – Tou Liang Huan Zhu
8. Openly repair the walkway but secretly march to Chen Cang – An Du Chen Cang	26. Point at the mulberry tree but curse the locust tree – Zhi Sang Ma Huai
9. Watch the fire burning from across the river – Ge An Guan Huo	27. Play a sober-minded fool – Jia Chi Bu Dian
10. Hide a knife in a smile – Xiao Li Cang Dao	28. Lure the enemy onto the roof, then take away the ladder – Shang Wu Chou Ti
11. Let the plum tree wither in place of the peach tree – Li Dai Tao Jiang	29. Flowers bloom in the tree – Shu Shang Kai Hua
12. Lead away a goat in passing – Shun Shau Qiang Yang	30. The guest becomes the host – Fan Ke Wei Zhu
13. Beat the grass to startle the snake – Da Cao Jing She	31. The beautiful woman stratagem – Mei Ren Ji
14. Borrow a corpse to return the soul – Jie Shi Huan Hun	32. The empty city stratagem – Kong Cheng Ji
15. Lure the tiger to leave the mountains – Diao Hu Li Shan	33. The counter-espionage stratagem – Fan Jian Ji
16. In order to capture, first let it go – Yu Qin Gu Zong	34. The self-torture stratagem – Ku Rou Ji
17. Toss out a brick to attract a piece of jade – Pao Zhuan Yin Yu	35. The stratagem of interrelated stratagems – Lian Huan Ji
18. To capture bandits, first capture the ringleader – Qin Zei Qin Wang	36. Running away is the best stratagem – Zou Wei Shang Ji

Source: Adapted from Ghauri and Fang (2002).[11]

or the knowhow they want. They normally want to buy the most modern technology and rely on the willingness of the Western firm to share such technologies with the Chinese. Moreover, they want to ascertain whether the Western firm will be able to fulfil the project or what they promise. This means it is a good idea to have a list of reference projects that have been delivered/completed by the firm. In the initial stages, therefore, it is imperative to build relationships and lobby the most important people and convince them that you have what they want. In most cases this is done through presentations of the company and its capabilities to several groups. Trust is built in these informal and early meetings that lasts throughout the negotiation process.

12.1.2 India

Following independence from British rule in 1947, India followed a self-sufficiency policy and introduced several restrictions on the amount and value of the foreign investment in the country. Most Western firms were not able to enter the Indian market. The economic liberalisation of India's economy commenced in 1991, and since then the country has been one of the largest recipients of inward foreign direct investment; Indian firms have also rapidly internationalised. In 2014, the Indian government launched the "Make in India" programme to encourage international companies to use the country as their manufacturing base. India is however not an easy place to do business in for Western firms. We will look at the question, what are some of the features of business negotiations in India that affect international firms? India, like China, is a geographically large country that is divided into 29 states and seven union territories. But unlike China, where the form of government is centralised, India is diverse in that across the country there are different state and sub-state regulations, different regional languages and different business practices. However, one consistent influence when conducting business activities in India is that of central government regulations. India has a history of bureaucratic rules and policies that affect the pace of business in the country.[12] International firms attempting to negotiate a business deal in India should consider the influence of the government and be aware that the business opportunity may be thwarted by the government, as was the case with Enron's power plant (see Example 12.2).

EXAMPLE 12.2
ENRON'S COSTLY NEGOTIATIONS IN INDIA

Enron corporation was an American energy company. At the start of the 1990s, Enron decided to diversify its geographic footprint and attempted to enter the Indian market. In June 1992, Enron engaged in negotiation with the government of India and identified the town of Dabhol in the state of Maharashtra for a major energy project. Enron proposed to construct a mega power plant worth $3 billion.

The state of Maharashtra was governed by the Congress Party. By 1995, the state was heading towards elections, and the opposition parties alleged that the deal with Enron was responsible for increased power tariffs. Playing the nationalist card, the opposition alliance of Shiv-Sena and the BJP claimed that the American firm's presence was hurting the poor in India. The coalition won the election and the agreement to purchase power through Enron's Dabhol power company was cancelled. By this stage, Enron and its partners had invested $300 million. Despite appeals and offers for renegotiations, the project never reached its production capacity, and the plant was finally closed after Enron's collapse in 2001.

Sources: Adapted from Pearl (2001);[13] and Rai (2002).[14]

Discussion Point: What are some of the impediments that negotiators face in countries with a complex and bureaucratic business system?

In terms of the institutional environment, India is a unique case. The country's institutions were developed by the British and follow the common-law system. However, the implementation of contracts and the application of laws are not as well developed as they are in the West. Additionally, the Indian business environment is dominated by large family-owned conglomerates like the Bajaj Group and Tata Group. Firms with limited international experience attempting to enter India may find working with a local Indian firm, with well-established networks and knowhow about the working of the local bureaucracy, helpful in addressing some of the uncertainties surrounding business in India.

Another consideration for negotiations in India is the pricing strategy used. Indian firms are known to be price-sensitive and have a successful history of cost reduction in the manufacturing process using reverse engineering. The former Renault–Nissan CEO Carlos Ghosn coined the term frugal engineering to describe the ability of Indian businesses to reduce the cost by eliminating unnecessary or costly processes. Indian companies also seek detailed information about the product and follow a rational decision-making process. International negotiators should, therefore, be prepared to make a detailed presentation, but should also be ready to deal with bargaining behaviour on the issue of pricing.

Indian firms display a combination of individualism and collectivism. While relationship-building may not be as important in the initial stages of discussion as it is in other collectivist societies, it is relied upon during the operational phase of the business and may need to be developed at that stage.[15] The relationship expectations can be thought of as being on a continuum, moving from low to high as the relationship moves from negotiations to operations.

India's neighbours in South Asia share some of these features in their business activities. The South Asian region includes three of the most populous countries in the world: India (1.3 billion people), Pakistan (210 million) and Bangladesh (161 million). Despite this large market size, intra-regional trade and investment have been hampered by political tensions between these states. A lot of international trade and business activities, however, are carried out with organisations and countries located outside of the region. While some of the countries in the region share commonalities in terms of the colonial institutional legacy that the British left, there are linguistic, religious and political differences that affect the business activities and negotiations. India is largely stable in political terms, whereas countries like Pakistan, Bangladesh and Sri Lanka have had periods of political uncertainty.

However, they are not different from India in terms of political risk, poor working conditions and the threat of contract breaches. For example, thousands of people were killed or handicapped in Union Carbide's leakage of poisonous gas in Bhopal, India. While people are still waiting for any compensation after several decades in India, more than 1,000 people were killed in the Rana Plaza incident in Bangladesh when a garment factory collapsed. The factory was contracted to manufacture clothes for many international brands. In the aftermath of the incident, many international firms signed the *Accord on Fire and Building Safety in Bangladesh*, a legally binding agreement that focuses on worker safety.[16] Due to these incidents, any agreements arising from negotiations related to contract manufacturing would need to include standards on working conditions and provisions for carrying out safety inspections. The risk of doing business in these countries is also high due to threats of religious extremism, and frequent changes in political leadership due to coups or dissolution of the government. This directly affects where the negotiations are held and the overall deal. Disruptions to the supply chain and reputational harm are some of the concerns that may influence a company's decision to undertake business activities in these countries. The use of agents may be useful in conducting some of the negotiation activities, but firms may want the assurances and guarantees of supranational organisations (like the World Bank or the Asian Development Bank) for megaprojects that involve a large amount of financial investment. Doing so can provide assurance that any contracts signed between the foreign firm and the government will be honoured, even if there is a change in the country's leadership.

12.2 NEGOTIATING IN THE ARAB WORLD

The Arabic-speaking world spreads from West Asia to North Africa and is sometimes referred to as the Middle East and North Africa (MENA) region. In addition to the use of the language, the countries classified as part of the Arab world share the same religious beliefs. In Hofstede's seminal work on culture classification, the Arabic-speaking countries are presented under the label of the Arab world. Hofstede, in his book *Cultures and Organizations: Software of the Mind*, explains that he would have preferred to keep the countries separate as his experience was that the countries were different, and cited the example of Lebanon and Egypt as two countries with distinct cultures.[17] Nonetheless, he was provided with data that had been combined, with the individual country-level data not being available. The research in the international business negotiations area, therefore, tends to mention the Arab world, even when the data is collected from one or two countries in the region.

Negotiators should acknowledge that there remain individual country-level differences in negotiations, especially as far as openness to trade and investment is concerned. However, there are some business practices that are similar across the Arabic-speaking countries, and we discuss them in this chapter. As Muslim majority countries, a significant portion of the population believes that while people should work hard, the outcome of any activity is godly determined. Hence, if the activity is meant to be, so it will be. Negotiators are, therefore, not as anxious about achieving a quick and favourable outcome as they are about building relations and thinking beyond one deal or a particular deal. For Arab companies, the opportunity to extend business is important, but who they work with is very important. Since the countries in the Arab world are highly collectivist, they seek to establish interpersonal relations with individual negotiators to ensure that there is trust between the parties before work is discussed.[18] The Arab word for these relations is *wasta*,[19] which is loosely translated as "business networks", that is, who knows who and to which network of relations do you belong?[20] Example 12.3 highlights the importance of *wasta* in negotiations in the Arab world.

EXAMPLE 12.3
***WASTA:* NEPOTISM OR INSIDERSHIP?**

The use of business networks is an accepted practice in many collectivist societies. Countries in the Arabic-speaking region of Middle East and North Africa (MENA) are highly collectivist and having these networks can help in developing trust between parties and sharing information. This form of *insidership* is considered to be a critical asset for firm internationalisation. From a Western perspective, the networks in the Arab countries may be seen as a form of nepotism. However, one should be mindful of not using self-reference criterion in judging these networks. The nature of these relations is different to what one might associate with nepotism or cronyism. One could compare *wasta* with the Western business practice of networking. In today's e-connected world, professional networking platforms like LinkedIn provide opportunities for individuals to enhance their networks. *Wasta* is similar, except the network-building is undertaken face-to-face and the relations involve real give and take and are developed over time and maintained.

As many Arab countries are shifting away from relying on natural resources for their economic growth, we are seeing a rapid move towards acquiring business relationships to improve their manufacturing and services sectors. For non-Arab managers, it is important they invest time in developing deep-level relations with the Arab managers, which in turn would facilitate the development of trust and the communication and sharing of information between the parties.

Sources: Adapted from ICLG (2019);[21] and Tashakova (2015).[22]

Discussion Point: How can negotiators develop and use business networks without being accused of cronyism or nepotism? Do you believe the use of networks for business activities will reduce once the formal institutions in these countries mature?

The use of time in the Arab world is meant to be flexible, and negotiators need to be aware of this when carrying out planning for negotiations.[23] A late start to a meeting or delays are common features of negotiating in the Arab world as time is seen to be flexible.[24] Individuals are not expected to abruptly cut a conversation or leave a social gathering if it runs overtime. The emphasis on personal relations means that people expect delays and are tolerant of it. This can be a source of frustration for negotiators who follow the monochronic time approach and adhere to strict deadlines. Being flexible about the use of time in negotiations and operations, such as delivery date, can help reduce some of the angst that negotiators and businesses may face when attempting to finalise and action the terms of the agreement.

The MENA region has experienced significant political changes in the past decade. The Arab Spring event, along with a sharp spike in the number of armed conflicts in countries in the Arab world, has added to the uncertainty of working in these countries. Intra-regional conflicts, for example between Qatar and some neighbouring countries like the United Arab Emirates (UAE) and Saudi Arabia, have further added to the risk of operating in a highly volatile region. International negotiators would be well advised to avoid discussions about politics, faith or, at the early stage, family. This uncertainty in countries in the region can increase the bargaining power of the foreign negotiator, who may choose the location of the negotiation and seek greater concessions from the other side.

As is the case in other markets with high levels of uncertainty, firms can use the services of local agents to negotiate on their behalf. However, firms need to be careful when selecting the agents as studies show that Arab agents tend to overstate their networks and connections in the business community to gain international contracts. Negotiators should also be aware that there is a large variation in the purchasing power of buyers across the countries in the Arab world, and the product and service offerings they make in the region would need to be adapted to better meet the needs of the individual market, weather conditions and consumption patterns.

12.3 NEGOTIATING IN RUSSIA

The Russian economy, like that of China, has recently transitioned from a pure command to a market-based economy. The geographic location and size of the country makes it an important player in international business. However, the majority of Russian negotiators have limited experience in international business activities and may take a bargaining/haggling approach to negotiations. The limited international experience does not mean that Russian negotiators are not skilled. In fact, they display characteristics such as patience, being persistent and unwillingness to make concessions that make them tough negotiators.[25]

The ethicality of negotiating practices can be questioned as Russian negotiators can use deceptive techniques such as sending fake non-verbal cues, misrepresenting the value of items and misleading the other side to obtain concessions. In terms of the negotiating strategy, Russian negotiators are known to use pressure techniques and may qualify their initial offer by claiming that it is the "best offer" possible. Russian negotiators may also play the power-distance card by claiming limited authority to provide concessions, which is consistent with their approach to not compromise on the offer made. Russian negotiators are also known to be rather aggressive and may threaten to walk away from a deal if their demands are not met.

Other considerations when negotiating with Russians are around the rules and regulations under which the deal will be structured. Business deals structured under Russian laws are preferred. However, the laws have some limitations, such as lack of recognition of warranties, and in such circumstances, negotiating deals under international laws may be preferred. Most communication in Russia is conducted in Russian or English; however, it is expected that official documentation that requires government approval will be produced in Russian.[26] Negotiating parties may rely on translators to facilitate the negotiations and preparation of relevant documents. In fact, Russians make extensive use of interpreters while negotiating with foreign parties.

A point of frustration when negotiating with Russians can be their use of time. It is common to face delays, especially when waiting for a response from the Russian side. In some instances, this may be a deliberate strategy, but in most cases this is a reflection of the way time is used in the society. Similarly, Russian negotiators may introduce new information at the last moment that may end up delaying the agreement and may require further discussions.[27] It is therefore important that firm deadlines for exchange of information are set and negotiators are willing to take a tough stance to avoid being dictated to by the Russian side as to how the negotiation process will take place.

Perhaps the most challenging aspect of negotiating business deals in Russia concerns bribery and corruption. As discussed in Chapter 10, what constitutes unethical behaviour varies across countries. The exchange of gifts between negotiating parties may be considered a way of building relations between parties in some countries, but in other countries such exchanges are frowned upon as they are seen to influence outcomes and decisions. Russia's corruption perception score, as published by Transparency International, suggests that people believe that the level of corruption in the public sector is high, and the payment of bribes to government officials has been observed in the country. International business negotiators need to be aware of this issue and should ensure that they do not fall into this trap and instead focus on winning the deal based on their own merit. As depicted in Example 12.4, the issue of corruption in Russia remains a challenge.

EXAMPLE 12.4
CORRUPTION IN RUSSIA

International firms attempting to conduct business activities in Russia need to be aware of the widespread issue of bribery and corruption in the country. Perhaps one of the most infamous cases of corruption and dishonest business practices was one dubbed "the Russian laundromat". The scheme, which is thought to be the world's biggest attempt at money laundering, involved moving $20-$80 billion out of Russia to be laundered into countries around the world. The scheme was exposed in 2017 by the Organized Crime and Corruption Reporting Project (OCCRP).

Surveys conducted in Russia found that the general population are aware of the high level of corruption in the country and believe that the country will never be able to be free of it. So much so that even Russia's top auditor has claimed that Russia's economic growth is being hampered by corruption in the legal system.

To address these concerns and to improve the opportunities for Russian firms to conduct business internationally, Aeroflot, the Russian airline, has proposed to develop a Transnational Anticorruption Compliance Strategy. The strategy aims to introduce an anti-corruption policy for Russian companies and streamline the country's legislation to reflect global best practices aimed at tackling corruption in the country.

Sources: Adapted from Aeroflot (2019);[28] Levinson (2019);[29] OCCRP (2017);[30] and The Moscow Times (2019).[31]

Discussion Point: What are the reputational risks for organisations who conduct business activities in countries with high levels of corruption? How can these risks be mitigated?

12.4 SUMMARY

In this chapter we detail the negotiating behaviour found in different countries around the world. The focus on China, India, countries in the Arab world, and Russia highlights how politics, religion and cultural differences can influence the negotiations process. Although the negotiation process differs between countries, there are also differences that one can observe across deals. A team negotiating with two parties from the same industry and cultural background may still encounter many differences and would need to respond accordingly. However, while there is no one correct way to conduct negotiations, there are some guidelines that negotiators should consider as best practice. For example, the relevance of relationship-building is higher in emerging or developing economies, especially in instances where the formal institutions and regulations are not strictly implemented. However, even in developed economies, making an effort to build interpersonal relations holds value. In the contemporary business environment, social and professional networks are highly valued, and allocating time in the negotiation process to build interpersonal relations can have long-term benefits extending beyond the current deal being negotiated.

QUESTIONS

1. How does the Chinese government influence international business negotiations?
2. Explain the relationship-building process followed by Indian negotiators.
3. Using the institutional lens, explain the use of *guanxi* and *wasta* in negotiations with Chinese and Arab negotiators.
4. What pricing strategy is/strategies are appropriate when negotiating with Chinese and Indian negotiators?
5. When dealing with firms from politically unstable countries, what steps can companies take to secure their business interests?

NOTES

1. World Population Review (2019) Continent and region populations 2019. Available from: http://worldpopulationreview.com/continents/.
2. Paik, Y. and Tung, R.L. (1999) Negotiating with East Asians: how to attain "win-win" outcomes. *Management International Review*. **39**(2), 103–22.
3. US Census Bureau (2019) *Current Population*. Available from: https://www.census.gov/.
4. Ghauri, P.N. and Fang, T. (2001) Negotiating with the Chinese: a socio-cultural analysis. *Journal of World Business*. **36**(3), 303–25; Ghauri, P.N. and Fang, T. (2000) Understanding Chinese business negotiating behaviour. In: Lau, C.-M., Wong, C.-S., Law, K.K.S. and Tse, D.K. (eds) *Asian Management Matters: Regional Relevance and Global Impact*. River Edge, Imperial College Press, pp. 373–89; Tung, R.L., Worm, V. and Fang, T. (2008) Sino-Western business negotiations revisited: 30 years after China's open door policy. *Organizational Dynamics*. **37**(1), 60–74.
5. Fortune (2019) *Global 500*. Available from: https://fortune.com/global500/2019/.

6. China Daily (2004) Lenovo buys IBM's PC unit for $1.25 billion. 8 December.
7. Spooner, J.G. (2004) IBM sells PC group to Lenovo. *Cnet.com*, 8 December.
8. Wright, G. (2004) Lenovo buys IBM PC business. *The Guardian*, 8 December.
9. Ghauri and Fang (2001) op. cit.
10. Liu, H. (2017) Chinese stratagem culture: nature, formation, and implications. *Journal of Transnational Management*. **22**(1), 53–68.
11. Ghauri and Fang (2001) op. cit.
12. Stacey, K. (2018) Battling India's bureaucracy for babies and businesses. *Financial Times*, 10 January.
13. Pearl, D. (2001) Dispute between Indian State, Enron casts a shadow over other projects. *The Wall Street Journal*, 14 March.
14. Rai, S. (2002) Seeking ways to sell Enron's plant in India. *The New York Times*, 11 April.
15. Kumar, R. (2005) Negotiating with the complex, imaginative Indian. *Ivey Business Journal*. March/April.
16. Accord on Fire and Building Safety in Bangladesh (2020). Available from: https://bangladeshaccord.org/.
17. Hofstede, G. (1991) *Cultures and Organizations: Software of the Mind*. London, McGraw-Hill.
18. Feghali, E. (1997) Arab cultural communication patterns. *International Journal of Intercultural Relations*. **21**(3), 345–78.
19. Cunningham, R.B. and Sarayah, Y.K. (1994) Taming *wasta* to achieve development. *Arab Studies Quarterly*. **16**(3), 29–41.
20. Khakhar, P. and Rammal, H.G. (2013) Culture and business networks: international business negotiations with Arab managers. *International Business Review*. **22**(3), 578–90.
21. ICLG (2019) United Arab Emirates. *Mergers and Acquisitions 2019*. The International Comparative Legal Guides.
22. Tashakova, O. (2015) Nepotism versus wasta in business globalisation. *Khaleej Times*, 15 September.
23. Lewis, R. (2014) How different cultures understand time. *Business Insider*, 1 June.
24. Alon, I. and Brett, J.M. (2007) Perceptions of time and their impact on negotiations in the Arabic-speaking Islamic World. *Negotiation Journal*. **23**(1), 55–73.
25. Zhuplev, A. (2016) *Doing Business in Russia: A Concise Guide*. Vol. II. New York, Business Expert Press.
26. Ivory, I. (2012) Negotiating a Russian deal. *The Moscow Times*, 10 April.
27. Ivory (2012) ibid.
28. Aeroflot (2019) Aeroflot to develop a strategy to harmonise anti-corruption requirements for Russian business. 16 September. Available from: https://www.aeroflot.ru/gb-en/news/61503?_ga=2.47137952.682276264.1569542864-1675422004.1569542864.
29. Levinson, A. (2019) Corruption dies hard in Russia. *The Moscow Times*, 1 April.
30. OCCRP (2017) The Russian laundromat exposed. The Organized Crime and Corruption Reporting Project, 20 March.
31. The Moscow Times (2019) Russia's top auditor Kudrin blasts corruption in legal system. 6 June.

FURTHER READING

Brett, J.M. (2007) *Negotiating Globally: How to Negotiate Deals, Resolve Disputes, and Make Decisions across Cultural Boundaries*. 2nd ed. San Francisco, John Wiley & Sons.

Ghauri, P.N. and Tony, F. (2002) Negotiating with the Chinese: a socio-cultural analysis. *Journal of World Business*. **36**(3), 303–25.

Kam-hon, L., Guang, Y. and Graham, J.L. (2006) Tension and trust in international business negotiations: American executives negotiating with Chinese executives. *Journal of International Business Studies.* **37**(5), 623–41.

Mayfield, J., Mayfield, M., Martin, D. and Herbig, P. (1998) How location impacts international business negotiations. *Review of Business.* **19**(2), 21–4.

Sharma, H. (2018) Indian negotiation style. *International Journal of Indian Culture and Business Management.* **17**(1), 94–108.

13
Guidelines for international business negotiations

In this chapter we extract the essence of previous chapters and present some guidelines that can be useful for planning and conducting international business negotiations to achieve the best possible results. We do that in three sections: checklist for negotiations, build relationships, and do we need an agent? As we mentioned earlier, negotiations skills are not in our genes but can be learned and mastered through careful planning and practice. The most crucial aspect of negotiations is careful preparation and planning. If our first experience is not so positive, that does not mean we are poor negotiators. It just means that we need to prepare and practise more. The more we get involved in negotiations, the more we learn and become better negotiators. Here are some guidelines to follow.

13.1 CHECKLIST FOR NEGOTIATIONS

It is important for negotiators to have a checklist upfront that covers what aspects of the forthcoming negotiations we need to prepare for and have ready before we enter them. This checklist should include clear objectives, information gathering, cultural understanding, knowledge of the other party and knowledge of our limits. In this section we will deal with these and other aspects one by one.

13.1.1 Have clear objectives

The first and most important aspect is to be clear on what we can expect to achieve from the coming negotiations. This should be done first by considering our own position. Can we really achieve what we want to achieve at this point of time and from this party? If we are to negotiate a partnership deal with, say, a Chinese party, do we want to get access to the large market or do we want to get access to a resource that this party has, such as cheap labour or a certain input that we need in our products? Depending upon our objectives, our negotiations strategies and behaviour might change. We need also to look at our situation and how badly we need this deal. Do we need this deal because we do not have any other orders and need to pay salaries to our staff and cover other running costs? Or do we need the deal to make a handsome profit as we are not short of orders?

Objectives are a limited set of core outcomes which are expected by a party as a result of the negotiation process. This may concern a reservation price, a certain type of contractual arrangement, keeping a technology and so on, and may include:

1. A limited range of favourable outcomes: it is not "all the cake" which is desired but just a certain part of it which is significant to a party.
2. A clear definition of what is negotiable and what is not negotiable.
3. A plan that may facilitate the extent and timing of concessions and enable a party to avoid yielding too much.

A similar analysis should be done for the other side: what are their objectives and how badly do they need this deal? What are their strengths and limitations and do their objectives match with your own? Do they want to have a one-off transaction as they need your technology, or do they want to establish a profitable business relationship? It is important to judge whether there is an overlap between their objectives and yours.[1]

13.1.2 Gather information

Once we know what we want to achieve from these negotiations and have made a judgement that these are achievable with this party, we then need to gather factual as well as intangible information about the deal and the other party. We need to gather factual information about the financial position of the other party and intangible information about their reputation and dealings with foreign partners/firms. This information is not difficult to gather; however, entering into negotiations with a party without having this information can lead to several complications and delays later in the process or even after the agreement. We also have to gather information about the country in which we are going to do business, including the rules and regulations about foreign firms and particularly for the specific industry. Some industries, such as food, pharmaceuticals and even high-tech computer technologies, often have specific rules in each country.[2]

Information about the negotiators coming to the table from the other side is of utmost importance. What type of individual will be coming from the other side? Their background and profession (such as engineer, marketer or politician) is important. People with a technical background behave differently from people with a commercial background and we need to prepare ourselves accordingly. We should also gather information about the level of management coming from the other side, as we have to match that level. For example, if a vice-president is coming then we need find an equally senior manager from our side to negotiate with them. Matching in this respect will facilitate the process.

13.1.3 Understand cultural differences

Many firms do not pay enough attention to cultural differences. The bigger the firm the more arrogant they are, as they believe that as they already work in several countries they have enough cultural understanding to tackle any market or people coming from any country. Moreover, firms coming from an Anglo-American culture, particularly from the United States and United Kingdom, believe that the whole world is used to their way of doing business and therefore they need not understand or adapt to other cultures. They thus automatically adopt the *self-reference criteria*.[3] This is, however, a misconception. Even if the other party, say from Pakistan, Indonesia or China, may speak good English, it does not mean that they follow an Anglo-American business culture.

BOX 13.1

KNOWING ME, KNOWING YOU

In negotiations, "know thyself" also means "know your culture". We cannot understand another culture without first understanding our own. We must start with recognising our own point of reference – the values and norms we ourselves operate within. Generalisations about business practices in Asia, for example, mean nothing unless we can compare them with generalisations about business practices in our own culture. Without understanding the ways in which these practices differ, we cannot effectively deal with them.

The better negotiators and more successful businesspeople are not those that have memorised thousands of dos and don'ts, but those that have developed an international feel, a global mindset and an empathetic approach towards doing business with people from other cultures. Certainly, they do try to learn about the people of the country they are negotiating with, and certainly those with experience of a particular country will have an advantage over the less experienced, but first and foremost, the better negotiators understand the broader process of establishing effective communication with business associates whose cultural baggage is different from their own. And they know the importance of understanding cultural differences in order to prevent these from undermining the negotiations.

Source: Adapted from Foster (1992).[4]

Discussion Point: What are some of the steps negotiators can take to evaluate their own strengths and weaknesses and identify the differences between the negotiating teams?

The key here is to understand the cultural differences, that is, how the culture where we are going to do business differs from our culture. In other words, we need to know about both our culture and the other culture, otherwise we work with our self-reference criteria and cannot see the differences. This also means that a list of "dos and don'ts" is not enough when doing business with different cultures.[5] Once we can see the differences, we can prepare ourselves and will not be surprised to discover a different behaviour. It is, for example, very important to have advance knowledge about how people treat time, rather than be surprised or get irritated when somebody is 20 or 30 minutes late. Do people use *monochronic time* or *polychronic time*? By knowing, we can be prepared for the fact that while negotiating with us the other side might still be receiving telephone calls or directing subordinates in their day-to-day work.[6]

13.1.4 Assess the communication pattern

For negotiations to take place, parties need to communicate with each other. The better the communication, the more effective and smoother the negotiation process. For international business negotiations, language and cultural differences are some of the impediments that disturb effective communication. It is, therefore, necessary to understand the communication style and pattern of the other side. As we have learnt, languages are different: some languages are exaggerative (Arabic), some are too precise (German) and some are high context (Chinese and Japanese). These languages influence our communication style and behaviour even if we are speaking a third language. In some cultures people talk a lot (Americans and Spanish), while in others people do not (Sweden and Finland), meaning there are many silent moments in the negotiation process. In such a negotiation process, people from the opposite culture get confused or worried and parties often misunderstand each other. A prior understanding or knowledge of these communication patterns is therefore important to avoid these misunderstandings.

If one party is speaking her/his native language and the other is not, or when both parties are speaking a third language (for example, a Swedish manager negotiating in Pakistan), parties need to speak very slowly, articulating each word and not being in a hurry, as the other party has to translate in her/his mind the message s/he receives and then translate her/his message that s/he wants to convey from her/his native language to the third language. To be a good listener is an important quality in these negotiations and it facilitates the communication to a great extent. Communication is thus a two-way process: listening and speaking. We need to manage both. Moreover, the more you demonstrate that you are listening carefully (for example, by nodding your head or adding yes now and then), the more you convey the message that you respect the other party and that you are keen to do business. Listening is therefore a useful negotiation tactic. On the other hand, the more we talk the more we disclose our position, and too much talking annoys the other party.

BOX 13.2
THE COMMUNICATION PROCESS

1. First there is a feeling: this is the very beginning of communication. Something that one of your six senses is picking up and that you want to get in somebody else's mind or body in the way that you are experiencing it.
2. Then there is an awareness of that sensation or thought: from that physical experience you get an idea, or you feel a need that demands expression.
3. This leads to the formation of words in your mind: these words are an attempt to capture that sensation or that idea you are experiencing.
4. These words and/or conduct are then put out to others: they are communicated verbally, in sign language, through other non-verbal means (body language) or on paper. These are the only means of sending the feelings or words that are in your mind to someone else.
5. The words and/or conducts are then received and processed by the other person: you must be able to convey them to another person's eyes and/or ears.
6. The receiver will process your words and/or conduct: whatever the other person sees

and/or hears will be reinterpreted into his own words and understanding. At this point the receiver may also have his own internal conversation and thoughts, which is stimulated by his interpretation.

7. The interpretation, internal dialogue and thoughts will in turn create feelings and images in the receiver's mind and body: the receiver's ultimate feelings in response to what you have sent out may be very different from what you were feeling or intending to communicate.

Source: Adapted from Edelman and Crain (1993).[7]

13.1.5 Control and observe body language

Earlier in the book we discussed *non-verbal communication* (body language) at length and explained how important it is as part of overall communication, particularly in negotiations. Non-verbal communication includes culture-based gestures and behaviour as well as body language that is intrinsic in human behaviour. Different cultures use body language differently, for example by nodding in a certain way (as in India when people move their head from one side to the other to show that they understand), by sitting in a certain way and by having more or less eye contact while communicating.[8] It is easy to prepare for culture-based gestures and signs and to follow these. For example, in the Middle East you cannot point a finger to the person you are talking to or talking about, in many Asian cultures you cannot show/direct the sole of your shoe to the other side and in Brazil you cannot give the OK sign (holding index finger and thumb) to show your affirmation. Body language strengthens the message we want to convey, and sometimes our body speaks louder than, and gives contradictory messages to, our words. It is therefore important to observe and understand body language to get the full message. In the same way we should be careful when sending messages that our words and body language are in sync.

BOX 13.3
COMMUNICATING THROUGH NON-VERBAL CUES

Arabs may watch the pupils of your eyes to judge your responses to different topics.

The pupil is a very sensitive indicator of how people respond to what they see or to a situation. When you are interested in something, your pupils dilate; if I say something you don't like, they tend to contract. But the Arabs have known about the pupil response for hundreds if not thousands of years. Because people can't control the response of their eyes, making them a dead giveaway, many Arabs wear dark glasses, even indoors.

These are people reading personal interactions on a second-by-second basis. By watching the pupils, they can respond rapidly to mood changes. That's one of the reasons why they use a closer conversational distance than Westerners do. At about one metre, the normal distance between two Westerners who are talking, we have a hard time following eye movement. But if you use an Arab distance, about half a metre or two feet, you can watch the pupil of the eye.

Direct eye contact for a Westerner is difficult to achieve since we are taught in the West not to stare, not to look at the eyes that carefully. If you stare at someone, it is too intense, too sexy or too hostile. It may also mean that we are not totally tuned into the situation. Maybe we should all wear dark glasses.

Source: Adapted from Ghauri and Cateora (2014).[9]

Discussion Point: One of the challenges that negotiators face in a cross-cultural setting is that they may inadvertently send messages through non-verbal cues that they are unaware of. Can you think of ways that can reduce the chances of miscommunication?

13.1.6 Know your limits

Before entering a negotiation it is important that we know exactly what our limits are in respect of price, delivery time and terms of payment, and other crucial issues to be negotiated. We should establish the minimum/maximum we want to achieve on these issues. Although we advocate negotiating for a *Pareto-optimal* solution, that is, the outcome which is beneficial for both parties, it is important to know our walk-away option, that is, the maximum and minimum limits of concessions we are willing to make and receive or the priority which we absolutely want to achieve and that if this is not possible we will be ready to walk away. It is good not to give the impression that this is the only deal we are willing to accept and that we want to get it at any price. This is just one of the possible business deals and a walk-away option should always be envisioned and decided upon before the formal face-to-face negotiations start. The walk-away option may be used due to unexpected changes in the environment or competitive conditions, a change of objectives or in the strategic direction of our own company, or a realisation during the negotiations that this deal will not help us achieve our objectives. In fact, we should also try to envisage the walk-away point of the other party. This will make our strategies and tactics more relevant and fruitful.

13.1.7 Formulate a strategy and tactics

Before we enter a face-to-face negotiation, we must formulate an overall strategy. Are we going to practise a tough, a soft or an intermediate strategy? A *tough strategy* means that we start by demanding a high initial offer and do not give any concessions until the other party has given one. A *soft strategy* means that we do not commence with a high initial offer and start giving concessions in a hope that the other party will reciprocate. An *intermediate strategy* means that we look for a settlement that is beneficial for both sides and if such an offer is made, we can accept it without haggling. In the case where we are planning to use the tough strategy, it is useful not to be tough on every issue – we can be soft on some issues that are relatively less important for the achievement of our objectives. Negotiation teams often play good cop/bad cop, where one of the team members uses a tough strategy and another a soft strategy to balance out the overall strategy.

When formulating our strategy, we should also try to envisage the other party's strategy. Even if we surmise that they will not come with a tough strategy as they need our technology, we should still be prepared for such a strategy.[10] If we are prepared, we will not be surprised or caught off guard. It is always better to counter the tough strategy with tough strategy and not be afraid of the resulting deadlock, as in that case both parties, and especially the other party, will have to reconsider their strategy. In the case of deadlock both parties will go away to reconsider their strategy, and when returning to the negotiations they will bring more options to the table.

In terms of *tactics*, the first aim should be to see if we can negotiate in our home country as there are several benefits associated with being the home team. This can be done by inviting the other team to our country so they can see the machines/products they intend to buy. One way to convince them to come is to offer to pay all the local expenses, including hotels, meals, some sightseeing and so on. In many cases customers, especially those from emerging markets, will be happy to do that. If it is not possible to convince them to come, then quite often foreign firms prefer to do negotiations at the hotel they are staying in. In this case, arguments that this saves time by not having to sit in traffic, and that the hotel has excellent conference facilities and serves good food and drinks that can be paid by the foreign firm, quite often work.

13.1.8 Control your concessions

Formulating tactics for your concessions is important. Plan and time your concessions beforehand. Concessions can often be viewed and interpreted in opposite ways, either as a sign of openness and willingness to cooperate or as a sign of weakness and readiness to yield as you are desperate to do the deal. When to give what, to have the maximum impact on the process, is perhaps the most crucial aspect of face-to-face negotiations. Do we give a concession to attract a concession, or do we give a concession to respond to the other party's concession? We need to prepare a list of possible concessions and rank them, either the most important one to the least important one or the easiest ones to give to the most difficult ones to give. Once this is done, we can then decide which one to give when. Do not give too many concessions in a row as it will harm your credibility.

Sometimes it is good to give concessions to create a positive *atmosphere*, to show that you are willing to give and that you are keen to do business with this party, thus increasing their expectations. Quite often we reserve some of our concessions for a particular concession that we want from the other side. For example, we are willing to give a 5 per cent discount on the price if they are willing to pay cash or pay for more than 50 per cent of the goods at the time of the signing of the contract. Negotiators who profess tough strategy advise that we should not give any concession for free. For each concession we give we need to get something in return. Or we only give a concession after we have received one from the other side. In other words, it is more like "take and give" than "give and take".

13.1.9 Patience is a virtue

Patience is a virtue and perhaps the biggest asset in negotiations. To allow yourself to be patient, you should not reveal your timetable. Never tell the other side when you will have to leave because this gives them the opportunity to put your team under time pressure. Allow yourself plenty of time and even some more. In particular, give yourself time to digest; do not respond too quickly to new propositions, as even small interruptions of the negotiations may

BOX 13.4
THE SILENT LANGUAGE

Here is a rather standard situation:

> After lots of stalling around, I finally put forward my price, and was met with silence. This made me very nervous. It must have gone on for three or four minutes, but it felt like an hour. Then I thought that maybe he realised that I was bluffing and was waiting for me to make a better offer. So, I did. I expected him to respond, say something like that it was closer to what he expected, but he went silent on me again! Now I was really nervous, so I gave him the absolute lowest price I was willing to go. He takes in a big suck of air, pauses, says that the proposal needs further study, and thanks me for my time. Well, I was confused, but I felt like he was calling the meeting to an end, and since the price was fair, I left feeling that we had a good shot. The funny thing was, we never heard from him again.

Source: Foster (1992).[11]

prove useful to think over complex issues or to discuss and find a common position within your own negotiation team. It is fine to show your dissatisfaction over difficult sessions and complex issues and discuss the reasons and possible solutions first within your team. The timing of verbal exchange is crucial in negotiations. Some Westerners, especially Americans, find gaps or pauses in conversations to be disturbing, while people from other cultures prefer to leave a moment of silence between statements, to give themselves and the other side time to digest the new issue/offer and counteroffer.

When planning, try to set realistic dates and deadlines and, if needed, plan conservatively, introducing time slack that allows for delays to be absorbed without ruining the flow of the whole venture. Remember – it is better to plan modestly and realistically than to miss deadlines and create major delays that ruin your credibility and the credibility of the whole planning process.

BOX 13.5
THE USE OF TIME AROUND THE WORLD

Time is cultural, subjective and variable. One of the most serious causes of frustration and friction in cross-cultural business dealings occurs when counterparts are out of sync with each other. Differences often appear with respect to the pace of time, its perceived nature and its function. Insights into a culture's view of time may be found in their sayings and proverbs. For example:

"Time is money." (United States)
"Those who rush arrive first at the grave." (Spain)
"The clock did not invent man." (Nigeria)
"If you wait long enough, even an egg will walk." (Ethiopia)
"Before the time, it is not yet the time; after the time, it's too late." (France)

Sources: Adapted from Hall and Hall (1990);[12] Pillai (2003).[13]

Discussion Point: How can negotiators balance demands to meet deadlines with being flexible during negotiations?

13.1.10 Be flexible with the agenda

In the negotiation literature there is a lot of discussion about whether to prepare an agenda beforehand and who should prepare the agenda. There are both advantages and disadvantages with preparing the agenda. If you prepare an agenda, you can prepare it according to your thoughts regarding what is important and what is not so important. This means that in a way you disclose your position and your priorities. However, even if you do prepare an agenda, be flexible with it if the other party does not stick to the agenda. It may be somewhat frustrating to see that a negotiation agenda has been agreed upon but is subsequently not followed. It is natural that the other party has its own priorities and ranks issues differently. It may also be the case that the other party prefers a global to a step-by-step negotiation, and that they do not see negotiation as a linear process in which issues are addressed and settled one after the other before moving on.

In face-to-face negotiation, the maintenance of flexibility of parties on issues is important, especially when the negotiation concerns issues like terms of payment, credit facilities, delivery time and price. These issues are interrelated and cannot be discussed or agreed upon separately. The process of give and take usually occurs after both sides have tested the level of commitment and have sent and received positive signals about the potential outcome and expectations are high on both sides. For example, the price can often be reduced if the party offers better terms of payment. It is also important to include some incentives that can be traded off but which cannot be evaluated in monetary terms, such as a reference project or future market access where the potential is much larger than the present sale.

13.2 BUILD RELATIONSHIPS

Although some scholars advise that while negotiating with different cultures we need to focus on the issues and not on the individuals,[14] we strongly believe that other than in Anglo-American culture and few others, developing relationships with the individuals from the other side is very important to do business. For example, in China and in the Middle East, unless you develop good relationships at an individual level, it is very difficult to do business. In fact, it is the same in many big emerging markets such as Indonesia, Pakistan and Bangladesh. As we mentioned earlier, if you want to do business in China, you need to do people first. The better the relationship we have with the local people the easier it is for us to understand and adapt to the new cultural settings and requirement. It is, therefore, very important to socialise with individuals from the other side whenever you get a chance. In some cultures, people do invite foreign guests to their homes, for example in India or Pakistan, while in other cultures it is customary to take foreign guests sightseeing and to restaurants, for example in China and the Middle East.

13.2.1 Position against the competitors

We need to gather information about our competitors – the firms that are going to compete with us on this project – as this will help us to position ourselves. It is important to remember that we are in a race against our competitors to win this contract, not against our buyer or seller. We need to see if the competitors have an earlier relationship with the other party or not. The idea is to develop a better relationship with the other party through social interactions, such as inviting them to your offices/factories/country. The party that has a better relationship with individuals from the other side has a greater chance of winning the contract.

Once we know who the competitors are, we need to gather information on their strengths and weaknesses as compared to ours. In cases where they are strong, we need to formulate arguments to convince the buyer with whom we are negotiating why it is beneficial for them to do business with us and rather than with the competitors, despite their strength. It is good to know the weaknesses of our competitors as this knowledge can be used in cases where we need to convince the other party to work with us.

We need to know about all aspects of our competitors: their technology, the individuals who work for them and whether they have done business with the particular buyer before. In the case where they have done business with this buyer before, we need to prepare arguments of why the buyer should do business with us this time. It is always better to position your technical solution as being superior to that of the competitors. Another way to persuade the buyer is to offer better financial terms.

13.2.2 Find the decision maker in the other team

In some cultures, for example in China, it is often difficult to find the real decision maker and parties end up building relationships with the wrong or not so important people. To be able to build useful relationships, it is essential to know the right people, that is, the people who make or influence decisions/choices in the opposite side. Once you know who the decision makers are, you can try to develop a trustworthy relationship with them. Trust can also be established through indirect communication, for example by sending material from your earlier projects and through finding friends and other network members of these individuals. It is much better if a friend of this person talks to them positively about your firm or individuals in the firm.

13.2.3 Develop and use your reputation

Although reputation develops over time, it cannot be left to chance. Smart negotiators develop and enhance their reputation in every meeting they have with the other party. This can be done by demonstrating a consistent and fair behaviour. For example, negotiators who say yes to everything that the other side asks for do not create a good reputation as the other side can see that the party in question is just saying yes even to issues that are difficult to achieve, and that he will not be able to deliver all he promises. On the other hand, if a negotiator says "yes" to things they can easily do, "they will try" to some of the things they see as difficult but doable, and "no" to things that will be very hard to achieve, they will enhance their credibility. The other side will trust this negotiator more than the one earlier who said yes to everything. In international business negotiations, people may have different understandings as to what is rational, fair or normal. We have a tendency to follow our self-reference criteria and thereby not understanding the other side's point of view. The negotiators who try to understand the other side's perspective and to find a collective meaning of what is fair are more appreciated by the other side.

As we know, reputation is developed over time; this means that while negotiating we should realise that our behaviour in this negotiation, or even in this session, will influence your future reputation. We should avoid at all costs getting a reputation that we do not keep our word or promises, and that our statements are not completely true. If our reputation is good, the other side will believe in what we promise and say. If our reputation is not so good, then the other side will need to independently verify/check our statements and whether the promises we are making are doable or not.[15]

13.2.4 Be prepared to negotiate beyond agreement

We often hear about the experiences of negotiators who talk of "negotiating beyond negotiation". This phrase typically refers to a significant element of international business negotiation, that is, deal making, and at the same time goes far beyond simple agreement on different issues. A relationship often develops through a series of successive negotiation rounds, with the signing of the contract and the implementation phase being the final round. Negotiation is often a continuous rather than discontinuous activity; although certain rituals, such as the signing of a contract, seem to put in place definite time boundaries, in the real world that is often not the case. Negotiators need to wait for the negotiation process to extend beyond the face-to-face sessions to the post-negotiation stage, as quite often formulating the contract draft is a negotiation in itself. For most cultures there is no clear timeline defined by the signing of a contract. The most important time frame is that of the relationship, not that of a particular deal. The better the relationship the parties have developed during the negotiations process, the easier and smoother this phase goes. However, if the parties have not been able to develop a good and trustful relationship, then both of them will be rather suspicious and want to check each and every sentence so that they can be sure that the agreement is in line with what they think they agreed.

13.2.5 Avoid the possibility of litigation

Whether one should have a formal signed contract or not is debatable, because you may be at risk of signing an agreement which will afterwards be considered detrimental to one party. A simple memorandum of understanding that allows further refinement may be better when the parties have not reached full agreement within a negotiation round. The idea that having a deal is better than having no deal may be dangerous. To sign an unclear or ambiguous contract can lead to enormous problems in the implementation stage. It is thus wiser to spend one more session discussing and clearing the ambiguity than signing the contract there and then.

In some cultures, the agreement or contract is just an agreement in principle or a formality. The implementation does not need to follow this document literally and should instead be based on mutual trust. Westerners normally like to rely on written contracts, while some Asians (for example, the Chinese) and Arabs will rely on mutual trust and understanding for the implementation. Because of these differences, there are often lengthy discussions on the language of the contract to be signed. It is thus important to make sure during the entire process that you and your counterpart have the same understanding of the issues being agreed upon. The contract should then be written in simple and clear language to avoid ambiguity or future conflict.

The presence of lawyers, especially early in the process, along with a very meticulous attitude when drafting the agreement may be interpreted as a sign of distrust. On the other hand, the role of lawyers in formalising the final agreement is standard in the world of international business. The advice, therefore, would be to exclude lawyers, as well as accountants, from the negotiation table in the early stages of the negotiation and even in the later stages of negotiation. They may, however, do a counselling job working behind the scenes. Litigation damages the relationship, which generally does not survive the legal process. Discussions are always preferable to court rulings. Even very detailed contracts can never be fully perfect, and misunderstandings can occur. In such a case, there is always an element of "renegotiation". Avoiding litigation, and even the possibility of it, must be a major concern for both parties, as if it happens it will destroy the relationship and will result in a "lose-lose" solution.

13.3 DO WE NEED AN AGENT?

In international business negotiations it is important to ask the question "do we need an agent?" The problem is that firms are often somewhat arrogant and believe that they can handle negotiations with every culture or country. In fact, the bigger the company the greater this belief. However, having done several negotiations in Latin America does not mean that you can also do business in Asia. If you have negotiated several deals in Japan, that does not mean that you can also handle negotiations in China or Indonesia. All these countries have their own peculiarities and cultural norms. In some countries it is difficult to handle the practicalities such as booking a hotel, renting a car with a driver, estimating the travel time between the hotel and the negotiation venue or the offices of the local party, and so on. For all these matters a foreign firm is better off having a local agent.

13.3.1 You need a door opener

As mentioned above, foreign firms do need a local agent to handle the practicalities. In some bigger deals, foreign firms need to meet with local authorities, politicians or civil servants. These people are very difficult to pin down and even more difficult to arrange a meeting with. In some countries, if you do not have a local agent you cannot even arrange a meeting with them. A local agent is therefore very helpful in opening these doors for you. The local agent can also open the doors to the local party's world: how serious are they about doing this deal and about doing future business with your company? How many other competitors are in the picture? Unless we have a local agent, it will be very difficult, if not impossible, to get this type of information. The agent can also help us in finding the right decision maker or influencers for the particular deal.

13.3.2 Ethical considerations

As mentioned earlier, in most deals ethical issues are involved, and foreign firms are at a disadvantage to understand the importance and the seriousness of ethical correctness in a particular market. According to the Foreign Corrupt Practices Act,[16] all American companies must apply universal rules for ethics, particularly in relation to bribery and illegal payments. However, many European and other countries turn a blind eye to these restrictions and even allow payments to officials as long as it is done abroad and not in the home country. At the same time, most of these unethical practices are illegal in the majority of countries, and if a firm or individual is caught practising these, the firm or individual can be prosecuted and the latter even sent to jail. The firm can be banned from doing business, both now and in the future, in that country. These are therefore serious matters, and negotiators should not be involved in carrying out these activities. Many companies thus find agents to be very useful in these matters, partly because they can give the right information about the country and partly because firms find it easier to let the agents deal with these matters. Agents are independent companies and the foreign firms, other than simply paying them a certain commission, which is a contractual and perhaps legitimate relationship between two independent companies, can claim not to be aware of what agents do.[17]

13.4 SUMMARY

This final chapter of the book builds on the material covered in the earlier chapters and provides guidelines for international business negotiations. A checklist for negotiators is provided that includes topics such as clear objectives, information gathering, cultural understanding, knowledge of the other party and knowledge of our limits. Other considerations for negotiators include the importance of relationship-building and deciding whether an agent is required in negotiations. These guidelines and the checklist can help prepare the protocol for negotiations and can help negotiators reflect on their actions, behaviours and the strategies they employ during the process.

QUESTIONS

1. What items should a checklist for negotiators include?
2. Being punctual and delivering on time are behavioural traits that are highly valued and expected in certain cultures. However, it is suggested that being flexible during negotiations can help parties reach an outcome. Explain how flexibility in the negotiation process can be beneficial, as well as the possible limitations of it.

3. "When preparing for negotiations, one should extend information gathering to beyond the other negotiating party by including competitors as well." Discuss this statement.

NOTES

1. Lewicki, R.J., Barry, B. and Saunders, D.M. (2007) *Essentials of Negotiation*. 4th ed. New York, McGraw-Hill.
2. McCall, J.B. (2003), Negotiating sales, export transactions and agency agreements. In: Ghauri, P. and Usunier, J.-C. (eds) *International Business Negotiations*, 2nd ed. Oxford, Pergamon/Elsevier, pp. 223–42.
3. Ghauri, P.N. and Cateora, P. (2014) *International Marketing*. 4th ed. London, McGraw-Hill.
4. Foster, D.E. (1992) *Bargaining across Borders*. New York, McGraw-Hill, pp. 4–5.
5. Fisher, R., Ury, W. and Patton, B. (1991) *Getting to Yes: Negotiating Agreements without Giving In*. 2nd ed. New York, Penguin.
6. Ghauri, P.N. and Fang, T. (2003) Negotiating with the Chinese: a process view. In: Ghauri, P.N. and Usunier, J.-C. (eds) *International Business Negotiations*. 2nd ed. Oxford, Pergamon/Elsevier, pp. 420–21.
7. Edelman, J. and Crain, M.B. (1993) *The Tao of Negotiation*. New York, Harper Business, pp. 62–3.
8. Ghauri and Usunier (2003) op. cit.
9. Ghauri, P.N. and Cateora, P. (2014) *International Marketing*. 4th ed. London, McGraw-Hill.
10. Ghauri, P.N. (1994) Negotiating projects with China (PRC) Fourth Seminar of the European Network on Project Marketing and System Selling, 21–23 April, Pisa, Italy.
11. Foster (1992) op. cit., pp. 98–9.
12. Hall, E.T. and Hall, M.R. (1990) *Understanding Cultural Differences*. Yarmouth, Intercultural Press, p. 196.
13. Pillai, R.K. (2003) *Reaching the World in Our Own Backyard: A Guide to Building Relationships with People of Other Faiths and Cultures*. Colorado, Waterbrook Press, p. 50.
14. Fisher et al. (1991) op. cit.
15. Lewicki et al. (2007) op. cit.
16. The United States Department of Justice (2020) Foreign Corrupt Practices Act. Available from: https://www.justice.gov/criminal-fraud/foreign-corrupt-practices-act.
17. Ghauri and Usunier (2003) op. cit.

FURTHER READING

Dinkevych, E., Wilken, R., Aykac, T., Jacob, F. and Prime, N. (2017) Can outnumbered negotiators succeed? The case of intercultural business negotiations. *International Business Review*. **26**(3), 592–603.

Ghauri, P. (1986) Guidelines for international business negotiations. *International Marketing Review*. **3**(3), 72–82.

Heiba, F. (1984) International business negotiations: a strategic planning model. *International Marketing Review*. **1**(4), 5–16.

Khan, M.A. and Ebner, N. (2019) *The Palgrave Handbook of Cross-Cultural Business Negotiation*. London, Palgrave Macmillan.

End of Part IV cases

CASE 1
GOOGLE AND THE GOVERNMENT OF CHINA: A CASE STUDY IN CROSS-CULTURAL NEGOTIATIONS*

The team of Google executives assigned to negotiate with Chinese government officials began to arrive at San Francisco International Airport two hours before their scheduled departure. The seasoned team had been briefed on Chinese culture throughout the past two weeks by a special consultant retained for the negotiations. They had also been provided with an executive summary of press coverage on China and China's most recent policy announcements regarding the Internet. The flight across the Pacific would give the executives valuable time to prepare for the negotiations concerning the acquisition of a Chinese domain name for Google and to reflect on just how far the company had come.

By the summer of 2005, Google had matured from a cutting-edge Silicon Valley start-up to emerge as one of the world's Internet titans. In only eight years the brainchild of two Stanford University graduate students had transformed an industry and was generating impressive earnings from advertising and the licensing of its search engine technology. Google's publicly traded stock had skyrocketed since it began trading a year before (Exhibit 1). The company was admired for its audacious goals (nothing short of organizing and providing access to "the world's information"[1]), its corporate principles (famously and succinctly encapsulated in three words: "Don't be evil"[2]), and its healthy balance sheet. By combining a Microsoft-like aggressiveness, an Apple-esque zest for innovation, and seemingly rigid adherence to utopian ideals, Google had captivated its users, customers, and investors. The company's flagship Web site, Google.com, stood among the most visited sites on the Internet (Exhibit 2).

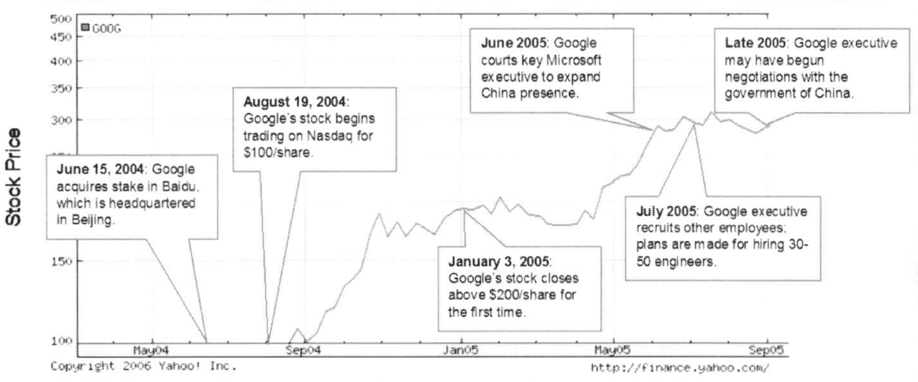

Exhibit 1 Timeline of key events and Google's stock price

Exhibit 2 Top ten most popular web sites in the world, March 2006

www.yahoo.com
www.msn.com
www.google.com
www.baidu.com
www.yahoo.co.jp
www.sina.com.cn
www.ebay.com
www.sohu.com
www.myspace.com
www.qq.com

Source: http://www.alexa.com/site/ds/top_sites?ts_mode=global&lang=none.

A company that sought to organize "the world's information" would never be content with limiting its presence to the U.S. market. As Internet usage in other countries had grown, so had Google's presence in those countries (for estimates of Internet usage in various countries, see Exhibit 3). Google had gradually expanded its geographic presence and established itself as one of the most visited sites in the world. During this expansion, it had added other domain names to assist non-American customers with their searches. These names, such as Google.fr for French users, could be viewed as brand extensions of the original Google.com, and captured a great number of international users. This in turn netted Google additional revenue. By 2005 nearly 40 percent of Google's revenue and more than half its user traffic came from outside the United States (see Exhibit 4 and Exhibit 5). Google had also added a number of complementary services to its core search engine business, including both consumer and commercial applications (see Exhibit 6 for a partial list of Google's other products and services). While the company had made strong inroads into Europe and Asia, the team of executives headed to Beijing was keenly aware that one market remained beyond their reach: China.

Exhibit 3 Worldwide Internet usage rates

#	Country or Region	Internet Users, Latest Data	Population (2006 Est.)	Internet Penetration (%)	Source and Date of Latest Data	% of World Users
1	United States	207,161,706	299,093,237	69.3	Nielsen//NR Aug. 2006	19.1
2	China	123,000,000	1,306,724,067	9.4	CNNIC June 2006	11.3
3	Japan	86,300,000	128,389,000	67.2	eTForecasts Dec. 2005	7.9
4	India	60,000,000	1,112,225,812	5.4	ITU Sept. 2006	5.5
5	Germany	50,616,207	82,515,988	61.3	Nielsen//NR Aug. 2006	4.7
6	United Kingdom	37,600,000	60,139,274	62.5	ITU Sept. 2006	3.5
7	Korea (South)	33,900,000	50,633,265	67.0	eTForecasts Dec. 2005	3.1
8	France	29,521,451	61,004,840	48.4	Nielsen//NR Aug. 2006	2.7
9	Italy	28,870,000	59,115,261	48.8	ITU Sept. 2005	2.7
10	Brazil	25,900,000	184,284,898	14.1	eTForecasts Dec. 2005	2.4
11	Russia	23,700,000	143,682,757	16.5	eTForecasts Dec. 2005	2.2
12	Canada	21,900,000	32,251,238	67.9	eTForecasts Dec. 2005	2.0
13	Spain	19,204,771	44,351,186	43.3	Nielsen//NR Aug. 2006	1.8
14	Mexico	18,622,500	105,149,952	17.7	ITU Sept. 2006	1.7
15	Indonesia	18,000,000	221,900,701	8.1	eTForecasts Dec. 2005	1.7
16	Turkey	16,000,000	74,709,412	21.4	ITU Sept. 2006	1.5
17	Australia	14,189,557	20,750,052	68.4	Nielsen//NR Aug. 2006	1.3
18	Taiwan	13,800,000	22,896,488	60.3	C. I. Almanac March 2005	1.3
19	Netherlands	10,806,328	16,386,216	65.9	Nielsen//NR June 2004	1.0
20	Poland	10,600,000	38,115,814	27.8	C. I. Almanac March 2005	1.0
Top 20 Countries		850,166,585	4,064,319,458	20.9	IWS Sept. 2006	78.3
Rest of the World		236,084,318	2,435,377,602	9.7	IWS Sept. 2006	21.7
Total World Users		1,086,250,903	6,499,697,060	16.7	IWS Sept. 2006	100.0

Source: http://www.internetworldstats.com/top20.htm.

Exhibit 4 Google's sources of revenue ($)

	Three Months Ending September 30,		Nine Months Ending September 30,	
	2004	2005	2004	2005
	(unaudited)			
Advertising revenues				
Google Web sites	411,671	884,679	1,058,645	2,278,848
Google network Web sites and magazines	384,285	675,012	1,064,263	1,889,369
Total advertising revenues	795,956	1,559,691	2,122,908	4,168,217
Licensing and other revenues	9,931	18,765	34,814	51,251
Revenues	805,887	1,578,456	2,157,722	4,219,468

Source: Google's Third Quarter 2005 10-Q SEC Statement.

Exhibit 5 Google's revenue - United States vs. international (%)

	Year Ending December 31,				
Segment	**2001**	**2002**	**2003**	**2004**	**2005**
United States	86	79	71	66	61
International	14	21	29	34	39

Note: Google slightly revised its 2003 figures in its 2005 10-K filing. Moreover, it supplied additional data beginning in 2006 as to how much of its international revenue was earned in the United Kingdom. In 2003 earnings in the United Kingdom accounted for 10 percent of revenue, and rose to 13 and 14 percent in 2004 and 2005, respectively.

Sources: Google's S-1 Statement (filed in 2004) and Google's 2005 10-K Statement.

> *The growth in international revenues from the three and nine months ended September 30, 2004 to the three and nine months ended September 30, 2005 is the result of our efforts to provide search results to international users and deliver more ads from non-U.S. advertisers.* **We expect that international revenues will generally continue to grow as a percentage of our total revenues during 2005 and in future periods.** *While international revenues accounted for approximately 39% of our total revenues in the nine months ended September 30, 2005 and 33% in the nine months ended September 30, 2004,* **more than half of our user traffic during these periods came from outside the U.S.**

Source: Google's Third Quarter 2005 10-Q SEC Statement, p. 24 (emphases added).

Though Google.com was periodically available to Chinese users, it did not provide reliable and efficient service to that market. The company had tried to protect its financial interest in the Chinese market by acquiring a stake in the Chinese search engine company Baidu, but Chinese law prohibited Google from holding more than a minority stake. Therefore, Google decided to expand its own presence in China. In the summer of 2005, plans for an expansion became more public - and appeared more concrete - after Google finally succeeded in hiring Dr Kai-fu Lee away from Microsoft. Lee was a world-renowned computer scientist widely praised and highly regarded in China and among the Chinese high-tech community. Court documents made public during Google's efforts to pull Lee away from Microsoft revealed that Google intended to establish a new Chinese research and development center supporting thirty to fifty engineers, headed by Lee. The executives on the flight were aware that these revelations had fueled speculation that Google was planning to establish a more permanent presence in China.

Although users in China could access any of Google's censorship-free offshore sites (e.g., Google.com or Google.co.uk), their searches were monitored by the Chinese government, and results found unacceptable were blocked by the censors. One notable example of this censorship was the difference in the results of searches for Tiananmen Square on Google.com and Baidu.cn (see Exhibit 7 and Exhibit 8). Because Google's searches could return results deemed contrary to China's interests, the government tried to block access to Google's site. This interference slowed the Google site's speed and actively interfered with its efficiency.

The Chinese government was able to accomplish this monitoring and blocking using its "Great Firewall," a system "that includes a blacklist of foreign sites blocked in China and filters that can

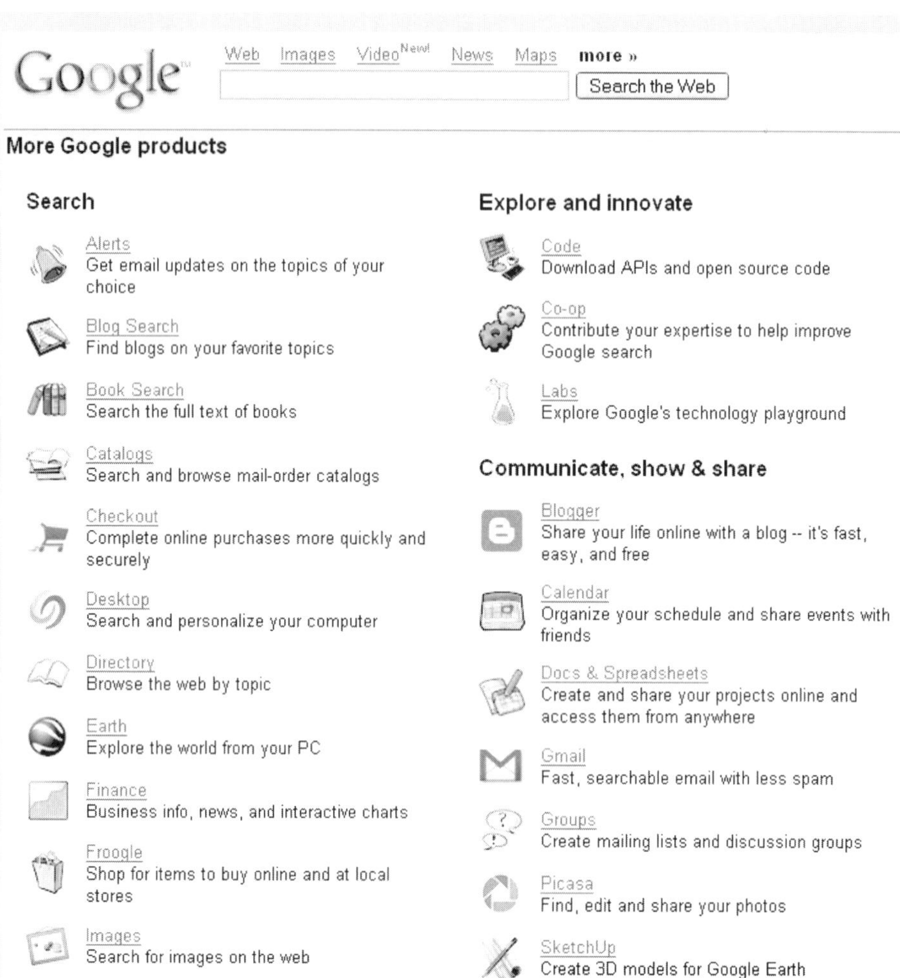

Source: http://www.google.com/intl/en/options/.

Exhibit 6 Partial list of Google's services

stop e-mail and make Web pages inaccessible if they contain certain keywords."[3] China's Great Firewall was the result of laws and regulations that required Chinese Internet service providers (ISPs) to extensively filter all Web sites for illegal information. Sites targeting the Chinese market therefore faced a choice: establish a server presence in China (and submit to state regulation on the front end of the search) or maintain an offshore server and force users to endure significant delays caused by the Firewall acting on the back end of the search. Google had operated offshore in an attempt to skirt Chinese law, so its users' results had to pass through the Great Firewall on their way to and from the

Exhibit 7 **First images returned when searching for "Tiananmen Square" on Google.com (accessed March 2006)**

Exhibit 8 **First images returned when searching for "Tiananmen Square" on Baidu.cn (accessed March 2006)**

company's offshore servers. Search results were slow, if not blocked entirely. Thus, to improve performance and its users' experiences, Google desperately needed to place servers behind the Chinese firewall. Once its servers were located in China, Google's search speed would be more competitive. Yet obstacles remained, and time was of the essence. Baidu was gaining momentum and Google's management was very concerned about the possibility of losing market share. The executives began to formulate their negotiation strategy shortly after takeoff.

GOOGLE'S PERSPECTIVE

The negotiations team had received a list of Google's management's concerns prior to leaving the company's Mountain View, California, headquarters. Management wanted to enhance the company's legitimacy with Chinese users, but knew doing so might be difficult for a company labeled as another Silicon Valley success story. China was a nationalistic culture, and the Chinese consumer was less willing to accept foreign brands when Chinese alternatives existed. As an example, Zhao Jing, a journalist well known for his provocative, political blogs about the Communist Party, was sharply criticized by some Chinese bloggers for moving his blog to an American site - MSN's Spaces - instead of a Chinese blogging site.[4] The sooner Google could acquire a ".cn" domain name, the sooner it could distance itself from its American roots. Only then would it become a member of the "in-group."[5] This in turn could lead to greater revenue streams from advertising to Chinese users.

However, Google's goals were not all financial. One nonfinancial consideration concerned governmental regulation of the site through monitoring and filtering. Because the company's primary goal was to satisfy users' preferences for "instant gratification"[6] of their information needs, it opposed any interference that might slow down or restrict a user's ability to retrieve information. This was a major motive for acquiring a ".cn" domain name. However, censorship could harm Google's credibility among Chinese and non-Chinese users, which would conflict with its goal of building "the most loyal audience on the Web."[7]

Google's management also would have to reconcile any action in China that could be viewed as censorship with its most famous principle: "Don't be evil." If Google were to agree to the level of censorship required by the Chinese authorities, it would likely face fierce criticism in the United States for appearing to act antithetically to its philosophy (see Exhibit 9 for excerpts from Google's code of conduct). The Google negotiations team had witnessed the media furor that Yahoo had faced when it turned over information transmitted by Chinese users of its e-mail services to the Chinese government. That information was later used to sentence three cyberdissidents to prison terms ranging from three to ten years.[8]

Yet even though the Google team would seek to avoid "evil" actions, the company's policy also required it to comply with local laws and regulations. Google complied with requests from authorities not to list neo-Nazi sites returned in searches in France and Germany and not to list results in the United States that violated the U.S. Digital Millennium Copyright Act. Google's adherence to these forms of state-mandated censorship demonstrated its willingness to abide by local laws.

The negotiations team had an alternative approach to entering the Chinese market, though it was not particularly attractive. The company could lobby China for access to a larger stake in Baidu. By upping its investment in a "homegrown" search engine company, Google could comply with the Chinese government's regulations governing Internet firms, maintain an uncensored Google.com site, and maintain its integrity. However, access to Google.com would remain painfully slow, and the result would likely be user frustration and lost market share. Further, because of regulatory limitations in China, Google might not be able to obtain a controlling interest in Baidu. Without complete control over Baidu, Google's revenue from China would be limited. Fortunately, Google's negotiations team would be assisted by Dr. Lee, who had gained experience dealing with the Chinese government while working for Microsoft. He also brought with him an element of prestige as a result of the admiration that many Chinese scientists and programmers held for him.

Exhibit 9 Excerpts from Google's Code of Conduct

PREFACE

Our informal corporate motto is "Don't be evil." We Googlers generally relate those words to the way we serve our users—as well we should. But being "a different kind of company" means more than the products we make and the business we're building; it means making sure that our core values inform our conduct in all aspects of our lives as Google employees.

The Google Code of Conduct is the code by which we put those values into practice. This document is meant for public consumption, but its most important audience is within our own walls. This code isn't merely a set of rules for specific circumstances but an intentionally expansive statement of principles meant to inform all our actions; we expect all our employees, temporary workers, consultants, contractors, officers and directors to study these principles and do their best to apply them to any and all circumstances which may arise.

The core message is simple: Being Googlers means striving toward the highest possible standard of ethical business conduct. This is a matter as much practical as ethical; we hire great people who work hard to build great products, but our most important asset by far is our reputation as a company that warrants our users' faith and trust. That trust is the foundation upon which our success and prosperity rests, and it must be re-earned every day, in every way, by every one of us.

So please do read this code, and then read it again, and remember that as our company evolves, The Google Code of Conduct will evolve as well. Our core principles won't change, but the specifics might, so a year from now, please read it a third time. And always bear in mind that each of us has a personal responsibility to do everything we can to incorporate these principles into our work, and our lives.

* * *

I. Serving Our Users

Google has always flourished by serving the interests of our users first and foremost. Our goal is to build products that organize the world's information and make it accessible to our users. Here are several principles that all Googlers should keep in mind as we work toward that goal.

a. Usefulness

Our products, features and services should make Google more useful for our users, whether they're simple search users or advertisers, large or small companies. We have many different types of users, but one primary goal for serving them all. "Is this useful?" is the one question every Googler should keep in mind during any task, every day.

b. Honesty

Our communications with our users should be appropriately clear and truthful. Our reputation as a company our users can trust is among our most valuable assets, and it is up to all of us to make sure that we nourish that reputation.

c. Responsiveness

Part of being useful and honest is being appropriately responsive: recognizing relevant user feedback when we see it, and doing something about it. We take pride in responding to communications from our users, whether in the form of comments or questions, problems or compliments.

d. Taking Action

Saying that Google, and the products and services we produce, should be useful, honest and responsive is one thing; achieving that goal 100 percent of the time is, of course, quite another. That means that improving our work over time is largely contingent on the vigilance of our staff. Any time you feel our users aren't being well served, don't hesitate to bring it to the attention of the appropriate person. Googlers don't sit back and say nothing when the interests of the user are at stake. When you feel it's warranted, we encourage you to take a stand.

* * *

VII. Obeying the Law

Google takes its responsibilities to comply with the laws and regulations applicable to it very seriously. Although we recognize that it is probably impossible for you to understand all aspects of every applicable law, please take the time to try to generally familiarize yourself with the major laws and regulations that apply to your work and take advantage of our Legal Department to assist you and answer questions. We must all always remember that our reputation is the foundation of our present and future success—and that earning, and then maintaining, that reputation requires attention and effort to stay in compliance with the law.

a. The Foreign Corrupt Practices Act

Google requires full compliance with the Foreign Corrupt Practices Act, export control regulations, antitrust laws and other trade regulation statutes.

The Foreign Corrupt Practices Act prohibits any "corrupt" offer, payment, promise to pay, or authorization to pay any money, gift, or anything of value to any foreign official, or any foreign political party, candidate or official, for the purpose of: influencing any act or failure to act in the foreign official or party's official capacity; or inducing the foreign official or party to use influence to affect a decision of a foreign government or agency, in order to obtain or retain business for anyone, or direct business to anyone.

What does all this legal jargon mean to you? Simply put: that any attempt on the part of any Google employee or contractor to bribe or otherwise unethically influence any United States or foreign official, in either the public or private sector, is probably illegal and regardless, is completely unacceptable and against Google's Code of Conduct.

As always, though, there's a gray area here: you should take great caution with any gifts or other inducements that could be perceived as bribes. That doesn't mean all minor gifts or promotional and marketing materials are unacceptable (although, in general, government officials in the United States and in many other countries may be very reluctant to accept any gifts or items of value to avoid the appearance of impropriety); just that the care we all take to stay on the right side of ethical business practices also must be adhered to in the international arena.

* * *

CHINA'S PERSPECTIVE

After discussing its options, the negotiations team began to review its executive summary on China. The documents made it clear that the two parties would have different objectives during the negotiations. While the Google team would focus on profits and brand management, China would focus on a number of other considerations. The Chinese government had a goal of achieving technological parity with the United States, and consistently strove to provide its citizens and companies with access to the very best technology. Allowing Google to have a Chinese domain name and set up a research and support facility site in China would give some Chinese engineers access to Google's proprietary research technology. This access might help curtail the "brain drain" (loss of technologically talented students and engineers to the United States and other countries) and create jobs for Chinese citizens. The possibility of retaining key talent might have been reinforced by the hiring of Dr. Lee, whose continued presence in the country might encourage other scientists and engineers to remain in China.

It was also clear that China's leaders viewed the issue of Internet regulation (or censorship) as extremely important. They recognized how important Internet access and use was to China's economic development, but also sought to control the Internet's power. In order to squash dissent and limit political opposition, the government had long had a policy of strict media control. Content in newspapers, radio, television, and now the Internet was heavily controlled by the state, and these sources were prevented from reporting on or providing access to news deemed contrary to the Chinese government's interests.

The report provided to the Google negotiations team noted China's leaders' desire to improve their nation's economy while preserving political stability. This balancing act was conducted "bearing in mind the history and culture of China."[9] In a September 2004 address to the Central Committee of the Communist Party, President Hu had warned that outsiders were attempting to westernize China.[10] The government was striving to prevent this process, and an unambiguous mode of doing so was to censor political discussions. The Internet was "unwittingly ushering an age of startling social change" in China, and the government was willing to employ censorship, including more than 30,000 Internet policemen to patrol the Internet, to put the brakes on it.

The summary also discussed China's leaders' bureaucratic efforts at self-preservation. Both the functionaries in the Internet Propaganda Management Department and the Ministry of Information Industry (which issued the Internet content provider [ICP] licenses) sought to please the party hierarchy to ensure their jobs and political longevity. The media had reported that despite initial hopes that President Hu would introduce democratic reforms, the president "has placed particular emphasis on tightening the party's control over public opinion, presiding over a crackdown to restore discipline to state media and intimidate dissident intellectuals."[11] Thus, it was firmly in the interest of the Chinese bureaucracy to insist that, as a condition of getting a license to establish a server within China, Google had to agree to censor its content and search results.

Finally, in restricting westernizing elements of the Internet through censorship, China could affirm its status as an independent actor in the global marketplace. As head of a hierarchical culture that valued status, the Chinese government sought to promote China as a powerful and independent actor in world forums. The government had in the past been critical of other Internet businesses that refused to follow its objectives and directives. For example, the online encyclopedia Wikipedia was completely

Blocking Wikipedia

A look at Wikipedia and China

- **Jan. 15, 2001:** Wikipedia project officially begins.
- **October 2002:** The first article is written in the Chinese-language Wikipedia.
- **June 2-21, 2004:** China blocks Wikipedia for the first time. After the block, the numbers of new users, articles and edits on Chinese Wikipedia sharply decline for more than six months.
- **Sept. 23-27, 2004:** Wikipedia is erratic or unavailable to some users in China.
- **Oct. 19, 2005:** People in China can longer access any of Wikipedia's articles.
- **Oct. 10, 2006:** The ban on Wikipedia in China seems to be partially lifted, although users are still unable to access the Chinese-language site.

Source: Wikipedia

Note: Though users were able to access Wikipedia in China in October 2006, many pages remained blocked. There was speculation that the government of China was blocking only pages (as opposed to entire sites) deemed contrary to its interests.

Source: Loretta Chao, "Beijing Eases Ban on Wikipedia; Chinese-Language Filter Remains," *Wall Street Journal*, October 17, 2006.

Exhibit 10 Wikipedia's experience with the Chinese Government

banned in China until 2006 (see Exhibit 10). An anonymous post on the Wikipedia site claimed that Wikipedia's users had been acting as "running dogs for American imperialism."[12] "Running dog" is an expression in Mandarin that means servile follower or lackey.[13] Many Chinese suspected the post had been made by a government agent. The government would likely seek to prevent any loss of face that might accompany a decision to cave in to any of Google's demands concerning Chinese law and the government's official policy on the availability of information deemed contrary to the state's best interests.

China had another option as well. Instead of allowing Google access to a ".cn" domain name, China could deny Google the license and continue to rely on local search engine alternatives to provide Chinese consumers with Internet searching services. Baidu had been steadily gaining market share, and was already one of the most visited sites in the world. It was a known entity and the Chinese government was already monitoring its compliance with Chinese law. The site was very similar in substance and style to Google. Though failure to bring a technologically advanced company such as Google to China would damage the regime's international reputation, it would likely produce fewer domestic repercussions.

Issue	Google		Chinese Government	
Issue 1	Priority	Position	Priority	Position
	Interests		Interests	
BATNA				
Reservation Price				

Directions: First identify the issues to be negotiated, putting each issue in a separate box in the issue column. In the Google column, identify Google's position on each issue, then the interests underlying that position. After you have completed all the positions and issues for Google, prioritize the issues, with 1 being the most important. Follow the same steps to identify the positions, interests, and priorities for the Chinese government.

Exhibit 11 Planning document

SEARCHING FOR A RESOLUTION

As the Google negotiators arrived in Beijing, several concerns lingered. Chief among them was how the team would be able to reconcile the company's principles with its profit motives. The Chinese government officials assigned to negotiate with the Google team had concerns as well. Given the distance between the two parties on a number of important issues, neither party was confident that a deal would be reached. It would take a keen understanding of each other's issues, positions, and interests to understand their motivations. Moreover, each party would have to understand how the culture of its counterpart might influence the outcome of the discussions. The Google team settled into its accommodations and prepared to meet with government officials later that day.

PREPARATION FOR THE CLASSROOM DISCUSSION

1. Develop a negotiations planning document using the Kellogg format in Exhibit 11.
2. Come to class prepared to support and explain the priorities that you see for the Chinese government and Google, and discuss their respective best alternative to a negotiated agreement (BATNAs).[14]
3. What ethical dilemmas do you foresee for Google? Is there any way to resolve them?
4. Do you see any potential for an integrative agreement that creates value for both parties?

CASE 2
SNØHETTA-RAS AL-KHAIMAH NEGOTIATIONS OVER THE DESIGN OF AN ICO: DISCUSSION GUIDE FOR "THE SAND CASTLE: BUILDING A CITY IN THE DESERT OF RAS AL-KHAIMAH" (FILM)*

I. BACKGROUND INFORMATION

In mid-summer 2006, the Norwegian architecture firm Snøhetta was invited by Crown Prince Saud bin Saqr of Ras Al-Khaimah to participate in a design competition for a new capital city. Sheikh Saud envisioned a city that would support a population of 500,000 people on 10 square kilometers with zero emissions and other environmentally friendly features. He expected to complete construction in 15-20 years. As one of his advisors put it, the Crown Prince wanted a "beautiful" city - one that would draw people to Ras Al-Khaimah.

Snøhetta AS was a group of 120 professionals in architecture, landscape architecture, and interior design. Founded in 1989, the firm won the first major design competition that it entered, for the Bibliotheca Alexandrina in Egypt, and thereafter gained international acclaim for striking designs and innovative use of materials. While most of the firm's projects during the 1990s were in Norway, one third of its 33 projects in 2002 originated outside of the country. In the Middle East, Snøhetta won the 2000 design competition for the Sheik Zayed Knowledge Center in Abu Dhabi and completed the new library in Egypt in 2001.

When Sheikh Saud's representatives approached Snøhetta in 2006, the firm was 3 years into supervising construction of the Norwegian Opera House (an 8-year project originally scheduled for completion in 2008) and deeply involved in designs for the World Trade Center Memorial in New York City. Snøhetta was also just about to enter the design competition for an Aramco-sponsored cultural center in Dhahran, Saudi Arabia. And yet, the Ras Al-Khaimah project represented the firm's biggest commercial opportunity since its founding. (Building the new city would cost billions of dollars.)

---

* This guide was written by Stephen E. Weiss, Associate Professor of Policy and International Business, York University, Schulich School of Business. It is intended to provide a basis for class discussion, not serve as a complete factual record or assessment of the actual events. The author gratefully acknowledges the assistance of Kjetil Thorsen and Elin Helgeland at Snøhetta and James McKellar, Tamara Abi Saab and Kathrine Varn at Schulich. Any errors in the document are solely the author's responsibility. (Orig. Nov. 10, 2010; rev. Oct. 2012.)

Snøhetta's total revenue for 2005 was approximately NOK 62.5 million (US$9.3 million). At this point in its evolution, the firm was led by two of its multiple founders: Norwegian Kjetil Thorsen, based at the main office in Oslo, and American Craig Dykers, who worked out of a smaller office in New York City.

Ras Al-Khaimah (RAK) was located in the northernmost corner of the United Arab Emirates on a promontory separating the Persian Gulf and Arabian Sea. The smallest of the seven emirates, it had a population of 300,000. RAK had no major oil deposits, so its government concentrated on developing an industrial sector. Pioneer Cement, which was established in the 1970s, became the UAE's largest cement producer. RAK Ceramics was founded in 1991 and within 10 years, grew into one of the world's largest ceramics manufacturers, with exports to over 130 countries. Then in 2005, the government set up Ras Al-Khaimah Investment Authority (RAKIA) to attract foreign firms to the emirate's free trade and industrial zones.

All of these enterprises contributed to the long-term plan of Crown Prince and Deputy Ruler Sheikh Saud bin Saqr al Qasimi. The fourth son of RAK Ruler Sheikh Saqr bin Mohammad al-Qassimi, Sheikh Saud had been educated in Lebanon and the USA, where he earned an MBA at the University of Michigan. Since 1979, he had held various government positions, and in June 2003, he was named Crown Prince. He intended to develop the emirate into a regional hub for industry, manufacturing, knowledge and tourism. The new city lay at the heart of this broad vision.

The advisor to the Crown Prince on the new-city project - and on many others - was Dr. Khater Massaad. The Lebanese-born Massaad, who held a doctorate in geophysics from the University of Lausanne, moved to RAK in the mid-1980s to test minerals. By 2006, he held multiple positions in the emirate: CEO of RAKIA; Executive Chairman of RAK's development authority/property developer, RAKEEN; CEO of RAK Ceramics; Chairman of Pioneer Cement; and more. He was Snøhetta's principal contact in RAK.

Unlike a public design competition with a priori specifications and explicit guidelines, the RAK competition was rather open-ended and directed toward a single, individual client: Sheikh Saud. Any architectural competition was expensive. According to Kjetil Thorsen, firms typically spent at least $200,000 just to participate, and winning was a low-probability event. Even 2 wins out of 10 competitions was considered a good success ratio.

Thorsen and Partner Robert Greenwood led the Snøhetta team that worked on the proposal for Sheikh Saud and his representative, Dr. Massaad. The team began in Oslo by studying a wide range of subjects including the history and culture of the region. Then they organized a week-long, public workshop in RAK at which they sought local input for architectural designs. No one showed up. Ultimately, the team's challenge was to find - or create - a design concept acceptable to their client. Massaad wanted something "genius, [a] new concept with something very unique and not too expensive."

II. THE NEGOTIATIONS

Snøhetta-RAK discussions and negotiations about a design took place over several months, from June 2006 to January 2007. Nearly all meetings were held in RAK and specifically, in the conference room at RAK Ceramics. Typically, two teams of 3 to 4 people participated, and the meetings lasted a brief 20 to 25 minutes. (For participants' names and roles, see below "Exhibit 1: Player Map.")

Four main negotiations took place during this period. Parts of each negotiation were filmed by a Norwegian film crew that was in the process of shooting a year-long, authorized documentary

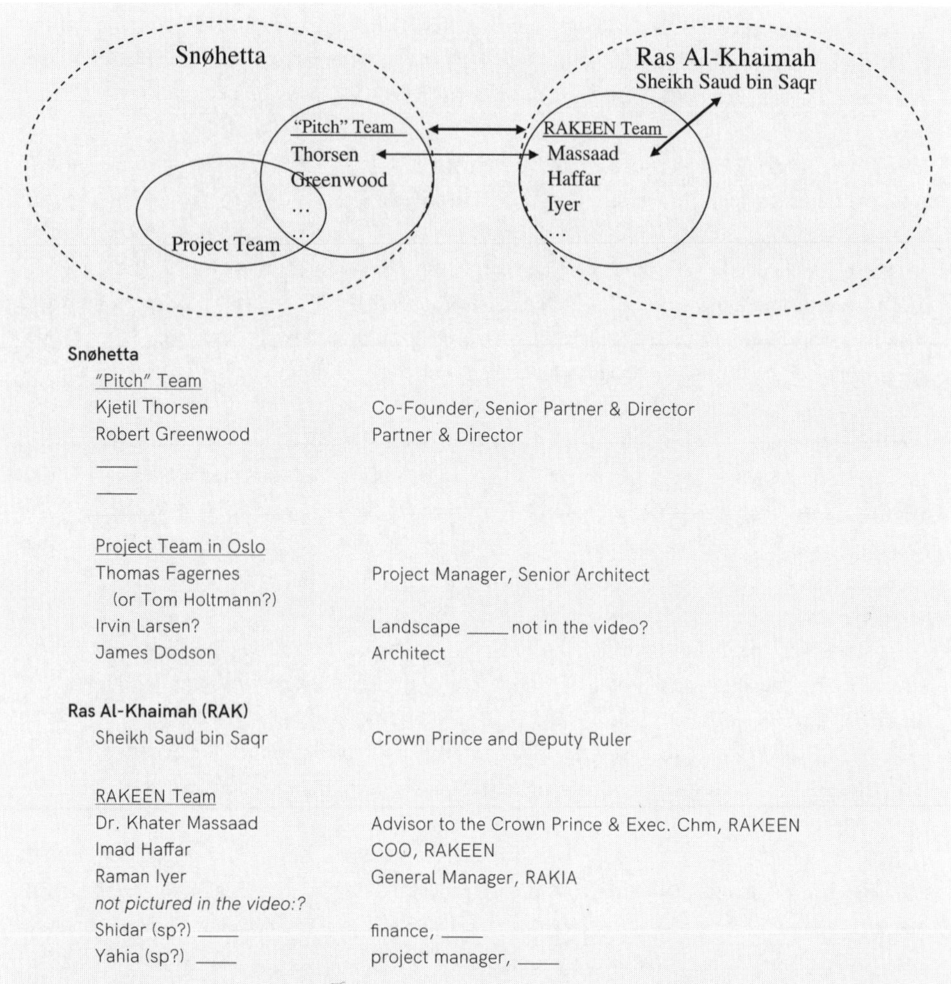

Snøhetta

"Pitch" Team

Kjetil Thorsen	Co-Founder, Senior Partner & Director
Robert Greenwood	Partner & Director
____	
____	

Project Team in Oslo

Thomas Fagernes (or Tom Holtmann?)	Project Manager, Senior Architect
Irvin Larsen?	Landscape ____ not in the video?
James Dodson	Architect

Ras Al-Khaimah (RAK)

Sheikh Saud bin Saqr	Crown Prince and Deputy Ruler

RAKEEN Team

Dr. Khater Massaad	Advisor to the Crown Prince & Exec. Chm, RAKEEN
Imad Haffar	COO, RAKEEN
Raman Iyer	General Manager, RAKIA
not pictured in the video:?	
Shidar (sp?) ____	finance, ____
Yahia (sp?) ____	project manager, ____

Exhibit 1 Party map from Snøhetta's perspective

about Snøhetta. When the RAK invitation arrived at Snøhetta, the film company sought and received permission from Massaad to continue filming in RAK. "The Sand Castle" includes video segments from each of the main negotiations.

III. QUESTIONS FOR DISCUSSIONS ABOUT FILM SCENES

The four lettered sets of questions below pertain to excerpts from "The Sand Castle."[15] (The teaching note for this case designates the excerpts.) For each set, you (or your instructor) may play the video excerpt then discuss the corresponding questions. They should be addressed in order. Sets B, C and D will make more sense to you after you have discussed prior sets, but they are all listed below for your convenience. Exhibit 1: may be used for reference during video viewing.

A. Developing the Concept of a "Beautiful" City

1. What is Snøhetta's mandate? [Discuss this before showing the video.]
2. What do the architects think is Massaad's – and the Crown Prince's – vision of beauty?
3. What does Snøhetta reveal about their understanding of their client's interests?
4. What is Snøhetta's basic concept for the design, and how did they conceive it?

B. Presenting the Design for the New City and Interpreting the Client's Reaction

1. What's your general sense of this client-architect relationship?
2. What verbal and nonverbal signals from Massaad are most revealing about his attitude toward the design of the new city and toward Snøhetta as a potential partner?
3. To what extent do the parties' respective cultures seem to influence their behaviors and relationships in this meeting?
4. If you were Thorsen, would you continue to try to win the business (the design contract) from Massaad and the Crown Prince?

C. Different Visions of an "Icon" (Convention Center): Maneuvering within the Architect-Client Relationship

1. Should an architect try to shape a client's aesthetic sensibility?
2. How does Snøhetta influence – or "negotiate" – Massaad's vision of beauty and the "iconic?"
3. (a) What communications from Massaad are encouraging for Snøhetta? (b) What is discouraging?

D. Changes in the Snøhetta-Massaad Relationship

1. What key differences do you notice between the communications of the Snøhetta principals and Massaad in this meeting and their communications in the first meeting (Clip 1)?
2. How optimistic are you about the capacity of the architects and the client to work together effectively in the future?

General Lessons about Negotiation

1. Why did Snøhetta and RAK reach an agreement on a convention center design?
2. What general negotiation concepts are illustrated in "The Sand Castle?"
3. What major lessons does this film suggest for effective negotiation behavior?

NOTES

1. Kopytoff, V. (2006) Google bows to China pressure. *San Francisco Chronicle*, 25 January.
2. Kopytoff (2006) ibid.
3. Pan, P.P. (2006) The click that broke a government's grip. *Washington Post*, 19 February.
4. Pan, P.P. (2006) Bloggers who pursue change confront fear and mistrust. *Washington Post*, 21 February.
5. See Jeanne M. Brett (2001), *Negotiating Globally*. San Francisco, Jossey-Bass, p. 16 (discussing the importance of belonging to the "in-group" in collectivist cultures, such as China).
6. http://www.google.com/intl/en/corporate/tenthings.html.
7. Ibid.
8. Kristof, N.D. (2006) China's cyberdissidents and the yahoos at Yahoo. *New York Times*, 19 February.

9. DeLong, J.V. (2006) Google is right on China. *TCS Daily*, 31 January, http://www.tcsdaily.com.
10. Pan, P.P. (2005) Hu tightens Party's grip on power. *Washington Post*, 24 April.
11. Pan (2005) ibid.
12. Pan, P.P. (2006) Reference tool on web finds fans, censors. *Washington Post*, 20 February.
13. Dictionary.com, available at: http://dictionary.reference.com/search?q=running%20dog.
14. See Roger Fisher, William Ury and Bruce Patton (1991) *Getting to Yes*. New York, Penguin Books.
15. Set A does not entail a Snøhetta-RAK negotiation, and Set C relates to more than one negotiation.

Role play exercise: a milk plant to Saudi Arabia

SCENARIO

British Dairies Limited (BDL) is one of the leading manufacturers and suppliers of complete milk plants. At present, BDL is negotiating to sell a milk plant to Saudi Arabia. Earlier, ten years ago, it sold a small plant to Kuwait. That is the only experience BDL has had in that part of the world.

Two other competitors, Danish Dairies A/S from Denmark and Global Dairies Ltd from the USA, are also negotiating to get the project. These two firms always compete with BDL in international projects.

BDL came into contact with the Saudis at an exhibition in Munich. The buying firm, Jeddah Food Industries Ltd (JFI), is a private concern owned by a powerful group related to the royal family. The group owns several other industries and also a bank. The background of the project is an explicit ambition of the Saudi authorities to become self-sufficient in basic food industries. At present, around 70 per cent of the country's needs for dairy products are imported from Europe (specifically the Netherlands, Denmark and Switzerland). There are two dominating industrial groups in Saudi and JFI is one of these. The other group is already running a milk plant in Riyadh which they bought from the Danish firm.

The project group from BDL has visited Saudi Arabia a number of times and discussed the offer for the project with the buyer. In these meetings, people from both sides met and discussed technical specifications and other terms for the project. BDL has been invited to visit Saudi Arabia for final negotiations. Most of the technical details and some other terms have been agreed upon and all parties are quite optimistic about an agreement.

NEGOTIATION TEAMS

BDL

Peter Plan is the Vice President responsible for the Milk Plant division. Earlier, he was working as Marketing Manager and has enough experience of international projects of this type. He was also involved in negotiations for the project in Kuwait, as a team member.

Sam Sceptic is an engineer and has prepared all the technical specifications several times together with the buyer's representative, Alex, the buyer's consultant.

Nicky Control is a relatively young MBA from London Business School who has been working with BDL for the last three years. This project is the largest so far and the first one with an international dimension. Nicky is very ambitious and has been working intensively with the offer.

James Thesaurus is an interpreter from a communication consulting firm in London. He has extensive experience of working with Arab countries and has been helping different British and Irish firms in Saudi Arabia (his wife is from Egypt).

Jedda Food Industries Ltd

Sheikh Rahim is the President and owner of JFI. He is also the leader of the negotiation team. He is around 50 and has studied law at Oxford. He owns several industries and is very rich and influential. He controls most of his industries himself and is therefore a very busy person.

Mohammed Mustafa is an engineer and is expected to be the first Managing Director of the proposed milk plant. He is 45 years old and has been studying in Europe and the USA. He has a solid background in the technical side of the food industry.

Alex Moneypenny (a relative of Mrs Moneypenny, secretary to James Bond's Boss, M) is Vice President of Sahara Consulting Group in Jeddah, a British Saudi consulting firm which specialises in projects between Saudis and Western firms. Moneypenny was responsible for the project feasibility study, carried out for JFI.

Faisal Mahmood is Secretary of State for the Department of Industries. He takes part in the negotiations for all big projects between Saudi and Western firms and is responsible for questions on taxes, custom duties, residence permits and other government rules and regulations.

THE PRESENT SITUATION

This is BDL's first project in Saudi Arabia, and there is a good chance that if it gets this project it will be possible to get more projects in Saudi. At its head office in Manchester, BDL has recently invested in new machinery and equipment, and its capacity has thus been enhanced.

BDL offered the project at a price of €350 million with the following terms of payment and a guarantee period of 12 months.

- 20 per cent at contract signing
- 30 per cent when installations start
- 30 per cent after first prove run
- 20 per cent three months after the first prove run.

Danish Dairies A/S has earlier delivered a project to Saudi to another party in Riyadh which is functioning very well. Alex Moneypenny has disclosed to Sam Sceptic (perhaps with the consent of Sheikh Rahim) that the price offered by the Danish firm, for the same project, is much lower. However, he also said that BDL's technical solution is perhaps considered a bit better.

BDL does not know much about the American offer. However, they know that Moneypenny has all the information on them. There is a rumour that the Americans have very good contacts with some important local people, so-called "Middlemen", and that they are working on Sheikh Rahim and the government representative Faisal Mahmood.

ASSIGNMENT

1. Both the groups formulate a strategy for the coming face-to-face negotiations, that is, what they want to achieve on each issue. The groups are not allowed to contact each other while formulating the strategy.
2. The parties now meet and negotiate. This is the last session and you have to either arrive at an agreement or finish negotiating, accepting that there will be no deal between the two parties.
3. The outcome of the negotiation should show the price, terms of payment and delivery time and any other terms agreed.

TIME

1. Negotiations: 30 minutes (maximum including the break).
2. Time out: Negotiators may take a two to three-minute break ("time out") for their own consultations or for informal contact with one or more of the other party's team members. However, not more than two breaks can be taken.

Index